▪STRATEGY▪

Formulation, Implementation, and Control

James M. Higgins

Rollins College
Roy E. Crummer Graduate School of Business

The Dryden Press
Chicago   New York   Philadelphia   San Francisco   Montreal   Toronto
London   Sydney   Tokyo   Mexico City   Rio de Janeiro   Madrid

Acquisitions Editor: Anne Elizabeth Smith
Project Editor: Jan Doty
Managing Editor: Jane Perkins
Design Director: Alan Wendt
Production Manager: Claire Roth
Permissions Editor: Doris Milligan

Cover Designer: Jeanne Calabrese
Copyeditor: Bonita Coors
Indexer: Lois Oster
Compositor: G&S Typesetters, Inc.
Text Type: Times Roman

Library of Congress Cataloging in Publication Data
Higgins, James M.
   Strategy: formulation, implementation, and control.
   Includes bibliographical references and index.
   1. Corporate planning. 2. Management. I. Title.
HD30.28.H513   1984   658.4'012   84-8176
ISBN 0-03-070639-4

Printed in the United States of America
567-039-987654321

Copyright 1985 CBS College Publishing
All rights reserved

Address orders:
383 Madison Avenue
New York, NY 10017

Address editorial correspondence:
One Salt Creek Lane
Hinsdale, IL 60521

CBS College Publishing
The Dryden Press
Holt, Rinehart and Winston
Saunders College Publishing

Much of the material in this edition was previously published in *Organizational Policy and Strategic Management: Text and Cases*, Second Edition, by James M. Higgins. Copyright 1983 by CBS College Publishing.

Contents

Preface	vii
Chapter 1 Strategic Management Begins with Mission, Policy, Information, and Strategists	3
Strategic Management in the Organization	6
The Plan of This Book	9
Mission	11
Organizational Policy	15
Organizational Policy at the Strategic Level	16
The Organizational Strategists	17
Strategic Management in the International Arena	26
Strategic Management in the Not-for-Profit Organization	29
Chapter 2 Internal and Environmental Information	37
SWOT	40
Information	43
The Internal Information Sought	49
The External Information Sought	50
Competitor Analysis: Another Perspective	60
Making Use of the Data: Analytical and Forecasting Techniques	67
Internal and Environmental Information in the International Arena	71
Nonprofits and Their Usages of Information to Determine SWOT	73
Appendix to Chapter 2	77
Chapter 3 Determining Strategic Objectives and Formulating the Master Strategy	81
Determining Strategic Objectives	82
Organizational Objectives as Integration Mechanisms—MBORR	85
The Objectives Established	88
Prioritizing Objectives	91
The Master Strategy	92
Levels of Strategy	94
Enterprise Strategy	96
Corporate Strategy	97
Business Strategy	108
Functional Strategy	108
The Grand Strategy	108

Preemptive Strategies	110
Some Important Characteristics of Plans	112
Impacts of Multinational Operations on Strategic Objectives and Master Strategy Formulation	113
Impacts of the Not-for-Profit Situation on Strategic Objectives and Master Strategy Formulation	114

Chapter 4 The Master Strategy at the SBU Level — 119

The Corporate Strategy for the Single-Business Enterprise	120
The Business Strategy for the Single-Business Enterprise	123
The Contingency Approach to Business-Level Strategy Formulation	129
The Behavioral Theory of Strategy Formulation	137
Functional Supportive Strategies	148
International Master Strategies at the SBU Level	155
Nonprofit Strategies at the SBU Level	157

Chapter 5 The Master Strategy in Multiple-SBU Firms — 163

Corporate Strategy at the Level of the Total Organization	164
Portfolio Management Techniques	166
Difference in Perspective: Divisional versus Corporate Strategists	183
The Master Strategy for Multinational Multiple-SBU Firms	186
The Master Strategy for Multiple Primary Mission Nonprofits	189

Chapter 6 The Strategic Decision Process—A Behavioral View — 191

The Complexity of Organizational Decision Making	191
The Strategic Decision Process	194
The Component Phases of Strategic Decision Making: A Closer Examination	195
Three Common Strategic Planning Modes	207
Managerial Comprehension of the Behavioral Process	209
Behavioral Aspects of Strategic Decision Making for Multinational Firms	209
The Behavioral View of Strategic Decision Making in Nonprofits	212

Chapter 7 Implementation — 215

Organization and Implementation	216
Organizational Structure	216
Implementation Systems	230
Human Resource Management, Organizational Behavior, and the Individual Manager	237
A Note on Implementation Policies	239
An Additional Perspective on Strategy/Structure/Implementation Relationships—The 7-S's Framework	239
Multinational Aspects of Organization and Implementation	241
Implementation in the Nonprofit Sector	243

Chapter 8 The Evaluation and Control of Organizational Strategy — 245

Control and Strategy	246
Strategic Control: The Evaluation of Corporate Strategy	248
Management Control	249

Operational Control	252
Strategic and Management Control Measures of Performance	252
Other Aspects of Control	261
What Should Be Measured?	263
Descriptive Characteristics and *The Search for Excellence*	264
The Emergent Strategy	265
Evaluation and Control in Multinational Enterprises	272
Strategic and Management Control in Nonprofit Organizations	273

Appendix I   Introduction to the Case Method — 277

Objectives	278
Approaches	278
Types of Organizations Encountered	278
Planning Level of Problems, Opportunities Encountered	279
Classroom Pedagogy	279
Case Bias	281
A Suggested Course of Action	281

Appendix II   The Strategic Audit—A SWOT Appproach — 285

Management Audit	285
Environmental Analysis	292

Appendix III   Financial Ratio Analysis — 293

Liquidity	293
Leverage	293
Activity	294
Profitability	294

Appendix IV   Economic and News Information — 297

Information to be Used with Cases Whose Decision Year is 1984	297
Information to be Used with Cases Whose Decision Year is 1983	298
Information to be Used with Cases Whose Decision Year is 1982	299
Information to be Used with Cases Whose Decision Year is 1981	300
Information to be Used with Cases Whose Decision Year is 1980	301
Information to be Used with Cases Whose Decision Year is 1979	302
Information to be Used with Cases Whose Decision Year is 1978	303
Information to be Used with Cases Whose Decision Year is 1977	304
Information to be Used with Cases Whose Decision Year is 1976	305
Information to be Used with Cases Whose Decision Year is 1975	306
Information to be Used with Cases Whose Decision Year is 1974	307

The Dryden Press Series in Management
Arthur G. Bedeian, Consulting Editor

Albanese and Van Fleet
**Organizational Behavior:
A Managerial Viewpoint**

Bedeian
**Organizations: Theory and Analysis, Text and Cases,
Second Edition**

Bedeian and Glueck
Management, Third Edition

Boone and Kurtz
Contemporary Business, Fourth Edition

Bowman and Branchaw
Business Report Writing

Chen and McGarrah
Productivity Management: Text and Cases

Compaine and Litro
Business: An Introduction

Gaither
**Productions and Operations Management:
A Problem-Solving and Decision-Making Approach,
Second Edition**

Higgins
Strategy: Formulation, Implementation, and Control

Higgins
**Organizational Policy and Strategic Management:
Text and Cases, Second Edition**

Hodgetts
**Management: Theory, Process, and Practice, Third
Edition**

Hodgetts
Modern Human Relations at Work, Second Edition

Holley and Jennings
Personnel Management: Functions and Issues

Holley and Jennings
The Labor Relations Process, Second Edition

Huseman, Lahiff, Penrose, and Hatfield
**Business Communication: Strategies and Skills,
Second Edition**

Huseman, Lahiff, and Penrose
**Readings and Applications in Business
Communication, Second Edition**

Jauch, Coltrin, Bedeian, and Glueck
**The Managerial Experience:
Cases, Exercises, and Readings, Third Edition**

Lee
Introduction to Management Science

Miner
Theories of Organizational Behavior

Miner
Theories of Organizational Structure and Process

Paine and Anderson
Strategic Management

Paine and Naumes
**Organizational Strategy and Policy: Text and Cases,
Third Edition**

Ray and Eison
Supervision

Robinson
**The Internationalization of Business: An
Introduction**

Robinson
International Business Management, Second Edition

Smith
**Management Systems:
Analyses and Applications**

Stone
Understanding Personnel Management

Tombari
**Business and Society:
Strategies for the Environment and Public Policy**

Trueman
**Quantitative Methods for Decision Making in
Business**

Zikmund
Business Research Methods

Preface

Strategy: Formulation, Implementation, and Control is intended to increase the student's knowledge of strategic management and organizational processes; to improve the skills necessary for carrying out the work of the strategist; and to enhance the appreciation of the general management attitude.

Objectives

This text is designed around the commonly recognized objectives of a course in strategy and policy. It develops the student's general management perspective, including an understanding of the role of the general manager-strategist, in a variety of domestic and international strategic situations.

It also integrates the functional business disciplines (marketing, finance, operations, human resources management, and information systems) with the management process to illustrate their interdependencies. The environment of business and its multiple roles within society, especially in regard to external constraints, are considered.

The student's analytic and research skills are applied in a decision-making setting. This text teaches the student how to make decisions, how to identify major issues in complex situations, and how to propose alternative solutions. The student will learn to determine appropriate choices from among these alternatives and to defend those choices.

A fourth objective is to acquaint the student with concepts in strategic management—its formulation and the resulting strategy content, policy, implementation, and control—and the incorporation of these concepts into practice. The student will be able to recognize the role of policy in the organization. Finally, this text is intended to relate the purposes of functional activity and to encourage the student to be objective-oriented as opposed to activity-oriented.

Special Features

This book features three models that explain organizational strategic management. The first model, shown in Figure 1.1, portrays the strategic process in five steps: mission determination, establishment of objectives, strategy formulation, implementation, and control. The chapters in this book follow the order of this model. The second model, portrayed in Figure 1.2, examines in detail the processes of objective determination and master strategy formulation. This model is the basis for discussions in Chapters 1 through 6. The third model, shown in Table 3.5, defines the contents of the master strategy. Much of Chapters 3, 4, and 5 expand on the information in this model.

In conjunction with the master strategy model, Table 3.5, basic action strategies and grand strategies (for example, growth through diversification, retrenchment, stabilization, niche, concentration, and combination) are explained in sufficient detail to enable the student first to understand and then to use these terms.

The process of determining strengths, weaknesses, opportunities, and threats (SWOT) is discussed at length throughout. Organizations and their environments are analyzed to determine SWOT, and social issues are integrated into these analyses. Information is presented to help the student forecast SWOT.

Each chapter contains key terms and concepts to guide the student. Information Capsules (anecdotes describing specific situations to illustrate major points in the text) are presented in all eight chapters. At the end of each chapter, brief commentaries explain how the material covered in that chapter is affected first by international circumstances and then by nonprofit situations.

The appendices are designed to increase the student's ability to analyze strategic situations. Appendix I discusses the case method. Appendix II provides a strategic audit, including questions to analyze organizations and their environments. This audit is based primarily on the master strategy shown in Table 3.5. Appendix III further defines and discusses the ratios presented in Table 8.1. Appendix IV contains economic and news data for 1974 through 1983. A separate appendix to Chapter 2 provides a list of information sources.

Use of the Text

Strategy: Formulation, Implementation, and Control is intended primarily for use in the capstone policy course by senior-level undergraduate students and by second-year MBA students. This book can be employed in an instructional situation using several different pedagogical approaches. It can stand alone for a text-only approach to the policy course, or it can be used with a case book, with an instructor's own cases or lectures, or with simulations or field exercises. It can also be used with analyses of real-life organizations, such as those that appear in each issue of *Business Week*.

This text may also be used by managers in management development courses or by any manager individually as a means of "getting up to speed" in this area. The state of the art of strategy and policy are reviewed, with a focus on both research and concepts in the rapidly expanding field of strategic management.

Any opinions, criticisms, praise, or other comments in regard to this text are welcome. Please write to the author at the following address:

James M. Higgins
Crummer Graduate School of Business
Rollins College
Winter Park, FL 32789

Acknowledgments

Many persons contributed to this book. First, I would like to thank the many scholars whose works are cited herein and who have contributed so much in recent years to our understanding of the strategic management process. Secondly, Marty Schatz, dean of the Crummer Graduate School of Business, has provided an organizational climate conducive to writing, and for that I am extremely grateful. Cid Stoll and Al Prast, graduate assistants, aided in various stages of the process. The reviewers of the original manuscript assisted in making some significant improvements, especially Art Sharplin of Northeast Louisiana University; Richard R. Merner of the University of Delaware; and James B. Thurman of George Washington University.

At Dryden Press I would like to thank Anne Smith, Associate Publisher, who supported and encouraged me throughout. Special thanks are due to Ruta Graff, who worked on the first version of this text as it appeared in *Organizational Policy and Strategic Management: Text and Cases*, and to Jan Doty, who has guided the production effort of this rendition. Alan Wendt, the designer, has done an outstanding job on this book. The copyeditor, Bonita Coors, deserves praise for her efforts.

Finally, my wife and two daughters are greatly appreciated for enduring another one.

James M. Higgins
October 1984

To Marty Schatz, Dean of the Crummer School

He has demonstrated sound leadership in formulating, implementing, and controlling strategy.

Chapter 1
Strategic Management Begins with Mission, Policy, Information, and Strategists

Effective business strategy is an essential requirement for an outstanding company. Of all the contrasts between the successful and the unsuccessful business, or between the corporate leader and its followers, the single, most important differentiating factor is strategy.
J. Thomas Cannon

Whether an organization will succeed or fail ultimately hinges upon the appropriate administration of the subjects of this book: strategic management and organizational policy. IBM, General Electric, Xerox, and Mazda all share at least three common factors—success, competent strategic management, and viable organizational policy. W. T. Grant, Minnie Pearl's Fried Chicken, WUV's Hamburgers, and Braniff Airlines, at the time of their demise, also possessed three common factors—failure, inadequate strategic management, and dysfunctional organizational policy. In the short run, any firm with a strategic advantage can survive and even prosper; but in the long run, only the organizations which practice sound strategic management and which have viable policies will continue to possess that strategic advantage and will therefore be able to survive and prosper!

> **Strategic management is the process of managing the pursuit of organizational mission while managing the relationship of the organization to its environment.**

Strategic management is principally concerned with executive actions that involve

1. The determination of the organization's mission, strategic policies, and strategic objectives.

2. The formulation of a master strategy to accomplish those objectives. This strategy is most often based on a grand strategy combining basic actions and marketing considerations.
3. The formulation of policies to aid in the implementation and control of the master strategy.
4. Managing, through subordinates, the process of implementation, which translates strategic plans into action and results.
5. The practices of evaluation and control to determine whether the mission and objectives have been achieved and whether the plans and policies for reaching them are functional.

Strategic management stresses managing the organization's relationship with its environment as a means to mission accomplishment. Strategic management recognizes that most organizations operate in increasingly volatile and often hostile environments. Historically, organizational strategic management revolved around basic action strategies and competitive marketing actions. Currently, more and more organizations recognize that the strategic process is much more complex; they therefore focus their efforts on virtually all key environmental and internal factors, not just on customers, suppliers, and the competition.

> **Organizational policy comprises broad forms of guidance established to aid managers in determining strategic objectives and in formulating, implementing, and controlling the master strategy.**

The guidance given by organizational policy ranges from very broad statements to somewhat more specific constraints that set out allowable or intended courses of action. Such guidance is necessary if the actions taken by organization members are to be consistent with the organization's mission. Policy provides a framework within which organization members can function, within which the master strategy can be formulated, implemented, and controlled.

> **The master strategy is the group of strategic plans formulated to achieve the organization's strategic objectives as it manages the organization's relationships with the major constituents of its internal and external environments affected by its actions, known as environmental stakeholders.**

> **Strategic objectives are major, comprehensive objectives for accomplishing mission. They define mission in more specific, achievable terms.**

> **Strategic plans are major, comprehensive, and usually long-term plans for accomplishing strategic objectives and, hence, mission.**

> **The grand strategy is that combination of basic action strategies, such as concentration, growth, conglomerate diversification, etc.; and marketing strategies; and for very large firms, portfolio techniques that define the driving force of the organization—that central character attribute to which all else should adhere.**

All organizations' master strategies have four common components: a societal response strategy, a mission determination strategy, a primary mission strategy, and a mission supportive strategy. In business, these strategies are referred to respectively as the enterprise strategy, the corporate strategy, the business strategy, and the functional strategy. The societal response strategy tells how the organization plans to relate to its external societal constituents. The mission determination strategy defines the organization's fields of endeavor and how it plans to conduct itself in those endeavors in very broad terms. The primary mission strategy indicates how the organization plans to achieve its primary mission. The supportive strategies tell how the organization plans on supporting its primary mission strategy. The content of the master strategy varies principally with the mission and with the type of organization.

Business organizations can be placed in two primary groups. Which of the four major components of the master strategy is emphasized depends upon which group a business fits into. The first group includes organizations that sell a single product or few products, largely in a single industry. This type of organization is known as a strategic business unit (SBU). Examples of single-SBU firms include Delta Airlines, individual McDonald's franchises, the maker of Arrow shirts, and most accounting firms. The second group is made up of organizations that market their products in many industries and have many SBUs. General Mills, Westinghouse, IBM, General Electric, Mitsubishi, Xerox, and EXXON are examples of multiple-SBU firms.

When formulating strategy at the SBU, or business level, strategists are most concerned with developing a strategic advantage through the use of the primary mission strategy of marketing (although some firms may emphasize other areas—production for example). Successfully competing in the marketplace is the aim of SBU strategy. Critical to the achievement of this aim are: supportive strategies in the economic functional areas of finance, operations/production, and human resource management; supportive strategies in the managerial functional areas, such as planning, organizing, implementing, and controlling; and the choice of basic corporate strategies, such as the decision to compete or find a niche, grow or stabilize, and so forth.

In multiple-SBU firms, the overall organizational master strategy consists of plans for obtaining a strategic advantage over other conglomerates by achieving a synergistic balance among all the SBUs. The techniques employed to achieve this balance are known as portfolio management. These emphasize corporate strategies. In addition, the master strategy at this level must examine the same fundamental issues as those portrayed in Table 3.5 of this text. That is, all major components of the master strategy must be addressed from the total organizational perspective, albeit if only from a policy viewpoint in terms of informing major divisions of total organizational objectives and plans in those areas . . . to which divisions would be expected to adhere.

In addition to strategies for corporate, SBU (business), and functional areas, the master strategy component for coping with the total organizational environment, known as the enterprise strategy, is a critical ingredient in the successful organization's master strategy. Chapter 3 discusses these types of strategies in much greater detail.

In nonprofit organizations, strategic planning units exist. A hospital, for example, is a SBU. A state government has numerous agencies, each corresponding to a SBU. The terms used in nonprofit organizations often differ from those used in business, but the concepts are the same.

The wise leader considers the days that are yet to come. —Persian Proverb

Strategic Management in the Organization

The role of strategic management in the organization can be examined through the use of a strategic management process model such as that presented in Figure 1.1 and an objectives determination and master strategy formulation model such as that presented in Figure 1.2, which provides more detailed information about the processes portrayed in the second and third steps of Figure 1.1. While Figures 1.1 and 1.2, as well as much of the accompanying narrative, portray the processes as sequential, they do not always occur as shown. Many times, objectives are established without exhaustive examination of information. Many times, objectives change after strategies have been formulated. Many times, objectives remain the same, but the strategies to achieve them are reformulated. However, most of the time, the processes shown in the figures occur sequentially at least once a year as firms complete their annual planning process.

Figure 1.1
The Organization—a Strategic Management Process Model

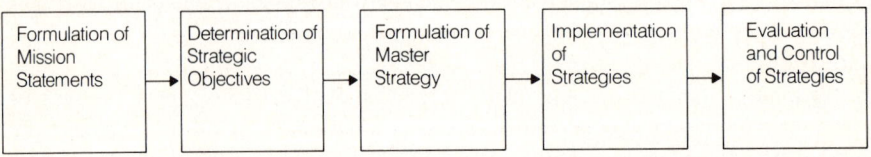

Strategic Policies   Policies that Aid Implementation   Control Policies

Figure 1.2
Objective Determination and Master Strategy Formulation

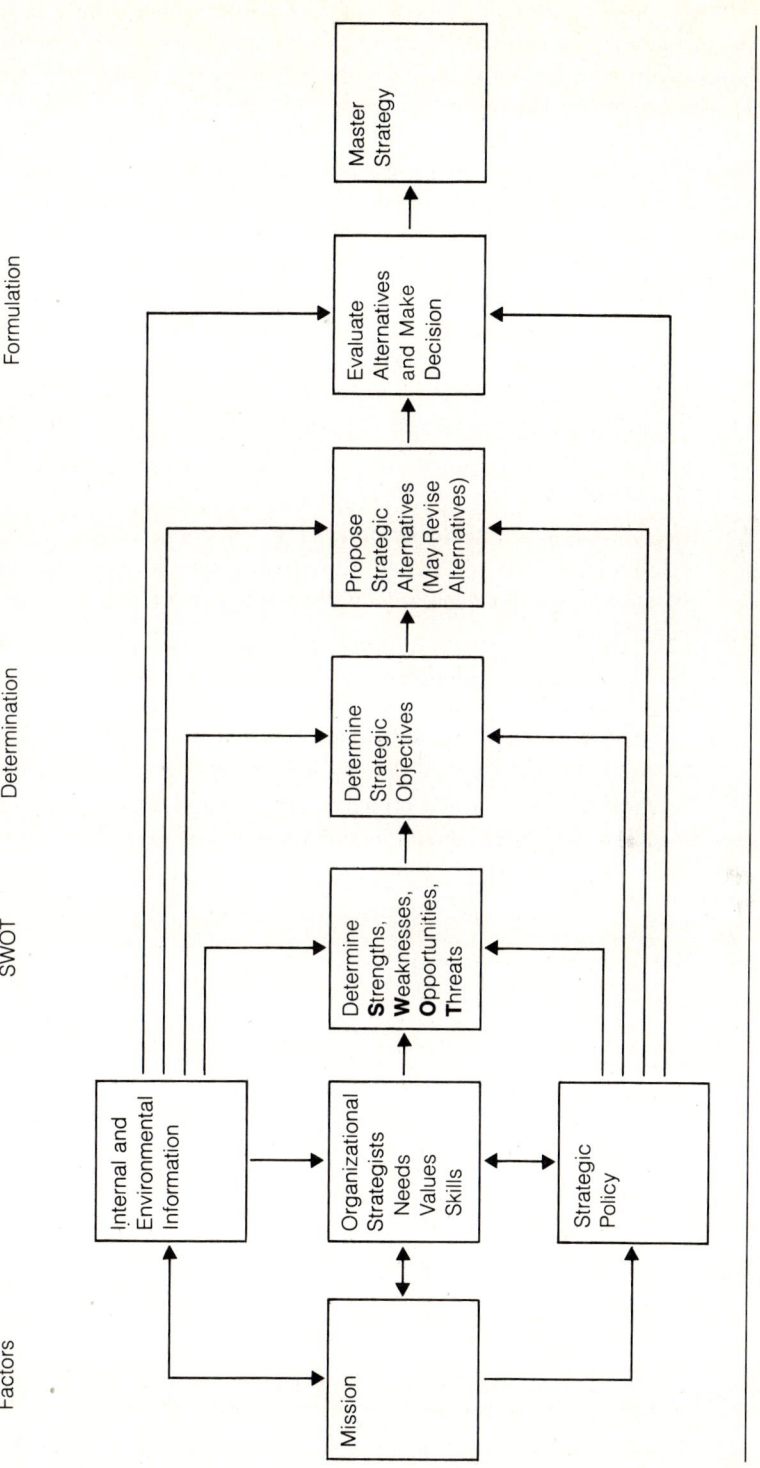

How these models are actually put into operation varies from organization to organization. Although specifics may vary, the strategic management process model contains the principal components of the effective organization. Numerous studies have indicated the importance of this strategic management approach and the processes depicted in the figures.[1] Not all are supportive, but most are, and most of those that are not can be explained by methodological reasons.

The contents of the model are as follows:

1. **Formulation of Mission Statements.** Organizations exist to accomplish a mission. Mission is the organization's reason for existence. Successful organizations have well-defined missions and function in accordance with them.

2. **Setting of Organizational Policy.** Broad, general guidance must be available for the entire strategic management process: strategic policies guide the objective setting and strategy formulation processes; additional policies derived from strategy and these strategic policies guide the ensuing actions, which lead to implementation of strategy; finally, selected policies guide control actions.

3. **Determination of Strategic Objectives.** Strategic objectives for achieving organizational mission in a complex environment must be determined. These objectives are simply more definitive statements of what constitutes mission accomplishment.

4. **Master Strategy Formulation.** Successful organizations establish strategic plans for reaching strategic objectives while managing relationships in a complex environment. In setting strategic objectives and in formulating strategy, organizational strategists examine mission, policy, and information.

5. **Implementation.** Three primary critical issues are involved in implementation: how the organization is organized, having appropriate implementation

---

[1] H. I. Ansoff et al., "Does Planning Pay? The Effect of Planning in Success of Acquisitions," *Long Range Planning*, December 1970, pp. 2–7; J. S. Armstrong, "The Value of Formal Planning for Strategic Decisions: Review of Empirical Research," *Strategic Management Journal*, July–September 1982, pp. 197–211; D. Burt, "Planning and Performance in Australian Retailing," *Long Range Planning*, June 1978, pp. 62–66; J. Eastlack, Jr. and P. McDonald, "CEO's Role in Corporate Growth," *Harvard Business Review*, May/June 1970, pp. 150–163; C. S. Guynes, "An Analysis of Planning in Large Texas Manufacturing Firms" (Ph.D. dissertation, Texas Technical University, 1969); H. W. Hegarty, "The Role of Strategy Formulation on Corporate Performance," *Proceedings: Midwest American Institute of Decision Sciences*, 1976; D. M. Herold, "Long Range Planning and Organizational Performance: A Cross Validation Study," *Academy of Management Journal*, March 1971, pp. 91–102; R. J. Kudla, "The Effects of Strategic Planning on Common Stock Returns," *Academy of Management Journal*, March 1980, pp. 5–20; W. M. Lindsay and L. W. Rue, "Impact of the Organization Environment on the Long Range Planning Process: A Contingency View," *Academy of Management Journal*, September 1980, pp. 385–404; Z. A. Malik, "Formal Long Range Planning and Organizational Performance: A Study" (Ph.D. dissertation, Rensselaer Polytechnic Institute, 1974); M. A. Najjar, "Planning in Small Manufacturing Companies: An Empirical Study" (Ph.D. dissertation, Ohio State University, 1966); L. C. Rhyne, "The Impact of Strategic Planning on Financial Performance" (Paper presented to the Academy of Management, August 1983); R. B. Robinson, Jr., and John A. Pearce II, "The Impact of Formalized Strategic Planning on Financial Performance in Small Organizations," *Strategic Management Journal*, July–September 1983, pp. 197–207; L. W. Rue, "Theoretical and Operational Implications of Long Range Planning on Selected Measures of Financial Performance in U.S. Industry" (Ph.D. dissertation, Georgia State University, 1973); L. W. Rue and R. M. Fulmer, "Is Long Range Planning Profitable?" *Proceedings: Academy of Management Meetings*, 1973, pp. 66–73; S. Schoeffler, R. D. Buzzell, and D. F. Heany, "Impact of Strategic Planning on Profit Performance," *Harvard Business Review*, March/April 1974, pp. 137–145; R. Stagner, "Corporate Decision Making," *Journal of Applied Psychology*, February 1969, pp. 1–13; S. S. Thune and R. T. House, "Where Long Range Planning Pays Off," *Business Horizons*, August 1970, pp. 81–87; S. C. Wheelwright, "Japan—Where Operations Really Are Strategic," *Harvard Business Review*, July/August 1981, pp. 56–66; D. R. Wood, Jr. and R. L. LaForge, "The Impact of Comprehensive Planning on Financial Performance," *Academy of Management Journal*, March 1979, pp. 81–87.

systems, and the proper managing of human resources. The components and relationships among these factors are revealed in Figure 7.6.

    a. **Organizing.** The tasks required by objectives and plans must be specifically defined, with objectives distributed to combinations of tasks known as jobs; and the authority to accomplish these tasks must be granted in order for implementation to occur satisfactorily. Jobs must also be grouped into departments. Choosing the primary macro structure can have a major impact on the success of the strategy and is a decision which must be carefully made. The structure must be appropriate to the strategy.

    b. **Implementation Systems.** Integrated planning and control systems are necessary to insure that strategies are converted into individual and work group objectives and actions, and that results occur. Leadership, motivation, and communication systems are necessary to insure that individuals and groups know and understand their tasks and objectives, and are motivated to accomplish them. Human resource management systems are necessary to insure that human resources are properly managed from the total organizational perspective. Concerns include personnel practices such as recruitment and selection, training and development, compensation, and performance appraisal. The organization's culture must be designed to be compatible with strategy if strategy is to succeed.

    c. **Management of Human Resources.** One of the major concerns of successfully implementing strategy, is the manner in which managers motivate and lead subordinates, and how they communicate to them. Of special interest in the top management levels is the nature of compensation. Furthermore, politics and understanding of organizational behavior are fundamental requirements to arriving at successful implementation.

6. **Evaluation and Control.** Strategists must determine whether the master strategy was or will be successful and take appropriate actions based on their findings.

In quite simple terms, the contents of the model address three basic issues common to all strategic situations:

1. Where are we now?
2. Where do we want to be?
3. How do we get there?

The Plan of This Book

The remainder of this text examines in more detail the two processes introduced in Figures 1.1 and 1.2. In Chapters 1 and 2, the objective determination and strategy formulation processes are reviewed. The remainder of Chapter 1 discusses mission, strategic policy, and the organizational strategists and how these three factors affect

"We've had to depend rather heavily on strategic management."

the processes outlined in Figure 1.2. Chapter 2 discusses the critical role of the fourth major influential factor in master strategy formulation, strategic information. Chapter 3 continues this discussion, concentrating on the steps in setting objectives and formulating strategy and on various techniques for improving the results of these processes. Chapter 4 discusses the principal contents of the master strategy at the SBU level, while Chapter 5 focuses on the major content of the master strategy and on the strategy formulation process in multiple-SBU firms. Chapter 6 examines the major behavioral aspects of the objective setting and strategy formulation processes. Chapter 7 continues the discussion of the strategic management process model, focusing on the stages of implementation. Chapter 8 concludes the discussion of the strategic management process with a review of how evaluation and control are carried out.

At the end of each chapter, the international and nonprofit applications of the topics examined are presented. The business organization is most often used as the example of the concepts presented in most of the text.

Following the textual material are four appendices. The first of these, "The Case Method" tells you how to approach cases and how to learn from them. The next is a strategic audit for your use in analyzing cases and actual organizations. The third is a section reviewing how to interpret financial statements. The fourth is a brief section containing key information on the economy and major news events during the period of the cases.

The following pages in this chapter and Chapter 2 examine the four factors that most strongly influence the setting of objectives. These same four factors and the strategic objectives determined from them also greatly affect strategy formulation. The role of these factors in that process is also discussed in this and the next chapter.

Purpose is the unifying principle around which human energy clusters in the organization. —Robert R. Blake and Jane S. Mouton

Mission

Mission, or purpose, is the organization's raison d'etre, its reason to be. Mission is the primary consideration upon which organizational objectives, policy, and strategy are based. Classifying organizations into various typologies is useful in understanding and predicting organizational strategy. Classification factors which might be expected to have an impact on strategy include

The organization's size—small, medium, or large.

Its geographic scope—local, national, or multinational.

The number and diversity of businesses it comprises—single-SBU firm or multiple-SBU conglomerate.

However, mission exerts the most basic influence on strategy composition. The most obvious segmentation of organizations according to mission uses categories of profit and nonprofit. More definitively, Peter M. Blau and W. Richard Scott have identified four major types of organizations according to the group which receives the greatest benefit from the organization's existence. This classification scheme is essentially based on mission. The classifications are not mutually exclusive; an organization may, in fact, be appropriately classified into more than one category. The typologies are[2]

1. The business concern, which benefits the owners (and, it might be added, the employees and most of those who transact with it)—for example, General Motors.
2. The mutual benefit association, which benefits the members themselves—for example, a union or a club.
3. The service organization, which benefits its clients—for example, United Way and the U.S. Department of Health and Human Resources.
4. The commonweal organization, which benefits society in general—for example, the U.S. Department of Defense.

One would anticipate that these differing basic missions would result in varying strategies. But these simple statements of purpose alone are insufficient to distin-

[2]P. M. Blau and W. R. Scott, *Formal Organizations* (New York: Chandler, 1962), pp. 250–253.

guish one organization's mission from another when both have the same primary beneficiary. For example, all members of the business organization classification seek profit, so profit alone cannot be an organization's complete definition of purpose. Rather, as Phillip Kotler suggests, an organization's mission is viewed as its stated definition of basic business scope and operations.[3] The primary thrust of this mission statement is external, focuses on markets and customers, and typically notes current fields of endeavor. In addition to these characteristics, many mission statements include descriptions of several additional basic actions. Among them are such factors as product quality, location of facilities, important aspects of perceived strategic advantage, and so forth.

Profit is the overriding purpose of all business organizations. Mission statements simply further identify how one business intends to achieve profit as opposed to how another firm might do so. These statements must be carefully worded, since they provide direction for policy, objectives, and strategy. Information Capsule 1.1 contains examples of mission statements abstracted from several organizations' annual reports or philosophies.

Mission statements change for numerous reasons; the appearance of opportunities or threats is a common reason for change. New management often introduces changes; for example, when Roy E. Winegardner was elected chief executive of Holiday Inns, he made major changes in the firm's mission. As he declared, "We are in the process of reshaping Holiday Inns into a different company . . . —a hospitality company." The principal result was to limit the company's scope to food, lodging, and entertainment, moving the company out of some businesses (Trailways) and into an active casino gambling position.[4]

Note the variations, and also the similarities and common components, among the mission statements in Information Capsule 1.1. As you can see, nonprofit organizations also have basic mission statements that are phrased in terms of primary markets. The basic question these statements seek to answer is "What business are we in or do we want to be in?" (If you look carefully at U.S. Steel's statement, you will find that steel is not really its principal business.)

It is critical to organizational success that this question of business engagement be answered properly. In 1975, W. T. Grant, a retail chain with almost $2 billion in sales and 1,000 stores, went bankrupt. One of the major underlying causes of its failure was that it overlooked this basic question. One Grant executive commented that the company could not make up its mind whether it wanted to be a full-service store like J. C. Penney and Sears or a discounter like K-Mart. The company compromised and "took a position between the two and consequently stood for nothing"[5]—and consequently went bankrupt.

Similarly, Braniff Airlines, in 1979, decided that it wanted to be a national airline, not just a regional one. The results were disastrous. The company lost $131

---

[3]P. Kotler, *Marketing Management: Analysis, Planning, Control* (Englewood Cliffs, N.J.: Prentice-Hall, 1980), pp. 50–54.
[4]R. E. Winegardner, as reported in "Holiday Inns: Refining Its Focus to Food, Lodging—and More Casinos," *Business Week*, July 21, 1980, pp. 100, 104.
[5]J. G. Kendrick, as quoted in "How W. T. Grant Lost $175 Million Last Year," *Business Week*, February 24, 1975, p. 75.

Information Capsule 1.1
Mission Statements

AT&T

. . . No longer do we perceive that our business will be limited to telephony or, for that matter, telecommunications. Ours is the business of information handling, the knowledge business. And the market we seek is global. . . . 1980 . . . was a year in which . . . we took the first steps toward a restructuring of the Bell System. . . . In the future we shall be operating in two modes. . . . Basic local and long distance service we shall continue to provide under regulation. At the same time, we will be afforded expanding opportunities to compete in unregulated markets.

AT&T, *Annual Report*, 1980.

Northwest Bancorporation

Northwest Bancorporation, also known as Banco [the nation's thirteenth largest bank in terms of income], . . . is one of only three major bank holding companies currently operating a multistate franchise. . . . Banco's banks are complemented by financial service activities: mortgage banking, venture capital, commercial finance, agricultural lending, leasing, insurance, trust management, international banking, and Eurobond and municipal bond underwriting. . . . The national network of financial service subsidiaries has offices in 16 states beyond the corporation's seven state banking region. As a consequence, Banco is well positioned to launch an aggressive expansion strategy when legislation reopens the door to interstate banking.

Northwest Bancorporation, *Annual Report*, 1980.

Dresser Industries

. . . Dresser Industries is a $4 billion corporation employing over 50,000 men and women and operating in virtually every country in the world. . . . Dresser Industries Inc. is one of the world's leading suppliers of technology, products, and services to industries involved in the development of energy resources—including petroleum, natural gas, coal, and synfuels. . . . Dresser is in the business of developing and managing a broad and balanced portfolio of engineered products and technical services that are marketed through five industry segments (petroleum, energy processing and conversion, refractories and minerals, construction and mining, industry specialty products) primarily to the oil, gas, coal and energy conversion industries throughout the world.

Dresser Industries, Inc., *Report on Your Investment*, 1980.

U.S. Steel

Steel is and has always been U.S. Steel's principal business and it will continue to be as long as it can return a competitive profit [steel accounted for only 12.1 percent of operating profits in 1980]. . . . Demand for steel is expected to grow at an average of 1½ to 2 percent per year—less than the rate of growth expected for the economy as a whole. Demand in many of our businesses (chemicals, resource development, manufacturing and engineering, domestic transportation and utility subsidiaries) is expected to grow at a faster rate than the Nation's economy. For U.S. Steel to grow as fast as the economy, a significant portion of facility investments must be directed to those markets having above average growth potential.

U.S. Steel, *Annual Report*, 1980.

The Crummer School—Rollins College

. . . The Roy E. Crummer Graduate School of Business is one of few collegiate schools of business to devote its efforts solely to graduate education. The faculty and administration believe that the best education for management consists of a broad-based undergraduate program coupled with a full two-year MBA program. It is on the undergraduate level that students should learn the fundamentals which give them the abilities to communicate and make ethical judgments, and it is the graduate level at which they should learn the skills that are necessary to make decisions concerning the management of an organization. . . . The goal is to apply that portion of the material which is appropriate for the particular problem being solved. It is important to note that we are not trying to substitute practicality for academic theory. Rather, we are trying to supplement the theory with the ability to implement it.

The full-time MBA program should be marketed on a national scale with the goal of becoming one of the nation's prestigious MBA programs. Students can be drawn directly from undergraduate school or from full-time employment.

The part-time MBA program will be marketed throughout the Orlando metropolitan area. Through close contact with corporate executives, recruitment efforts will emphasize a high quality program of private education featuring close student contact, and outstanding faculty.

Roy E. Crummer Graduate School of Business, *Structure, Governance, and Policies*, 1984.

---

million in 1980.[6] The president resigned; and eventually the airline went bankrupt. The mission statement must always reflect capabilities. Braniff's choice of mission overlooked its managerial, aircraft, and professional flight staff capabilities; it simply did not have enough managers, enough airplanes, or enough pilots and host personnel to meet the demands of rampant growth. Nor could it obtain planes or per-

[6]Braniff Airlines, *Annual Report*, 1980, p. 4.

sonnel, or train personnel quickly enough, to meet these demands.[7] Its future was predictable.

Practically as well as conceptually speaking, all organizational activity derives from the mission. Without a proper mission statement, the organization may ultimately be doomed to failure.

Undertaking the definition of a company mission is one of the most easily slighted tasks in the strategic management process. . . . But the critical role of the company mission as the basis of orchestrating managerial action is repeatedly demonstrated by failing firms whose short-run actions are ultimately found to be counterproductive to their long-run purpose.

—John A. Pearce II

Organizational Policy

The term *policy* is used here to designate broad guidance created to ensure the successful establishment of objectives and the successful formulation, implementation, and control of strategy. Most policies have a broad and major impact on the organization, but some have a more limited impact and are designed to guide decisions through the use of more specific constraints. Policies provide organization members, primarily managers, with a framework within which they can make decisions. Examples of policies include the following:

1. Only products with at least a 15 percent return on investment (ROI) will be considered as additions to existing product lines.
2. Only products with high quality will be chosen for inclusion in the product line.

Because of these policies, this firm's corporate, business, and division managers will not select products which do not provide at least this rate of return and which do not have high quality. Because the managers do not have to determine what level of ROI is appropriate or what level of product quality is sought, the policies save time and effort.

As with the term *strategy*, the usage of the term *policy* varies greatly. The student of strategic management should recognize this fact and should not allow semantic problems to interfere with organizational analysis. The term is often employed to describe what is defined—here and often elsewhere—as strategy. Or the term may be used to describe very specific rules, such as "no smoking" or "employees retire at age sixty-five." Often, policy is considered a component of strategy. In various contexts, strategies have a way of shading into policies, and vice versa.

Regardless of what we call them, however, an organization must have major plans of action in order to accomplish its mission. The organization must also have some form of broad guidance for formulating, implementing, and controlling these

---

[7]This is the author's personal analysis. Fall 1981.

plans. These components of effective organizations are labeled here as *strategy* and *policy*, respectively.

Business policy has a tendency for jargon that delineates and isolates the field from the uninitiated.

—*Milton Leontiades*

You will note that Figure 1.1 identifies three major types of policies: strategic policies, policies that aid implementation, and control policies. Let us now examine the first of these—strategic policies—in more detail.

Organizational Policy at the Strategic Level

The master strategy derives from the organization's mission and from the policies which exist to provide guidance in formulating it. These policies, which are called strategic policies here, are usually created by the owners, the board of directors, the chief executive officer (CEO), top line and staff personnel, top SBU managers, or professional planners; however, other organizational members may aid in their formulation. Some organizations refer to these policies as "basic assumptions." Others designate them "primary intents." Still others refer to them as "master policies." But regardless of its designation, certain guidance must be available to the organization's strategists as they determine strategic objectives and formulate the master strategy. In the business organization, this guidance normally relates to the following issues, although exact policies vary from firm to firm:

1. The return on investment desired and other performance criteria.
2. The scope of the strategy.
3. The basic actions in which the organization may engage: competition, growth, diversification, and so on.
4. The industries to be entered.
5. The qualifications of products to be offered.
6. The organization's climate and management philosophy.
7. The geographic location of the basic actions.
8. The role of the corporation in the total society.

Based on the issues above and on consideration of mission and internal and environmental information, the organization's strategists determine objectives and formulate strategies. After considering information related to internal and environmental factors, the organization's strategists may, from time to time, redefine the basic policies which guide the formulation of strategic objectives and of the master strategy and its component strategies. For example, examination of internal factors may reveal critical inabilities which preclude diversification. Or exploration of the external environment may reveal that new industry opportunities are available. Strategic policies must remain flexible if the organization is to be successful. Conceptually, strategic policies constitute a body of statements separate from strategic objectives and strategies. In practice, however, the three are often intermingled. Policies exist at every level of the organization. At the highest level, strategic policies guide the formation of strategic objectives and the master strategy. Lower-level policies should be subordinate to those at higher levels of the strategy formulation process. Oftentimes, strategic policies almost constitute a master strategy. Information Capsule 1.2 contains the strategic policies for a highly successful manufacturing firm—the Dana Corporation. Note that these policies contain some objectives and are so specific as occasionally to constitute a strategy.[8]

Once strategic, or master, policies are established, the organization literally lives or dies by them. Both implementation and control policies, discussed in later chapters, are based on the outcomes of these strategic policies. All three types of policies are critical. The title of this book stresses the importance of both strategic management and one of its principal components, policy. Neither can be overlooked. Since all actions will follow the guidance provided in policy, proper policy formulation is critical to organizational success. W. T. Grant had very few policies, and most of those it had were inappropriate. It went bankrupt. Firms such as Martin Marietta and K-Mart have highly functional policies based on mission and information. Such policies allow firms to survive and prosper.

Most battles are won—or lost—before they are engaged, by men who take no part in them; by their strategists. —K. von Clausewitz

The Organizational Strategists

In concept, organizational strategists, those involved in general management, include the owners, the board of directors, the CEO, and the top corporate and SBU line and staff officers, including professional planners. However, research by Henry Mintzberg has shown that an organization's strategic decision processes are normally dominated by an entrepreneurial chief executive, a coalition of high-ranking corporate or SBU officers, or a planning department.[9] Planning departments in multiple-SBU firms may be attached either to the corporate headquarters or to SBU headquarters or to both. Before we examine the roles of the three dominant strategists noted above, let's review the impact of boards of directors on strategic management.

The Board of Directors and Strategic Management

Research reveals that the board of directors has historically performed few of the classic functions conceptualized for it, such as strategic decision making. While the board may have passively approved the organization's objectives and strategies,

---

[8] Most of the early writings, which came from the Harvard School of Business, defined strategy as that "set of major policies which defined what the organization wanted to be or become."
[9] H. Mintzberg, "Strategy Making in Three Modes," *California Management Review*, Winter 1973, pp. 45–46.

Information Capsule 1.2
Dana Policy

EARNINGS . . . The purpose of the Dana Corporation is to earn money for its shareholders and to protect and increase the value of their investment. We believe the best measurement of the accomplishment of our purpose is the constant growth in the corporation's earnings per share.

GROWTH . . . We believe in a steady rate of growth consistent with protecting our assets against the erosions of inflation.

We must enter new diversified markets worldwide that are consistent with our goal and compatible with our management and technical abilities.

The corporation and the divisions share in this growth responsibility.

PEOPLE . . . We are dedicated to the belief that our people are our most important asset.

We will encourage all of them to contribute and to grow to the limit of their desire and ability.

We believe people respond to recognition, freedom to contribute, opportunity to grow, and to fair compensation. We believe that higher pay follows job performance and endorse the practice of an above average base compensation with a high incentive potential.

We believe in the philosophy of continued employment for all Dana people. We believe that they should identify with the company and that this identity should carry on after they have left active employment.

We believe that wages and related benefits are the concern and responsibility of supervisors. There are some benefits which are a corporate matter and participation in these—the Stock Purchase Plan, the Management Resource Program, some form of Income Protection, Matching Gifts, Tuition Refund, Relocation and Foreign Service Benefits—is a privilege of all permanent Dana people.

We believe that on-the-job training is the most effective method of teaching; that everyone must prove proficiency in at least one line of our company's work—sales, engineering, manufacturing, financial control, or personnel; second, these people should then demonstrate ability as supervisors and be able to get work done through other people; third, we recognize the importance of gaining this experience both internationally and domestically.

Periodic changes in duties are desirable but should vary with the individuals and their own capabilities. These changes should not conflict with the operating efficiency of the company.

We believe in utilizing cooperative student programs and summer employment as recruiting devices and for training of people.

In filling vacancies that result from job training and promotion, every effort will be expended to find candidates within the Dana Corporation and its affiliates and subsidiaries. Permanent people interested in other positions in the company are encouraged to discuss the Dana Management Resources programs with their supervisor.

We believe education of all of our permanent people who desire it is very important. Division presidents and general managers and staff vice presidents and directors are responsible for the education of the people in their organizations. The Policy Committee is responsible for the education of officers, division presidents and general managers, and staff vice presidents and directors.

The Dana Board of Regents is responsible for suggesting policies and providing programs to support and encourage the career and personal development of all Dana people.

PLANNING . . . We believe in planning at all levels of the organization.

Divisions will be responsible for detailed one-year and general five-year plans covering products, growth, profitability, investment, source and use of funds, people, etc. These plans will be reviewed and continually updated.

Corporate planning will also be done with a detailed one-year and general five-year plan. This corporate plan should consist of a reasonable summation of the divisions' plans plus the additional action that is necessary to fulfill the broad corporate objectives.

The practice of management by objective is a key part of this planning process. Naturally differences in the various divisions will dictate their own objectives in support of the broad corporate objectives.

ORGANIZATION . . . We believe in a divisionalized organizational structure with considerable responsibility for performance given to division presidents and general managers worldwide.

These managers must have operating latitude to accomplish their goals within corporate objectives and policies. This environment not only stimulates initiative and innovation, but develops the expertise of management that is the keystone of our success.

In keeping with this philosophy, we do not create corporate procedures. If procedures are mandatory for the operation of a division, it is the responsibility of the division president or general manager to create them.

Our divisions are based on products where products are the key and on markets where the markets are the key. In order to achieve stability of performance, we believe Dana's goal should be equal sales to our three market places: vehicular, service and industrial. Thus, the concept of a tripod with relatively equal legs (vehicular, service and industrial) targets our approach to balanced growth. New divisions will be added or existing divisions restructured as circumstances dictate.

We believe in a "store manager" concept because it results in management training. We also believe it allows operating situations to be broken down into sizes that are readily manageable.

We believe in a small, highly effective corporate support group to service the needs of the corporate groups and the divisions, as requested.

CUSTOMERS . . . We believe it is absolutely necessary to anticipate our customers' needs for both product and service, and toward the fulfillment of this policy we must exert every effort. In anticipating our customers' need for products and services, we must insure our delivery capability based on an internal capacity with an opportunity for outside procurement consistent with sound, economical employment of the corporate assets.

Once a commitment is made to a customer, every effort must be made to fulfill that obligation.

It is highly desirable to maintain a balance between make and buy not only to protect the continuity of employment for our people through the various swings of business cycles, but also to insure customer supply through these same cycles.

COMMUNICATION . . . We will communicate our goals, policies and objectives to the shareholders, customers, people, plant city public, and the financial community.

It is the job of the division presidents and general managers and staff vice presidents and directors to keep people up to date constantly through newsletters, bulletin boards, group meetings, etc. At least once every year they shall make sure that all their people are informed of the results of their particular operation and what is planned for the coming year.

It is the responsibility of supervisors to encourage opinions and ideas from their people. Supervisors shall implement those ideas and suggestions that have merit or explain the reasons why certain things cannot be utilized if they are impractical or improper.

CITIZENSHIP . . . The Dana Corporation will be a good citizen at the international, national, state and local levels. We will conduct our business in a professional and ethical manner when dealing with governments, customers, neighbors and the general public worldwide.

Laws and regulations under which we operate worldwide have become increasingly complex. The laws of propriety always govern. The General Counsel and each General Manager can give guidance when in doubt about legal or appropriate conduct. It is assumed that no one would willfully violate the law and subject themselves to disciplinary action.

We encourage active participation on the part of all of our people in community action.

We will contribute to worthwhile community causes consistent with their importance to the good of the community.

The Policy Committee

Approved by The Board of Directors

Reprinted with the permission of the Dana Corporation, Toledo, Ohio. Taken from "The Dana Story, 1979" (annual report), p. 26.

---

normally it has had very little impact on their formulation and has not scrutinized them in very great detail. Furthermore, the evidence indicates that most board members have been ill-prepared to make such decisions. However, during the 1970s, failures of several major boards to take appropriate actions combined with lawsuits and proxy actions by disgruntled stockholders and citizens' groups resulted in the board's becoming much more professional, diverse, and responsive, at least in major corporations.

The role of the board of directors, while historically not well understood and not followed operationally as outlined conceptually, has in recent years become of major concern to corporations. The result has been an emphasis on increasing the board's role in making strategic decisions, monitoring executive performance and compensation, assuring the soundness of budgeting, and determining the soundness of policies. The number of outside directors has significantly increased, and a definite trend toward use of professional board members has become apparent. While the actions of boards naturally vary from firm to firm, we can anticipate continued efforts by boards to take a more active part in the organization's strategic process.

The coalitions which may develop on the board are very important, since the board must finally approve the chosen strategies. Research reveals that top management often controls the board rather than vice versa, as is normally conceptualized.[10] The behavioral aspects of the strategic decision process are examined in detail in Chapter 6, with special attention given to the coalition process. Let us now examine in more conceptual terms how each of the three major groups of strategists may influence the strategic management process.

The principal function of the strategists in determining objectives and formulating strategy is to consider mission, strategic policies, and information and then determine objectives which best match the needs of the organization, given the information available about strengths, weaknesses, opportunities, and threats. Then the strategists look at these same three factors in determining plans to reach the desired objectives. How the three major types of strategists—the entrepreneurial CEO, the coalition, and the professionals—go about their tasks may vary, however.

The Chief Executive Officer as Strategist

The CEO clearly dominates strategy formulation in practically all smaller firms, in most medium-sized firms, and in many, if not most, large firms. Within multiple-SBU companies, total organization strategies are determined by corporate CEOs or other strategists, with the SBU corporate strategies being determined by SBU CEOs or other strategists. CEOs who affect strategy may be either owner/entrepreneurs or professional managers who take risks and who seek the power that such positions and decisions involve.

Almost all U.S. corporations were begun or made successful by entrepreneurially oriented owner/managers: Sears (Richard W. Sears), Xerox (Joseph Wil-

---

[10] K. R. Andrews, "Replaying the Board's Role in Formulating Strategy," *Harvard Business Review*, May/June 1981, pp. 18–20, 24–25; K. R. Andrews, "Corporate Strategy as a Vital Function of the Board," *Harvard Business Review*, November/December 1981, p. 175; W. W. Wommack, "The Board's Most Important Function," *Harvard Business Review*, September/October 1979, pp. 52–62; "The Board: It's Obsolete Unless Overhauled," *Business Week*, May 22, 1971, pp. 50–58; W. Boulton, "The Evolving Board: A Look at the Board's Changing Roles and Information Needs," *Academy of Management Review*, October 1978, pp. 827–836; M. Chandler, "It's Time to Clean up the Boardroom," *Harvard Business Review*, September/October 1975, pp. 73–82; N. C. Churchill, V. Lewis, and C. Ramsay, "Changing Strategic Requirements of Boards of Directors as Companies Develop and Grow" (Paper presented to the Strategic Management Society Conference, Paris, October 1983); W. D. Clendenin, "Company Presidents Look at the Board of Directors," *California Management Review*, Spring 1972, pp. 60–66; "End of the Director's Rubber Stamp," *Business Week*, September 10, 1979, pp. 72–77; S. M. Felton, Jr., "Case of the Board and the Strategic Process," *Harvard Business Review*, July/August 1979, pp. 19–22; P. B. Firstenberg and B. G. Malkiel, "Why Corporate Boards Need Independent Directors," *Management Review*, April 1980, pp. 26–28; J. A. Groobey, "Making the Board of Directors More Effective," *California Management Review*, Spring 1974, pp. 25–34; J. W. Henke, Jr., "Making Board of Directors' Involvement in Corporate Strategy Work" (Paper presented to the Strategic Management Society Conference, Paris, October 1983); M. Launstein, "Preserving the Importance of the Board," *Harvard Business Review*, July/August 1977, pp. 36–47; M. S. Mizruchi, "Who Controls Whom? An Examination of the Relation Between Management and Board of Directors in Large American Corporations," *Academy of Management Review*, July 1983, pp. 426–435; J. Montgomery, "New Direction: Citizens and Southern Shakeup Underscores Evaluation of Boards," *Wall Street Journal*, March 21, 1978; R. Mueller, *New Directions for Directors* (Lexington, Mass.: Lexington Books, 1978).

son), Eastern Airlines (Captain Eddie Rickenbacker), Jim Walters Corporation (Jim Walters), Eckerd Drugs (Jack Eckerd), the Coca-Cola Company (John Woodruff), Ford Motor Company (Henry Ford), Mary Kay Cosmetics (Mary Kay), Wendy's (R. David Thomas), George E. Johnson Company (George E. Johnson), Marriott Corporation (J. Willard Marriott), and McDonald's (Ray Kroc), to name a few. Many firms, including some of those just mentioned, have also been tremendously affected in their strategic courses of action by professional managers who took risks and acted as entrepreneurs—General Motors (Alfred P. Sloan), the Coca-Cola Company (J. Paul Austin), AT&T (John DeButts), Miller Brewing Company (John A. Murphy), and Radio Shack (Charles Tandy), for example.

Look around your town or city. How many businesses there are run by a CEO or a family dominated by one person? Almost all businesses are headed by one person, aren't they? These managers are the backbone of the system of free enterprise, which rewards the investor, the innovator, and the risk taker.

In recent years, substantial concern has been expressed that this entrepreneurial motivation is missing from large, dominant corporations.[11] Indeed, this concern appears to be well founded; and as a result, the ability of U.S. firms to compete in the international arena has been significantly reduced. This is especially true with respect to competing with Japanese firms, which actively seek to further the success of their organizations in the long run, not the short run.

As you progress through this text, the importance of taking the strategic management viewpoint will be further emphasized. U.S. firms do seem to have realized their overemphasis on the short term and do seem to be responding to the challenge of international competition. One of the biggest keys to success in this endeavor is to correlate the strategists' compensation to long-term successes and not to short-term successes such as those indicated by current profits and ROI. Information Capsule 1.3 discusses Japanese management systems and how they stress the strategic view.

The Coalition as Strategist

The business organization, whether a single- or multiple-SBU type, is a formal authority system composed of subsystems. Within this system and within these subsystems, informal social systems develop. These informal relationships often play a major role in strategy formulation.

Studies of the objective setting and strategy formulation processes have revealed that a powerful informal group of top managers may emerge within the formal planning group. This informal group, referred to as the coalition, may, in fact, establish an organization's objectives and strategies, depending on the nature of the entrepreneurial leadership characteristics of the organization's formal leader.

Bargaining often determines organization objectives, strategies, and policy. Members of the coalition negotiate strategic matters among themselves, with other powerful individuals, or with other coalitions which may develop inside or outside the organization. At the center of this bargaining process is the conflict which exists

---

[11] For example see the "Productivity" issue of *Business Week*, article entitled "Managers Who are no Longer Entrepreneurs," June 30, 1980, pp. 74–75.

Information Capsule 1.3
Japanese Management and the Strategic View

Examining the Japanese success story shows that several factors have contributed to the enormous strides the Japanese have made economically in the last ten years. Careful examination of the evidence reveals that the following five factors have especially contributed to this success:

1. *Cooperation between Government and Business.* Japan's government steers firms in the proper strategic direction, toward areas in which potential profits appear highest. Tax incentives, subsidies, import quotas, and R&D funding are used to this end.
2. *Cooperation between Labor and Business.* The confrontation which characterizes the U.S. labor/business interaction is absent in Japan.
3. *Management Style.* Employee participation in decision making, recognition of employees' performance and human needs, and employee job security are key ingredients in the Japanese management style which have clearly contributed to Japanese successes. These considerations are typically absent in U.S. managerial actions.
4. *Management Development and Education.* Japanese managers continually receive training on how to manage, especially interpersonal relationships. U.S. companies, in contrast, invest relatively little in such endeavors.
5. *Management Systems—Strategic and Quantitative.* Japanese managers take the strategic view. Their marketing actions, production actions, and personnel actions reflect a concern for the long-run viability of the firm. For example, they may stress market share more than profits; but in the long run, market share will lead to profits. This contrasts with U.S. management objectives, which often emphasize short-run results, such as annual profit. Because Japanese managers know their firms will be competitive in ten years, by which time they may have become top managers, they are willing to sacrifice now for that future success.

    Statistical analysis is employed at every stage of the production or service process to measure the quality of inputs, to make certain that the process is as it should be, and to measure the quality of outputs. This emphasis on statistics and quality control was suggested by an American consultant, William Deming of Washington, D.C., a prophet not recognized, until recently, in his own land. The Japanese success story has, however, brought recognition to his work.

between, on the one hand, the manager's desire to accomplish his or her particular subunit's objectives and to protect its interests (and his or her own) and, on the other hand, the requirement of the organization to accomplish organizational objectives. Because managers must seek to improve subunit performance in organizations with scarce resources, they must compete with other managers for those resources. But total competition would be detrimental to the firm; thus, bargaining and tradeoffs in strategy and policy matters occur. The result is often suboptimization and failure to accomplish the mission. (It is interesting to note that coalitions play a very prominent role in government and other nonprofit organizations.)

While many of the ideas presented here oppose the traditional view of the all-powerful chief executive officer, significant empirical support substantiates them. The evidence is reviewed in more detail in Chapter 6.

Planning Departments—Professional Planners as Strategists

When the duties associated with strategy formation become too extensive for the CEO to accomplish alone, he or she normally delegates many of these duties to a planning committee of top managers or, in larger organizations, to a professional planning department. The role of the professional planning unit usually involves collecting and analyzing data and making them available, and generating and evaluating alternatives. Professional planners and planning units exist most commonly in larger business organizations. However, as planning models become more widely computerized and as information sharing within an industry becomes more widespread, planning departments should become more common even in smaller business organizations. The size of these planning units vary from the planner and his or her secretary to a staff of fifty or more in the largest corporations. A study by Larry Greiner indicates that these planners spend up to half of their time reading reports. The areas which the planning department is expected to investigate in these reports include

1. Strategic surprises of all types.
2. Strategic contingency actions for known, recurring problems.
3. Research into new product and new market opportunities.
4. Forecasts involving all relevant data.
5. Competitors' strategies.
6. Economic situations—especially changes—and how they relate to the organization.
7. Technological changes.
8. Societal demands.
9. Government—legal and political trends.
10. Internal financial, production, marketing, and personnel information.
11. Other internal and external information.[12]

---

[12] L. E. Greiner, "Integrating Formal Planning into Organizations," *Formal Planning Systems*, by F. J. Aguilar, R. A. Howell, and R. F. Vancil (eds.) (Cambridge, Mass.: Graduate School of Business, Harvard University, 1970).

The professional planner should be the manager and designer of the strategy formulation system. The planner influences top and lower levels of management in their planning efforts. He or she provides information, establishes planning rules, consults, and integrates the various plans submitted. The planner's role in many firms is not so much to be a chief planner but rather to be a planning coordinator—a monitor, a controller, and a critic of subsystem plans and planning.

Another dimension of the planning function involves the professional futurist. While strategists might be concerned with five-year forecasts, futurists peer twenty years or more into the future to attempt to define major economic, social, governmental, and technological trends. One of their primary functions appears to be to ask discerning questions—"what if" questions about the results of traditional forecasting techniques. For example, population forecasts using traditional extrapolative techniques overlook the impact of possible changes in birth control practices. The futurist's duty is to query, "What if the use of birth control devices increases or decreases by X percent?" Even more dramatic questions can be asked by futurists: "What if the government of a certain country is overthrown by leftists (or by rightists)? How would overthrow by leftists (or by rightists) affect our business?" "What if there is another Arab oil embargo?"[13] Although a futurist's primary role is to question, he or she must also draw some implications from the suggested answers to the questions. Not all organizations would benefit from a futurist's predictions; but for many organizations, to ignore the areas in which the futurist deals would be folly.

Finally, from time to time, the professional planning department may in fact decide future courses of action for the organization. The power to do so results from its knowledge of and skill in strategy formulation and from its control of the information needed to make strategic decisions. This portion of its role will be discussed in Chapter 6.

Characteristics of the Effective Professional Planner. Objective setting and strategy formulation, like many management activities, have been described both as intuitive and as rational endeavors. In fact, both intuition and reason are required. The collection and analysis of data is a rational process, one which requires the ability to process massive amounts of information. But the effective utilization of the resultant information to generate alternatives and forecast the future requires creativity. It may occasionally call for the employment of nonrational techniques of alternative generation. In addition to these skills, the corporate planner must possess a keen ability to use the politics of the organization. The planner must possess social skills, since much of his or her effort involves group activity. Since these subjects are discussed in detail in other books, they will not be pursued further here. In summary, however, the effective planner needs a minimum of several skills: conceptual, creative, rational, political, and social.

The Future of the Professional Planner. The evidence indicates that organizational environments are becoming more variable and more volatile with each passing year. Businesses' major environmental concerns—society, government, tech-

---

[13]L. R. Galeese, "The Soothsayers: More Companies Use 'Futurists' to Discern What Is Lying Ahead," *Wall Street Journal*, March 31, 1975, pp. 1, 8.

nology, competition, labor, the economy, the international environment, and natural resource availabilities—are increasingly unpredictable. As a result, the organization will depend more on professional strategists to interpret the meanings of the changes and to establish objectives and create strategies which will fulfill the organizational mission. The time horizon of the objectives and strategies may be compressed, but objectives and strategies must nonetheless be formulated. In fact, numerous alternative contingency strategies will be produced to cope with numerous possible situations. Several firms are currently generating multiple strategies, each designed to be employed given a certain set of circumstances.

As the tasks of objective determination and strategy formulation become more complex, professional strategists will assume more of the strategic decision-making role. Computer simulations will become necessities, because as the environment becomes more turbulent, the need to ask "what if" questions becomes even greater. Overall, the professional planner would seem to have a promising future, one which could lead to the chief executive's office. The individual or group helping the organization cope with its problems gains power. As the planning unit is required to respond to greater challenges, it and its chief administrator should become more powerful.

I hardly need to point out that it is more difficult and demanding to be a successful business manager today, in our national and international environment, than ever before. Nevertheless, a basic component of management's job is to adapt effectively.
—James E. Lee, President, Gulf Oil Corporation

Strategic Management in the International Arena

Strategic management in the international arena follows the same basic patterns established earlier, in Figures 1.1 and 1.2. The conceptual processes are essentially the same, but the operating environment is so different that the resultant actions are frequently unrecognizable, especially in terms of implementation. The multinational corporation (MNC), the firm that conducts its business across national boundaries, will find itself confronted with four major problems:[14]

1. The international marketplace is highly competitive. Firms in France, Germany, Great Britain, Brazil, Japan, Korea, Taiwan, Canada, the United States, and numerous other countries have forged substantial, internationally competitive operating units. Many of these firms have significant strategic advantages, such as those involving labor cost or technology, that make competing with them very difficult.

2. Operations are conducted in widely varying economic, legal, political, social, and cultural environments. For example, a wide range of economies exist,

[14] Y. N. Chang and F. Campo-Flores, *Business Policy and Strategy* (Santa Monica, Calif.: Goodyear Publishing Company, 1980), Chapter 17; Y. L. Doz, "Strategic Management in Multinational Companies," *Sloan Management Review*, Winter 1980, pp. 27–46.

from developing to mature. Many of the customs so common to the parent country of the MNC are virtually unknown in the host country in which the MNC will do business.
3. The relative values of currencies vary rapidly, and currency translations can quickly turn a profit into a loss. For example, one major U.S. multinational lost one-third of its profits as the result of currency transaction losses. Some lose all their profits.
4. Government-to-government relationships and government-to-MNC relationships have a significant bearing on results. For example, the U.S. government often encourages U.S. firms to enter into international business, but then places severe restrictions on their rules of operation.

An additional factor might just be that management, and in particular strategic management, would be in a different stage of development in a country other than one's own. Therefore, adjustments in management practices, in strategic management practices in particular, would be necessary.

The evolution of multinational companies (MNCs) over the last decade has been characterized by a growing conflict between the requirements for economic survival and success (the economic imperative) and the adjustments made necessary by the demands of host governments (the political imperative). —Yves L. Doz, 1980

Strategic management is every bit as important in the international business situation as it is in the domestic market. Strategists must learn to cope with the variables in this environment just as they would in any other. Let us examine how the four factors listed above might alter approaches to the major points discussed earlier—mission, strategic policy, and strategists.

Mission

The four types of basic missions listed earlier remain; but in much of the world outside the United States and Canada, the service and commonweal missions are more often legally required for businesses than they are in these two countries. A close tie more often exists between business and government. There is an even closer alignment in many cases between business and labor; thus, the mutual benefit mission is sometimes more pronounced. For example, in much of Europe, it is illegal to terminate employees for other than the most grievous offenses, because government wishes full employment for the commonweal whether the firm remains productive or not. Thus, business assumes a commonweal mission. And in Japan, the organization is, in a sense, viewed by most of its employees as a mutual benefit organization. For example, the biggest firms guarantee male workers lifetime employment. On the other hand, employees work within the firm not so much to further their own interests but rather to further the interests of the organization for the benefit of society. In England, profit and service missions are apparently much more subordinate to the commonweal mission than they are in the United States and Canada. Service and quality have all but disappeared from many English industries as a result. Again, then, we see the priorities of the missions change. The results are most dramatically displayed in the marketplace and in the management of employees.

Strategic Policy

Because missions vary, strategic policy mixes (and, indeed, operational and control policies as well) must vary. For example, in most of the world, concern for employees and employee development is very low. The essential question in developing nations is how to make any profit. Organization climate and management philosophy policies are therefore quite different from what they might be in the United States and Canada and are most often not even addressed as strategic policies. Product quality is often of less concern in countries (for example, England) with close government/business ties, because in such countries protected internal markets exist. On the other hand, in Japan, a country with close business/government ties, quality is important, because the Japanese seek to be highly competitive in the international marketplace, although they do protect their home markets.

The Strategists

Again, because of varying mission significance and the related closer or more distant business/government relationships, variances exist in the composition of the strategist group. In countries with closer business/government relationships and more commonweal-oriented objectives, the government is often a full partner or even a managing partner in business endeavors. This is true to some extent in Germany and Japan, to a great extent in England and in Yugoslavia and most of the Soviet bloc countries, and to a limited extent in Brazil. It is increasingly true in the United States. And because of mutual benefit arrangements, unions and front-line employees may be in a position, usually elected, to aid in the strategic decision process. For example, in Germany, a law requires that approximately half of the board of directors of each of the larger business firms be composed of elected front-line employees.[15] In Poland, until the imposition of martial law in late 1981, the labor union Solidarity—uncharacteristically for a communist country—played a major part not only in strategic business decisions but in governmental decisions as well. And in the United States, there is a limited trend toward workers' participating at the strategic level; for example, the president of the United Auto Workers Union is now a member of the board of directors of the "new" Chrysler Corporation.

In most countries, governments have established policies demanding that a certain percentage of the MNC's top management be residents of the host country. Thus, the importation of management talent from the parent country of the MNC is often restricted, and in some cases even forbidden. Thus, the composition of the

---

[15] K. E. Agethe, "Mitbestimmung: Report on a Social Experiment," *Business Horizons*, February 1977, pp. 5–14.

group that formulates strategy varies and often includes people who do not speak the same language, further compounding an already complex problem. In terms of impact on organization and implementation, these laws are especially significant, because they virtually always require that all front-line, supervisory, and middle-management positions be filled by host country residents.[16]

The International Ball Game

The international ball game is different. It's not really a whole new ball game; it's more like playing in a different ball park, where you have to learn the factors unique to the playing field. The task of the MNC's strategist is essentially the same as that of other strategists, but he or she or they must learn to cope with numerous variables that are not frequently encountered in the domestic situation. The following chapters discuss more specifically the major ways in which information, policy, and various strategies are affected.

Strategic Management in the Not-for-Profit Organization

Strategic management in the not-for-profit organization follows much the same pattern as indicated in Figures 1.1 and 1.2, at least conceptually. However, a number of factors serve to alter that process, and indeed to alter the manner in which economic and management functions are practiced within them as well. The following paragraphs first identify the nature of the not-for-profit organization and then indicate in general terms how the strategic management process varies in a not-for-profit from that process in a for-profit organization.

The Not-for-Profit Organization

Philip Kotler advises that four major types of organizations exist when classifications of private, public, for-profit, and not-for-profit are considered:

1. The private for-profit includes private corporations, partnerships, sole proprietorships.
2. The public for-profit includes state owned airlines, utilities, and so forth.
3. The private not-for-profit includes private museums, charities, universities, associations, hospitals, and so forth.
4. The public not-for-profit includes government agencies, public schools, public hospitals, and so on.

---

[16]R. Hal Mason, "Conflicts between Host Countries and the Multinational Enterprise," *California Management Review*, Fall 1974, pp. 5–14.

The private, nonprofit organizations, are often referred to as the third sector (of the economy), not being for-profit and not being government based. These may be broken into eight major groups as follows:[17]

1. Religious organizations
   a. churches
   b. church associations
   c. evangelical movements
2. Social organizations
   a. service clubs
   b. fraternal organizations
3. Cultural organizations
   a. museums
   b. symphonies
   c. opera companies
   d. art leagues
   e. zoos
4. Knowledge organizations
   a. private grade schools
   b. private universities
   c. research organizations
5. Protective organizations
   a. trade associations
   b. trade unions
6. Political organizations
   a. political parties
   b. lobbyist groups
7. Philanthropic organizations
   a. private welfare organizations
   b. private foundations
   c. charity hospitals
   d. nursing homes
8. Social cause organizations
   a. peace groups
   b. family planning groups
   c. environmental groups
   d. racial rights groups
   e. consumerist groups
   f. women's rights groups
   g. anti-vice groups

Not-for-profits comprise a major portion of the national economy. Various forms of government collectively account for a third of the U.S. GNP.[18] Indeed, few would argue that government in its various forms is the most pervasive of all institutions. On the other hand, it is not monolithic; but as E. S. Savas observes, is actually comprised of some 80,000 units within the United States,[19] albeit, one—the federal government, seeming monolithic to many. The number of private not-for-profit organizations is also extremely large and their impact on GNP is also highly significant.

Perhaps the most distinguishing feature of not-for-profit organizations is the separation which exists between their clients or users and their resource contributors.[20] Marketing in this environment serves the same dual function as in a for-profit organization—to market the product or service, and to raise funds. In the for-profit organization, marketing accomplishes both at the same time (except for contributed stockholders' equity or debt); but in the nonprofit, these are usually accomplished separately. In the for-profit organization, the client or user pays for the product or service, thus providing cash flow and hopefully profits. This is not true typically of the user or client in nonprofits and, therefore, that type of organization must seek financial resources elsewhere.

---

[17] Philip Kotler, *Marketing for Nonprofit Organizations*, 2e, (Englewood Cliffs: Prentice Hall, 1982), pp. 12–14.
[18] E. S. Savas, *Privatizing the Public Sector: How to Shrink Government* (Chatham, New Jersey: Chatham House Publishers, 1982).
[19] Ibid.
[20] E. Greenburg, "Competing for Scarce Resources," *Journal of Business Strategy*, Winter 1982, p. 82.

Now let us examine the ways in which the various major factors in the strategic management process are affected by the nonprofit situation.

Mission

Two major problems in a nonprofit organization are the absence of a clearly defined mission and the absence of the related clearly defined objectives. While it seems a simple matter to establish these, in nonprofits, it is not—at least partly because of the political nature of most such organizations, and at least partly because of the aforementioned separation of users and clients from resource contributors. The political process affects their missions and subsequent objectives in a number of ways. First, in government and in many of the other nonprofits, top management is continually changing, and with that change, mission and objectives change. Second, it is more politically expedient not to have a specific mission and measurable objectives if one wants to retain an elected position. Then too, there are always numerous constituents seeking to have a nonprofit organization satisfy their particular needs. This leads to a series of conflicting objectives which may never be resolved. For example, a hospital is typically required by law (federal and often municipal) to provide care to indigent patients. It is also expected to provide paying patients with the lowest-cost care. Yet, because of one constituent's demand, that of government, as much as 30% of a hospital's patient costs are written off, thus raising the price of a paying patient's care. Obviously, this angers paying patients—who may be represented by insurance companies, consumer groups, and even state agencies seeking to lower hospital costs. Finally, many of these organizations are subject to the charismatic leader, who may substitute mystique for substance.

The separation of providers of funds from clients and users contributes to imprecisely defined missions and objectives in two major ways. First, the influence of the resource contributors on decisions related to mission is often great. Unfortunately, they are often not qualified to be setting mission and objectives. And since their time and interest are limited, they may react rather than think through the problem. And, frequently, customer influence in these same decisions is limited. Therefore, market driven (customer influenced) mission statements are not typical. And, one might question, if they should be, since in many cases, services, especially government services, are provided at less than cost or are free, clearly biasing rationality from the perspective of the taxpayer or other contributor.

Another factor posing problems in determining mission and objectives is the fact that service (which most of these nonprofits provide) is intangible and difficult to measure. This does not mean that it is impossible to establish measurable missions and objectives, but it is frequently difficult. Efforts have been made in recent years to improve the measurability of service organization objectives, for example, establishing specific percentages of welfare clients that should be taken off the welfare roles for a given period. But, nonetheless, it is still difficult to use quantified objectives in many instances and, therefore, qualitative objectives abound in nonprofit organizations.

Finally, one must always be conscious of how success is measured in these organizations. Many of these organizations have multiple missions, (as do many for-profit organizations). The mutual benefit mission noted earlier in the chapter can play an important role in determining mission and objectives. For example, since these organizations often work on a budgetary basis, for which there are many demands, an external pressure usually exists to reduce the spending level. If a unit is too successful in achieving objectives, jobs may be lost—even those of top management. So who would rationally opt to work oneself out of work? Too, survival is a measurement of success for many of these organizations. Therefore, the focus often is one of "breaking even," not one of accomplishment. Another measure of success is spending the budget, not exceeding it, but spending it. Because of the historical trend in many of these nonprofits to base next year's budget on last year's budget, most make certain that this year's budget disappears.[21]

Strategic Policy

The strategic policies are often vague for many of the same reasons that mission and objectives are vague. Clients keep changing, if only by political decree. The service's quality is difficult to define—should a person be out of the hospital in six days or seven for a particular operation? (The federal government is now defining the quality of service for all major diagnostic related groupings with respect to how much they will pay for Medicare Services.) The roles of these organizations in society are not always well understood. Top managers often change, so there is a lack of consistency in management philosophy. The basic actions in which these organizations can engage are often limited by law or other factors. For example, a charity seldom diversifies into another charitable cause. And, finally, performance criteria are hazy, and as noted earlier, difficult to define. It would be easy to say that the profit motive gives for-profits an advantage in establishing strategic policies. Perhaps, but as noted above, other factors, such as politics, increase the complexity of the strategic process in nonprofit organizations.

The Strategists

The strategists vary. They may be contributors, top managers, board members (who are often chosen for their financial contributions), professional staff, clients, members of various coalitions which may develop, and finally society at large through various pressure groups or the electoral process. Critically, the motivations of the members of the management group may vary. For example, you often have professional salaried managers working with volunteer managers. The volunteer wants certain objectives accomplished, has certain preferences for plans, that often are in conflict with those of the professional manager. And volunteers are often well inten-

---

[21] Based loosely on the following: W. H. Newman, and H. W. Wallender, III, "Managing Not-for-Profit Enterprises," *Academy of Management Review*, January 1978, pp. 24–31; M. L. Hatten, "Strategic Management in Not-for-Profit Organizations," *Strategic Management Journal*, April–June 1982, pp. 89–104; E. L. Greenberg, "Competing for Scarce Resources," *Journal of Business Strategy*, winter 1982, pp. 81–87; and M. W. Dirsmith, S. F. Jablonsky, and A. D. Luzi, "Planning and Control in the U.S. Federal Government: A Critical Analysis of PPB, MBO, and ZBB," *Strategic Management Journal*, October–December 1980, pp. 303–329.

tioned, but not particularly well trained nor skilled in management. And because board members are often chosen for their financial capabilities, and not their management skills, their inputs to strategy formulation may be less than adequate. Characteristically, in many of these organizations, government especially, bureaucracies arise and any strategic decision must be approved by numerous layers of managers whose personnel are affected by the decision.

Finally, many of these organizations are very small. The top manager's time is limited. He or she is stretched thin, yet expected to perform strategic management functions as well as many others. The task becomes almost impossible—to be a specialist in many areas, such as accounting and marketing, and yet also plan strategy.

The Nonprofit Environment

The environment is different. The stakes of the game are different in many respects. The decision makers vary. The purposes are often unclear . . . but are becoming more precisely defined, we hope. The field is largely unexplored. Yet, in concept, and perhaps in practice, with proper adjustment, strategic management can be utilized similarly in both for-profits and not-for-profits.

Summary

Failing to plan is planning to fail. —Robert M. Fulmer

This chapter examined the basic concepts of strategic management, organizational policy, and the master strategy, and introduced two models which form the basis for this chapter and for the remainder of the text. Strategic management emphasizes the relationship of the organization to its environment as it attempts to accomplish its mission. Strategic management differs from traditional policy and strategy concerns, because these areas are primarily concerned only with mission accomplishment, with virtually no attention given to the greater impacts of strategy on the total environment. The strategic management process begins with mission, which leads to the formulation of strategic objectives. Subsequently, a master strategy is determined to accomplish those objectives. Intermediate planning, organizing, and implementation and operational planning occur to carry out the master strategy. Finally, evaluation takes place to see if the mission was accomplished. Organizational policy guides the entire process from the setting of objectives to evaluation and control.

The objective setting and strategy formulation processes depend upon four factors. One factor is the organizational strategists. There are three primary groups of strategists—the chief executive, the coalition, and the planning department. These strategists view the other factors—mission, strategic policy, and internal and external information—and then determine strategic objectives and organizational strengths, weaknesses, opportunities, and threats (SWOT). Next they generate alternative strategies to achieve strategic objectives, and finally they choose a master strategy from among these alternatives.

The international business situation is often quite different from the domestic one, since four primary problem areas are encountered: additional competition; differing economic, legal, social, political, and cultural systems; currency translations; and significant differences in the role of government.

Key Terms and Concepts

Key terms and concepts with which you should be familiar include: strategic management, organizational policy, master strategy, the principal concerns of strategic management, the single-SBU organization, the multiple-SBU organization, the enterprise strategy, the corporate strategy, the business strategy, the supportive strategies, the major parts of the strategic management process model, the major parts in the objective setting and strategy formulation model, mission statements, the four types of mission according to benefit, the three major types of organizational policy, the common strategic policies, the historical and evolving role of the board of directors in strategic management, the three major types of strategists, and the ways in which the subjects of this chapter are affected by international business situations, and by their application in nonprofits.

Discussion Questions

1. What is the major concern of strategic management? How does strategic management differ from traditional approaches to strategy and policy?
2. Apply the strategic management process model to a profit and a not-for-profit organization with which you are familiar. What differences are there? What similarities?
3. Now apply the objective setting and strategy formulation model to any organization for which you can gather the information necessary to complete this model.
4. Explain how the strategists use information, mission, and policy in setting objectives and in formulating strategy.
5. What impacts on objective setting and strategy formulation might result from the control of these processes by each of the three major types of strategists?

References

Ackoff, R. L. "The Meaning of Strategic Planning." In *Business Planning and Policy Formulation*, ed. Robert J. Mockler. New York: Appleton-Century-Crofts, 1972.

Ansoff, H. I. "The Concept of Strategic Management." *Journal of Business Policy*, Summer 1972.

Bracker, J. "The Historical Development of the Strategic Management Concept." *Academy of Management Review*, April 1980, pp. 219–224.

Bryson, J. M. "A Perspective on Planning and Crisis in the Public Sector." *Strategic Management Journal*, 1981, pp. 181–196.

Carroll, A. "Strategic Planning for Boundary Spanning Relations." *Managerial Planning*, January/February 1976, p. 1. "Corporate Planning: Piercing Corporate Fog in the Executive Suite." *Business Week*, April 28, 1975, p. 47.

Cyert, R. M., and March, J. G. *A Behavioral Theory of the Firm*. Englewood Cliffs, N.J.: Prentice-Hall, 1963.

Frankenhoff, W. P., and Granger, C. H. "Strategic Management: A New Managerial Concept for an Era of Rapid Change." *Long Range Planning*, April 1971, pp. 7–12.

Frederick, G. D., "The State of Private Sector Strategic Planning in Canada," *Long Range Planning,* June 1983, pp. 40–46.

Hegarty, W. H., and R. C. Hoffman, "Strategic Decision Making Among European Firms" (Paper presented to the Strategic Management Society Conference, Paris, October 1983).

Hofer, C. W. "Research in Strategic Planning: A Survey of Past Studies and Suggestions for Future Efforts." *Journal of Economics and Business*, Spring/Summer 1976, p. 281.

Mintzberg, H. "Policy as a Field of Management Theory." *Academy of Management Review*, January 1977, pp. 88–103.

Newman, W. H. "Shaping the Master Strategy of Your Firm." *California Management Review*, 1967, no. 3, pp. 77–88.

Schendel, D. E., and Hatten, K. J. "Business Policy or Strategic Management: A Broader View for an Emerging Discipline." *Proceedings: Academy of Management Meetings, 1972*, pp. 99–102.

Schendel, D. E., and Hofer, C. W., eds. *Strategic Management: A New View of Business Policy and Planning*. Boston: Little, Brown, 1979.

Shuman, J. C. "Corporate Planning in Small Companies." *Long Range Planning*, October 1975, pp. 81–90.

Springer, C., "Human Resource Strategy," *Journal of Business Strategy*, Fall 1980, pp. 78–83 This article profiles the strategic planner.

Steiner, G. A. *Top Management Planning*. New York: Collier Macmillan Ltd., 1969.

Chapter 2
Internal and Environmental Information

Nothing is permanent, except change.
Heraclitus

Personal computers, digital watches, video disks, the Adam microcomputer, Wendy's national hamburger chain, Merrill Lynch Ready Asset Accounts, Reunite, and the space shuttle all came on the scene from 1975 to 1984. A prime rate of 21 percent, a federal debt of 2 trillion dollars, a Republican president attempting to eliminate government deficits and waste, devastation then recovery in the housing and domestic auto industries, national recognition of the need for improved quality and productivity, major changes in energy supplies—from rationing to surplus, an annual inflation rate of 12.5 percent, supply-side economics, the Pershing II missile deployment in Europe, and havoc in the bond markets occurred during about the same period. In 1984, the dollar was strong again. Once-strong foreign currencies, such as the Pound, Franc, Deutschemark, and Yen, showed definite signs of weakness. The Japanese had forged a formidable competitive position relative to U.S., European, and Canadian firms in numerous important industries. And in the 1980s, the Chinese decided to emphasize consumption instead of continuing to emphasize basic industries, as they had in the 1970s.

What do all of these and numerous similar events and facts have in common? The answer is that they all illustrate that business is currently facing an environment which is more changeful and more demanding than any business has previously encountered. And, unfortunately, the future holds little promise of a more stable situation.

Figure 2.1
The Organization—a Strategic Management Process Model

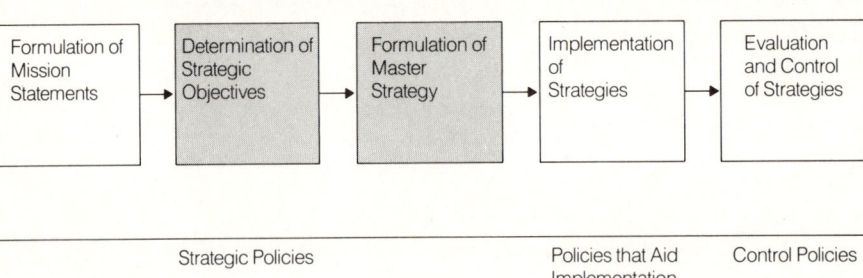

It can be argued that if a business is not growing, not changing, not meeting the new needs of the society, it is declining. To the unaware, strengths too soon become weaknesses, opportunities too soon become threats.

Just ask AAA Auto Club. Once masters of an undisputed and quite profitable niche, they now must struggle to stay ahead of competitors such as Wards Auto Club, which can deal through its credit card holders.[1] Or query a major airline about the impact that small airlines with fuel-efficient airplanes for shorter flights have had on its profits.[2] Or investigate the fortunes of the Victoria Station restaurant chain. That firm faces dire problems caused by the invasion by numerous others into its niche, the theme restaurant.[3] The examples are numerous and are readily found in the bankruptcy courts or in reports of management terminations and corporate takeovers.

Organizational strategists must make themselves aware of the changing world and of the organization's internal situation as well. The basis of successful strategic action is information. Chapter 1 discussed mission, strategic policy, and strategists, three of the four major influences on the determination of strategic objectives and the formulation of the master strategy. Information is the fourth major factor.

A danger facing all organizations is that top management's understanding of the environment can become obsolete.   —*R. T. Lenz and Jack L. Engledow*

This chapter reviews internal and environmental information and how this information can be gathered and used in the strategic management process. (Figures 2.1 and 2.2 show which components of this process are examined in this chapter.) The objective of obtaining information is to ascertain organizational strengths and weaknesses and organizational opportunities and threats in order to better determine objectives and strategy. This chapter first defines strengths, weaknesses, opportu-

---

[1] M. Yao, "As Auto Clubs Boom, AAA Is Scrambling to Keep Ahead of Its Aggressive Competitors," *Wall Street Journal*, August 5, 1980, p. 48.
[2] P. Nulty, "Friendly Skies for Little Airlines," *Fortune*, February 9, 1981, pp. 45–53.
[3] Author's personal analysis.

Figure 2.2
Objective Determination and Master Strategy Formulation

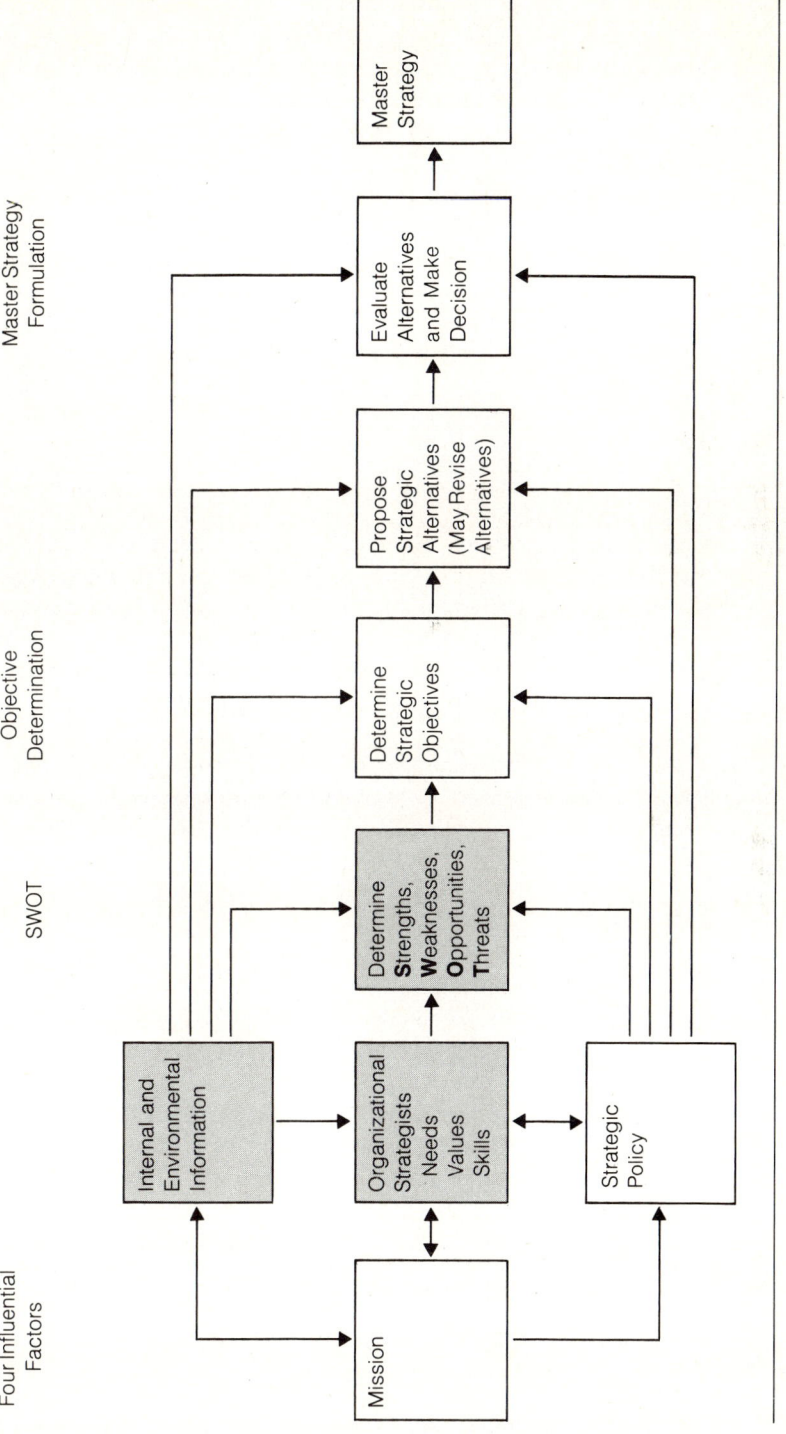

nities, and threats in order to provide the necessary background regarding what information is necessary. The discussion then moves to strategic information systems and the sources of information. The information sought at both the internal and the external level is reviewed. Special emphasis is given to environmental events and their impacts on the organization. The chapter then examines the analysis and forecasting of information. The appendix which follows this chapter provides a more detailed listing of sources of environmental information.

As you analyze any cases which might be used in a course on strategic management, you will use such environmental information. The knowledge gained from this chapter is important to you in class, as well as being important to strategists in business organizations. The second appendix to this book provides an extensive checklist similar to what organizations use in determining SWOT. You should use this "strategic audit" in examining any cases assigned to you.

SWOT

The organization's strategists observe mission, strategic policies, and current and forecasted information and then determine current and future organizational strengths, weaknesses, opportunities, and threats in order to determine where they are, where they want to be, and how they plan to get there—the essence of strategy. Strategists then perform their most important roles by determining strategic objectives and formulating the strategic plans to accomplish those objectives.

Organizations have certain characteristics—strengths—which make them uniquely adapted to carry out their tasks. Conversely they have other features—weaknesses—which inhibit their ability to fulfill their purposes. —Howard H. Stevenson

What Are SWOT?

Identifying SWOT is essential if the organization is to be successful. The process is complicated; and there are no simple solutions, as you will see in later chapters. First, though, exactly what are SWOT?

Strengths. Strengths are positive internal abilities and situations which might enable the organization to possess a strategic advantage in achieving its objectives.

At the business level, strengths are defined in terms of how the SBU can market its products competitively. There are five primary variables in marketing strategy: target market, product, promotion, price, and distribution. The strategies developed in these five areas are essential to success; but functional strategies, both economic and managerial, can make important contributions to a successful marketing effort. For example, in 1979 and 1980, Texas Instruments (TI) spent millions of dollars robotizing its production lines.[4] Why? Because in the electronics industry, price and

---

[4] "Texas Instruments Shows U.S. Business How to Survive in the 1980s," *Business Week*, September 18, 1978, pp. 66–92.

product quality are essential ingredients in successful competition, especially against the highly efficient and highly productive Japanese firms. Only through such investments could TI hope to remain competitive in the future.

Strengths at the corporate level for multiple-SBU firms are defined most often in terms of the synergy and balance among the SBUs within the firm. Synergy is the degree to which SBUs reinforce each other in pursuit of objectives. For example, an organization such as General Electric is considered to have very strong synergy among its SBUs. All are essentially technologically based and have strong profit margins or potentials. Balance refers to the relative cash requirements of the SBUs. The balance among GE's SBUs is also good; some are growing, some are stable, and some have strong cash flows that can support the total company's growth efforts.

Weaknesses. Weaknesses are internal inabilities and situations which might result in or have resulted in the firm's not achieving its objectives. Weaknesses are the opposite of strengths.

At the business level, marketing is still the principal concern. Wendy's found itself vulnerable to inflationary cost/price/demand factors in 1978, 1979, and 1980 because its product line at that time depended totally on beef, which underwent significant price increases during that period. This dependence was a weakness. Sales stagnated and profits dropped. Wendy's partially solved this problem by expanding its product base to include chicken and salads.

At the corporate level in the multiple-SBU firm, weaknesses are again a function of synergy and balance.[5] In 1976, Donald A. McMahon, the new president of the Royal Crown Cola Company, found that the firm's SBUs had little synergy. The required management skills were diverse and the industries totally unrelated. No balance existed. There were many money-losers. He immediately divested (sold off) many of these SBUs and then acquired Arby's in a successful effort to provide cash flow.[6]

Opportunities. Opportunities are external factors and situations which will assist the organization in achieving or exceeding its objectives. At the business level, they, too, are almost always expressed in terms of market potentials. The founders of Apple Computers saw a need for a personal computer at a low price. They created one and made a fortune. At the corporate strategy level in multiple-SBU firms, opportunities usually involve acquisitions or mergers. The Coca-Cola Company acquired the Taylor Wine Company because it saw that the corporation could become less dependent on soft drinks—and on its single most important product, Coke—and move into a rapidly expanding industry. It was correct in its evaluation of the opportunities. (However, industry profits diminished and Coke divested Taylor in 1983.)

Threats. Threats are external factors which might result in or have resulted in the firm's not achieving its objectives. Historically, threats have been defined in terms

---

[5] "The Penalties of Short-Term Corporate Strategies," *Business Week*, June 30, 1980, pp. 70, 71.
[6] "The Royal Crown Cola Gets a Lot More Fizz," *Business Week*, March 14, 1977, pp. 84, 85; "The Graying of the Soft Drink Industry," *Business Week*, May 23, 1977, pp. 68–72.

of the firm's competitors, but more recently the focus has expanded to include government, unions, society, and other stakeholders. At the business strategy level, an example of a threat is a technological innovation introduced by a competitor. Within a few months of the introduction of the digital watch, time had begun to run out on the Bulova Watch Company as a dominant force in the industry. It still depended upon pin-lever watches. Digital watches quickly captured Bulova's traditional markets. An example of how government can be a threat to business is the safety and environmental legislation which has placed demands on the U.S. auto industry. An example of a societal threat is the successful campaign of environmental groups to keep the Disney corporation from building a ski area in King's Mountain, California, when Disney badly needed an enterprise strategy.

At the corporate strategy level in multiple-SBU firms, threats are often the same as at the SBU level. Additional threats involve acquisitions and mergers. Rival multiple-SBU firms may compete to acquire the same SBU. A threat is also represented by an unfriendly response to a takeover attempt. In 1980, for example, InterNorth, Inc., attempted to acquire Crouse-Hinds Company. The offer was perceived as unfriendly, and Crouse-Hinds sought a friendly merger with Cooper Industries, Inc. Crouse-Hinds succeeded in obtaining pledges of allegiance to Cooper from several large stockholders; and InterNorth's bid was unsuccessful.[7]

At any time many businesses are confronted with a host of external technological threats. Managements of threatened firms realize that many threats may not materialize, at least in the short run. However, one or more of those potential threats may develop in ways that will have devastating impact.

—Arnold C. Cooper and Dan Schendel

How Managers Define SWOT. H. H. Stevenson studied fifty managers in six diverse business organizations to find out how they defined organizational strengths and weaknesses. He found that while the steps for defining strengths and weaknesses were essentially the same, the specific factors examined and the criteria used in judging these factors varied, and many factors modified the exact definitions. Strengths tended to be relatively well known and based on historical data; but weaknesses were less well known, and often little relevant data about them was available. Further, interpretation of data by the managers was partly a function of the managers' position and responsibility in the organization, their personality, and their perceived role in the organization.[8]

The implications of this study are important. Stevenson notes that in conducting an internal evaluation, managers should view the evaluation as an aid to task accomplishment; develop areas of examination tailored to the responsibility and authority of each manager; make criteria explicit to provide a common framework; understand the differences in use of identified strengths and weaknesses; and recognize the strategic importance of defining these attributes. In addition, it also seems pos-

---

[7] P. Blustein, "More Companies Use 'the Lockup' to Ward Off Unfriendly Takeovers," *Wall Street Journal*, January 28, 1981, p. 31.

[8] H. H. Stevenson, "Defining Corporate Strengths and Weaknesses," *Sloan Management Review*, Spring 1976, pp. 51–66.

sible that having the evaluation conducted by an external consultant would alleviate most of the problems mentioned above.

On the basis of a single research study, one can hardly discount all evaluations of strengths and weaknesses (or threats and opportunities). However, this study points out the need to be aware of the human variable in the strategic decision process. While this chapter is devoted to the techniques involved in strategic decision making, Chapter 6 concentrates on this human variable. As will be seen, the strategic decision process is extremely complex, much more so than the models which describe it usually depict. In fact, much of the rationality desired and built into the decision system through techniques is negated by the human variable.

Information

To manage a business well is to manage its future; and to manage its future is to manage information. —Marion Harper, Jr.

Information has two primary roles in objective setting and strategy formulation. First, information indicates the existence of strengths, weaknesses, opportunities, and threats. Second, information on the strengths and weaknesses of the organization in relation to environmental opportunities and threats is used to set objectives and formulate strategies. Strategists generate and evaluate alternatives based on this information.

Information systems indicate the existence of many strengths, weaknesses, opportunities, and threats. Most of them will not require the reformulation of the master strategy, but they often cause strategy objectives to be changed. Most threats are resolved and most opportunities taken advantage of at lower levels of planning, control, and implementation. Occasionally strategic information systems may indicate the need to formulate or reformulate the master strategy and cause the strategic decision process to be pursued.

Strategic Information Systems

Getting an idea from one place to another is as important as getting an idea.
—Advertisement by TRW, 1983

It is the function of the Strategic Information System (SIS) to provide the informational inputs required in the strategic decision process. Any decision, and specifically the strategic decision, can be only as satisfactory as the information upon which it is based. An information system which provides accurate, timely, and relevant information for use in the strategic decision process is an important organizational resource, because executives can be virtually overwhelmed by information. Various structural arrangements exist in organizations to provide strategic information. In larger organizations, sizable professional planning units utilizing elaborate Management Information Systems (MIS) provide this information. In smaller organizations, the CEO may scan the environment and assess his or her organization in an attempt to collect information to help determine where the organization is and where it ought to be. Numerous variations exist between these two extremes. In addition to providing strategic information, major functions of the MIS include communication of objectives and plans and provision of information related to performance control.

If our friend Winfield (see cartoon) had used an MIS, the $100 million liability probably would not have "appeared out of nowhere." It might not even have appeared. On the other hand, information doesn't always ensure success—especially when not enough is gathered, as Information Capsule 2.1 illustrates. Strategic information systems can be either formal or informal. Both types play a vital role in strategy formulation. The formal SIS is a component of the formal MIS. Of special concern to SBU strategic planning are demand forecasts for products and services balanced against the capacity and capabilities to produce them. Ultimately these balances are reflected in the operating plan and the operating budget. Also appearing in the operating budget are resource distribution actions and actual production commitments.

"I must have heard you wrong, Winfield. I thought you said this little $100 million pension liability just appeared out of nowhere."

Source: Buck Consultants, Inc. Two Pennsylvania Plaza, New York, New York 10121.

Information Capsule 2.1
A Matter of Taste

Pillsbury has learned an important lesson about gathering enough information. Based on insufficient information and erroneous assumptions, the company developed a quick, cheap, easy-to-fix dessert that no one liked.

According to marketing surveys conducted by Pillsbury, the public wanted a hot, fast, fruit dessert. Pillsbury developed Appleasy—a dessert made with apples, cinnamon, and "strudel crunch"—to fit the bill. All the preparer had to do was add hot water. But Pillsbury made a big mistake: As the price of apples increased, it decreased the number of apples in the dessert and increased the starch and sugar, assuming the consumer would not want to pay a higher price. This assumption proved to be wrong.

Although the earlier product had fit the description of what the consumer wanted, the company changed to a product the consumer did not want because it underestimated the consumer's willingness to pay a higher price for a better product.

But Pillsbury's marketing strategy isn't always wrong. Trying to capture a larger part of the frozen pizza market, Pillsbury asked the question "What do people not like about frozen pizza?" The answer to their question was "the crust." Most persons commented that the crust tasted like cardboard. After long and intensive testing, Pillsbury developed and patented a formula for frozen pizza crust that tasted good.

The advertising campaign launched by Pillsbury for its new Totino's Pizza stressed that "Our crust doesn't taste like cardboard." Most other frozen brands claimed their frozen pizzas tasted "just like pizzeria" pizza. Since most consumers don't believe that frozen pizza can taste as good as pizzeria pizza, Pillsbury's ad campaign was more successful than those for other frozen pizzas.

Source: Adapted from "A Matter of Taste—There's No Way to Tell if a New Food Product Will Please the Public," by Laurence Ingrassia, *The Wall Street Journal*, February 26, 1980, pp. 1, 23. Reprinted by permission of *The Wall Street Journal*, © Dow Jones & Company, Inc. 1980. All Rights Reserved.

Most organizations plan strategy on an annual, cyclical basis. For such purposes, routines for data storage and reporting may exist. Since strategic decision making may occasionally be crisis oriented, however, there are few predictable boundaries as to the types of information which might be needed. It is therefore necessary to store almost all conceivable types of information, often in a "raw" form, in order to meet the demands of various situations.

As shown in Figure 2.3, a centralized formal data bank stores the data necessary for generating both routine and nonroutine reports on internal and environmental phenomena. Internal information is presented in this figure as being reported on a functional basis. It could be sorted on a division/functional or other basis if neces-

Figure 2.3
Strategic Information Systems

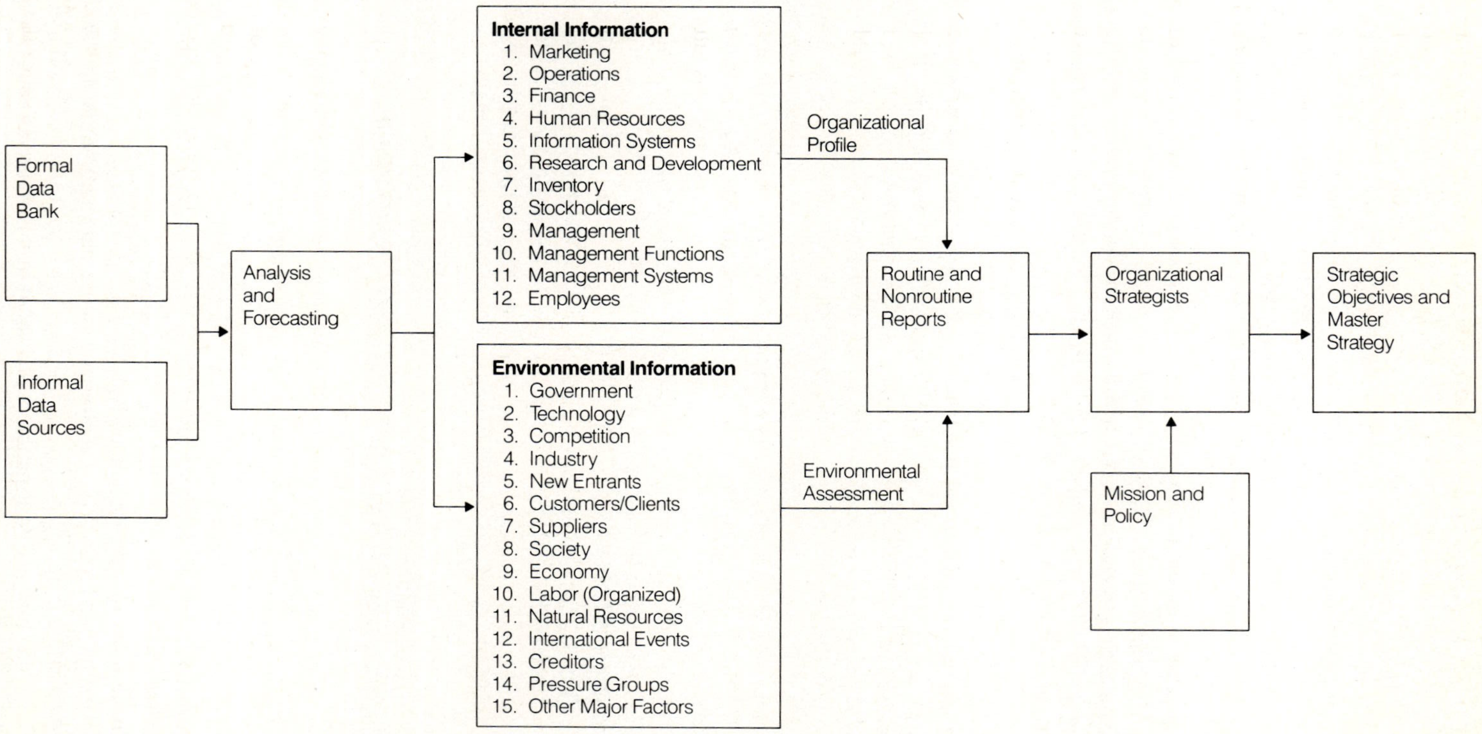

Internal Information
1. Marketing
2. Operations
3. Finance
4. Human Resources
5. Information Systems
6. Research and Development
7. Inventory
8. Stockholders
9. Management
10. Management Functions
11. Management Systems
12. Employees

Environmental Information
1. Government
2. Technology
3. Competition
4. Industry
5. New Entrants
6. Customers/Clients
7. Suppliers
8. Society
9. Economy
10. Labor (Organized)
11. Natural Resources
12. International Events
13. Creditors
14. Pressure Groups
15. Other Major Factors

Formal Data Bank

Informal Data Sources

Analysis and Forecasting

Organizational Profile

Environmental Assessment

Routine and Nonroutine Reports

Organizational Strategists

Mission and Policy

Strategic Objectives and Master Strategy

sary. Much of the strategic information routinely exists in reports and reporting formats already in use in the firm, especially formal internal data such as financial statements, cost control reports, quality control reports, inventory level reports, division performance reports, absenteeism and turnover reports, and the like.

One manifestation of the computerized information system is the corporate "war room" with comprehensive computer-linked visual data display systems. While "war rooms" have existed for many years, in the past they used hand printed charts on limited subjects. Now any corporate information can appear instantaneously on large television screens.[9]

To this point the discussion of the SIS has stressed the formal information system. But the importance of informal information should not be overlooked. Many times, personal contacts with individuals inside or outside the organization produce significant information related to the future. For example, tips on federal government legislation may prove extremely beneficial. Or rumors about a competitor's strategy may, when investigated, prove to be an important indicator of profitable strategic actions. The evidence strongly suggests that, while the formal system may be proposed as the critical element, the informal system is the most consistently used basis for many top management decisions. Research indicates that 40 to 75 percent of the information used by top managers comes from informal sources.[10]

Finally, a pragmatic note: management must make forecasts based on planning information, especially internal information—not simply based on past history. Normally, this necessity is understood with respect to environmental information, which often has already been changed in time horizon before it reaches top management. Strategists often overlook forecasting when dealing with internal strengths and weaknesses. Even though the decisions must be made now, it is future as well as current strengths and weaknesses that must be compared with future as well as current threats and opportunities in the strategic decision process.

In the ideal strategic decision situation, the processes of information gathering and analysis described above would be accomplished in the formal information system, preferably under the direction of members of the professional planning group. At the opposite extreme, the CEO of a small organization may occasionally find it necessary to search for information or perform analyses personally.

Sources of Internal and Environmental Information

As suggested earlier, information related to the internal strengths and weaknesses of the organization should be available in the organization's MIS. This information may also be gathered through informal sources. Typically, this type of information will be found in annual, quarterly, and monthly financial reports; in cost analyses; in capital budget statements; in cost/benefit analyses; in personnel reports on major

---

[9] "Corporate 'War Rooms' Plug Into the Computer," *Business Week*, August 23, 1976, pp. 65–67.
[10] C. R. Adams, "How Management Users View Information Systems," *Decision Sciences*, April 1975, pp. 337–345; J. Dearden, "MIS is Mirage," *Harvard Business Review*, January/February 1972, pp. 90–99; R. E. Linnemann and J. D. Kennell, "Shirtsleeve Approach to Long-Range Planning," *Harvard Business Review*, March/April 1977, pp. 141–150; P. Lorange, "The Planner's Dual Role—a Survey of U.S. Companies," *Long Range Planning*, March 1973, pp. 12–16; K. S. Ringbaak, "Organized Corporate Planning Systems: An Empirical Study of Planning Practice and Experiences in American Big Business" (Ph.D. dissertation, University of Wisconsin, 1968); R. N. Taylor, "Psychological Aspects of Planning," *Long Range Planning*, April 1976, pp. 66–74.

human resource concerns; in marketing reports on sales and related information; and so forth. Few problems should exist in obtaining relevant internal information if the MIS is properly designed and implemented (A big "if"). However, the human resource information contained in most systems is limited in nature. Organizations are only beginning to recognize the need for and application of this type of information. While organizations usually collect data on absenteeism, tardiness, turnover, and so forth, seldom do they measure organizational climate, satisfaction, leadership style, and the like—important ingredients in explaining human resource productivity.

In addition to standardized control reports, nonroutine control activities may be desirable. These activities include organizational climate surveys, management audits, social audits, operational audits (of any subsystem), productivity audits, financial audits, strategic audits, and so forth. Both routine and nonroutine control activities are discussed at greater length in Chapter 8.

The strategic purpose of obtaining information on internal strengths and weaknesses is to compare them with perceived environmental threats and opportunities and to make decisions based on these comparisons. F. J. Aguilar has described four modes of scanning the external environment for information about threats and opportunities:[11]

1. Undirected viewing—general exposure to information with no purpose other than exploration.
2. Conditioned viewing—directed exposure to, but not active search for, specific kinds of data, which will be assessed as they are encountered.
3. Informal search—search for specific information carried out in a limited and relatively unstructured manner.
4. Formal search—active, deliberate, structured search for specific information undertaken with a purpose in mind.

Most organizations use all four types of scanning, depending on the cost benefit of each. These four approaches form a continuum from general exposure to information to active and deliberate search for specific information. Every firm must remain alert to the general environment and to its own operations. As bits and pieces of information obtained in this scanning indicate changes in factors relevant to the formulation of strategy, then other, more directed types of scanning should begin. Conducting formal searches is desirable any time specific information is needed for strategy formulation.

Information on environmental factors can be obtained through various sources; for example, the *Wall Street Journal*; *Fortune*; *Business Week*; *Harvard Business Review*; numerous scholarly, popular, and trade journals; and newspapers are important sources. Any number of government, industry, news media, research, and reporting services provide additional information. The appendix to this chapter lists sources for each of the major environmental factors identified in Figure 2.3.

The various information sources vary in validity and reliability, as well as accessibility and timeliness. Much of the information used is gathered from secondary

[11] F. J. Aguilar, *Scanning the Business Environment* (New York: MacMillan, 1967).

sources, but primary data gathering through research may be undertaken if the organization can afford the cost. While internal information sources may allow the organization to approach a real-time (or up-to-date), on-line MIS, constraints on environmental sources make a real-time environmental MIS unlikely. The informal information system may be used more than the formal system. Information sharing among organizations is useful and has proved successful.

We've named some sources of information and how we find them and what we want them for, but we have not yet examined exactly what types of information we seek. Internal information regarding existing situations and external information related to government, technology, competition, society, the economy, labor, natural resources, international events, and other major variables are critical to the success of the organization. First, let us examine the internal information needed.

The Internal Information Sought

Whatever information can be gathered regarding strategic strengths and weaknesses is important. Each business unit should concern itself with identifying the results of its efforts and its strengths and weaknesses, both current and potential, with respect to

Functional areas such as marketing, finance, operations, human resources, information systems, R&D, and inventory.

Management values and capabilities.

Performance of management functions.

Performance of management systems.

Stockholder orientations.

Employee perspectives.

This information is best obtained through a total management audit covering every facet of the business, performed annually in conjunction with routine control reports. What the unit wants to know is where it is; and, if it is not where it wants to be, why it isn't there and how it can get there. (Such an audit follows as part of the strategic audit in Appendix II to this text and is useful in analyzing cases or other organizational situations.)

The oil companies have a tremendous strength in cash flow, but several are weak because they lack diversification. Delta Airlines has a vital strength in its personnel and in the way that it has historically chosen and financed its aircraft. W. T. Grant was especially weak in strategy, control, and merchandising. The Japanese auto firms have a crucial competitive edge in the product—its design, fuel economy, and cost—resulting from a highly productive and quality-oriented work force. All of these and many more examples tell us that firms must build on strengths and overcome weaknesses to be successful. This information does not stand alone, however. Many internal factors are strengths or weaknesses only in relation to external opportunities and threats.

The External Information Sought

At one level, environment is not a very mysterious concept. It means the surroundings of an organization; the "climate" in which the organization functions. The concept becomes challenging when we try to move from simple description of the environment to analysis of its properties. —William R. Dill

External information that will have a direct impact on opportunities and threats or provide inputs for defining strengths and weaknesses should be sought. Typically, this includes information in the following areas:

Government.
Technology.
Competition.
The industry.
New entrants.
Customers/Clients.
Substitutes.
Suppliers.
Society.
The economy.
Labor (organized).
Natural resources.
International events.
Pressure groups.
Creditors.
Other factors.

The purpose of seeking this information is to assess the environment and determine the fit between this environment, its opportunities and threats, and the organization's strengths and weaknesses as revealed in the organizational profile above.

Now let us examine in more detail the types of information sought and the reasons for seeking this information in each of these areas.

Government

During the 1960s and 1970s, government dominated the external business environment. While competition was of concern, businesses probably spent as much time complying with governmental requirements as they did worrying about competition, perhaps more time.

Table 2.1 presents a list of major federal laws in several vital areas. Some were recently passed; some have been enforced more stringently in recent years. As can

Table 2.1
Laws That Affect Business

Recent Laws
Environment
Federal Insecticide, Fungicide, and Rodenticide Act of 1947
Federal Water Pollution Control Act of 1956
Clean Air Act of 1963
Solid Wastes Disposal Act of 1965, as amended
Water Quality Act of 1965
A federal court broadly interprets the provisions of the Refuse Act of 1899 in 1966
Air Quality Act of 1967
National Environmental Policy Act of 1970
Noise Abatement and Control Act of 1970
Resource Recovery Act of 1970
Clean Air Act Amendments of 1970

Equal Employment Opportunity
Equal Pay Act of 1963 as amended by the Education Amendments of 1972
Title VII of the Civil Rights Act of 1964 as amended by the Equal Employment Opportunity Act of 1972
Presidential Executive Orders 11246, 11375, 11478, 11758 (1967–1975)
Age Discrimination in Employment Act of 1967
Sections 500 and 503 of the Rehabilitation Act Amendments of 1974
Veteran's Employment and Readjustment Act of 1972, as amended

Consumerism
Meat Inspection Act of 1906
Federal Food, Drug and Cosmetic Act 1938, as amended by presidential executive order: The Office of Consumer Affairs, 1964
National Traffic and Motor Vehicle Safety Act of 1966, as amended
Fair Packaging and Labeling Act of 1966
Federal Cigarette Labeling and Advertising Act, 1967
Consumer Credit Protection Act, 1968
Toy Safety Act, 1969
Truth in Lending Act of 1969
Consumer Product Safety Act of 1972
Fair Credit Billing Act of 1974
The Equal Credit Opportunity Act of 1974
Consumer Product Warranties Act of 1975
Consumer Goods Pricing Act of 1975
Fair Trade Laws repealed, 1977
Fair Debt Collection, 1978

Energy
Federal Energy Administration Act of 1974
Energy Reorganization Act of 1974 (establishes ERDA)
Energy Supply and Environmental Coordination Act of 1974
Energy Policy and Conservation Act of 1975

Economics
Chrysler Loan Guarantee Act of 1979
Revised Bankruptcy Act of 1980
Tax Act of 1981
Deregulation of Airlines; Trucking 1979–1981
FCC allows AT&T to sell nonregulated services, 1979
The Federal Reserve Bank permits banks to pay interest on checking accounts, 1980
AT&T divests itself of its local telephone companies, 1984

Table 2.1 continued

Labor
Occupational Safety and Health Act of 1970
Employee Retirement Income Security Act, 1974

Other Laws
Interstate Commerce Act of 1887
Sherman Act, 1890
Pure Food and Drug Act, 1906
Sixteenth Amendment, 1913 (income tax)
Clayton Act, 1914
Federal Trade Commission Act, 1914
Federal Communications Act, 1934
Social Security Act, 1935
Wagner Act, 1935
Robinson-Patman Act, 1936
Fair Labor Standards Act, 1938 (Wage and Hour Act)
Taft-Hartley Act, 1947
Anti-Merger Act, 1950
Automobile Information Disclosure Act of 1958
Landrum-Griffin Act, 1959

---

be seen by this table, in each of several major categories, business has had many of its strategic alternatives limited. These laws have served to increase business's social responsibility. Alternatives may be limited additionally through the enforcement of these laws, since enforcement varies from law to law and geographic area to geographic area. For example, the operations of almost all manufacturing organizations have been affected by the environmental protection requirements, resulting in significant additions to production costs. Also, virtually all organizations of any size have had to make comprehensive changes in their personnel practices as the result of equal opportunity laws. For many organizations, personnel practices have been dictated by federal agencies as the result of these laws. The consumer issue has resulted in numerous recalls of automobiles to Detroit and of other products to other manufacturers in other cities. And the energy problem and related laws have caused U.S. auto makers to completely redesign their automobiles, making them lighter, smaller, and more fuel efficient.

But these laws are not the only government constraints on business. There are regulatory agencies whose primary functions involve the control and observation of business. Indeed, the number of agencies and individuals at the federal level whose function is to regulate business is extremely high. In addition, there are state regulatory agencies, which control, for example, all public utilities; state environmental protection agencies, which are the true enforcement mechanisms of the federal environmental law; state consumer protection agencies; various state agencies related to the building of houses; and various licensing and permit-granting organizations—state, federal, and local. These agencies, as well as various pressure groups such as the NAACP, the Sierra Club, and Ralph Nader and his group, have significant impact upon the strategy formulation of many businesses. As can be seen in some of the cases presented in this book, it is often necessary to change the major plans of action known as strategy in order to accommodate the demands of these organizations.

Many times, companies have abandoned plans or strategies because of their demands. For example, as mentioned earlier, Disney abandoned a ski resort project at King's Mountain because of pressure from environmentalists. Similarly, many nuclear power projects have been halted. Finally, numerous steel plants have been shut down because of the cost of adding environmental protection equipment. It should be noted that the demands of these external organizations may be appropriate, given the greater requirements of the society. Sometimes businesses take actions which are highly questionable with respect to overall benefit to society. Regardless of the moral perspective, however, these external forces act as constraints on business.

It is clear that international trade and international business are affected greatly by government legislation.

The future holds some promise of less constraint; in 1981, public attitudes and the presidential administration seemed to favor fewer constraints. But the task of deregulation is not simple. Business's future appears to be one of continued regulation and control by federal, state, and local governments, especially the federal government. Because of these constraints and the frequent changes in them, business must continually monitor the environment and adapt to it or change it. Legal, ethical, and socially responsible political actions and lobbying are important strategic actions. All strategic actions depend on awareness.

Technology

Many, if not most, businesses depend on some type of technology for a competitive advantage or for products to sell. The American way of life has come to involve consuming more and more of the latest and greatest, and that involves technological advances. Since business is so dependent on technology, it must be ever mindful of technological surprises from competitors. In addition, because of the secondary impacts of technology, especially on the natural physical environment, business must guard against future environmental catastrophes such as the damage done by DDT.

There are few major industries in this country which do not depend on technology. Television, computers, calculators, airplanes, pacemakers, Corningware, lasers, and photocopy machines are just a few of the many examples of major industrial products which are technology-based. When a major technology comes into existence, an entire new industry may be created, such as occurred with the computer industry or the photocopying industry.

Businesses must first of all concern themselves with new technology in their particular industry—that is, with the technological developments of their competitors. This concern has often led to industrial espionage. Moreover, the rapid changes occurring in the business technological environment have resulted in an increase in business's efforts to forecast technology. This process involves using many judgmental forecasting techniques. Technological forecasting is not easy, nor is it very accurate. With luck the management of strategic surprises is a 50–50 proposition. Most competitors' technologies are unknown until their products are brought to the market. These odds would be more favorable if information systems were more widely used and more sophisticated.

In an interesting study of responses to technological threats, A. C. Cooper and others found that traditional firms encounter great difficulty in responding successfully to major technological innovations introduced into their industry, especially during maturity or saturation stages of the product life cycle. While their sample was small, virtually no well-established firm studied was able to launch a successful counterthreat to the introduction of a new technology into its industry. This finding suggests that even when firms know about new technologies and respond to them, the response strategy may be ill-advised.[12] When we consider the product life cycle, we can see that when new technology is introduced, the introducer gains a distinct strategic advantage over those who do not have the technology. If it is successfully able to capture a considerable share of the market, then the competitor who previously had the market has no advantage over any other firm coming into the market for this new product. J. M. Utterback and M. J. Abernathy found that firms in early stages of growth tended to introduce more technological innovations than did firms which were very large and complex in nature. This suggests that as firms mature, they may stagnate.[13]

In sum, these studies suggest that technological innovation may be difficult to counteract for a firm in the mature stage of the product life cycle. The available information also suggests that technology is the source of product innovation, and that new firms and new industries can be successfully based on such innovation.

The Japanese have been quite successful in adopting someone else's technology and underpricing their international competitors through highly productive management and marketing systems and strategies. However, only a few U.S. and Canadian firms have been able to achieve the high levels of productivity which allow firms to take advantage of others' technological advances. Clearly, technology is an advantage, and so is information. The firm that does not keep pace is destined for decline, as Information Capsule 2.2 indicates.

While technology plays an important role in business success, it also poses problems for many companies. The unexpected consequences of a new technology can sometimes result in damage to the physical environment. All organizations, not just business, must engage in ongoing assessment of the impacts of technology on the physical environment. Nuclear waste (governmental and commercial), oil spills, and PCB contamination are all examples of technology out of control. Even less dramatic wastes and products of industry and government can in mass damage the environment. Such is the case with automobile exhaust fumes, waste water, and garbage. From a strategic viewpoint, industry must be responsive not just to the profit motive but also to the greater needs of the society and to the quality of life. This is not only a moral position, but also hard reality. Where business has not been responsive to these needs, it has in the past often been forced by society and by government to respond in a manner that is ultimately more costly and less profitable.

Technology assessment recognizes that within the ecosystem, all systems are interrelated and what affects one ultimately affects another. Technology assessment requires environmental surveillance. Business must chart a careful course of technological action. Indeed, the Environmental Protection Agency and other federal

---

[12] A. C. Cooper et al., "Strategic Responses to Technological Threats," *Proceedings, Academy of Management*, 1974.
[13] J. M. Utterback and M. J. Abernathy, "The Test of a Conceptual Model Linking States in Firms' Process and Product Innovation," Working Paper no. 74–23, Harvard School of Business, 1974.

Information Capsule 2.2
New Home-Computer Design May Revive Japanese Market

Microsoft Corporation of Bellevue, Washington, previewed its new MSX computer at the preeminent Japan Electronics Show in Osaka, Japan, in October 1983. By all measures of success, the MSX promises to be the dominant type of personal computer in the next five years. The MSX incorporates a new computer design that allows it to handle programs written for most other personal computers—something unheard of previously. In addition, the MSX is inexpensive, is the only computer to operate while several memory cartridges are plugged into it, and is expected to be able to incorporate disk-drive features currently under design—making it superior to computers such as Coleco's Adam which incorporate less desirable tape memory systems.

The MSX incorporates a new master control program, the MSX-DOS to control the flow of information to and from magnetic disks. The program is quite similar to the popular CP/M control program used on IBM's personal computer. As a result, software firms should be able to readily adapt current programs to the new system. The MSX computer will be sold first as a game system, but will move rapidly into the personal computer line. Earlier MSX systems are to be manufactured to accommodate readily later modifications to the system. The MSX will be sold first in Japan for approximately one year, but after that, it is likely to be introduced into the U.S. market by a number of manufacturers. Industry experts estimate that the MSX system will cause computer prices to drop significantly.

Source: Excerpted from "New Home-Computer Design May Revive Japanese Market," by Richard A. Shaffer, *The Wall Street Journal*, October 14, 1983, p. 33. Reprinted by permission of *The Wall Street Journal*, © Dow Jones & Company, Inc., 1983. All Rights Reserved.

---

and state agencies require that such plans be made and recorded in environmental impact statements for areas of obvious impact. Business and other organizations must be ever alert to the less obvious impacts of their actions as well. The activities of various pressure groups must also be monitored. The attitudes of society should be determined. Governmental responses should be anticipated. All of this requires a satisfactory strategic information system.

Competition, Industry, New Entrants, Customers/Clients, Substitutes, Suppliers

In recent years, considerable interest has been shown in what has come to be known as "competitor analysis." The subjects of this section of the chapter-competition, industry, new entrants, customers/clients (buyers), substitutes, and suppliers, are

Figure 2.4
Forces Driving Industry Competition

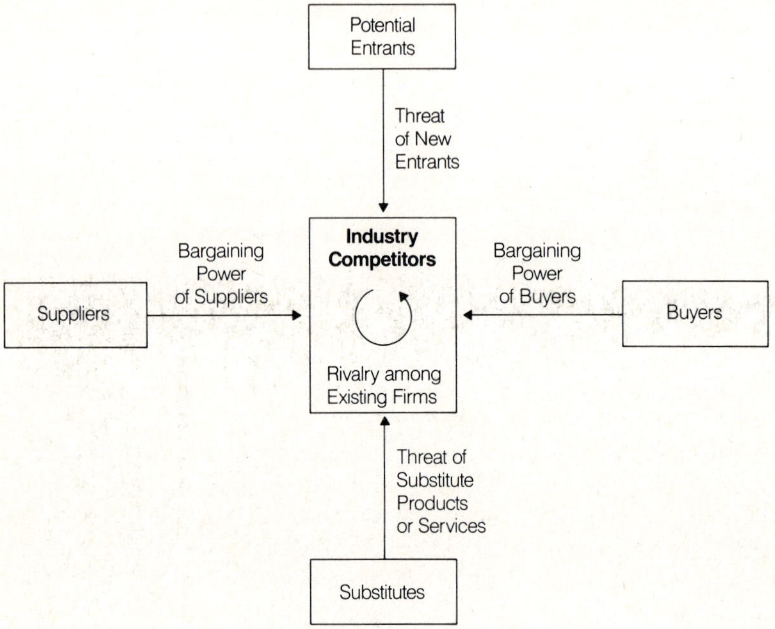

```
                    ┌──────────────┐
                    │  Potential   │
                    │   Entrants   │
                    └──────┬───────┘
                           │ Threat
                           │ of New
                           │ Entrants
                           ▼
┌───────────┐  Bargaining  ┌──────────────┐  Bargaining  ┌─────────┐
│ Suppliers │──Power of ──▶│   Industry   │◀── Power ────│ Buyers  │
│           │   Suppliers  │  Competitors │   of Buyers  │         │
└───────────┘              │      ↻       │              └─────────┘
                           │ Rivalry among│
                           │Existing Firms│
                           └──────▲───────┘
                                  │ Threat of
                                  │ Substitute
                                  │ Products
                                  │ or Services
                           ┌──────┴───────┐
                           │  Substitutes │
                           └──────────────┘
```

Source: M. E. Porter, *Competitive Strategy* (New York: Free Press, 1980), p. 4. Copyright © 1980 by The Free Press, a division of Macmillan Publishing Co., Inc. Reprinted by permission.

all related to the subject of competitor analysis through the works of **Michael E. Porter.**

Porter's Competitor Analysis. M. E. Porter proposes that the intensity of competition is the most critical element in the firm's environment. Porter suggests that the level of this intensity is a function of five basic competitive forces as depicted in Figure 2.4. Porter contends that, "The collective strength of these forces determines the ultimate profit potential in the industry, where profit potential is measured in terms of long-run return on invested capital."[14]

According to Porter, a corporation must carefully monitor its environment to determine the impact of these five factors on the firm's potentials for success.[15]

1. *Threat of New Entrants*. New entrants typically
   - have substantial resources.
   - pursue actions which increase industry capacity.
   - attempt to increase their market share.

---
[14] M. E. Porter, *Competitive Strategy*, New York: Free Press, 1980, p. 3.
[15] The sections on Porter's model are taken from Ibid., pp. 3–33.

As a consequence
- prices often go down.
- incumbents' costs may become inflated.
- incumbents' profits may therefore go down.

Because of the above factors, new entrants must be viewed as threats to incumbents. Miller's entry into the beer industry is a classic example of this type of situation.

Porter identifies seven major sources of barriers to entry into an existing industry. These barriers assist incumbents because they reduce the number of potential new entrants:

- economies of scale—to obtain these requires high entry investment.
- existing product differentiation which leads to customer loyalty.
- capital requirements.
- switching costs—for buyers switching from incumbent's product to the new entrant's product.
- access to distribution channels.
- cost disadvantages independent of scale.
- government policy.

2. *Intensity of Rivalry Among Existing Firms.* Porter views rivalry as a process of move and countermove among existing, mutually dependent, competitors employing tactics such as price competition, advertising, new products, and so forth. He sees intense rivalry as resulting from any number of critical industry factors which can and do change:
   - numerous or equally balanced competitors.
   - slow industry growth.
   - high fixed or storage costs.
   - lack of differentiation or switching costs.
   - capacity augmented in large increments.
   - diverse competitors.
   - high strategic stakes.
   - high exit barriers.

3. *Pressure from Substitute Products.* "All firms in an industry are competing, in a broad sense, with industries producing substitute products."[16] These substitutes result in a price lid on industry products.
   - The key to identifying substitutes is to look for those products that perform the same "function" as the product of the industry even though they may not appear to be obvious substitutes.

[16] Ibid., p. 23.

- Firms should pay attention to those products whose price-performance tradeoff with the industry's products is improving.
- Furthermore, the higher the industry's profits, the more likely that substitutes will be sought.

A good example of substitution is the problem faced by the security guard industry. Electronic alarms are a strong substitute. They are cheaper to operate and effective. Their advantage should increase in the future as labor costs increase and the cost of the electronic devices decreases.

4. *Bargaining Power of Buyers.* Customer/Clients (buyers) compete with the industry in the sense that they are able to force prices down, bargain for higher quality or more goods and services, or play one competitor in the industry against another. A particular buyer or group of buyers is powerful in the industry if
   - it purchases a large portion of the seller's total sales.
   - its purchases from the industry are a significant portion of its cost of goods sold.
   - its purchases from the industry are standard or undifferentiated.
   - switching costs are low.
   - it earns low profits.
   - it has the potential for backward integration.
   - the industry's product is unimportant to the quality of the buyer's product.
   - the buyer has full information.

5. *Bargaining Power of Suppliers.* Suppliers can impact on an industry through their abilities to control prices and product/service quality. The conditions making suppliers powerful tend to mirror those that make buyers powerful. A supplier group is powerful if
   - it is dominated by a few companies, and is more concentrated than the industry to which it sells.
   - there are few substitutes.
   - the supplier's products are differentiated or switching costs are high.
   - suppliers pose a threat of forward integration.
   - labor, by the way, is a supplier group.

With respect to obtaining the information necessary to determine the characteristics about the industry and its competitors, suppliers, new entrants, substitutes, and buyers, Porter suggests the sources depicted in Figure 2.5. An additional list of general information sources is provided as an appendix to this chapter. Furthermore, W. E. Rothschild has prepared a more detailed list of sources and concerns specifically with regard to competitors, and his approach is discussed in the next section. One final note, Porter recommends certain types of "generic" strategies for competing, and these are reviewed in more detail in Chapter 4.

Figure 2.5
Sources of Data for Industry Analysis

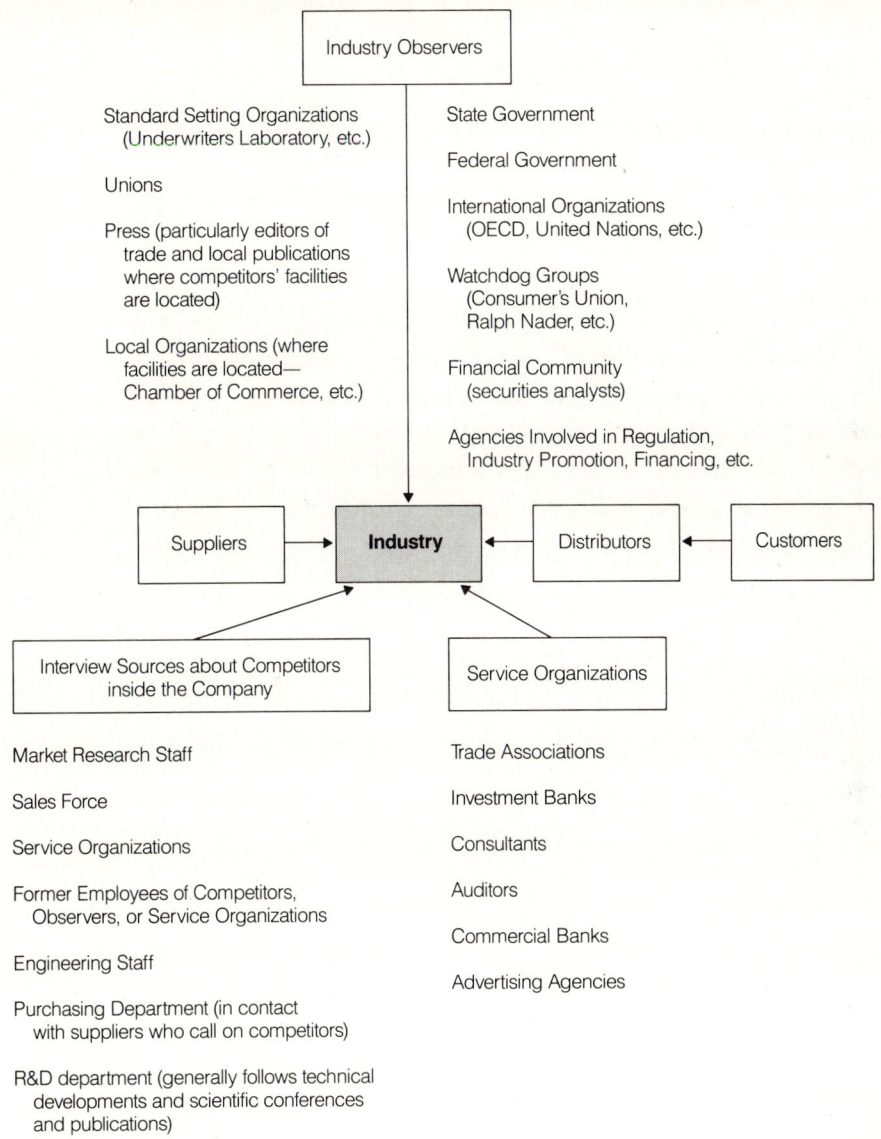

Source: M. E. Porter, *Competitive Strategy* (New York: Free Press, 1980), p. 378. Copyright © 1980 by The Free Press, a division of Macmillan Publishing Co., Inc. Reprinted by permission.

Competitor Analysis: Another Perspective

Induce your competitors not to invest in those products, markets, and services where you expect to invest the most. That is the most fundamental rule of strategy. —Bruce D. Henderson

At the business level of strategy formulation, competition is of critical concern. Any business must know what its competition is doing and is going to do and how these actions will affect it. William E. Rothschild, author and integrative strategist for General Electric, suggests that the following key questions must be answered if a firm is to be successful:[17]

Who is the competition now and who will it be in the future?

What are the key competitors' strategies, objectives, and goals?

How important is a specific market to the competitors, and are they committed enough to continue to invest?

What unique strengths do the competitors have?

Do they have any weaknesses that make them vulnerable?

What changes are likely in the competitors' future strategies?

What are the implications of competitors' strategies on the market, industry, and one's own company?

As Rothschild suggests, these questions boil down to "Who are they?" and "What are they up to?"

Although these questions seem rather straightforward, answering them, according to Rothschild, is complicated by three problems:

1. Many managers are overconfident. They have won the previous battles and assume they'll win the next ones. Laxity results.
2. Many strategists do not know what they need to know or how to obtain information.
3. Many strategists are concerned that it may be necessary to act unethically to obtain the necessary information.

In response to problems 2 and 3, Rothschild assures strategists that the environment abounds with information. To help them find it, he provides a table indicating the information required and another giving sources for this information. These tables appear here as Tables 2.2 and 2.3.

The inputs from competitor analysis contribute to the identification of SWOT. Without such inputs, management is operating as would the captain of a ship without maps of the waters.

---

[17] W. E. Rothschild, "Competitor Analysis: The Missing Link in Strategy," *Management Review*, July 1979, pp. 22–39.

Table 2.2
Information Needed for Competitor Analysis

Conceptive Design	Physical Resources	Market	Finance	Management
Technical resources	Capacity	Sales force	Long-term	Key people
Concepts	Plant	Skills	Debt/equity ratio	Objectives and priorities
Patents and copyrights	Size	Size	Cost of debt	Values
Technological	Location	Type	Short-term	Reward systems
sophistication	Age	Location	Line of credit	Decision making
Technical integration	Equipment	Distribution network	Type of debt	Location
Human resources	Automation	Research	Cost of debt	Type
Key people and skills	Maintenance	Skills	Liquidity	Speed
Use of external technical	Flexibility	Type	Cash flow	Planning
groups	Processes	Service and sales policies	Days of receivables	Type
Funding	Uniqueness	Advertising	Inventory turnover	Emphasis
Total	Flexibility	Skills	Accounting practices	Time span
Percentage of sales	Degree of integration	Type	Human resources	Staffing
Consistency over time	Human resources	Human resources	Key people and skills	Longevity and turnover
Internally generated	Key people and skills	Key people and skills	Turnover	Experience
Government supplied	Work force	Turnover	Systems	Replacement policies
	Skills mix	Funding	Budgeting	Organization
	Unions	Total	Forecasting	Centralization
	Turnover	Consistency over time	Controlling	Functions
		Percentage of sales		Use of staff
		Reward systems		

Source: Reprinted by permission of the publisher, from, "Competitor Analysis: The Missing Link in Strategy," W. E. Rothschild, *Management Review*, July 1979, © 1979 by AMACOM, a division of American Management Associations, p. 26. All rights reserved.

Table 2.3
Sources of Information for Competitor Analysis

	Public	Trade/Professionals	Government	Investors
What competitors say about themselves	Advertising Promotional materials Press releases Speeches Books Articles Personnel changes Want ads	Manuals Technical papers Licenses Patents Courses Seminars	Security and Exchange reports FTC Testimony Lawsuits Antitrust	Annual meetings Annual reports Prospectuses Stock/bond issues
What others say about them	Books Articles Case studies Consultants Newspaper reporters Environmental groups Consumer groups Unions "Who's Who" Recruiting firms	Suppliers/vendors Trade press Industry study Customers Subcontractors	Lawsuits Antitrust State/federal agencies National plans Government programs	Security analyst reports Industry studies Credit reports

Source: Reprinted, by permission of the publisher, from, "Competitor Analysis: The Missing Link in Strategy," W. E. Rothschild, *Management Review*, July 1979, © 1979 by AMACOM, a division of American Management Associations, p. 27. All rights reserved.

Society

Until the 1960s, business apparently considered itself a closed system, one which operated without having significant transactions with those outside. But the events of the 1960s and the 1970s (which came as a surprise to most businesses)—the marchers, the protests, the demonstrations, the riots, and the bombings—convinced business that society did not hold the same view. Society was concerned with the impact business had on it. Government responded to society's concerns and created numerous laws which affected the operation of business. The perceived role of business was expanded to include much more than the mere production of goods and services. Business is now expected to contribute to the society in other ways, for example, through the employment of the economically and culturally disadvantaged. Information search must be continually maintained in order that no surprises occur in the area of societal demands. Business has learned that it must respond to the demands of the society, especially the demands of those groups which can bring significant pressure on business.

This responsiveness can lead to a reduction of strategic alternatives. In fact, E. A. Murray, Jr., has suggested that for many businesses, especially those who are regulated to a great extent by the federal government or against whom significant action has been taken by large pressure groups, decisions are more negotiated than formulated from within. Murray has proposed the following:[18]

1. The less the effective power of the firm relative to that of other institutions in its environment with which it must interact, the more the change in strategy of the firm over time will be disjointed and incremental rather than integrated and comprehensive, irrespective of nature and environmental opportunities and threats facing the firm.

2. The greater the degree of fragmentation of decisions of strategic significance to the firm yet external to it, the more the change in the strategy of the firm over time will be disjointed and incremental rather than integrated and comprehensive, irrespective of nature and environmental opportunities and threats facing the firm.

The concept of incremental decision making and coalition bargaining will be discussed in Chapter 6. While that chapter stresses internal coalitions, Murray's comments relate to planning that results from the need to adapt to powerful external influences. Murray examined a public utility and its frustration in attempting to comply with requirements of its environment—specifically, environmentalists and the federal government. His examination of this utility and its problems supported both of his propositions. He also found that many organizations must often comply with what seem to be irrational or contradictory regulations and requirements of different groups—or more commonly, requirements levied upon them by different agencies of the federal government. Often even the same agency of the federal government may issue contradictory requirements. Murray has raised an important is-

---

[18] E. A. Murray, Jr., "Limitations to Strategic Alternatives," *Proceedings, Academy of Management*, 1976, pp. 140–144.

sue as to whether strategy under these circumstances—circumstances which are increasingly common—can be described as having been formulated.

Businesses must continually explore the issues of social responsibility to better determine their impacts. No surprises should occur. Again, information is critical.

The Economy

Significant changes in the economy are often caused by the actions of the federal government, either through its fiscal policies or through the monetary policies of the Federal Reserve Board. It is often argued that deficits in federal spending have been the main contributors to double-digit inflation, that the monetary policies of the Federal Reserve have increased unemployment, and that its high interest rates have devastated the housing and banking industries. Whatever the causes, the results have often dictated the level and composition of business activity.

The nature of federal expenditures, which has been changing in recent years, also clearly impacts on the economy. For example, direct benefit payments to individuals, almost nonexistent 20 years ago, now account for 42 percent of the federal budget, and expenditures by the Department of Defense (DOD), which not too many years ago constituted almost 60 percent of the total federal budget, now account for 29 percent of the budget. Within departments, expenditures are also changing in nature, and these changes greatly affect the economy. For example, a few years ago, procurement accounted for nearly 60 percent of the DOD allocation. In 1984, procurement accounted for only 30 percent of DOD's budget, but this was up significantly from the Carter administration years when procurement hit a low, and military pay and benefits accounted for over 50 percent of the DOD budget, as opposed to their current combined level of about 33 percent.

Another major impact of federal spending in these two major areas, transfer payments and DOD, is the manner in which these expenditures are funded. In 1984, the national debt will require 103 billion dollars in current expenditures for debt service. This constitutes a little over 12 percent of the federal budget, up significantly from past years. It is no secret that the huge deficits in current federal budgets are a matter of major concern to all because of their impact on the long-term viability of the economy. At the very minimum, these deficits raise interests rates in the business money markets and tighten the supplies of monies available for business expansion.[19]

Businesses must respond to these changes. Firms must gear up to produce the military hardware to be procured, and/or to enter basic industries that typify the spending of transfer payments. They must also be prepared for the changing monetary conditions and be able to respond accordingly. Change is the name of the game. To keep on top of change, businesses must have information.

---

[19]*The Budget of the United States Government, Fiscal Year 1984* (Washington, D.C.: Government Printing Office, 1984), pp. MS.2, 3–38, 5–1 to 5–16.

Labor

Organized labor has made significant strides over the years in securing increased wages and benefits for workers; and its efforts to organize both blue-collar and white-collar workers, especially in the South, can be expected to continue. Organized labor has an extremely powerful influence on the national economy and on the supportive strategies and policies of the businesses which operate within that economy. There is significant evidence to indicate that in the states in which organized labor is strong—those, for example, in the East, the Northwest, the Midwest, and much of the Far West—it can elect its candidates to both the state and federal legislatures. And labor's impact on the presidential as well as gubernatorial and mayoral races has historically been significant. But labor's impact on government and on the economy appears to be lessening, and business must be attuned to that change.

Changes in employees' attitudes also affect business. Significant changes in the attitudes of all employees, whether organized or not, occurred during the 1960s and 1970s. These changes are primarily related to the work ethic and to the extent to which lower-level employees help the organization's management make decisions, sometimes strategic as well as operational.

One factor often cited as significant in the much-discussed decrease of productivity in the United States is a change in workers' attitude toward work. Many surveys have found that the "Protestant work ethic" has diminished, especially among younger workers (though competition for jobs is evidently increasing). Working hard is no longer all-important to many people. An apparent shift from emphasis on equality of opportunity to equality of reward regardless of effort was seen in the United States in the 1970s, although the country now appears to be moving away from this approach. Workers at all levels of the organization have also begun to expect more personal satisfaction from their work and more participation in decision making.

These and other factors make the successful implementation of strategy difficult, because they make motivation difficult. The manager today who must motivate employees is highly constrained by numerous conditions, many of which he or she cannot control. Since many businesses must increase productivity to survive, they must pay close attention to the attitudes of workers.

Natural Resources

Energy is not the only resource in questionable supply in the United States. Government studies have revealed that several major metals and other primary manufacturing materials are in short supply. Living space in large cities, clean air and water, and natural areas of beauty are also scarce. And, on a worldwide basis, food is in extremely short supply for most of the population. In short, the earth's inhabitants face an ever-increasing population with a limited amount of supplies with which to support this multitude. This creates great problems for businesses and for governments. The resource shortage problem will be further compounded in the future as developing nations seek to emulate industrialized nations. The United States depends upon many developing nations for the provision of scarce materials, a situation which has led and will continue to lead to a bargaining advantage for the providing nations.

While stockpiles of some of the metals and other materials which are needed may be created, stockpiling of some resources—for example, energy—is rather difficult. And while the United States has made significant strides toward energy independence, this goal will probably not be achieved until the late 1980s. Yet the tremendous positive changes in energy supply caused by reduced consumption led in 1981 to a short-term energy glut. This oversupply has caused problems for certain businesses and opportunities for others. Business must be prepared to react quickly to changing conditions. This requires information!

While material shortages appear to be the key resource problems of the United States, the inadequate supply of food is the most critical resource shortage for most nations. And while the United States is able to produce a great deal of food, its food technology is highly energy-dependent. It is clear that the nations of the world must come to grips with the reality that the supply of materials is not inexhaustible and that the number of people who are to live upon this planet must be somehow limited if each of the individuals in the world is to enjoy a desirable quality of life. The impact upon business of these worldwide problems include expropriation, import or export quotas, higher prices, and political power demonstrations by the underdeveloped nations who possess natural resources. Again, the needs for materials change and supplies diminish. Astute strategists observe and predict such changes. More importantly, they anticipate them, preparing their organizations for these events.

International Events

There appears to be one major factor in the international situation which business must recognize, and that is the change taking place in economic, political, and social power structures.

Immediately after World War II, the United States was clearly the most powerful nation in the world, since it alone possessed the atomic bomb and it had the most successful economy. Now, however, several European nations, the U.S.S.R., China, India, Brazil, Canada, the OPEC nations, and Japan, among others, have economic or military power significant enough to create major spheres of influence which can counteract the efforts of the United States both economically and militarily.

Furthermore, many nations are undergoing internal social change to achieve redistribution of wealth. Frequently, this change is accomplished through violence and under the banner of communism. The ability of businesses to engage in trade with communist countries is limited. Why? Because many communist nations are unwilling or unable to trade with the United States or Canada on a large scale, especially the new emerging nations. Furthermore, trade with communist countries is sometimes reduced to barter, since some of their currencies have little value outside of the communist bloc countries. These factors restrict both the number of potential consumers and the sources of raw materials for U.S. businesses.

Other problems in doing business in foreign countries include cultural differences, lack of local managerial talent, double taxation, and monetary translations.

As a result of the difficulties of coping with various problems in foreign countries, many firms are reassessing the need to operate in many of these countries.

Yet, the world is full of consumers. The problem is finding them and meeting their needs. Wealth changes drastically. The newly wealthy OPEC countries consume. Business need only find out what these countries want to consume and whether it can supply it. If people in the United States and Canada seek fuel-efficient cars, are U.S. and Canadian firms content to let the Japanese supply them? Where are the international markets? What are the needs of international consumers? Without information, a company will never know the answers to such questions.

Other Significant Factors

Numerous other factors affect individual businesses; perhaps the most significant remaining factor affecting most businesses is demographics.

Demographic Changes. Perhaps the most significant demographic changes which will affect businesses are increases in population, geographic shifts in population, and changes in the population's composition by age group. In the United States, the median age of the population has increased as the "baby boom" generation has aged and the birth rate has fallen. It is also expected that many people who currently live in the North, Northeast, and Midwest will move to the South and the West.

On an international basis, the most significant demographic factor is the sheer increase in population, especially in the developing nations. In 1979, the world's population was over 4.4 billion. Some estimate that world population could double by the year 2000; and most believe that it will certainly reach 7 billion by then. The consequences of this enormous population growth have not even begun to be imagined. One current negative impact on the United States has been an increase in the entrance of illegal aliens into this country. On the other hand, the increasing population represents a huge potential market if the developing nations can achieve economic success. Businesses must continue surveillance of these critical population changes if they are to take advantage of the opportunities created and negate the threats involved.

Other demographic changes are expected to occur. For example, more white-collar jobs will be created in proportion to those in the blue-collar occupations. Incomes may rise, but it is difficult at this time to determine the impact which inflation will have upon this rise in income. The shifts in market areas, as well as the shifts in the composition of the market, will provide growth opportunities and problems for the business community.

Making Use of the Data: Analytical and Forecasting Techniques

Forecasting is difficult, especially about the future. —Chinese Proverb

Once strategic data have been accumulated, they must be transformed into information which will enable decision makers to make appropriate decisions. These decisions, while made in the present, relate to future events. Techniques designed specifically to provide inferences about the future are called forecasting techniques. Other methodologies, labeled descriptive techniques, provide information about current situations; decision makers can draw inferences about the future after examining the information provided by these methodologies. Some forecasting methods with which you may be familiar include regression, correlation, Delphi, Box-Jenkins, seasonal trend, and expert opinion. Simulation, one of the most important forecasting techniques, is reviewed later in this section.

The role of forecasting in strategic management is to reduce uncertainty and aid in decision making. In strategic decision situations, uncertainty can never be totally eliminated. Ultimately, decision makers attempt to quantify the uncertainty that remains. This process is usually referred to as risk analysis.

Compounding the problem of reducing uncertainty, there is evidence that the amount of uncertainty is increasing as the environment becomes more volatile and previously unknown strategic problems confront organizations. These events are made more pronounced because of the long time horizons present in most strategy formulation situations. Three or more years frequently may transpire from conception to the actual marketing of a new product or the acquisition or divestment of an SBU. During this time the assumptions (premises) upon which the strategy was based may change significantly.

However, much uncertainty can be reduced, and the strategic manager should become familiar with those uncertainty reduction techniques at his or her disposal. Put simply, forecasting is vital. While it is assumed as given in most planning models, forecasting is not an easy task.[20]

Simulation Modeling and Other Uses of the Computer

One of the most significant analytical/forecasting techniques is simulation modeling. Simulation allows the strategist to ask "what if" questions—for example, "What if the price of raw material rises 1 percent?" "What if the union negotiates a 10-percent increase in benefits?" "What if our firm raises prices by 5 percent?" The answers to these and many other vital questions can be rendered quickly and accurately if the organization possesses a valid simulation model of its operations. Simulation models are expensive; so not every organization can afford one. For those who can, such models are becoming a necessity, not a luxury. To date, only simulations of internal operations are available; environmental simulations, with the exception of models of the national economy, are not widely available. However, such simulations are in the developmental stages.

---

[20] J. C. Chambers, S. K. Mullick, and D. D. Smith, "How to Choose the Right Forecasting Technique," *Harvard Business Review*, July/August 1971, pp. 45–74; W. Bouton, "The Changing Requirements for Managing Corporate Information Systems," *MSU Business Topics*, Summer 1978, pp. 1–12; W. K. Hall, "Forecasting Techniques for Use in the Corporate Planning Process," *Managerial Planning*, November/December 1972, pp. 5–10, 33; D. Lebell and O. J. Krasner, "Selecting Forecasting Techniques from Business Planning Requirements," *Academy of Management Review*, July 1977, pp. 373–383; S. Makridakis and S. Wheelwright, "Integrating Forecasting and Planning," *Long Range Planning*, September 1973, pp. 53–63; J. Utterback, "Environmental Analysis and Forecasting," in *Strategic Management, A New View of Business Policy and Planning*, Charles Hofer and Dan Schendel, eds. (Boston: Little/Brown, 1979).

Simulations are computerized models which aid management in decision making. Simulation models abstract reality—normally an organization's internal flows—in terms of logically arranged, algebraic equations, expressed symbolically. These models are interactive; that is, they allow managers to "talk" with them. Simulations in business are usually accomplished on the basis of computer time sharing. The normal use of simulations is to assume a change in one or more inputs to the system and view the resulting changes in the system as portrayed by the model. Simulations have evolved over a period of years but have been important only since 1970, when appropriate systems-oriented software packages were developed and time sharing became feasible. J. B. Boulden and E. S. Buffa summarized the requirements for an "on-line, real-time" shared computer system as follows:[21]

Simplicity.

Secrecy.

Conversational capability (user friendly).

Fast response.

Accessibility.

Data availability.

Flexibility.

Economy.

A simulation commences with an exhaustive analysis of the actual interrelationships of the organization, its subsystems, and the subsystems' components. Most simulations use a modular approach. They develop models for each of the major structural divisions, functions, or subsystems, combining them at an interface point into a total corporate model. The modules comprising the total model are usually at the business or functional level.[22] Eventually, every quantifiable internal resource, event, or flow is incorporated into a modular model. Modules are then combined and interrelationships interfaced.

The evidence indicates that the number of business firms employing simulations is large and growing. Numerous types of simulations are utilized, but few totally integrated corporate models exist. That is, few firms have combined simulations of various aspects of their operations to develop a model of the total corporation. Firms most frequently employ models in the areas of financial analysis and planning and evaluation of policy alternatives.

The development costs of "tailor made" simulations have been as high as $1 million, but more recent prices commence at $75,000. Because of the initial cost, most simulation users are firms that have annual sales of over $250 million, although one rule of thumb is that annual sales of at least $10 million are necessary in

---

[21] J. B. Boulden and E. S. Buffa, "Corporate Models: On-Line, Real-Time Systems," *Harvard Business Review*, July/August 1970, pp. 65–67. Also see, for a more recent view, P. S. Bender, W. D. Northrup, and J. F. Shapiro, "Practical Modeling for Resource Management," *Harvard Business Review*, March/April 1981, pp. 163–173.

[22] "Breakthrough in Management Planning" (Chicago: Planmetrics); "'What If' Help for Management," *Business Week*, January 21, 1980, pp. 73, 74; E. R. McLean and G. L. Neale, "Computer-Based Planning Models Come of Age," *Harvard Business Review*, July/August 1980, pp. 46–48; both EPS (Environmental Planning Systems) and IFPS (Interactive Financial Planning Systems) are computer simulation software packages which use this approach.

order to justify the initial development costs. Packaged simulation software is available through software distributors. Use of these packages substantially reduces cost; unfortunately, it often also reduces the comprehensiveness and accuracy of the resultant output.

There is limited use of simulation in state, city, and local governments. More frequent use is found at the federal government level. Most of these simulations do not model the total entity, except again for the model of the national economy. Little evidence of simulation use is found in the nonprofit, nonpublic sector, probably because of cost. Use of simulations is almost nonexistent in firms with sales less than $10 million a year. However, with the increased usage of minicomputers and microcomputers by small businesses and other small organizations, it would seem to be only a matter of time before relevant simulation software packages become available.[23]

In addition to simulation modeling, uses of the computer in strategic management include the provision of timely information at lower levels, which should eventually improve strategic decision making; the provision of more common models for financial analysis, forecasting, descriptive statistical analysis, capital budgeting, and so on; and even the training of executives to ask the right questions in strategy formulation.

It is important to remember that the computer only aids the strategist; it does not and cannot replace him or her. The strategist must use a certain amount of intuition as well as science in the strategic management process. It is this ability to meaningfully interpret and relate the scientifically derived information and to make appropriate strategic decisions that separates the strategist from the operational manager.

The Micro Advances Our Ability to Forecast

Information and information processing have become accessible to a much larger segment of the management population than before was possible with the advent of the microcomputer. This computer has given access to many who were previously financially or technologically denied the opportunity to employ the computer in managing their organizations. Of critical importance are the numerous software programs available to assist individuals and corporations in managing strategically. For example, spread sheet analyses, which allow managers to forecast the impacts of selected changes in financial performance, enable even the smallest organizations and their managers to make more sophisticated, more rational decisions with respect to their strategies. Numerous manipulations of balance sheets, income statements, and cash flows are also available. And, quite frankly, for the first time, many smaller organizations will now consequently develop such fundamental planning statements as budgets, which, while apparently simple, are time consuming and much more readily accomplished using appropriate software packages. Similar advances have been made in word processing, in ratio analyses, in capital needs fore-

---

[23] "Missing Computer Software," *Business Week*, September 1, 1980, pp. 46–56; W. M. Bulkeley, "Calculated Move: Computer Makers Feel Key to Sales Edge Lies in Better Programming," *Wall Street Journal*, September 29, 1980, pp. 1, 25.

casting, in sales forecasting, and so forth. Even such complicated programs, such as those employing Box Jenkins, the Program Evaluation Review Technique or the Critical Path Method, or Environmental Planning Systems are available for microcomputers. The ability to crunch numbers better and faster does not guarantee that improved decision making will occur, but the improvement in both hardware and software does suggest, at least, that better decisions are possible, if not more likely.

Analytical Techniques: A Comment

Numerous forecasting techniques exist. For example, virtually hundreds of methodologies have been suggested for societal and technological forecasting; but there is not space to discuss all of them here. The important points to remember are these:

1. Numerous techniques exist, some better than others for a particular situation.
2. Using more than one technique should improve forecasting.
3. The output of a technique is no better than its inputs and its assumptions.
4. Cost-benefit analysis should be performed before expensive techniques are undertaken.
5. The techniques should be evaluated.
6. Regardless of the amount of time and money invested, the environment is uncertain and is undergoing an increasing amount of change. Forecasting failures will occur. Flexibility must be maintained.
7. Somebody has to put it all together. Someone must make the decision as to what the information means. That person is not always right, as Information Capsule 2.1 revealed.

Internal and Environmental Information in the International Arena

The information requirements are greater for multinational firms than for domestic ones, because the multinational firm must know about more economic, cultural, social, political, legal, and monetary systems. Sources of this information vary, and they are often less accessible than in the parent country. Furthermore, because the transmission of information depends on language, language differences also present problems. Unfortunately, management information systems are often less sophisticated than managers might be used to or might desire. Informal sources must often be relied upon.

Research shows that multinationals historically have not done a thorough job of environmental analysis.[24] Indeed, they often attempt simply to replicate "back-home" strategies in lieu of assessing external situations and developing strategies accordingly. That such practices are foolhardy is shown by the following examples:

---

[24] "A Survey of International Research Practices by American International Corporations," (New York: International Research Associates, 1969).

1. A major razor blade firm tried to sell razor blades in a foreign country in drug stores and grocery stores, as it had back home. It didn't know the people in that country bought their razor blades in hardware stores.
2. Kentucky Fried Chicken, very successful in Japan, failed dismally with the same strategy in Hong Kong because social customs regarding the eating of chicken were different from those in Japan.
3. A U.S. company attempted to sell a gelatin dessert in a South American country where only 3 percent of the population had refrigerators.

The overriding purpose of obtaining information—identifying SWOT in order to better formulate objectives and strategies—remains the same in the international arena. The problem with fulfilling this purpose is twofold: first, SWOT changes; second, the appropriate strategies often differ. Fundamental marketing approaches must be altered, as suggested above. Leadership and motivation strategies must also be changed, because underlying basic cultural motivations differ.[25] Even more fundamentally, the choice of basic action strategies and their combinations must be altered to meet the demands of the situation. The variances which occur in mission, policy, and the composition of strategist groups; the resultant differences in objectives and strategies; and the differences in the environment require that information be gathered beyond that or instead of that which would routinely be gathered if the organization were operating only in the parent country.

Typically, multinationals possess some resource advantage, either capital, technology, or managerial expertise. Depending upon host country and parent country requirements, the multinational corporation's capital may or may not be invested in foreign countries, its technology may or may not be fully shared with others, and its managerial expertise may or may not be exported. Typically, licensing and joint ventures have replaced the capital investment and direct ownership basic action strategies of the 1950s and 1960s. The primary causes for this shifting of strategies are the potential for expropriation and the demands of host countries.

As a result of the potential for expropriation, the assessment of political instability is a critical strategic step, and the information needed for this assessment is complex and difficult to obtain and assimilate. Many foreign governments have political structures different from those of the parent country; and most governments are quite secretive about internal affairs. F. T. Haner has developed one useful system for classifying investment risks abroad. He uses a series of factors rated from 1 to 5, with total points being accumulated for the series. Acceptable levels of risk are defined and then compared to the estimates for various countries.[26] Investing is quite risky in some countries; on the other hand, stable countries such as the United States and Canada offer sound investments for firms from other nations.

In summary, the information requirements are greater at the international level than at the domestic level, because they involve learning the basic economic, cultural, social, political, and legal structures for each country. The purpose and process of information gathering remains the same, but differing SWOT and strategies may result.

---

[25] S. H. Robock and K. Simmons, *International Business and Multinational Enterprises* (Homewood, Ill.: Irwin, 1973).
[26] F. T. Haner, "Rating Investment Risks Abroad," *Business Horizons*, April 1979, pp. 18–23.

Nonprofits and Their Usages of Information to Determine SWOT

Nonprofits examine themselves for strengths and weaknesses, they assess their environments for threats and opportunities, but the nature of what is examined, both internally and externally, will vary from what for-profits might consider. Because the organizational category of nonprofits encompasses such a wide spectrum of organizations, in terms of size and purpose, it is virtually impossible to characterize their situations specifically. Rather, what can be done is to make some very general observations about common characteristics of certain of these nonprofits, and to make some observations about their usages of information in determining SWOT.

Internally, most nonprofits would seem to consider much the same factors as appear in Figure 2.3. The target groups, the techniques, the processes, however, will be somewhat different for the economic functions such as marketing, and some of the management functions, such as leadership. In smaller nonprofits, as in smaller for-profits, the performance of these functions is likely to be less sophisticated than in larger organizations. And, it is generally recognized that most nonprofits have less sophisticated management systems and fewer skilled managers than for-profit organizations. In another area, significant differences would probably occur with respect to major power/influence groups. Only on limited occasions would there be stockholders. Rather, contributors, taxpayers, or members (in cases of dues-collecting associations, for example, unions) would be more appropriate persons to examine for their expectations and influence. Similarly, the nature of the management group will be somewhat different in that nonpaid volunteers will often serve in upper management and on the board of directors or similar governance unit. Government will be an internal factor to consider for all government organizations. Those governments external to a particular government organization will, of course, need to be monitored. Employees may not be members of organized labor groups; but in larger nonprofits, bureaucracies tend to dominate the everyday decision process, and often, the strategic one as well.

Externally, major differences would include the role of government, the definition of "competition" and "the industry," relationships with society and the reaction to societal pressure groups, the role of labor, and the influence or absence of influence of the client group. The role of government is more significantly increased. Many nonprofits will, of course, be governmental units, so government may be an internal factor to assess. For most governments, other governments will still remain an influence to consider. The city must consider the state and federal governments, and so forth. For nonprofits such as health care institutions, governments of all types, but especially the federal government, are a major force in determining proper actions. Administrators must carefully monitor federal legislative action and federal agency interpretations thereof, for the impacts of these. For example, hospitals in 1983, encountered significant changes in federal government Medicare payment procedures. Payments were standardized for any procedure in a given area according to diagnostic related groupings (DRG). Many hospitals found their costs exceeded these standard payments. For unions, charities, and several of the other nonprofits, government plays an important regulatory, if not an administrative, role. Thus, in most cases, for nonprofits, government must be carefully considered in strategic decisions. The definition of competition and the industry changes some-

Figure 2.6
Competitive Alternatives to Hospital Care

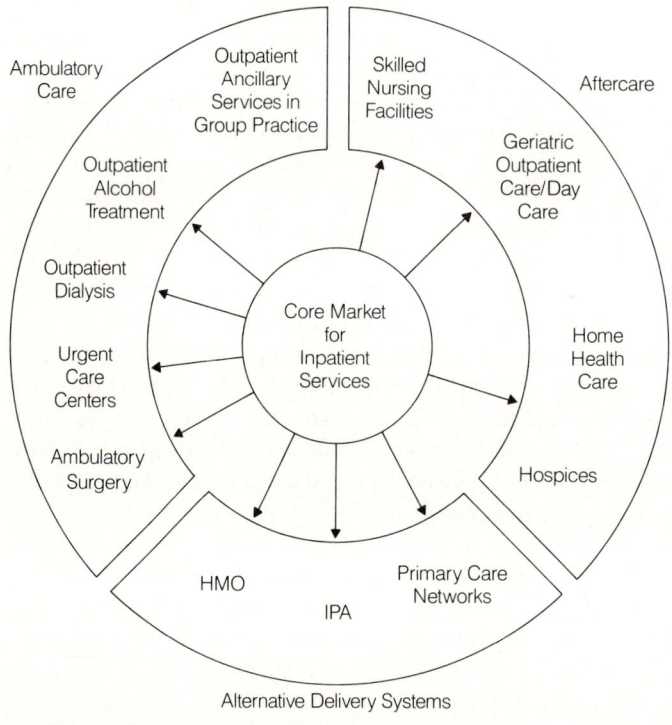

Source: Jeff Charles Goldsmith, *Can Hospitals Survive?*; Homewood: Dow Jones, 1981, p. 17. Reprinted by permission of Jeff Charles Goldsmith.

what for nonprofits. While profit competition does not exist, there will be competition for resources, for personnel, for clients, for expertise and experience, and for prestige and influence.[27] The competition for funds is especially intense. There are only so many contributors, so many tax dollars available. Known charitable sources, such as business corporations, receive multiple donation requests daily (at all of their geographic locations). Most sources can only give so much, and thus the competition for funds becomes very intense among nonprofits.

A specific example of factors that a not-for-profit (or for-profit) hospital would consider in competitor analysis is indicated in Figure 2.6. This figure suggests that a number of competitors exist in each of a hospital's three major, traditional client service areas. Hospitals must develop strategies for coping with such competition, just as any business would.

Normally, nonprofits are very sensitive to societal demands and to those pressure groups which arise. Government at all elected levels is responsive, if slowly, to

[27] E. Greenberg, "Competing for Scarce Resources," *Journal of Business Strategy*, Winter 1982, pp. 83–86.

pressure groups, although it would appear that only the "squeakiest wheels" get greased. (But too, the internal bureaucracies that emerge are not particularly responsive, so strategic managers must be attuned to this problem.) Labor is highly unionized in public education, in certain municipalities in the lower paying jobs, and in many health care institutions. But for most nonprofits, organized labor does not pose the same threat that it does to many for-profits. This is especially true of the federal government. Although some federal employee unions do exist, their powers are significantly less than their for-profit counterparts. Among other things, they do not have the right to strike legally, as President Reagan demonstrated to members of PATCO, the air traffic controller's union. Finally, the client, if he or she is a member of a strong pressure group, may have tremendous influence on the organization. If not, then clients typically have little influence since they are normally going to be receiving services free or at below cost.

The consequence of the above differences is that the strategists must incorporate their knowledge of these differences into their strategic information systems and into their strategic decision processes. They must monitor more closely various factors depending upon the importance of each strategic factor. As would any strategist, they must consider those factors that are going to have the most impact on their futures. Perhaps one of the most important points to be made in this section is that for those of us who are not as familiar with nonprofit organizations as we are with for-profit organizations, we need to keep these differences in perspective when examining nonprofit situations.

Summary

Change typifies the environment of all organizations, but the pace of change seems to be accelerating, especially in multinational situations. The purpose of obtaining internal and external information is to determine strengths, weaknesses, opportunities, and threats in order to better establish objectives, formulate strategic alternatives, and decide upon courses of strategic action. Strengths and weaknesses, threats and opportunities are not always perceived in the same ways or determined in the same ways. Differences in approaches to managing them consequently result.

The strategic information system is a critical element in achieving success. Both formal and informal sources are used to identify and determine the nature of internal and external factors. Strategists must continually scan the environment for information which could necessitate changing strategies. The internal information sought relates at the corporate level to SBU performance, and at the SBU level to functions such as marketing, production, finance, human resource management, and so forth. Management systems and techniques are examined at both levels, as are management values and capabilities. Externally, the organization monitors information related to government, technology, competition, society, the economy, labor, natural resources, and international situations.

It must be remembered that strategic decisions are based on forecasts related to current information. Any number of forecasting techniques exist, each better in some situations than in others. Modeling seems to offer much hope for the future, especially in terms of helping strategists understand how changes will affect the organization.

In the multinational firm, information has the same purpose and is used in the same process as in a domestic firm; but the SWOT, the information needed, the strategies that result, and the problems encountered are more complex and involve more difficulty because of the differences between host country's and parent country's economic, cultural, social, legal, political, and monetary systems.

Key Terms and Concepts

After completing this chapter, you should be familiar with the following terms and concepts: how change affects the need for information; why information is critical to strategy formulation; the definitions of strengths, weaknesses, opportunities, and threats; how SWOT are defined operationally; strategic information system (SIS); management information system (MIS); major sources of internal and external information; scanning; the internal information sought; the external information sought, including major factors involved in each; the importance of forecasting; modeling; the impacts of the international situation on the information component of strategy formulation; and the impacts of the nonprofit situation on the information component of strategy formation.

Discussion Questions

1. Discuss any organization with regard to the contents of this chapter and the key terms and concepts noted above.
2. Now that you have examined all four of the primary formative factors in the strategy formulation process, which do you believe is the most critical, and why?
3. Review an international organization and describe how its information function might operate outside of the parent country.

References

"Business is Turning Data into A Potent Strategic Weapon," *Business Week*, August 22, 1983, pp. 92–95.

Hofer, C. W. "Research on Strategic Planning: A Survey of Past Studies and Suggestions for Future Efforts." *Journal of Economics and Business*, Spring/Summer 1976, pp. 261–272.

Mintzberg, H. "Planning on the Left Side and Managing on the Right." *Harvard Business Review*, July/August 1976, pp. 49–58.

Steiner, G. A. *Pitfalls in Comprehensive Long-Range Planning*. Oxford, Ohio: The Planning Executives Institute, 1972.

Summer, C. E., *Strategic Behavior in Business and Government*, Boston: Little/Brown, 1980.

Tipgos, M. A. "Structuring a Management Information System for Strategic Planning." *Managerial Planning*, January/February 1975, pp. 10–16.

Appendix to Chapter 2
Sources for Environmental Information

1. Government.
   a. *Code of Federal Regulations*, *Federal Register*, other federal publications.
   b. Various publishing house services—Commerce Clearing House (CCH), Bureau of National Affairs (BNA), Prentice-Hall (PH), and the like.
   c. Lobbyists.
   d. *Kiplinger Washington Newsletter*.
   e. *Monthly Catalog of United States Government Publications*.
   f. Monthly checklist of state publications.
2. Technology.
   a. *Statistical Abstract of the United States*.
   b. *Applied Science and Technology Index*.
   c. Scientific and Technical Information Service.
   d. Congressional hearings, university reports, "think tank" reports.
   e. Department of Defense and military department publishers.
   f. Industrial reports.
   g. Computer-assisted information search.
   h. National Science Foundation, *Annual Report*.
   i. *Research and Development Directory*.
   j. Industry contacts, salespeople, professional meetings.
   k. Patents.
3. Industry and Competition.
   a. Annual reports of companies in question.
   b. Securities and Exchange Commission—10-K Report.
   c. *Fortune 500 Directory*, *Forbes*, *Wall Street Transcript*, *Barrons*.
   d. Investment services and directories: Dun & Bradstreet, Standard & Poor's Value Line, Moody's, Starch Marketing.
   e. Trade association publications.
   f. Professional meetings, salespeople, industry contacts.
   g. Espionage.
   h. Surveys, for example, market research.
   i. *County and City Data Book*.
   j. *County Business Patterns*.
   k. Standard and Poor's *Industry Surveys*
4. Society.
   a. Pressure group publications and pronouncements.

b. Books which might affect societal attitudes.
   c. Government (see section 1 in this list).
   d. Surveys.
   e. Judgment, opinion, scenario forecasting (Delphi).
   f. The media, especially television and newspapers.
   g. Articles in sociological, psychological, and political journals.
   h. Various institute and foundation reports such as the Ford Foundation's and the Brookings Institute's.
5. Economy.
   a. National Economy.
      i. U.S. Department of Commerce.
         (a) Bureau of Census—*Survey of Manufacturers*, *Statistical Abstract of the United States*, *Current Population Reports*, census reports on various industries, housing, population, and so on.
         (b) Office of Business Economics—*Survey of Current Business*.
         (c) Bureau of Economic Analysis—*Business Conditions Digest*.
         (d) Business and Defense Services Administration—*U.S. Industrial Outlook*.
      ii. Council of Economic Advisors—*Economic Indicators*, *Annual Report*.
      iii. Securities and Exchange Commission—"Quarterly Financial Reports," "Quarterly Report of Plant and Equipment Expenditures of U.S. Corporations," "Quarterly Report of Working Capital of U.S. Corporations."
      iv. St. Louis Federal Reserve Bank—"Quarterly Report."
      v. The Conference Board.
      vi. Trade Association Publications.
      vii. Federal Trade Commission.
      viii. U.S. Chamber of Commerce/American Manufacturers Association.
      ix. INSEAD (The European Institute of Business Administration); IMEDE (Management Development Institute, Lausanne).
      x. University of Michigan Survey Research Center.
      xi. *Federal Reserve Bulletin*.
   b. International Economic Conditions.
      i. U.S. Department of Commerce.
         (a) Bureau of Census—"Guide to Foreign Trade Statistics."
         (b) Bureau of International Commerce—"Overseas Business Reports," "Foreign Economic Trends and Their Implications for the United States."
      ii. O.E.C.D.—*Economic Outlook and Main Economic Indicators*.
      iii. United Nations—*Statistical Yearbook*.
      iv. O.I.T.; International Labor Office—*Yearbook of Labor Statistics*.
      v. Business International newsletters.
      vi. St. Louis Federal Reserve Bank.
      vii. National plans of European countries.

6. Labor.
    a. *Labor Law Journal* and other related journals, including law school journals.
    b. Various publishing house services, such as CCH, BNA, PH.
    c. Various labor union publications.
    d. U.S. Department of Labor publications, *Monthly Labor Review*.
    e. U.S. Department of Commerce.
7. Natural Resources.
    a. U.S. Department of the Interior, Bureau of Mines—*Minerals Yearbook*, *Geological Survey*.
    b. U.S. Department of Agriculture—*Agricultural Abstract*.
    c. Federal Power Commission statistics of electric utilities/statistics of gas pipe companies.
    d. Publications of various institutions: American Petroleum Institute, U.S. Atomic Energy Commission, Coal Mining Institute of America, American Steel Institute, Brookings Institute.
8. General Information.
    a. Indexes and periodical directories.
    b. Bibliographies and special guides.
    c. Other basic sources.

Sources: C. R. Goeldner and Laura M. Kirks, "Business Facts: Where to Find Them," *MSU Business Topics*, Summer 1976, pp. 23–76; Francois E. deCarbonnel and Roy G. Donance, "Information Sources for Planning Decisions," *California Management Review*, (Summer 1973), pp. 42–53; and A. B. Nutt, R. C. Lenz, Jr., H. W. Lanford, and M. J. Cleary, "Data Sources for Trend Extrapolation in Technological Forecasting," *Long Range Planning*, February 1976, pp. 72–76.

Chapter 3
Determining Strategic Objectives and Formulating the Master Strategy

The thing to do with the future is not to forecast it, but to create it. The objective of planning should be to design a desirable future and to invent ways to bring it about. —Russell Ackoff

This chapter continues to examine, primarily from a conceptual perspective, the major issues involved in a situation that requires strategy formulation:

1. Where are we? (current performance; SWOT)
2. Where do we want to be? (future objectives; forecasted SWOT)
3. How do we get there? (master strategy; forecasted SWOT)

The chapter focuses on the processes involved in determining strategic objectives and in formulating the master strategy and discusses the corporate strategy in particular. The objective determination process is studied. Then objectives as integrative mechanisms are discussed. Management by objectives, results, and rewards (MBORR), a management planning and control system as well as a management philosophy, is outlined. Most of the second half of the chapter examines the master strategy, especially corporate strategy alternatives. Finally, some of the important characteristics of all plans are noted. Figures 3.1 and 3.2 show what subjects are presented in the chapter.

"Would you tell me, please, which way I ought to go from here?" said Alice. *"That depends a good deal on where you want to get to,"* said the Cheshire cat.
—Lewis Carroll, Alice's Adventures in Wonderland

Figure 3.1
The Organization—a Strategic Management Process Model

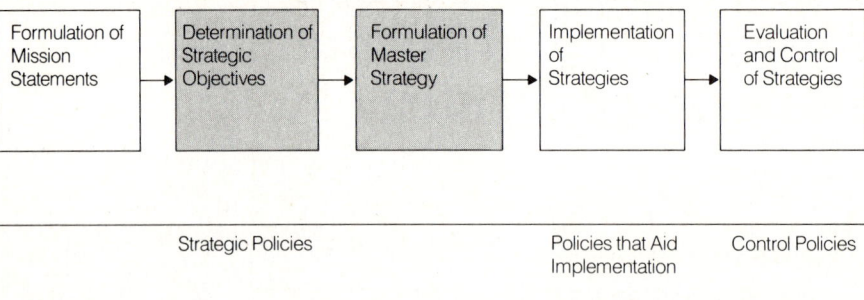

Determining Strategic Objectives

To fulfill the promise of the mission, strategic objectives—the results intended—must be identified. Without objectives, the organization is assured of eventual failure. The objectives depend on mission, policy, the strategists, and SWOT. Objectives state "where we want to be."

The Objective Setting Process

All objectives possess four components:

1. The attribute sought.
2. An index for measuring progress toward the attribute.
3. A target to be achieved or hurdle to be overcome.
4. A time frame within which the target or hurdle is to be achieved.[1]

Figure 3.3 portrays these components for several typical objectives. Typical strategic business objectives include concerns for the impacts of operations on both the organization and the external environment. But looking at Figure 3.3, you can see that fundamental internal concerns of the organization include the attributes of efficiency (profits, profits in relation to sales), growth (sales), utilization of resources (return on investment, ROI), contribution to owners (earnings per share), and contribution to employees (wages, employee development). Externally, the organization must be concerned with contribution to customers (quality, price) and contribution to society (taxes paid, corporate citizenship). It has also been observed that contribution to other major stakeholders—those on whom the actions of the organi-

---

[1] C. W. Hofer and D. Schendel, *Strategy Formulation: Analytical Concepts* (St. Paul, Minn.: West, 1978), pp. 20–22.

Figure 3.2
Objective Determination and Master Strategy Formulation

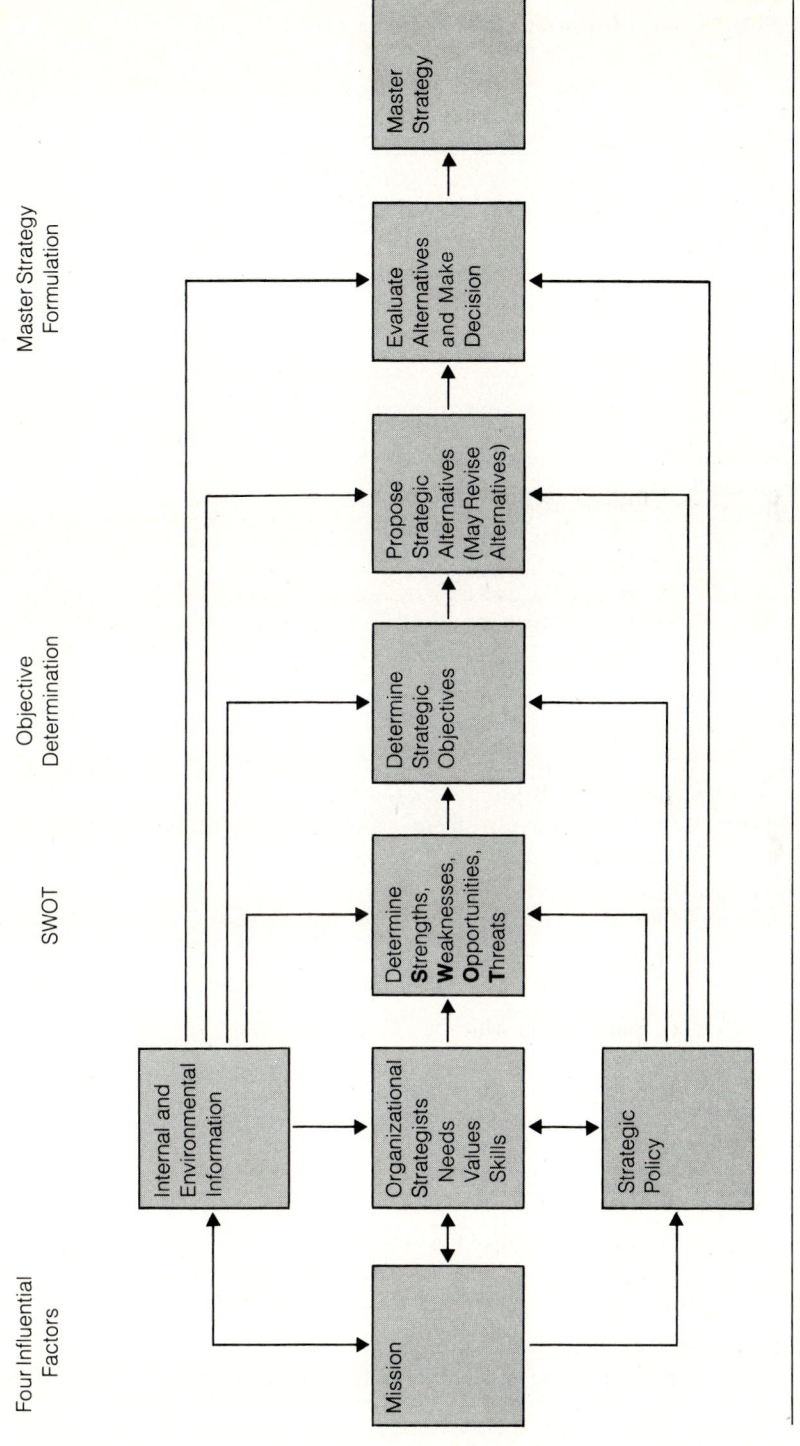

Figure 3.3
Some Typical Business Objectives

Possible Attributes	Possible Indices	Targets and Time Frame		
		Year One	Year Two	Year Three
Growth	$ sales	$100 mil	120 mil	140 mil
	Unit sales	× units	1.10 × units	1.20 × units
Efficiency	$ profits	10 mil	12 mil	15 mil
	Profits/sales	.10	.10	.11
Utilization of resources	ROI	.15	.15	.16
	ROE	.25	.26	.27
Contribution to owners	Dividends	$1.00/share	$1.10/share	$1.30/share
	Eps	$2.00/share	$2.40/share	$2.80/share
Contribution to customers	Price Quality Reliability	Equal to or better than competition	Equal to or better than competition	Equal to or better than competition
Contributions to employees	Wage rate	$3.50/hour	$3.75/hour	$4.00/hour
	Employment stability	< 5% turnover	< 4% turnover	< 4% turnover
Contributions to society	Taxes paid	$10 mil	$12 mil	$16 mil
	Scholarships awarded Etc.	$100,000	$120,000	$120,000

Source: C. W. Hofer, "A Conceptual Scheme for Formulating a Total Business Strategy," Dover, MA: Case Teacher's Association, #BP-0040, p. 2. Copyright 1976 by C. W. Hofer. Reproduced by permission.

zation have a direct impact—is also of vital concern. Similar objectives exist for nonbusiness organizations, but not in profit terms.

Objectives steer the organization in the direction its mission has pointed out. As has often been said, "If you don't know where you are going, any road will get you there." Without objectives, "there" is usually "nowhere"! The Cheshire cat was right. First you must decide where you are going, then you can decide what road to take. Objectives provide direction and motivation. The objective setting process also provides valuable communication within and among organization subunits.

Levels of Objectives

There are three major levels of planning within the organization: strategic, intermediate, and operational (see Figure 3.1). Hence, there are three major levels of objectives and plans.

The objectives toward which strategic plans are directed should be specific. For example, a firm might set objectives of a 15-percent return on investment, a 20-percent penetration of the product market, a 10-percent increase in sales per year, and so forth. However, at the strategic planning stage, the plans need not be stated so specifically; in fact, these plans are usually broadly stated. But as planning progresses through the next two stages, intermediate and operational, the plans set out more specifically how objectives will be accomplished. Intermediate plans translate strategy into more specific courses of action for major organizational subsystems. Operational plans translate intermediate plans into very specific courses of action for lower-level subsystems and for individuals. Usually, the planning process in-

Information Capsule 3.1
Hewlett-Packard's Strategic Objectives

The following is a brief description of the Hewlett-Packard objectives in 1981:[2]

1. Profit Objective: To achieve sufficient profit to finance company growth and to provide resources we need to achieve our other corporate objectives.
2. Customer Objective: To provide products and services of the greatest possible value to our customers, thereby gaining and holding their respect and loyalty.
3. Fields of Interest Objective: To enter new fields only when the ideas we have, together with our technical, manufacturing, and marketing skills, assure that we can make a needed and profitable contribution to the field.
4. Growth Objective: To let growth be limited only by our profits and our ability to develop and produce technical products that satisfy real customer needs.
5. People Objective: To help Hewlett-Packard people share in the company's success, which they make possible; to provide job security based on their performance; to recognize individual achievements; and to help them gain a sense of satisfaction and accomplishment from their work.
6. Management Objective: To foster initiative and creativity by allowing the individual great freedom of action in attaining well-defined objectives.
7. Citizenship Objective: To honor our obligations to society by being an economic, intellectual, and social asset to each nation and each community in which we operate.

Source: Hewlett-Packard Company, Inc., 1981 Statement of Objectives.

cludes a series of increasingly complex and detailed subobjectives, subplans, subpolicies, and so forth, until objectives and actions are parcelled to individual workers. Again, as with most management terminology, there are no generally accepted definitions which describe the various levels of plans established to accomplish the master strategy. Differences in terminology should be allowed for in the examination of strategy and in the practice of strategic management.

Organizational Objectives as Integration Mechanisms—MBORR

Let us now examine a program for establishing effective objectives and then consider types of objectives which organizations establish. The program is called management by objectives, results, and rewards—MBORR. The need for specific

---
[2] As depicted in internal corporate documents and described to the author by Hewlett-Packard personnel.

objectives must be emphasized. Vague objectives, at the very least, lead to misinterpretation and a lack of accountability for performance. It is precisely to deal with such problems that MBORR-type programs were established. MBORR as used here embodies specific objective setting programs and does not focus on the more behavioral concepts of subordinate development often associated with such programs.

MBORR: Concepts and Implications for Strategy

Management by objectives, results, and rewards is a management planning, control, communication, and subordinate development system. This type of program in its various forms—MBO, management by objectives; MBR, management by results; and MBC, management by compensation; as well as MBORR—is probably the most frequently discussed management practice in the last thirty years. Few can agree on specific contents, but most would agree that four common dimensions should be considered:

1. Establishment of objectives.
2. Employee participation.
3. Evaluation and control of performance.
4. Rewards for results.

The normal MBORR process involves the establishment of specific objectives by top management in all performance areas. These objectives are then communicated to the next lower level of management, which may or may not have participated in their development. At each level, objectives may then be distributed to the appropriate managers for their acceptance or rejection. Or these managers may submit to their superiors proposals which state their commitments to the accomplishment of the objectives. What evolves is a negotiation meeting between a manager and his or her superior manager involving give and take with respect to the subordinate's objectives. Once agreement is reached, the process shifts to the next lower level of management and continues until objective distribution reaches the supervisory level. The process usually terminates at this level, because first-line positions often cannot properly utilize this technique.

MBORR-type techniques were first introduced to the public as MBR by Peter Drucker, who had observed the method's successful functioning at General Motors. Since that time, countless studies and reviews of its effectiveness and ineffectiveness have been reported, variations in its methodology suggested, and corrective actions for its weaknesses proposed. George Odiorne popularized the concept as MBO. I have added the RR to emphasize the importance of measuring results and rewarding them.[3] Below are listed just a few of the major findings regarding MBORR-type programs. Positive results include the following:

1. Performance—both quantity and quality—are improved.

[3] J. M. Higgins, *Human Relations Concepts and Skills* (New York: Random House, 1982), Chapter 13.

2. Communications and understanding are improved.
3. Job satisfaction is improved.
4. Individual growth is enhanced.
5. Role prescription is clarified.

Negative results include the following:

1. Managers may become more critical.
2. Managers may use MBORR objectives as a "whip."
3. Establishing objectives entails all sorts of problems: scale unit bias may exist, objectives may be set too high or too low, they may not be accepted, they may be inflexible, they may be difficult to set for nonquantifiable areas.
4. The process may be too short-run oriented.
5. The process seems to lose its effect over time.
6. Monetary rewards are sometimes insufficient and hence fail to maintain performance.
7. The process often takes too much time.
8. Group dynamics are usually not taken into consideration.
9. There are physical and mental limitations for the individual.
10. Goals established become maximums even where they could be exceeded.

The negative results reported here far outnumber the positive effects, and at least twenty more could have been listed. However, studies of the technique's effectiveness have been performed in widely varying situations, causing results to vary. More importantly, many have reported that the technique's implementation, not the technique itself, was the problem. It appears that when an appropriate implementation procedure is followed and top management is involved and concerned, MBORR is effective.

Latham and Yukl, in reviewing published and unpublished field research, report that, whether or not MBORR-type programs were specifically used, the setting of objectives led to superior performance.[4] Some have suggested that specific objectives are not necessary in every situation, and indeed M. B. McCaskey's "directional planning," which does not require objective setting, may be sufficient for certain limited situations.[5] In general, though, John Mee's "Principle of the Objective" is relevant: "Before initiating any course of action the objectives must be clearly determined, understood and stated."[6] In summary, without specific objectives, the strategy eventually fails to elicit performance.

---

[4]G. P. Latham and G. A. Yukl, "A Review of Research on the Application of Goal Setting in Organizations," *Academy of Management Journal*, December 1975, pp. 827–832.

[5]M. B. McCaskey, "A Contingency Approach to Planning: Planning with Goals and Planning without Goals," *Academy of Management Journal*, June 1974, pp. 281–291.

[6]J. Mee, "The Principle of the Objective," in "Management Philosophy for Professional Executives," *Business Horizons*, December 1956, pp. 5–11.

Table 3.1
Objectives Stipulated in Plans

Industry	Number of Firms	Sales	Earnings	Return on Investment	Capital Growth	Share of the Market	Sales/Earnings Ratio	No Quantified Objectives
Mining	19	16	18	14	8	4	3	0
Food	26	26	26	21	17	15	18	0
Textiles and paper	28	24	27	23	14	13	16	0
Chemical	46	42	46	35	22	24	22	0
Oil	17	9	16	13	8	5	4	1
Steel and aluminum	18	17	18	15	9	9	7	0
Machinery	42	40	42	33	23	29	24	0
Electrical	49	47	47	38	23	29	26	1
Vehicles and accessories	29	27	28	27	15	19	14	0
Transport and communication	12	9	10	8	8	7	4	0
Wholesale and retail	34	33	33	26	22	8	21	0
Services	8	6	7	6	2	2	3	0
Total	328	296	318	259	171	164	162	2

Source: From Leslie W. Rue, "Tools and Techniques of Long-Range Planning," *Long Range Planning*, October 1974, p. 62. Reprinted by permission of Pergamon Press Ltd., Oxford, England.

The Objectives Established

Objectives are needed in every area where performance and results directly and vitally affect the survival and prosperity of the business. —Peter Drucker

Organizations establish many types of objectives. Some are specific, some are not. Many organizations set no specific objectives. Some organizations establish only a limited number. Others establish objectives for many areas of operating performance. The following paragraphs report on three research studies which deal with the nature of business objectives.

Les Rue, reporting on a survey of 400 predominantly large firms in several major industries, found that most firms have multiple, quantitative, written objective statements like those presented in Table 3.1. This table indicates that more firms established earnings and sales objectives than return objectives. Rue also examined financial analyses associated with the objectives established and found that profit (the income statement) was of primary concern but that most firms were also concerned with balance sheet and cash flow analysis (see Table 3.2).[7]

[7]L. W. Rue, "Tools and Techniques of Long Range Planning," *Long Range Planning*, October 1974, pp. 61–65.

J. W. Dobbie, in an examination of fifty large California-based firms (all with over $100 million in annual sales), found the firms tended to express objectives according to the type of strategy they employed. His strategy classifications included: personal (the aims of the chief executive); opportunity; geographic expansion; financial growth; and business (for planning or diversified firms). The types of objectives examined were: various return methods; growth in sales or earnings; and pro-forma financial statements or resource control. His findings are summarized in Table 3.3. Dobbie also observed that managerial style and the position of the planning unit within the organization structure affected the type of objectives chosen.

Table 3.2
Pro-Forma Statements Used in Planning

		Pro-Forma Statement			
Industry	Number of Firms	Balance Sheet	Income Statement	Cash Flow	None
Mining	19	13	18	17	0
Food	26	20	24	23	0
Textile and paper	28	22	26	24	2
Chemical	46	34	45	43	0
Oil	17	11	16	17	0
Steel and aluminum	18	16	17	16	0
Machinery	42	33	41	37	1
Electrical	49	43	43	39	3
Vehicles and accessories	29	26	27	24	1
Transportation and communication	12	6	11	8	1
Wholesale and retail	34	30	33	31	1
Services	8	6	8	7	0
Total	328	245	294	287	9

Source: From Leslie W. Rue, "Tools and Techniques of Long-Range Planning," *Long Range Planning*, October 1974, p. 64. Reprinted by permission of Pergamon Press Ltd., Oxford, England.

Table 3.3
Primary Statement Form of Long-Range Goals versus Form of Strategy

	Form of Strategic Plan				
Primary Form of Long-Range Goals	Business	Financial Growth	Geographic	Opportunity	Personal
Various Returns Methods	4		1		
Growth in Sales and/or Earnings	7	7	1	2	
Pro-Forma Financial Statements or Resource Control	14	9	3	1	6

Note: Basis: 55 Firms.
Source: John W. Dobbie, "Guides to a Foundation for Strategic Planning in Large Firms," paper presented to the 34th Annual Meeting of the Academy of Management, Seattle, Washington, August 1974, p. 14. Reprinted by permission of the Academy of Management.

Table 3.4
Range of Corporate Goals for Eighty-Two Firms

Category	Number	Percent[a]
Profitability	73	89
Growth	67	82
Market share	54	66
Social responsibility	53	65
Employee welfare	51	62
Product quality and service	49	60
Research and development	44	54
Diversification	42	51
Efficiency	41	50
Financial stability	40	49
Resource conservation	32	39
Management development	29	35
Multinational enterprise	24	29
Consolidation	14	17
Miscellaneous other goals	15	18

[a] Adds to more than 100 percent because most companies have more than one goal.
Source: Y. K. Shetty, "New Look at Corporate Goals," *California Management Review*, Winter 1979, p. 73. © 1979 by the Regents of the University of California. Reprinted from the *California Management Review*, Volume XXII, no. 2, p. 73, by permission of the Regents.

While Dobbie's sample size limits generalization, his study at least suggests that as complexity of operations and experience in strategy formulation increase, the number of objectives and their diversity increase.[8]

Y. K. Shetty, in an examination of eighty-two companies, found a wide range of corporate objectives, as indicated in Table 3.4. Most companies had five or six goals. However, one company had only one objective, while another had eighteen. As can be seen from the table, economic objectives dominated corporate concerns. Shetty found that objectives varied by industry; for example, social responsibility was the second most frequently cited objective in the chemicals and drugs group of companies, but the fifth most frequently cited objective in the electrical and electronics group. Finally, Shetty concluded that as organizations grow, their environments tend to become more turbulent; and as a result, their objectives change as they become more responsive to stakeholders outside the immediate economic constituency.[9]

As you can see from these studies, objectives which organizations employ in their strategies are dominated by, but not limited to, economic objectives. Other types of objectives include employee development and social responsibility. And while it is apparent that most business organizations are today primarily concerned with mission objectives, other issues are expected to become increasingly important as society (and government) continue to demand more of business.

---

[8] J. W. Dobbie, "Guides to a Foundation for Strategic Planning in Large Firms" (Paper presented to the 34th Annual Meeting of the Academy of Management, Seattle, Washington, August 1974).
[9] Y. K. Shetty, "New Look at Corporate Goals," *California Management Review*, Winter 1979, pp. 71–79.

The key to successful planning is the process of establishing specific objectives at each succeeding level of the organization. Objectives tie the organization together.

Prioritizing Objectives

One of the most perplexing problems confronting the strategic manager is the prioritizing of objectives. Many seem important, and in the hectic day-to-day crisis management environment, it's easy to forget that the swamp still needs draining. Even during the cyclical or periodic planning process, the task of establishing priorities for objectives is not an easy one. There exist certain natural conflicts among objectives. For example, observing the objectives in Figure 3.3, one would expect that contributions to society and employees might be financially in conflict with returns to owners (short term at least), and perhaps customers. There are also often conflicts between corporate and business, or business and functional objectives. There are almost always conflicts between strategic and operational objectives. And the problem of prioritizing is further compounded when one realizes that objectives are normally to some degree interdependent, and often reciprocally causal. There are power centers that demand attention to their objectives in every organization. Finally, one's personal objectives may in fact be in conflict with appropriate organizational priorities. How then does the strategist determine which objectives are most important?

First, there are few proven decision rules for determining appropriate priority. Rather, there are rules of thumb which guide many managers. To begin, managers may simply react to problems as they arise, establishing the solution to the most current issue as having the major priority. Granted, this does not seem the proper action for a strategic planner, but it happens. And in fact, sometimes it's necessary to be flexible and recognize that something very current is very critical and strategic and needs to take priority. One must recognize that major decisions are not as infrequently made on the spur of the moment, in a reactive mode, as one would like to think. We would like strategists to be proactive, but many times, reaction is necessary. Thus, general managers respond to crises as they evolve. For example, when Bendix attempted the takeover of Martin Marietta, it was imperative for the CEO of Martin to be reactive, to launch an immediate defense of the company. He had to seek to satisfy those objectives that were dominant at the moment. Urgency, and the order of their attracting the attention of the strategist, should not, however, determine the order in which objectives are routinely going to be prioritized.

More desirable is a rational approach to the prioritizing of objectives. Certainly in the periodic strategic planning process, there is the opportunity among participants to evaluate critically and weigh alternative objectives and give them priority. The preponderance of evidence suggests a participative approach involving the key managers involved—here strategists. Simple ranking, paired comparisons ranking, the employment of nonparametric statistics, or any other generally organized fashion of ranking objectives, as long as it is supported by appropriate information, and as long as implementers are participants, would seem to move in the right direction.

Every enterprise needs a central purpose expressed in terms of the services it will render to society. And it needs a basic concept of how it will create these services. Since it will be competing with other enterprises for resources, it must have some distinctive advantages—in its services or in its methods of creating them. Moreover, since it will inevitably cooperate with other firms, it must have the means for maintaining viable coalitions with them. In addition, there are the elements of change, growth, and adaptation. Master strategy is a company's basic plan for dealing with these factors. —William H. Newman

The Master Strategy

Once strategic objectives have been determined, organizational strategists formulate the master strategy. Strategies tell "how we get to where we want to be."

The term *strategy* derives from the ancient Greeks' word for general, *strategos*. Until the nineteenth century, the term related to the plans of action used by a military force in battle. More recently, *strategy* has taken on new meanings and is frequently used to refer to the endeavors of various organizations, primarily business organizations, to anticipate, respond to, and generally survive in their environments. As mentioned in Chapter 1, the term *strategy* is defined differently in the various organizational contexts in which it may be encountered; however, there is general agreement that a strategy is a major organizational plan of action to reach a major organizational objective.

An Overview of Strategy

Historically, most organizations have concentrated their strategic efforts on the development of either of two primary strategies (or sometimes both in combination): a focal basic action strategy, such as internal growth, conglomerate diversification, or retrenchment; and/or a focal marketing strategy. They have viewed strategy largely as simply requiring some basic action, perhaps internal growth, towards which their remaining efforts would be directed. And/or, they have focused on some element of the marketing strategy, such as a high-quality product. This focal basic action strategy or marketing strategy, or combination of the two, has come to be known as the "grand strategy." (This grand strategy is discussed in more detail near the end of this chapter.) And while most organizations have established a "grand strategy," they have not typically formulated a true, all-encompassing master strategy. But that is changing. For example, as the importance of managing environmental relationships became evident, more firms, both single- and multiple-SBU organizations, incorporated enterprise strategies into their master strategies. (In contrast, most nonbusiness organizations have historically lacked objectives and strategies, but this is now changing.)

The emphasis placed on the enterprise strategy is exemplified by Union Carbide, which has a complex strategy for improving its environmental protection activity. Its Environmental Impact Analysis program (EIA) is headed by a high-ranking corporate official. Each company plant is rated on numerous aspects of the impacts of its products and processes on several environmental areas of concern—air and water quality, noise, and the like. Potential problem areas are immediately observable. Public opinion is also rated. Most of the rating system is computerized, as are the corporation's processes. Inputs and outputs are measured; levels of waste and pollution are determined and controlled; and corrective actions are taken.[10]

Most firms have yet to appreciate fully the importance to strategic success of a fourth area, functional strategies, although the events of the late 1970s showed most business firms the need to pay greater attention to these strategies. For example, finance strategies have become critical in periods of high interest rates and tight money. Operations strategies are being given substantive attention in many industries, such as electronics and automobile manufacturing, in order to meet foreign competition, especially from the Japanese. Finally, human resource management (along with all of the management skills) have become vital to the reindustrialization efforts of U.S. and Canadian businesses.

Typical of master strategy statements based on the corporate and business strategy components is the following example.

In 1965, Heublein's stated strategic objectives were three in number:

1. To make Smirnoff the number one liquor brand in the world.
2. To continue a sales growth of 10 percent a year through internal growth, acquisition, or both.
3. To maintain a return on equity above 15 percent.

The essence of its strategic plans of action to accomplish these objectives involved the following elements:

1. Substantive advertising.
2. Certain types of distribution.
3. Careful selection of products and acquisitions with high cash flows (to allow substantive advertising).

Heublein, in these statements, quite succinctly captured what it wanted to be and how it was to accomplish these ends. Note that Heublein did not embellish its master strategy with any considerations not associated directly with its focal basic action or focal competitive activity.[11] There has, of course, been renewed interest in competitive strategies, as the works of Michael Porter (discussed in Chapter 2) and others in the field, have become more widely known.

In contrast to the Heublein example, IBM takes a broader approach to master strategy formulation. IBM's master strategy contains two principal components: mission, which includes elements of enterprise, corporate, business, and functional strategies; and strategic issues, which are managed separately and include the enter-

---

[10] "How Union Carbide Has Cleaned Up Its Image," *Business Week*, August 2, 1976, p. 46.

[11] G. A. Smith, Jr., C. Roland Christensen, and N. A. Berg, *Policy Formulation and Administration* (Homewood, Ill.: Irwin, 1968).

prise strategy. That is, the strategic issues strategy is concerned with environmental response strategies, while the mission strategy is concerned with operating the business.

Each year IBM reviews its master strategy as its SBUs and its support functions (for example, production facilities) establish objectives and plans for the year. This process occurs within the framework of corporate policies established for strategy formulation. Certain corporate strategy considerations, such as diversification and divestment (when necessary), are constraints to business and functional strategies. Strategic issues, as mentioned earlier, are managed separately.[12]

In summary, the master strategy is an umbrella beneath which specific strategies for coping with society, with the business choice decision, with competition, and with functional operations may be found.

We must plan for the future, because people who stay in the present will remain in the past. —Abraham Lincoln

All organizations have master strategies, whether or not they are consciously determined. Many business firms and other organizations can be quite successful in the short run without consciously formulating strategic objectives or plans to reach those objectives. Almost never, however, is any firm successful in the long run without first determining what it wants to be (mission, policies, and objectives) and how it plans to achieve that vision (strategy).

Levels of Strategy

As we saw in Chapter 1, organizations have four major components in their master strategies. The terms this book has used for the levels of strategy for businesses—enterprise, corporate, business, and functional—were first used by Dan Schendel and Charles Hofer.[13] (See also Table 3.5.) These levels can be described as follows:

Enterprise—the societal response strategy; how the organization relates to society.

Corporate—the mission determination strategy; criteria for defining the organization's fields of endeavor; and how it will fundamentally conduct itself.

Business—the primary mission strategy; how the organization will achieve its mission within a chosen field of endeavor.

Functional—the mission supportive strategy; how the organization will support its primary mission strategy.

---

[12] D. G. Thoroman, "Strategic Planning in IBM," *Long Range Planning*, January/February 1971, pp. 2–6.
[13] D. E. Schendel and C. W. Hofer, eds., *Strategic Management: A New View of Business Policy and Planning* (Boston: Little/Brown, 1979), pp. 11–14.

Table 3.5
The Master Strategy for Business

Enterprise Strategy (Societal Response)

Strategies to ensure that the firm acts properly as a corporate citizen.

Corporate Strategy (Mission Determination); (What many call "The Grand Strategy")

Strategies to determine what business or businesses the firm is in or should be in and how the business or businesses should be conducted.
1. Is there some business in which the organization has a natural strategic advantage or an innate interest?
2. Does the company want to compete or find a niche?
3. Does the company want or need to grow, stabilize, engage in investment reduction, or turn around company fortunes?

Basic action strategies available to single-SBU or multiple-SBU corporations (relate to questions 2 and 3 above):
  A. Competing or finding a niche
  B. Concentration or multiple products
  C. Growth
    1. Intensive, integrative, or diversified
    2. Regional, national, or international
    3. Internal, by acquisition, by merger, by joint venture
    4. Speed
  D. Stabilization
  E. Investment reduction
    1. Retrenchment
    2. Divestment (for multiple-SBU firms only)
    3. Selected asset reduction
    4. Cost cutting
    5. Liquidation
    6. Selling out
    7. Profit extraction
  F. Turnaround
  G. Combination

Business (SBU) Strategy (Primary Mission)

Competitive strategies.
Economic Functional Strategies
  A. Marketing
    1. Target market
    2. Product
    3. Promotion
    4. Distribution
    5. Price

Functional Strategy (Mission Supportive)

Strategies that support other strategies.
  A. Economic functional strategies
    1. Operations—production or service generation
    2. Finance
    3. Personnel/Human Resource Management
    4. Information systems
    5. R&D, market research
    6. Other significant areas

Table 3.5 continued

B. Management functional strategies
    1. Planning
    2. Organizing
    3. Implementing
    4. Controlling
    5. Staffing
    6. Leading
    7. Motivating
    8. Communicating
    9. Decision making
    10. Representing
    11. Integrating

C. Strategic issues strategies
    1. Known contingencies (energy)
    2. Surprises (competitor changes strategy; major economic changes; etc.)

The main difference between the way Schendel and Hofer use these terms and the way this text uses them is that, while they include marketing under functional strategies, this text includes it in business strategies.

Enterprise Strategy

Organizations need an enterprise strategy to cope with their largely uncontrollable external governmental and societal environment. This strategy does not deal with product/market concerns but rather with the broader issues of corporate citizenship. It integrates the organization with society.

    As Chapter 2 pointed out, the events of the 1960s and 1970s taught business leaders an important lesson—business is an open system. It has transactions not only with customers, suppliers, and unions but also with society, government, and members of pressure groups such as environmental groups and minority interest organizations. Contrary to popular opinion and widespread antibusiness sentiment, business does not act solely in accordance with its own self-interests in search of profit. It does consider the demands of other systems. It must consider them if it is to accomplish its mission in the long run. Business today faces many severe problems as a result of these demands, but it is learning to cope with them. Meeting these challenges is the function of the enterprise strategy.

Social power requires social response.   —Keith Davis and Robert L. Blomstrom

One of the major problems with which business has been confronted is the inability to define exactly what constitutes corporate social responsibility. Numerous pressure groups, such as the NAACP, the Sierra Club, the state and federal government, and Ralph Nader's Raiders, have made varying demands on the organization. Many times these demands are contradictory. The organization is caught in a dilemma: To whom does it respond? Clearly, it must respond to the law and to those who can bring the most pressure upon the organization or who have been able to define their demands most explicitly. But business cannot react to all of the demands with which it is confronted, nor should it.

Society's major demands have been fairly well-defined, at least legally. Business is legally required to protect the natural physical environment, provide equal employment opportunity, treat the consumer fairly, maintain satisfactory relations with government, and practice business in an ethical manner. In addition, energy conservation has become an important and major responsibility of business as well as the nation as a whole. Interestingly, many individuals are now concerned that business renew its efforts to produce goods and services at a profit, and more specifically to increase productivity and provide jobs. The demands seem to have come full circle.

Many corporate social policies are not as specific in content as they should be. While not all contingencies can be anticipated, social issues have usually given sufficient warning to allow for development of more than "do good" statements. However, many firms have been noticeably deficient in planning to meet external societal pressures. Appropriate corporate social strategies and policy should result from the same sort of rigorous analysis required of other anticipated corporate interactions affecting the accomplishment of organizational goals. Social pressures change, but so do other elements in the corporate environment. Change must be accepted and adapted to; otherwise, the costs to the firm will be high, in terms of both immediate measurable dollars and those nebulous factors such as image, morale, and productivity which eventually affect profits.

With proper planning and control, corporate social problems can be realistically and satisfactorily solved. Business's leaders must consider value orientations other than those economic values traditionally held. Responsiveness to societal demands and ethical considerations must be emphasized. Most importantly, business must remember that the consequence of social power is social responsibility.

Corporate Strategy

The corporate strategy focuses on the questions: "What business or businesses are we in or should we be in?" and "How shall we fundamentally conduct that business or those businesses?" The answer to the first question derives directly from mission, and is in fact often identical to it. The answer to this question is critical, because being in the wrong business is usually fatal. The railroads, for example, decided at the turn of the century to stay out of the automobile industry, and later to stay out of the air travel industry. They saw themselves as being in the railroad business, not the transportation business. Xerox, on the other hand, saw itself as being in the information business, not the photocopying business. Xerox moved into new business areas and has been able to prosper, despite intense competition in its primary line of business, photocopying.[14] (See Figure 3.4.)

The answer to the second question is also critical, because these basic actions position a firm in an industry or across industries. A poorly positioned firm has little

---

[14] Based on an address by Xerox Vice-President for Corporate Planning at the August 1979 Academy of Management Meetings, Atlanta.

Figure 3.4
Basic Action Strategies

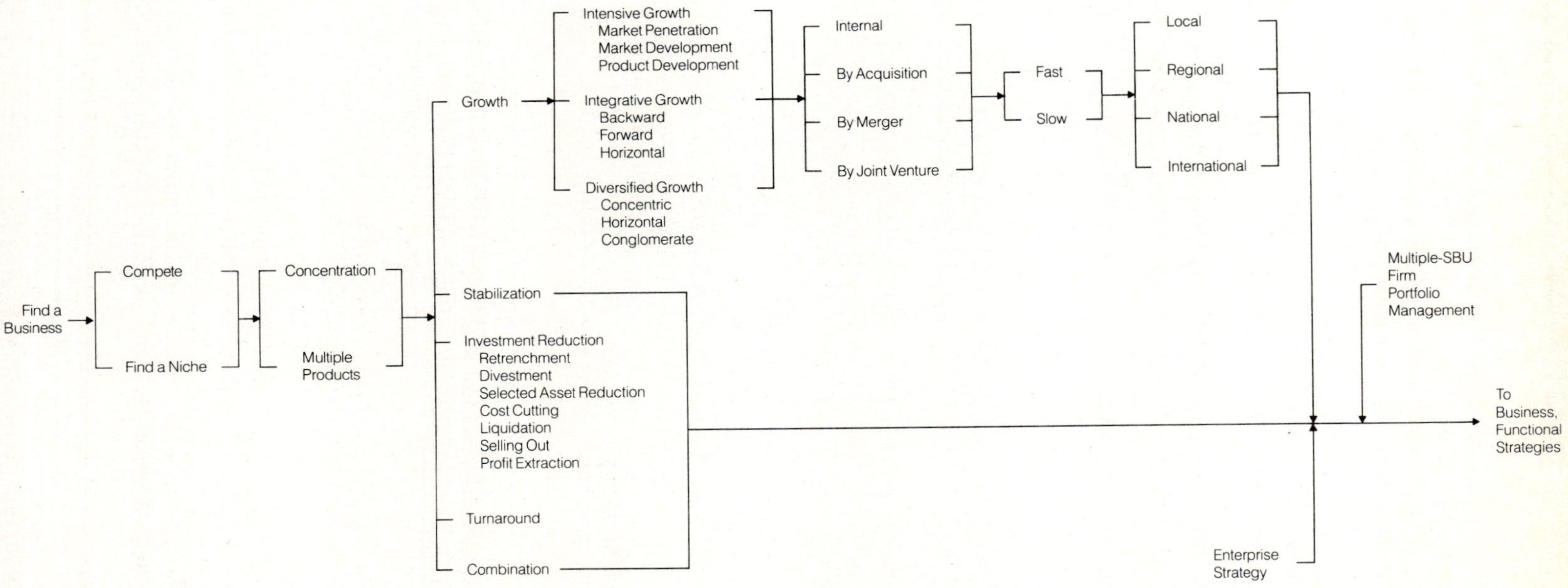

```
Find a
Business
   ↓
Compete ─────────────┐
                     │
Find a Niche ────────┤
                     │
         Concentration ──┐
              ↑          │
         Multiple        │
         Products ───────┤
                         │
                    Growth ──┬── Intensive Growth      ─┐
                             │     Market Penetration   │
                             │     Market Development   │
                             │     Product Development  │
                             ├── Integrative Growth     │
                             │     Backward             │──┬── Internal
                             │     Forward              │  ├── By Acquisition ──┬── Fast ──┬── Local
                             │     Horizontal           │  ├── By Merger        │          ├── Regional
                             ├── Diversified Growth     │  └── By Joint Venture └── Slow ──┼── National
                             │     Concentric           │                                  └── International
                             │     Horizontal           │
                             │     Conglomerate        ─┘
                    Stabilization
                    Investment Reduction
                      Retrenchment
                      Divestment
                      Selected Asset Reduction
                      Cost Cutting
                      Liquidation
                      Selling Out
                      Profit Extraction
                    Turnaround
                    Combination
                                                                  Multiple-SBU
                                                                  Firm Portfolio
                                                                  Management
                                                                        ↓
                                                          ──────────────→  To Business,
                                                                            Functional
                                                                            Strategies
                                             Enterprise
                                             Strategy
```

or no chance of long-term success. At one time, GE's SBU alignment included a computer division. GE's decision to compete head on with IBM was unsound, and it eventually sold this SBU. (Interestingly, GE is now considering reentering a portion of the computer market because it needs this capacity for its other products.)[15]

The answers to the two questions above in turn depend on the firm's answers to the three basic questions listed below. The first question concerns what business or businesses the firm will enter. The second and third concern how the firm will engage in its business or businesses—what its action strategies will be.

1. Is there some business in which the organization has a natural strategic advantage or an innate interest?
2. Does the company want to compete or find a niche?
3. Does the company want or need to grow, stabilize, engage in investment reduction, or turn around company fortunes?

How a firm's corporate strategy is affected specifically by its answers to these three questions varies with many factors. The following paragraphs provide some insights into these specifics.

Clearly, whether a firm has a single business or whether it is a multiple-SBU organization has a major bearing on the details of strategy. The single-SBU organization is primarily caught up in competition—the business strategy—and has much less concern with many of the available basic action strategies than do multiple-SBU firms. Many firms engage in only one business and have no intention to leave that field of enterprise. But, for many, there should be no such intention. Similarly, how the organization conducts its business often follows a set pattern; but for many, it should not.

1. Natural Strategic Advantage or Innate Interest

Many companies enter a field of endeavor because a perceived customer need exists that no one is satisfying. The founder of Federal Express, Frederick W. Smith, saw the need for overnight package deliveries between major cities. He believed that a fleet of small jet airplanes could do what no other mail service could. He was right. Other examples of natural strategic advantages include Wendy's movement into the high-priced hamburger field, the selling of various forms of technology to developing countries, and the gas mileage advantage that Japanese cars had over U.S.-manufactured autos during the 1970s.

Many businesses, on the other hand, are entered simply because the owner or top manager wanted to be in that business. Also, many small businesses are based on the founder's area of expertise. For example, many people start restaurants because they have always wanted to own a restaurant. Or someone may start a service station because he or she is a good mechanic. Finally, the top manager of a larger organization may move the firm into new businesses simply because he or she wanted to own a publishing house, or a foundry, or a restaurant chain, etc.

---

[15] "The Opposites: GE Grows While Westinghouse Shrinks," *Business Week*, January 31, 1977, pp. 60–66; "General Electric: The Financial Wizards Switch Back to Technology," *Business Week*, March 16, 1981, pp. 110–114.

"Don't laugh—he was doing that the day he figured out how to scoop up Trans-American Romex, Inc."

Source: Drawing by D. Reilly: © 1979 *The New Yorker Magazine*, Inc.

2. *Competition or Niche*

Organizations, whether single-SBU or multiple-SBU, must decide whether to compete directly with others or find a niche. Of course, all businesses always compete with other businesses in some way. The question is whether the firm chooses to compete head-on with other firms in the same business or seek a niche—a market which no other firm has chosen to enter. Most businesses compete head on with others; for example, Sears, J. C. Penney, and Montgomery Ward have historically competed directly with each other. On the other hand, Gibsons, a loosely federated group of discount stores franchised to several different ownership groups, seeks primarily to locate in small towns where there is no competition. It does not usually choose to compete head-on with Kmart or other discount stores.

Niches are not always secure; successful niche-finding strategies tend to provoke competition. After sales of the Excalibur specialty car (a replica of a 1933 Mercedes Phaeton, priced in 1981 at about $40,000) showed there was a market for high-quality, high-priced, unusual cars, a half-dozen or so competitors jumped into the same market, including one competitor whose car is priced at about $75,000. Occupying a niche can involve other disadvantages. Wendy's had the high-priced hamburger niche all to itself but found that its high prices made it vulnerable to chicken and seafood competitors.

Niche strategies are, however, a good way for the smaller firm—the firm with fewer financial resources—to make a good return on its investment. For example, one plastic extrusion firm which makes plastic trash bags and refrigerator containers distributes its products only in the southeastern United States and has primarily established a market based on its prices' being lower than those of national brands. (This form of niche strategy involves a geographic niche rather than a product-related one.) The firm considered going national but decided against it. As the production manager related, "If we went national, the big boys would notice us and could wipe us out if our market share got too big. Right now, they consider us to be a minor nuisance. But if we began to get too big, then they might consider us a threat and take action to eliminate us."

3. *Concentration or Multiple Products/Businesses*

Concentration is the focusing of the organization on one product, in essentially one market, using primarily one type of technology.[16] It is by far the most frequently encountered "grand strategy." Most businesses are concentrated in one field. "Kentucky Fried Chicken only does one thing," and therefore they "do it right." There are obvious reasons for choosing a concentration strategy. Most entrepreneurs begin this way because it is in their field of innate interest and/or expertise. There is less risk, at least in terms of resources, for starting up an enterprise. The competition can be more readily identified and more carefully analyzed. As the firm grows, the expertise required to manage properly is going to remain essentially the same. The competitive advantage comes from employing a highly developed focal marketing strategy. The contents of this strategy will vary, but would most frequently include product quality and/or price, sensitivity to the demands of the customer or client, and some element of recognition in the marketplace. Firms using a concentration strategy would, at the next level of choices in Figure 3.4, choose those strategies which would allow them to grow, but only through this one product or service. However, there are problems associated with this strategy as well.

Concentration exposes the organization to the vagaries of the marketplace, the economy, and to changes in technology. Furthermore, growth is going to reach its peak once the market is saturated. Investment opportunities are fewer. Long-term profit potentials decline as new entrants emerge in the industry. (Watch out KFC, here come: Bo Jangle's, Brown's, Popeyes, and a host of others.) Thus, firms may choose, in the next basic action choice stage, to pursue the types of growth that result in multiple products.

---

[16]J. A. Pearce II, "Selecting Among Alternative Grand Strategies," *California Management Review*, Spring 1982, pp. 23–31.

4. Growth, Stabilization, Investment Reduction, Turnaround, or Combination

Once the firm has decided whether to compete or find a niche and be concentrated in one product area or pursue multiple products—whether the answer applies to a particular SBU or to several—the next major issues are whether the firm wants to grow, stabilize, reduce investment, turn around company fortunes, or pursue a combination of these goals. At the corporate level for multiple-SBU firms, answering these questions is the crux of the corporate strategy. The techniques used are known as portfolio techniques and are explored further in Chapter 5. At the single-SBU level, these critical decisions depend on a multitude of SWOT factors.

Growth. Growth involves four primary considerations: type of growth—intensive, integrative, or diversified; where it will be geographically focused—at the regional, national, or international level; how it will take place—internally or through acquisition, merger, or joint venture; and how fast it will take place.

Types of Growth.[17] The choice of type of growth—intensive, integrative, or diversified—is critical. Intensive growth is appropriate for the firm which has not fully exploited the opportunities existing in its current products and markets. There are three types of intensive growth—market penetration, market development, and product development.

Market penetration consists of seeking increased sales for present products through a more aggressive marketing effort. Market penetration is characteristic of the mature industry with homogeneous products. When Phillip Morris acquired the Miller Brewing Company in 1970, Miller management immediately employed a market penetration strategy. It significantly expanded the advertising budget and changed advertising themes. The now-famous "Miller time" ads depicted Miller beer as the drink of he-men. The results have been almost unbelievably successful.

Market development involves taking existing products into new markets. When Disney created Disney World, it was, as many commentators noted, creating a Disneyland East; it was taking its product, Disneyland, to a new market, the East Coast. When the Miller Brewing Company successfully introduced the 7-ounce container into the market (others had tried but failed), it was taking its product to new markets—primarily to women who preferred a smaller container and were less likely to drink a lot of beer at one time than were men. The market development strategy is especially important to firms whose products, while sound, have not reached all markets.

Product development consists of developing improved products for current markets. When you see "new, improved" Cheer, you are witnessing this strategy in action. Product development is extremely important to maturing products because of the need to extend the product life cycle. The Datsun 240Z became the 260Z which became the 280Z which became the 280ZX which has become the 300 ZX, "awesome," "driven," and a "major motion." Why? Because of competition in a maturing industry, the high-performance sports car industry.

---

[17] Philip Kotler, *Marketing Management* (Englewood Cliffs, N.J.: Prentice-Hall, 1980), pp. 48–53.

The second type of growth, integrative growth, can move in three directions—backward, forward, and horizontally. In backward integration, the organization attempts to acquire control over its suppliers. Sears has historically followed a pattern of acquiring its suppliers—for example, J. C. Higgins. This acquisition strategy is typically followed for the purpose of reducing costs and making the firm's sales and distribution functions more cost competitive, or more responsive to the needs of the acquiring company. This strategy is particularly important to the firm in a mature industry in which price becomes a major strategic weapon.

In forward integration, the firm attempts to acquire control of its distributors. When Royal Crown purchased Arby's in 1976 (a conglomerate diversification effort), one of its first acts was to arrange for long-term markets for Royal Crown Cola through its wholly owned Arby's locations, thus assuring the company of increased distribution for its products. When Xerox established its consumer retail stores in 1980, it too was seeking to assure control of distribution for its current and future products. Interestingly, the major oil companies began a program of divesting their forward integration instruments—service stations—in the late 1970s, apparently because of the low profit margins involved in distribution of their products.

When a firm attempts to acquire its competition, it is practicing horizontal integrative growth. Lone Star Industries has acquired much of its competition, and many experts predict that by 1985 it will dominate a commodity which will most assuredly be in short supply—concrete.[18]

The final major type of growth is diversified growth. Diversification becomes an important alternative when an organization has "all of its eggs in one basket" and has the internally generated expertise and the extra cash flow with which it can expand into other areas. Diversification can be used to smooth out corporate revenues; this strategy is desirable for highly seasonal businesses—for example, areas that specialize in providing recreational snow skiing, such as Vail, Colorado. Diversification is also advisable where current businesses or products are in mature or decline stages of the product life cycle and revenues will ultimately be threatened. Diversification may also be desirable when external opportunities are significant. Information Capsule 3.2 indicates just how important diversification can be.

There are three types of diversification—concentric, horizontal, and conglomerate. With concentric diversification, the business seeks to add new products that are technologically related to current products. These products will normally be marketed to new customers. When Texas Instruments added personal computers to its product lines, it was practicing concentric diversification. When Levi Strauss added women's clothing to its men's line, it, too, was practicing concentric diversification.

Horizontal diversification also involves adding new products to the firm's product line, but these products are not technologically related to existing ones and are aimed at current customers. Over the years, AMF has added pleasure boats, bicycles, snow skis, and other athletic equipment to its original offerings in order to provide new products for its current customers.

Conglomerate diversification involves both new products or businesses and new customers. The firm usually enters into conglomerate diversification to offset some

---

[18] D. D. Holt, "Lone Star Industries: Flying High on Cement Wings," *Fortune*, July 28, 1980, pp. 46–48.

Information Capsule 3.2
Expanding the World of Coca-Cola

In 1960, all of the Coca-Cola Company's revenues resulted from sales of soft drink syrups—principally Coca-Cola—to bottlers. Shortly thereafter, Coca-Cola made its first diversification effort, acquisition of the Minute Maid Corporation. In 1964, the company merged with Duncan Foods Company and thus became a major force in the coffee importing, processing, and distribution industry. In 1970, it purchased Aqua-Chem, Incorporated, a water purification firm. Additional acquisitions included several Coca-Cola bottling plants.

But in the mid-1970s, about 90 percent of the company's profits still came from sales of soft drinks, nationally and internationally. As a consequence, the company began to seek additional diversification. The primary reason was that it saw its market shrinking nationally in absolute terms. Furthermore, it foresaw increased competition from Pepsi-Cola and others and thus saw that its market might shrink in relative terms as well. The absolute market was shrinking because of demographics. Soft drinks had historically been consumed mostly by people aged 13 to 24. This segment of the population was predicted to have 4 million fewer persons in 1985 than in 1975. Thus, the soft drink market was expected to lose some 3.3 billion cans a year in sales. Given this fact and the anticipated increased competition from Pepsi, Dr. Pepper, 7-Up, and others, Coca-Cola felt it had to take action to diversify.

It was this concern that resulted in acquiring Taylor Wine Company in January 1977, and Sterling Vineyards (in California) and Gonzales & Co., which operated Monterey Vinyards (in California), later in 1977. The company then pursued a strategy of using the Taylor name combined with the California production capacity to move boldly and with substantial advertising into the wine market, becoming an important force in the industry by 1980. (Coca-Cola's marketing blitzes have in fact changed the way the staid old wine industry functions, much as Phillip Morris's acquisition of Miller Beer and its later product/marketing strategies did to the beer industry in the early 1970s.) (Taylor was divested in 1983 due to sagging profits in the wine industry.)

But the wine acquisition and subsequent other acquisitions—for example, those of the Atlanta Coca-Cola Bottling Company and of a plastics company—still did not alter the company's basic dependence on soft drinks, which in 1980 still accounted for 71 percent of sales and 83 percent of profits. In 1980, profits turned flat as the "Pepsi challenge" (a taste test comparison which Pepsi won) was heavily advertised, forcing the company to reexamine its situation. Something else was apparently needed. It was with much fanfare that Coca-Cola announced the acquisition of Columbia Pictures in 1981. Apparently, Coca-Cola had decided it was time to get serious about diversification.

deficiency, but it may also pursue this strategy to take advantage of a significant opportunity. Technically, of course, once a firm enters into more than one business, it ceases to be a single-business firm. Organizations such as InterNorth, GE, EXXON, and Esmark are conglomerate companies.

Where to Grow. Most firms start in a particular geographic region, move to a national sales effort, and eventually attempt to repeat domestic successes in foreign countries. Geographic growth is of course highly desirable, because it increases total market size. Of course, not all firms can be national. King's, a regional restaurant chain prominent in the northeastern United States, has stated that it does not believe it should go national and attempt to compete with other major chains. It intends not to grow, at least not geographically. But for most firms, geographic growth and success go hand in hand. What is imperative is that such growth not come too quickly. International growth, in particular, involves many difficulties. It is not simply an extension of domestic efforts, but requires an understanding of numerous complex cultural, logistical, social, economic, and political differences.

How to Grow. The organization can grow in four ways—internally, by acquisition, by merger, or by joint venture. Internal growth offers many advantages; one of the most important of them is continuity of management style. Internal growth also has its limitations. It takes much longer to become larger and more diverse through internal growth than through the three external forms of growth. Nonetheless, many firms have grown to substantial size primarily through internal growth—the Coca-Cola Company, Radio Shack (Tandy), Schlitz Brewing Company, and Trans World Airlines, for example. On the other hand, firms such as PepsiCo, Allegheny Ludlam, TransAmerica, and First Northern Bank have grown externally, primarily through acquisition. Recently, as you will learn in Information Capsule 3.2, Coca-Cola has become more acquisition-oriented in an effort to become less dependent upon one major industry, the soft drink industry.

Typically, businesses begin as single-SBU firms, commonly with one product. As they grow, normally internally, and if they are successful, they begin to look for growth into new markets; new products; or areas of supply, distribution, or competition. It is at this point that growth often ceases to be internal and comes primarily through external sources.

Both acquisition and merger involve combining organizations; they differ mainly in the nature of the remaining organization. In acquisition, one firm retains its identity as the dominant firm, while the other becomes subordinate in authority to that dominant firm. When Heublein acquired Kentucky Fried Chicken, top management at KFC began to report to Heublein top management. Typically, acquisitions occur for the purpose of diversification. In mergers, a new organizational entity emerges. When Nabisco and Standard Brands merged, a new entity, Nabisco Brands, resulted. A new management structure was formed, with members of top management of both organizations taking various positions in the new management hierarchy.

Joint ventures are temporary partnerships formed for one specific purpose. For example, Blount Brothers Construction Company joined with the French construction firm Bouygues to land one of the biggest single construction projects in history—the University of Riyadh's new campus in Saudi Arabia. In all likelihood, neither firm could have obtained the contract alone, much less have completed the project. Entering the joint venture allowed both firms to overcome these problems.[19] Historically, firms outside the United States and Canada have utilized the joint venture much more than firms from these two countries; but in recent years, U.S. and Canadian firms have made increasing use of this mechanism.

Speed of Growth. One of the greatest mistakes a firm can make is to grow beyond its capacities. Such a mistake was one of the major causes of the downfall of the W. T. Grant Company. It takes time to develop the managers and management systems necessary to cope with the problems of increasing size. W. T. Grant simply did not foster this development. Different problems are encountered at various stages of growth and with various types of growth. Organizations must manage their way through these problems before further growth is advisable.

Stabilization. Some organizations are satisfied not to grow (or to grow very little). The president of a large bank which had a 46-percent market share in a major, highly competitive metropolitan area told the author he would be quite happy just to maintain that market share. (That's understandable.) Many owners of smaller businesses, such as restaurants, insurance agencies, small manufacturers, and so forth, are satisfied to make only a certain amount of profit and do not wish to grow beyond a certain size.

While stabilization provides an opportunity to "catch one's breath" between growth periods or during turnaround periods, as a long-term strategy, it leaves the organization open to competition.

Investment Reduction. Firms may choose to follow a program of investment reduction, which simply means reducing the amount of capital investment in the organization or a specific SBU. This move may be necessitated by financial difficulties or, as in the case of profit extraction, may be an intentional program of removing assets from a successful business to create cash flow for other parts of the business or for distribution to owners. Several types of investment reduction exist.

Retrenchment is a major, across-the-board effort to reduce cash outflows in order to reduce the scope and size of the business, to lessen the exposure of the firm to risk, to concentrate on what the company does well in order to become more profitable, or simply to survive. It is generally viewed as a temporary measure.

At the corporate level in multiple-SBU firms, divestment—selling or liquidating individual SBUs—is the primary means of retrenchment. Often firms have acquired businesses which do not continue to provide sufficient ROI. When products fail to meet the goals which the organization has established to help it accomplish its mission, then these products should be eliminated, perhaps sold to others. Again, this process is known as divesting. Occasionally, losses must be taken; but long-term losses that might result from failure to divest must be estimated and balanced against short-term losses from divestment. Equity Funding, after its disastrous

[19] "Blount: Building More Than Buildings to Broaden Its Base." *Business Week*, April 23, 1979, pp. 108–110.

bankruptcy in the early 1970s, eventually became Orion Capital, with only two of the six original major SBUs remaining.[20] The company survived and even became profitable largely by eliminating unprofitable SBUs.

At the single-SBU level, selected asset reduction is the type of investment reduction which occurs most often. For example, a firm might decide not to build a new plant, thus limiting the number of markets it can serve. The decision not to give raises is a common form of asset reduction. Cost cutting is also often emphasized; for example, a manufacturer might cut costs by moving corporate headquarters from its plush rental facility back into the plant. This move might allow more markets to be served.

The next two options, liquidation and selling out, represent the ultimate in investment reduction, since the amount of investment is reduced to zero. At the single-SBU level, these options signify the ultimate disaster; but for the multiple-SBU firm, the cash received from these processes can be used to purchase other, more desirable SBUs.

Profit extraction is a strategy commonly followed by multiple-SBU firms for business subunits which are in profitable, usually mature industries in which growth is not possible or is not desirable for some reason. By reducing investment and extracting profits, the firm can utilize cash flows for the benefit of other SBUs. Typically, the SBU from which profits are heavily extracted will be sold to another organization. It is also common for an entrepreneur to follow the profit extraction strategy prior to selling the firm to an acquiring organization.

Turnaround. Turnaround strategies refer to efforts to turn around company fortunes when the firm has encountered a period of poor sales, poor revenues, or losses. A turnaround strategy usually involves some type of investment reduction, an attempt to stabilize, and then a growth strategy of some type. Schendel and Patton have studied various strategies organizations follow when they need to turn around corporate fortunes. They found that firms that turned around company performance had sound investments and stressed expansion in order to generate rapid sales growth. It appears that successful turnaround may be a function of several variables; but it is difficult to tell exactly why some organizations succeed and others do not, even when the same strategies are used. For example, Schendel and Patton noted that one matched pair in their sample study, the Melvill Shoe Corporation and SCOA Industries, Inc., had almost identical turnaround strategies. Yet SCOA suffered continuous decline in fortunes from the 1950s through 1970, while Melvill was much more successful. Exactly why this occurred is uncertain, although SCOA's implementation appeared to be faulty.[21]

Combination. Firms, either at the SBU level or at the corporate level, normally employ a combination of the basic actions described above as they pursue their missions. Not all the strategies are mutually exclusive. If you will examine Figure 3.4, you will see that several can occur simultaneously.

---

[20] "Orion Capital: A Shady Ancestry Shapes an Insurer's Future," *Business Week*, July 1, 1980, pp. 102–106; "Orion Capital: Born Again," *Financial World*, July 1, 1979, pp. 26, 27.
[21] D. Schendel and A. C. Patton, "Strategic Responses to Technological Threats," *Business Horizons*, February 1976, pp. 61–69.

Business Strategy

Once the organization has determined its strategy for coping with its environment—its enterprise strategy—and once the organization has determined what business it wants to be in and how it will conduct each business—its corporate strategy—then it must determine how it will compete within each business—its business strategy. This strategy, in both profit-seeking and not-for-profit organizations, can be termed the primary mission strategy. In business, we could also entitle it the mission competitive strategy, because a single business' major concern is to develop a strategic advantage which allows the firm to beat the competition in the marketplace. This strategy is discussed in considerable detail in Chapter 4.

Functional Strategy

Organizations perform certain functions critical to the successful accomplishment of all other strategies. They are designated *functional strategies*. There are two major types of functional strategies. The economic functional strategies include those concerned with marketing, operations, finance, personnel, information, research and development, and others. The management functional strategies include those related to planning, organizing, implementing, controlling, staffing, leading, motivating, communicating, and decision making. In addition, functional strategies include a third, but important type, the strategic issues strategies. With the exception of marketing, which is here considered part of the primary mission strategy, these functional strategies are labeled as mission supportive strategies. Functional strategies support enterprise, corporate, business, and other functional strategies. These strategies, too, are discussed in more detail in Chapter 4.

The Grand Strategy

A number of authorities in strategic management have employed the term "grand strategy." Although subtle differences exist in the various definitions, they are usually similarly operationalized by their authors in terms of the basic action strategies enumerated in this chapter. In a representative definition, John A. Pearce II, describes the grand strategy as, "the comprehensive, general plan of major actions by which a firm intends to achieve its long-term objectives within its dynamic environment." Pearce suggests that 12 such major strategies exist: concentric diversification, conglomerate diversification, product development, market development, concentration on current activities, joint ventures, horizontal integration, vertical integration, innovation, retrenchment, liquidation, and divestiture.[22] What Pearce is suggesting here is that these appear to be the 12 most commonly utilized basic ac-

---

[22] J. A. Pearce II, "Selecting Among Alternative Grand Strategies," *California Management Review*, Spring 1982, pp. 23–31.

tion strategies, but more than that, that these strategies drive the remainder of the firm's master strategy (my words, not his). Others, such as Charles Hofer and Dan Schendel have identified "generic (basic action) strategies" which they suggest should be used in various stages of the product life cycle depending on the firm's relative competitive position. Their six strategies, share-increasing, growth, profit, market concentration or asset reduction, turnaround, or liquidation or divestment,[23] are discussed in more detail in Chapter 5.

As the definition of grand strategy in Chapter 1 indicates, it is my personal belief that grand strategies include more than basic action strategies. They may include marketing or other economic functional strategies; for the large conglomerate, they may include portfolio strategies. The primary issue is what constitutes that driving force of the organization—that characteristic to which all else must adhere? For example, Porter has developed three generic strategies: cost leadership, differentiation, and focus (discussed in more detail in Chapter 4). These strategies are marketing strategies.[24] At the business level, what normally drives the organization is the marketing strategy.

Given this more inclusive perspective, the above referenced strategies are but a few grand strategies currently under study in the field of strategic management. The next chapter examines a number of these as identified in various studies of firms and industries in specific types of situations. It is apparent that grand strategies exist and that they drive the supportive efforts of the organization. For example, Beatrice Foods has chosen the path of conglomerate diversification. That single grand strategy drives all else that it does as a company (not necessarily, however, what its individual strategic business units do). As many as 20 acquisitions and/or divestments have occurred in a single year as the firm attempts to improve its profits by improving its portfolio. Similarly, Disney has followed an internal growth through product and market development grand strategy, accompanied by an emphasis on quality of service or product. These focus points have driven the Disney philosophy and corporate culture since its inception.

This observation is not limited to anecdotal evidence. Michael A. Hitt, R. Duane Ireland, and K. A. Palia, in examining relationships in 93 industrial firms, found that depending on the type of (basic action) grand strategy employed by the firm, various of 7 different economic functional areas (marketing, finance, etc.) are more critical, more focused on than are others.[25]

Because of the large number of such strategies and their combinations, the limited research evidence to support various contentions, and the infancy of the research, it would seem best at this point simply to recognize their existence and the way in which they affect the remainder of the organization. In addition, individual industry-based, research-supported grand strategies, such as those discussed in the next chapter, might also be viable considerations in formulating strategies in similar situations. Beyond that, one must be quite careful in placing too much faith in unvarified recommendations. One must always choose among the basic action strategies and/or marketing strategies, making one the most central thrust of the

---

[23]C. W. Hofer and D. Schendel, *Strategy Formulation: Analytical Concepts*, (St. Paul, Minn.: West, 1978), pp. 104, 162–177.
[24]M. E. Porter, *Competitive Strategy*, (New York: Free Press, 1980), Chapters 1 and 2.
[25]M. A. Hitt, R. D. Ireland, and K. A. Palia, "Industrial Firms' Grand Strategy and Functional Importance: Moderating Effects of Technology and Uncertainty," *Academy of Management Journal*, vol. 25, no. 2, 1982, pp. 265–298.

master strategy, but exactly which one is most appropriate to choose is as yet an unknown in most circumstances.

Preemptive Strategies

Ian MacMillan has proposed that preemptive strategies are appropriate mechanisms for firms wishing to secure advantages over competitors. A preemptive action is defined as "a major move by a focal business ahead of moves by its adversaries, which allows it to secure an advantageous position from which it is difficult to dislodge because of the advantages it has captured by being the first mover." He offers a common example of such a move in the firm that expands capacity far ahead of industry demand, anticipating the gaining of market share through discouraging competitors from expanding.[26] Preemptive moves are based on the strategists' assumptions about the marketplace. If these assumptions are inaccurate, then the preemptive moves may leave strategists vulnerable. MacMillan provides the characteristics of an ideal preemptive move:[27]

- "It should be possible to rapidly occupy 'prime' positions, at any advantageous point, along the entire industry chain.
- "Once the move is made, it should be difficult for most of the adversaries to follow into these positions.
- "Conditions should exist that slow down the response rate of any competitors who can respond.
- "It should be relatively easy for the preempting business to reverse its move, if it so desires."

He feels that there are two basic classes of preemptive opportunities which a firm should seek:[28]

- Those opportunities that exploit rival weaknesses or its lack of commitment.
- Those opportunities that exploit rival strengths or its strong commitments.

In terms of exploiting a rival's weaknesses, MacMillan suggests the following:[29]

- Reshape the industry infrastructure—that which is necessary to ensure a smooth flow from raw materials to finished goods.
- Occupy prime positions—geographically, key accounts, distributors, service organizations, suppliers, government contracts.
- Secure critical skills—secure these across all functions.
- Preempt a psychological position—develop an appeal to the customer that is hard for competitors to overcome.

---

[26] I. C. MacMillan, "Preemptive Strategies," *Journal of Business Strategy*, Fall 1983, p. 16.
[27] Ibid., p. 18.
[28] Ibid., pp. 18–19.
[29] Ibid., p. 19.

In terms of exploiting a rival's strengths, MacMillan suggests the following:

- Cannibalize competitive advantages—make moves that force the opponent to have to cannibalize current advantages in order to respond. An opponent is not likely to do this.
- Damage the opponent's image, company tradition, or strategy.
- Threaten a major investment—for example in the competitor's production capacity, distribution system, or supply system.
- Force competitors to antagonize powerful third parties—by choosing preemptive moves which necessitate the competitor's upsetting powerful third parties, it is likely that the competitor will offer no response.

MacMillan suggests that major opportunities for preemptive strategies exist in the areas presented in Exhibit 3.1.

EXHIBIT 3.1
Sources of Preemptive Opportunities

Supply Systems
1. Secure access to raw materials or components
2. Preempt production equipment
3. Dominate supply logistics

Product
1. Introduce new product lines
2. Develop dominant design
3. Position
4. Secure accelerated approval from agencies
5. Secure product development and delivery skills
6. Expand scope of the product

Production Systems
1. Proprietary processes
2. Aggressive capacity expansion
3. Vertical integration with key suppliers
4. Secure scarce and critical production skills

Customers
1. Segmentation
2. Build early brand awareness
3. Train customers in usage skills
4. Capture key accounts

Distribution and Service Systems
1. Occupation of prime locations
2. Preferential access to key distributors
3. Dominance of distribution logistics
4. Access to superior service capabilities
5. Development of distributor skills

Source: I. C. MacMillan, "Preemptive Strategies," reprinted by permission from the Journal of Business Strategy, Fall 1983, Copyright © 1983, Warren, Gorham & Lamont Inc., 210 South Street, Boston, Mass., p. 20. All Rights Reserved.

MacMillan's preemptive strategy approach seems sound intuitively. There is, in fact, evidence from a host of research to suggest that such actions generally (not necessarily those he specifically suggests) are quite sound. One must always keep in mind the situation, and be cognizant of the SWOTs involved.

Some Important Characteristics of Plans

It is relevant to note that all plans should have certain characteristics and that the contents of strategy should reflect them. A few of these characteristics are listed below.

Flexibility. In today's volatile environment, organizations must remain flexible in their planning processes so that as changes arise, the organizations will be able to adapt. Some organizations have developed numerous contingency plans and multiple strategies for the purpose of coping with the changing requirements of the environment. Having already developed alternative strategies, the firm can implement the proper one immediately upon occurrence of various events.

Contents. Any plan should include, to the appropriate degree, specification of

Who will be involved—organization levels and individuals.
What will be required—resources.
Where action will occur—geographically and by organization level.
When action will occur—time horizon, implementation date.
Why action will occur—the objective.
How the objective will be accomplished—what actions are necessary (which is indicated somewhat by who, what, and where, the means of implementation).
Control—some provision for evaluation.

Consistency. Plans developed within a strategy should be consistent with one another, and strategies should be consistent within an organization. The objectives of the master strategy must be included in the development of intermediate and operational plans. These plans must also be consistent with organizational structure. Such considerations are especially important to the functional area division plans. These objectives often suboptimize the total strategy because functional area or product division needs are included without the proper analysis of their impact on overall organizational objective accomplishment.

Timeliness. To be effective, a plan must be timely. Had the Edsel been introduced just two years sooner or later, it might have succeeded. Although some believed it unattractive, its main failing was that it was a big car introduced when the consumer was looking for a small car.

Risk. Risk is the probability of return. To have a high probability of success, the strategy must have the proper level of risk. Max Richards has shown that risk is, in fact, the key factor in strategic failure.[30] Risk is extremely difficult to calculate and involves highly subjective probability estimation, usually under conditions of uncertainty. Obviously, it is an extremely complex issue.

Acceptance by Society and Government. Business's social responsibility is so important that every plan must be specifically concerned with societal impact analysis. If society and government do not accept an organization's actions as appropriate, profit may suffer. In addition, sanctions may be levied against the firm so that it will eventually be forced to change.

Impacts of Multinational Operations on Strategic Objectives and Master Strategy Formulation

Objectives and strategies result from the strategists' considerations of mission, strategic policy, and information. It follows that, since each of these factors is usually changed to some degree as the result of operating in a country other than the organization's parent country, strategic objectives and the master strategy will also be different. They usually are.

All organizations depend on some strategic advantage for their existence. Multinationals are no different. Typically, multinationals rely on some form of resource superiority. As noted in the previous chapter, these resource advantages usually include superior capital, technology, or management expertise. Sheer size, in terms of ability to provide markets for certain products or raw materials, may also be a strategic advantage in and of itself. The multinational business must convert one or more of these advantages into strengths to help it overcome weaknesses, such as an absence of host country management talent; take advantage of opportunities, such as a developing economy; and overcome threats, such as international competition. So far, so good. But the rules by which the game is played are often different in the international arena; and hence, objectives and strategies must be altered.

In further examining some of the constraints which face multinationals, Hal Mason reported that host countries often place restrictions on the following:

Ownership—typically, the host country or a firm from the host country must own a major or controlling interest.

Employment—almost always, host countries demand that certain positions in management and technological areas be held by host country nationals.

Profits and fees—typically, profits and fees are set at some maximum level.

Internal debt capital—often, internal debt capital is set according to a preestablished formula.

Training and development—insistence on training and development for host country nationals is common.

Host country markets—most host countries demand development of their exports.

---

[30]M. Richards, "Risk and Strategic Failure," *Proceedings: Academy of Management*, August 1974, pp. 40–46.

Technological bases—most host countries seek technologically based industry rather than extractive industry.[31]

As you can imagine, the impacts on objective setting may be significant. Reexamining the objectives noted in Figure 3.3, we find, for example, that growth may be legislatively limited; efficiency may be governmentally held to a lower level than desirable because of extra costs such as those for extensive training and development; utilization of resources is often set at certain levels; contribution to owners (profits) is almost always set at certain levels, as is the ownership itself; contribution to customers may be modified to meet government-set levels; contribution to employees focuses on technical training and often on guaranteed employment as opposed to true development; and finally, contribution to society is stressed through the government involvement outlined above but does not take the forms, such as emphasis on pollution control, that dominate this concern in the United States and Canada.

Similarly, if we review some of the major basic action strategies, we find, for example, that in Japan, diversification occurs earlier in the firm's history than in the United States, while in Europe, it tends to occur later.[32] In Japan, the supportive strategy of quality in production probably is emphasized more than in any other country. Firms in much of the rest of the world, including the United States, lag behind in this regard. The Japanese have also emphasized management philosophies different from those used in much of the rest of the world. These management styles are very work group/team oriented. And the Japanese have emphasized market share as opposed to profit strategies. On the other hand, firms from the United States have historically emphasized production and research technologies and new products. Foreign-country marketing of such products as Coca-Cola, McDonald's restaurants, and Kentucky Fried Chicken have, however, usually followed standard approaches found in the United States. Finally, in virtually all the countries of the world, negotiations with governments are becoming increasingly more critical than they have been historically in the United States and Canada.

From these few examples, you can see that both objectives and strategies will vary. Most of these differences are the result of cultural/historical factors, including negative experiences with colonialistic MNCs. Regardless of the cause, the multinational strategic manager must be alert to the necessity for changing strategic standard operating procedures.

Impacts of The Not-for-Profit Situation on Strategic Objectives and Master Strategy Formulation

If you examine the objectives in Figure 3.3, you will find that most of these are quite applicable to nonprofits. There is more orientation towards budgets than sales and profits. There are problems posed with identifying units of service, that is, spe-

---

[31] R. H. Mason, "Conflicts between Host Countries and the Multinational Enterprise," *California Management Review*, Fall 1974, pp. 5–14.

[32] Y. Suzuki, "The Strategy and Structure of Top 100 Japanese Industrial Enterprises, 1950–1970," *Strategic Management Journal*, July/September 1980, p. 285.

cific objectives. And, one would have to substitute contribution to resource providers in place of contribution to owners. But beyond that, the objectives could, not necessarily would, be similar. The priorities will probably vary however. One would anticipate less emphasis on objectives concerned with resource contributors (as opposed to this very necessary concern in a corporation or other business). There will probably be more stress on contributions to customers (users), employees, and society. And, historically, there has been less of a concern for efficiency and proper utilization of resources (in budgetary terms) in nonprofits than in for-profits. Most nonprofits are labor intensive, but labor seems to be taken for granted rather than as the subject of efficiency analysis. And, since nonprofits are often managed by politically motivated individuals, the opportunities for mismanagement of employees, especially in terms of inefficient empire building (growth objectives), are substantial. In addition, because of the tendency to manage by budgets, there has been a widely observed waste of resources in government, for example, in the military and in numerous state and federal civilian agencies. The point here is that, historically, it is likely that efficiency objectives were not established or perhaps were not stressed.

One group of authors even questions whether objective based management systems such as MBO (Management By Objectives), ZBB (Zero Based Budgeting), or PBB (Program Planning and Budgeting) will work in the federal government. They feel that such systems require a tolerance for uncertainty that government officials simply do not have and cannot afford to project.[33] On the other hand, government seems to have responded to societal demands for better planning, and if anything, such systems reduce uncertainty. It would seem to me to be better to force changes in administrator's behavior than to accept an abdication of responsibility for strategic management.

With respect to the strategies identified in Table 3.5, it is apparent that nonprofits employ very similar strategies. Nonprofits have societal response strategies, mission determination strategies, mission competitive strategies, and mission supportive strategies. Because not-for-profit missions are going to be more service, mutual benefit, and commonweal in nature (see Chapter 1) than in a business, their mission competitive strategies are going to reflect nonprofit-type concerns for gaining not only clients and customers, but also resource contributions—tax dollars, donations, or member assessments. Looking more specifically at government, intentional growth strategies are going to be fewer (except as an individual manager would want growth for power reasons). Similarly, acquisition, divestiture, and turnaround have comparatively little meaning, but market and product/service development strategies are likely. Support strategies have not always been as likely to focus on quality or efficiency of labor utilization as they might in business, although that seems to be changing. Labor is somewhat of a given, determined in the bureaucracy somewhere outside the manager's control, and this is another reason that labor efficiency is probably not stressed more. Motivation and leadership strategies are going to differ somewhat, because organizational members are not as likely to be money motivated as their for-profit counterparts.

---

[33] M. W. Dirsmith, S. F. Jablowsky, A. D. Luzi, "Planning and Control in the U.S. Federal Government: A Critical Analysis of PPB, MBO, and ZBB," *Strategic Management Journal*, 1980, pp. 303–329.

Figure 3.5
Hospital Feeder System, 1980

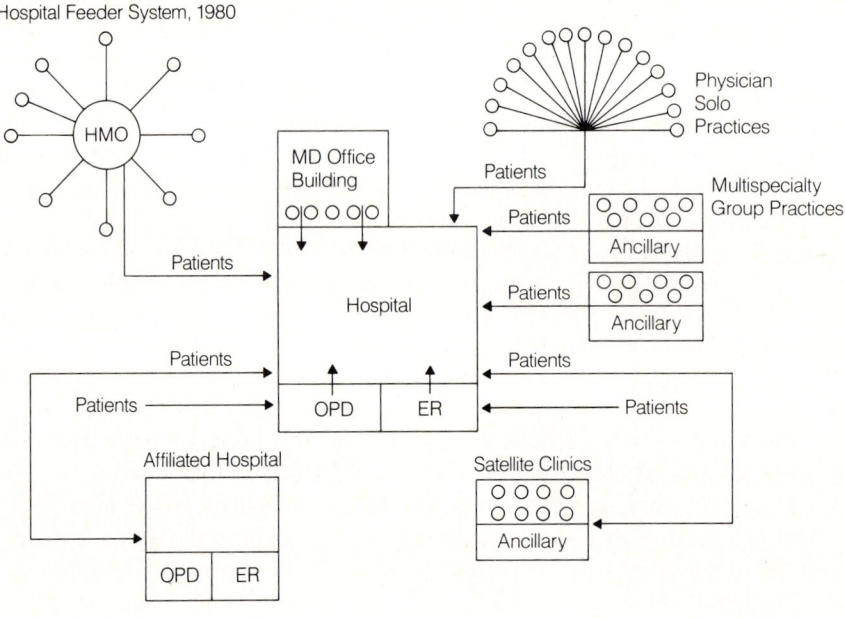

Source: Jeff Charles Goldsmith, *Can Hospitals Survive?*; Homewood: Dow Jones, 1981, p. 143. Reprinted by permission of Jeff Charles Goldsmith.

In other nonprofits, exclusive of hospitals, one would probably find an absence of intentionally formulated strategies. Rather, most strategies would simply be made on the spur of the moment, as needed, with the probable exception of the financing strategy. This will be especially true in the many smaller nonprofit organizations. If you will recall, survival is a major objective, so sophisticated strategies seem out of place in that type of environment. The hospital industry, on the other hand, has made rapid advances in recent years in terms of strategy formulation. Acquisition, divestment, conglomerate growth, and other strategies common to for-profit organizations are common in that industry as well. Figure 3.5 details some of the ways in which hospitals might in fact tailor basic action growth strategies to their particular situation. Terms such as vertical and horizontal diversification take on whole new meanings when "captured" doctors in HMO's, MD office buildings, satellite clinics, and so forth are added to more typical patient sources such as physician solo practices. Affiliated hospitals while providing horizontal diversification also provide referral patients and thus serve vertical diversification purposes as well. Service objectives are frequently quantified in hospitals and thus strategies are typically more well defined. Marketing strategies are also more sophisticated than in any of the other nonprofits, exclusive of government and a few large charities such as United Way. The motivation and leadership strategies in hospitals must focus on the higher need levels that employees possess, but also must satisfy their basic needs.

A good example of strategy formation in nonprofits is found in the Equal Employment Opportunity Commission (EEOC). The EEOC has as its mission the enforcement of Title VII of the Civil Rights Act of 1964, as amended. To that end, the EEOC developed a grand strategy to solve the problem of discrimination in employment. As a major objective, it sought to ensure that as many jobs as possible were opened to equal employment opportunity. Pressure, conciliation agreements, and legal suits were used against the largest, most visible employers, such as American Telephone and Telegraph, the entire steel industry, General Motors, and numerous others.[34] The EEOC's strategy recognized that, given its limited manpower, it might use the visual evidence of its enforcement efforts to scare other employers into compliance. This strategy emphasizes the accomplishment of the EEOC's primary mission and strategic objectives; it does not consider other aspects of the organization's environment.

The above commentary is limited both by space and by the fact that very little research or even observational analyses exist with respect to nonprofits, but by now, you probably have the gist of the major differences. The key is that when analyzing any organization's strategies, their SWOT, or their objectives, you must make certain that you recognize the difference in environments and in internal organizational profiles.

Summary

The major strategic objectives which exist in virtually all business organizations include: growth, efficiency, utilization of resources, contribution to owners, contribution to customers, contribution to employees, and contribution to society. Objectives serve not only to direct but also to integrate the organization. MBORR as a management system and philosophy has been shown to be highly related to organizational success.

The master strategy has four major components: a societal response strategy, a mission determination strategy, a primary mission strategy, and a supportive strategy. In business, these strategies are known as the enterprise strategy, the corporate strategy, the business strategy, and the functional (support) strategy. Each of these major strategies is composed of numerous subcomponent strategies. The enterprise strategy is concerned with how the organization functions as a member of the overall society. The corporate strategy is concerned with the business or businesses the firm is in and the basic action strategies that naturally follow. The business strategy is concerned primarily with marketing (and occasionally with other functional strategies). Business strategies are the primary driving force behind the organization's ability to compete. Finally, the supportive strategies focus on the efforts of both economic functional strategies—such as production, finance, and human re-

---

[34] "EEOC Steps Up the Pressure," *Business Week*, February 23, 1974, pp. 87–88.

source management—and managerial functional strategies—such as planning, organizing, implementing, and controlling—to support the business strategy.

Plans, and hence strategies, have important intrinsic characteristics, including flexibility, contents, consistency, timeliness, risk, and acceptance by society and government.

Key Terms and Concepts

By the time you have completed this chapter, you should be familiar with the following key terms and concepts: the objective setting process; typical business objectives and their major characteristics; the levels of objectives; the major MBORR processes; the positive and negative features of MBORR; the importance of objectives to performance; the four major levels of strategy for all organizations and for business in particular; the major component substrategies of the corporate strategy, including definitions and examples; the grand strategy; the major characteristics of plans; the impacts of international and nonprofit situations on the concepts discussed in this chapter.

Discussion Questions

1. Describe how each of the objectives from Figure 3.3 might be operationalized.
2. Why do organizations function better if they have objectives than if they do not?
3. Give examples of each of the major strategies discussed in this chapter, including the subcomponent strategies of the corporate strategy.
4. Discuss as many strategic mistakes of well-known large firms as possible, categorizing each of these mistakes in terms of the strategies outlined in Table 3.5.

References

Ansoff, H. I. "Managing Strategic Surprise by Response to Weak Signals." *California Management Review*, Winter 1975, pp. 21–33.

Gutmann, P. M. "Strategies for Growth." *California Management Review*, Summer 1964, pp. 81–86.

Odiorne, G. *Management by Objectives*. New York: Pitman Publishing, 1965.

Tosi, H. "Effective and Ineffective MBO." *Management by Objectives* 4 (1975): 7–14.

Chapter 4
The Master Strategy at the SBU Level

Never follow the crowd.
Bernard Baruch

Most business organizations engage in only one line of business. Your local auto dealer or flower shop; a wholly owned national restaurant chain such as Victoria Station; a subsidiary of a major conglomerate, such as Sylvania of GTE; or a retail grocery organization, whether it be Kroger, Safeway, Albertson's, A&P, or Grand Union, are all examples of business organizations with essentially one line of business. The master strategies of such organizations are the subject of this chapter.

The principal concern of single-business organizations is establishing a strategic advantage which allows them to beat the competition in the marketplace. At the business level, the organization's master strategy focuses primarily on marketing, but the roles of basic action strategies and supportive functional area strategies are critical and indeed may be the focal point of the competitive marketing strategy.

This chapter discusses the marketing strategy and how it can be used to gain strategic advantage. It also examines the role functional strategies play in obtaining strategic advantage at the SBU level. Of special importance to the marketing strategy is the product life cycle and the related contingency approaches. These factors are discussed in considerable detail. Figures 4.1 and 4.2 indicate which portions of the strategic process are examined in this chapter.

Figure 4.1
The Organization—a Strategic Management Process Model

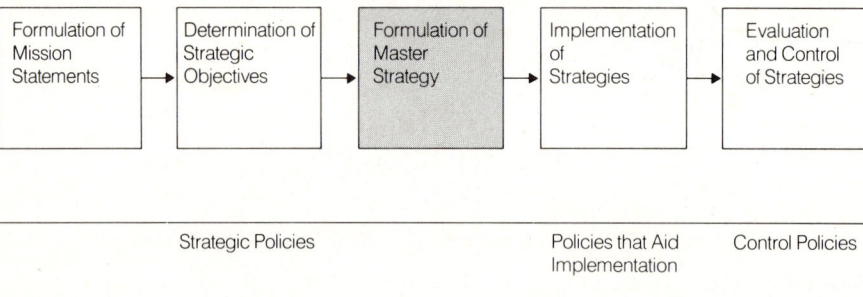

The Corporate Strategy for the Single-Business Enterprise

"What business are we in or should we be in?" As you have learned, all business firms must answer that question. In Chapter 3, we saw that the choice of business depends on the answers to three questions:

1. Is there some business in which the organization has a natural strategic advantage or an innate interest?
2. Does the company want to compete or find a niche?
3. Does the company want or need to concentrate, grow, stabilize, engage in investment reduction, or turn around company fortunes? A number of basic strategy options exist. While strategies such as diversification have been ruled out, at least for the time being, single business firms still have numerous basic action strategies from which to choose. These basic action strategies will lead to the formulation of the grand strategy as per the discussion in the previous chapter. Often, at the business level, the marketing strategy drives the organization as part of a concentration grand strategy.

Even after these questions have been answered, the single-business organization must always be alert to the possibility of redefining the business. The business changes over time; or more accurately, it should change with changes in strategic variables.

The owner of a medium-sized manufacturing company, when first asked what his business was, replied, "We make high-quality men's pajamas." Later, he realized that he was in the contract labor business. This realization opened many new product horizons to the firm; but just as importantly, it caused him to realize that his primary competitive strength lay in his workers, who were responsible for the high product quality which was the central focus of his competitive effort. He saw then

Figure 4.2
Objective Determination and Master Strategy Formulation

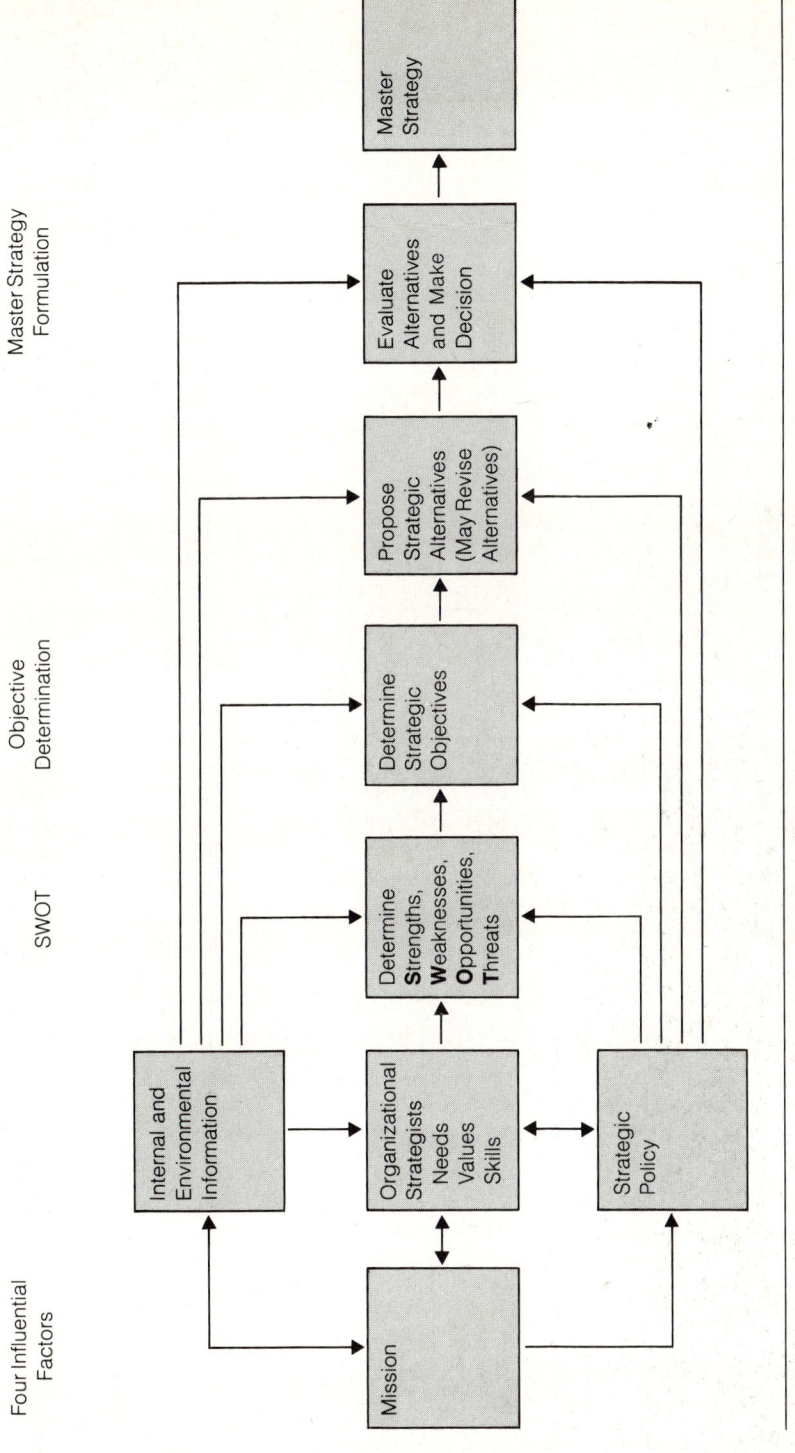

Figure 4.3
Relationships among Strategies in Single-SBU Firms

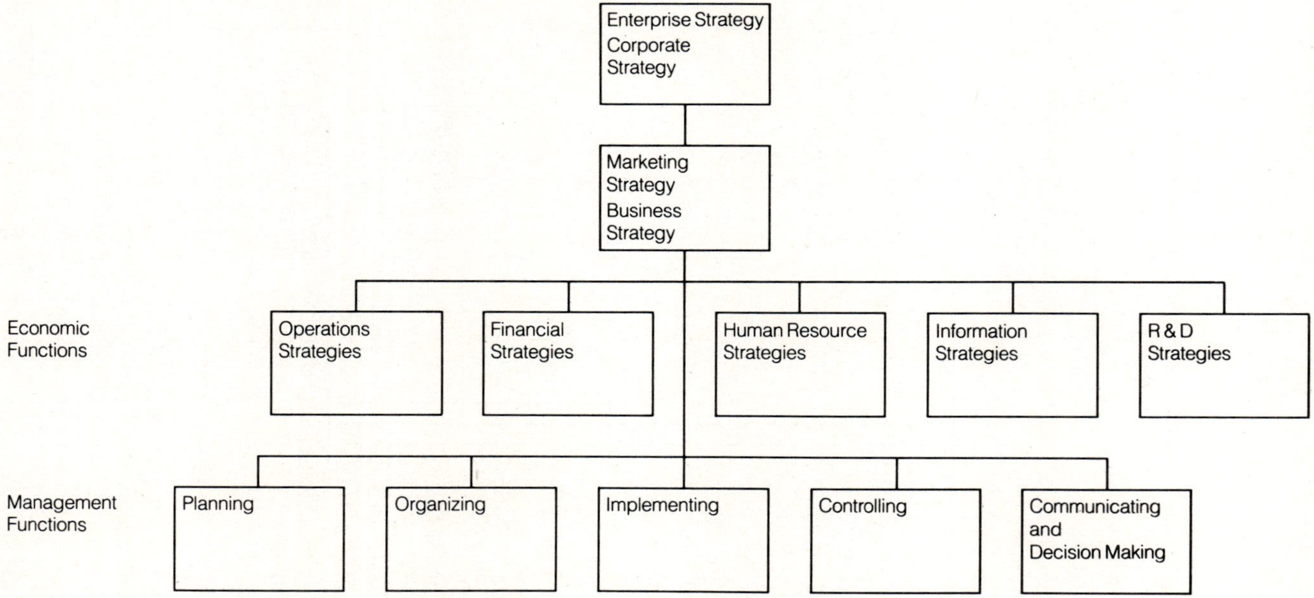

the need to emphasize human resources management in his organization to a much greater extent than he had been.[1]

In defining the business in a single-business firm, important points for any top manager to remember are to be flexible, to anticipate change, and to be responsive to changes, both internal and external.

The Business Strategy for the Single-Business Enterprise

Competition is the name of the game. For most single business companies, marketing plays the most critical role in strategic business success, but selected basic action and functional support strategies play integral roles. In some companies, certain functional support strategies, such as production or research and development, may dominate the business strategy.

The business strategy addresses the issue of how the firm is to compete in one business or in a particular product market segment. The objective is to obtain a strategic advantage over the competition. A business firm must either do something that no other firm does; do something better than its competition, or at least convince people it does; or do something in a location in which no other firm does the same thing. Any of these alternatives must be accomplished by use of the basic action strategies available in combination with a sound marketing strategy based on the fundamental marketing components: target market, product, promotion, distribution, and price. The business strategy integrates the various functional strategies which support the competitive effort. Figure 4.3 portrays the relationships among the various strategies in the single-SBU firm.

Marketing Strategy

Marketing is so basic that it cannot be considered a separate function. . . . It is the whole business seen from the final result, that is, from the customer's point of view. —Peter Drucker

Let us examine each of the marketing concepts listed above with particular attention to the strategic advantages that are sought in each of the components of the marketing strategy.

Target Market. To whom are you going to try to sell the product, whatever it is? The answer to this question identifies the target market. You usually cannot successfully sell iceboxes to Eskimos, but you can very successfully sell large, juicy hamburgers to the adult hamburger-eating market, as Wendy's has shown. And McDonald's has an excellent strategy of attracting children in order to sell not only them but also their parents its products. Both of these firms understand the concept of target market and have made the most of it.

---

[1] This anecdote is based on a personal consulting experience of the author's.

Typical target market strategic advantages include:

1. *Market Share.* Not even RCA or GE could successfully enter the main-frame computer market against IBM. IBM's market share was so large—well over 90 percent at one time—that its resources simply could not be matched. It had strong customer knowledge, strong products, strong cash flows to support the necessary research and development, and strong personnel throughout. Its management systems were excellent. Since the early 1970s, several firms have begun to take certain segments of the market from IBM, but none has yet directly challenged it successfully in its major business lines.

2. *Expanding the Market.* The Coca-Cola Company believes it must expand its market, because its traditional domestic demographic market, people between the ages of 13 and 24, is shrinking. The company is therefore showing more older people in its ads.

3. *Defining a New Market/Segmenting the Market.* Psychology Today successfully identified a portion of the population who wanted to read psychologically oriented articles written in understandable language and of interest to readers in their everyday lives.

4. *Knowledge of Customer/Market Research.* In analyzing the Phillip Morris acquisition of 7-Up, one is faced with two possible alternative uses of knowledge about the customer. First, colas dominate the U.S. market. Phillip Morris may have been betting that it could convert cola drinkers into lemon/lime drinkers via advertising, that is, expand its market. Or, it could have been basing its acquisition on the knowledge that in most other countries, lemon/lime is preferred to cola. In the first case, it may not have been using market research satisfactorily. In the second, it may have achieved a marketing coup. Only time will tell.

5. *A Balance among Target Markets.* Johnson Products, headed by George Johnson, ran into serious trouble in the mid 1970s when the large cosmetics companies moved into Johnson's niche—selling hair care products to minorities, primarily blacks. Had Johnson had other products aimed at other markets, its current financial situation would be better.

It doesn't matter how good the seller thinks the product is if no sizable customer group agrees. It doesn't matter how well you can make it, if no one wants to buy it. The essence of marketing is the socially responsible marketing concept, which states that for a product to be successful, it must satisfy a customer need without being detrimental to the overall society. The target market and the product, then, are closely related.

Product.

In the factory we make cosmetics, and in the drugstore we sell hope.
—Charles Revson

You have to have something to sell. The product, whether it is a manufactured physical object or some type of service, must exist because someone needs it. In addition to the physical product or service itself, other elements of the product include package design; brands and trademarks; customer protections such as warranties and guarantees; and product life cycle extension devices such as product improvements.

Once the customers and their needs have been identified, then the product can be created. (Many times a product is created and then a customer need is found; but this strategy often fails.) As you saw in Information Capsule 2.1, fulfilling a customer need is sometimes an uncertain proposition, even with proper market research. As was the case with Pillsbury's Appleasy, the company may not believe that the customer will pay the price to satisfy that need. Needs can also change. This was part of the problem facing the U.S. auto industry in the late seventies. Before the Iranian crisis, the auto companies were correct in assuming that they could still sell large cars. But the market changed too quickly for them to be able to react, and no contingency alternatives were ready.

Typical product strategic advantages include

1. *Quality.* The quality of Japanese products was once low. High quality is now associated with most of their products. As a result, many products manufactured by U.S. firms (notably automobiles, cameras, small appliances, and electronic goods) have suffered in the marketplace because the quality of these products is perceived to be lower than that of Japanese products.

2. *Product/Service Line Completeness.* People shop at Macy's, May Company, the Denver, Rich's, Jordan Marsh, Burdines, Neiman Marcus and other fine department stores instead of specialty stores because everything is under one roof. The enclosed shopping mall with three or four anchor stores and a hundred or more specialty shops expands this concept further.

3. *Service after Purchase.* Sears has always been known for its service after purchase. For example, if a Sears Craftsman brand tool ever breaks, Sears will replace it.

4. *Packaging.* When Marlboro introduced the "crush-proof box," the cigarette itself had not changed; but the package had, and thus the product had. In this case, the package helped significantly in selling the product, partly because it did protect the physical goods enclosed but also because the box integrated well with the image of the rugged "Marlboro man."

5. *New Product.* Wendy's introduced two new products to the national fast food market—chili and the big, juicy hamburger. An empire resulted.

6. *Patent Protection.* Polaroid has suffered financially since its patent ran out. Kodak has made substantial inroads in the Polaroid instant camera market.

7. *Positive Product/Company Image.* Frank Borman tells us that at Eastern Airlines "We have to earn our wings every day." He is trying to change Eastern's image from one of providing poor service, to one of providing good service, because airlines with a good service image are likely to make a more sizable profit than airlines with a poor one.

Smirnoff vodka, a product not unlike most other vodkas, was advertised in such a unique way, beginning in the 1960s, that in 1978, vodka became the number one selling liquor in the United States. Smirnoff, through advertising, successfully transformed an odorless, tasteless alcohol into a preferred product.

Promotion.

It's not the steak, it's the sizzle. —The World's Greatest Salesperson

If you can't sell the product, it doesn't matter how good it is. Without the proper combination of mass selling, personal selling, and sales promotion efforts, the product is doomed.

Typical promotion strategic advantages include

1. *Advertising Campaign/Theme.* The "Pepsi challenge," a Pepsi-Cola advertising campaign involving blind taste tests between Coke and Pepsi in which more participants preferred Pepsi than Coke, has enabled Pepsi to outsell Coke in several major markets. What makes for a successful campaign or theme is partly research, partly luck, and a great deal of creativity. Ideally, the campaign will help establish customer loyalty to the product.

2. *Effective and Efficient Sales Force.* It is critical that the sales force create customer knowledge and loyalty. This textbook and others are sold through sales representatives. Though advertising and sales promotions play a part, many people believe that the sales rep has the major influence over most professors where textbook adoption is concerned. The sales rep must be able to show the professor the advantages of the book in question. Ask your professor about the quality of the various sales reps that he or she encounters. How do the effective ones provide their companies with an advantage?

3. *Effective and Efficient Sales Promotion Efforts.* Look at a newspaper each day for several days and you will undoubtedly see that Arby's, Pizza Inn, Bonanza, or other food franchisers are offering coupon specials. These specials are an effective means for firms to draw customers into their retail establishments. Price is a critical element in this strategy, but it is brought to the customer's attention through sales promotion.

Distribution. The distribution strategy is concerned with the physical distribution of the product, including the selection of marketing channels. Distribution-related strategic advantages include

1. *Speed of Delivery.* Federal Express, by delivering on its promise "When it absolutely, positively has to be there overnight," created an entire new industry based on speed of physical distribution. This then became their product.

2. *Location of Delivery.* In moving to consumer retail stores, Xerox believes that it can successfully reach millions of small businesses and individual consumers that its sales force could not reach effectively or efficiently.

3. *Service during Distribution, Including Packaging.* Think of a restaurant where service is good. Now think of one where service is bad. Now you have the idea.

4. *Cost.* Wilsons, Service Merchandise, Leeds, and other discount distributors depend on direct delivery to their warehouses to cut costs and hence enable them to underprice many retail distributors of the same products.

5. *Selectivity in Distribution.* You can't buy a Hummel, a set of Wilson Staffs, an Izod shirt, Florsheim shoes, a Brooks Brothers suit, or a Butte Knit at K-mart. Selective distribution gives such products part of their appeal.
6. *Integration with Sales and Operations.* Distribution is often perceived as rather mundane; but distribution-related strategic advantages are often critical, and that is why so many firms today have established logistics departments. If a firm is to succeed, then the efforts of all its parts must be coordinated.

Price. High, low, or in between—what is the right price? Should the firm price for market share, for profit, to cover costs? These are difficult questions to answer. Is the price legally, socially, morally defensible? The pricing strategy must certainly meet these three criteria.

Typical price-related strategic advantages include

1. *A Price Lower Than the Competition's.* In 1980, Texas Instruments lost much of its market share in pocket calculators to firms such as Sharp, which charged significantly lower prices for essentially the same calculator. Lower price may be used to gain market share, which may then lead to long-term profits if customer loyalty can be established. Lower prices may also be used simply to make as much money as possible in a very short period of time.
2. *A Price Higher Than the Competition's.* Some products elicit greater demand as their prices increase relative to the prices of competitors' products. The Corvette, most diamonds, and Smirnoff Silver Label vodka are examples of products whose demand is not highly price elastic and may, in fact, increase as the price rises. Ralph Lauren clothing is a good example of a product that sells well partly because it costs more than its competition. Each item of Ralph Lauren clothing, while basically the same as competitors' clothing, has a polo player on it; so everyone knows the wearer paid more for it.
3. *A Price That Meets the Competition's.* Where price is not an important issue, then other factors may be used to compete; but the company first has to meet the competition's price to be able to sell its product. The airline industry, the auto industry, and the soft drink industry all compete most of the time on some basis other than price. So does the beer industry, from which some two hundred firms disappeared in a twenty-year period because those firms simply could not meet the prices of larger, more efficient brewers.

There's no customer loyalty that two cents can't overcome. —Anonymous

For firms that provide the right product to the right target market at the right price with the right promotion and distribution, the rewards are significant. Information Capsule 4.1 illustrates the economically satisfying results of this combination.

Marketing strategy is critical to success, and various strategic marketing advantages have been identified here. But how does a firm know what strategy to use? One approach to solving this problem is the contingency approach. This approach to strategy formulation and alternative generation is examined next.

Information Capsule 4.1
The Art of Making a Million

Anyone who still believes you have to have money to make money has never met Larry Ross and Martin Blinder. These two young men transformed their avocation into their vocation—and developed a thriving art-publishing business, making a million bucks in the process.

When the bearded team founded Martin Lawrence Limited Editions in 1975, they had little more to go on than determination and a keen appreciation for fine art. Both were art collectors and in their mid-20s. Their initial investment of only $500 went toward subleasing an office, buying a desk, and obtaining a telephone.

Today their business, based in Van Nuys, Calif., a Los Angeles suburb, grosses more than $20 million annually. They own four galleries in Hawaii and two in Southern California and distribute limited editions of fine-art prints to some 1,200 other galleries throughout the world. Among the prominent artists they distribute are Salvador Dali and Victor Vasarely.

Such artists have chosen to work in the print medium to make their work available to more collectors. The artist and the publisher together select which original prints are to be produced in limited editions. The work is designed by the artist, printed under his direct supervision and then numbered and hand-signed by the artist. Each print is original in that the artist personally works on the plates used to make the lithographs. When the predetermined number of prints has been "pulled," the plates are destroyed.

Ross and Blinder attribute the success of their company—it is now among the top four or five art publishers worldwide—to creative marketing in an otherwise staid industry. "We take a Madison Avenue approach to fine art," says Blinder.

For example, in 1977, they offered *Lincoln in Dalivision* in an edition of 1,190 hand-signed lithographs, heavily advertised and imaginatively packaged in portfolios that included special viewing monocles and framable certificates of authenticity. When seen through the monocle from the proper perspective, *Lincoln in Dalivision*, otherwise an abstract, is a portrait of the American President.

Two other factors have also helped them succeed: The first is the continuing interest in art as an investment. "Often, the appreciation in value far outstrips inflation," says Blinder. He ought to know. After graduating from Adelphi University, he became, at 21, Wall Street's youngest stockbroker.

When Blinder and Ross offered *Lincoln in Dalivision* four years ago, the prints were priced at $750 each; today they sell for as much as $12,000. The original oil painting by Dali is also owned by Martin Lawrence Limited Editions. Asking price: $1.9 million.

The second success factor was an unexpected meeting in 1976 with Dali himself. At the time, Martin Lawrence Limited Editions was doing respectably well, buying and selling art and publishing the works of talented but little-known California artists. But the firm still had not published the work of a renowned contemporary artist, something Ross and Blinder knew could rapidly propel their young enterprise to success.

They decided on Dali, the master of surrealism and a legendary recluse, who they knew was staying at a New York hotel. They tried calling him. Dali answered. Ross and Blinder were astounded. "We lucked out," says Ross.

Three days later, they arrived in New York for a meeting with Dali's business manager and left with the rights to publish many of Dali's works. "Everything seemed to snowball after that," says Blinder.

So booming is their international business that travel to Europe has become routine. In fact, it is not unusual for them to conduct business in, say, Paris in the morning, New York in early afternoon, and Los Angeles over a late dinner—all in the same day! For those days they draw straws, literally. "The loser goes," says Blinder. . . .

The $500 Martin Lawrence investment is still multiplying, with a gallery just opened in Sherman Oaks, Calif. Eventually they want to own a string of galleries around the world. They are also branching out into music publishing.

Financial success aside, Ross and Blinder derive personal fulfillment from what they do. "Many people think of art as being too expensive to own," says Blinder, "but we help make it possible for many individuals of modest means to enjoy both the esthetic and investment value of fine art."

Source: "The Art of Making a Million." Reprinted by permission from *Nation's Business*, April 1981, p. 18. Copyright 1981 by Nation's Business, Chamber of Commerce of the United States.

The contingency approach suggests that for a given set of circumstances, a "best" strategy exists. The approach is currently in a formative stage, but the related research is increasing rapidly. The approach has been applied only to profit-oriented organizations, but it may be extended to nonprofit organizations in the future.

The Contingency Approach to Business-Level Strategy Formulation

One does not plan and then try to make the circumstances fit these plans. One tries to make plans fit the circumstances. —George Patton

The science of strategic management has not yet reached the degree of sophistication that will allow executives to know the exact strategy which should be followed for every situation. However, research and theory have pointed towards a set of environmental and organizational variables which have significant impact on the content of strategy, at least with regard to strategy for a single product. Furthermore, for some specific situations, appropriate strategies have been identified, most of them also for a single product. In the following pages, major strategic variables will be reviewed and the few variable strategy combinations which have been identified will be discussed.

Table 4.1
Environmental and Organizational Variables Which Are Strategically Significant at Different Stages of the Product Life Cycle

Types of Variables[a]	Life Cycle Stages Introduction	Growth
Market and consumer behavior variables	Buyer needs Purchase frequency	Buyer needs Buyer concentration Purchase frequency
Industry structure variables	Uniqueness of the product Rate of technological change in product design	Type of product Rate of technological change in product design Number of equal products Barriers to entry
Competitor variables		Degree of specialization within the industry
Supplier variables		
Broader environmental variables	Interest rates Money supply	GNP trend Money supply
Organizational variables	Quality of products	Market share Quality of products Marketing intensity

[a] Within each category, the specific variables identified have been ranked in terms of their degree of significance for formulating viable business strategies. For instance, in the maturity stage of the life cycle, only two competitor variables are considered to be significant for the formulation of a business strategy; namely, the degree of specialization in the industry and the degree of capacity utilization, and of these, the degree of specialization is thought to be the more important.

Strategic Contingency Variables—Factors to Be Considered When One Product or Business Is Involved

After reviewing the research and the theories mentioned previously, C. W. Hofer concluded that the most important single variable in the determination of strategy is the life cycle stage of the product for which the strategy is being formulated.[2] Table

[2] C. W. Hofer, "Toward a Contingency Theory of Business Strategy," *Academy of Management Journal* (December 1975): 784–810.

Table 4.1 continued

Maturity	Saturation	Decline
Market segmentation Buyer needs Purchase frequency Buyer concentration	Market size Market segmentation Elasticity of demand Buyer loyalty Seasonality Cyclicality	Market size Buyer loyalty Elasticity of demand
Type of product Rate of technological change in process design Degree of product differentiation Number of equal products Transportation and distribution costs Barriers to entry	Degree of product differentiation Price/cost structure Experience curves Degree of integration Economics of scale	Degree of product differentiation Price/cost structure Marginal plant size Transportation and distribution costs
Degree of specialization within the industry Degree of capacity utilization	Degree of seller concentration Aggressiveness of competition Degree of specialization in the industry	Degree of specialization within the industry Degree of capacity utilization
Degree of supplier concentration	Degree of supplier concentration Major changes in availability of raw materials	Major changes in availability of raw materials
GNP trend Antitrust regulations	Growth of population Age distribution of population Regional shifts of population Life style changes	Interest rates Age distribution of population
Market share Quality of products Value added Degree of customer concentration Marketing intensity Discretionary cash flow/gross capital investment	Market share Quality of products Length of the production cycle P/S newness Relative wage rate Marketing intensity	Market share Quality of products Length of the production cycle Relative wage rate Degree of customer concentration

Source: Charles W. Hofer, "Toward a Contingency Theory of Business Strategy," *Academy of Management Journal* 18 (December 1975): 800–801. Reprinted by permission of the *Academy of Management Journal*.

4.1 portrays the key variables which his work has suggested are appropriate to each stage of the product life cycle. The table is arranged so that the first factor listed in each cell is the most important, the second is the second most important, and so on.

A business could use the table in this manner: For a product in a particular stage of the product life cycle, it would consult the table to determine what key variables should be considered in the formulation of strategy. For example, suppose a firm has a product in the maturity stage of the product life cycle. The firm's strategic managers would review information related to each of the factors listed under the

Table 4.2
Strategies for the Product Life Cycle

Strategic Area	Phase I Introduction	Phase II Growth	Phase III Maturity	Phase IV Decline
Objective	Introducing the customer to the product; promoting initial adoption by trade, customers	Increasing trade channels; establishing brand, franchises	Maintaining trade support; leveling production; lowering costs; maintaining market share by competitive pricing	Monitor contribution to total product offering and profit
Characteristics	Learning and development in the market and the product	Demand exceeds supply; competition enters market	Sales saturation; low product differentiation	Competitors leave the market
Product	Limited line; adaption to initial adoptors	Addition of variations, improvements	Cost considerations; uniformity for mass production	Simplification of the line
Promotion	Personal selling; missionary selling; awareness, interest; advertising, if any, usually introductory offers	Awareness; interest, evaluations; brand stress; personal selling decreases; advertisement	Mass advertisements as reminder; trade promotion	Minimal
Distribution	Exclusive or direct	Selective	Extensive	Customer option
Price	Introductory, high discounts to facilitate initial adoption by trade, customers	High unit margins or competitive for high market share	Highly competitive	Profit maintenance
Profit margin	Low	High initially to recover R&D, introductory cost, investment; lower as competition enters	Normal to low, as volume stabilizes	High to compensate for lower and declining sales

Source: Henry E. Metzner, Jerry L. Watt, and William F. Glueck, "Product Life Cycle and Stages of Growth, an Empirical Analysis," *Proceedings: Academy of Management*, 1975, Table 1, pp. 61–63. Reprinted by permission of The Academy of Management.

maturity stage for each of the types of variables listed. For example, under "Market and consumer behavioral variables," market segmentation is considered to be the most influential factor. Buyer needs, purchase frequency, and buyer concentration also influence strategy. The firm's strategic managers would gather information on these and the other factors listed for each of the other variables. Based on these factors, strengths and weaknesses would be assessed.

Note that no strategy is recommended in the table. That is left for the individual organization to determine. Strategies such as those presented in Table 4.2 or Table 4.3 might be employed. Research suggests that certain actions are more successful than others, regardless of the situation; these actions will be discussed later.

The conceptualization presented in Table 4.1 is extremely important and highly contributive to strategy formulation. Actual strategic decisions as well as their simulations in the classroom, such as are required by case analyses, can be improved through use of this table. Some caution is necessary, however. These factors have not been tested, as presented, in actual corporations. Furthermore, some very limited evidence suggests that product life cycle strategies are not appropriate to every product. Nonetheless, at this point, the stage of the product life cycle appears to be the single most important factor in determining strategy.

The Contingency Theory Applied

As mentioned earlier, contingency theories are based on the assumption that for a given set of factors in a situation, a best series of actions exists. In a situation where the given set of factors is predominant, the manager—here the strategist—should act in a certain way. The advantages of establishing contingency actions for a given set of circumstances are obvious: performance should improve.

As an example of how contingency theory is applied in strategy formulation for a single product, let us look again at C. W. Hofer's work. Hofer has suggested seven contingency strategy propositions for the maturity stage of the product life cycle. Two of these propositions are listed below as illustrations. Each defines a specific situation in terms of the key variables in Table 4.1 and then suggests an appropriate strategy.

N^2 *When the degree of product differentiation is low, the nature of buyer needs primarily noneconomic, the degree of market segmentation slight, the degree of specialization within the industry low, the marketing intensity high, the manufacturing economies of scale medium, and the ratio of distribution costs to manufacturing value added high, businesses should*

1. *Use universal rather than specialized marketing appeals;*
2. *Reduce their geographic scope or increase their marketing expenditures sufficiently so that their per capita marketing expenditures within their geographic service area are in excess of the industry average;*
3. *Attempt to keep their degree of capacity utilization high and their fixed assets relatively modern; and*
4. *Withdraw from the industry if their market share falls to less than 20 percent of that held by the industry leader within their geographic service area.*

N^3 *When the degree of product differentiation is high, the nature of the buyer's needs primarily noneconomic, the degree of market segmentation moderate to high, the product complexity high, the purchase frequency low, and the barriers to entry in the distribution or technology areas, businesses should*

1. *Focus their R&D funds first on modifying and upgrading their existing product line, second on developing new products, and last on process innovations;*

Table 4.3
Appropriate Business Strategies over the Product Life Cycle

	Functional Focus	R & D	Production	Marketing	Physical Distribution
Precommercialization	Coordination of R&D and other functions	Reliability tests Release blueprints	Production design Process planning Purchasing department lines up vendors and subcontractors	Test marketing Detailed marketing plan	Plan shipping schedules, mixed carloads Rent warehouse space, trucks
Introduction	Engineering: debugging in R&D production and field	Technical corrections (engineering changes)	Subcontracting Centralize pilot plants; test various processes; develop standards	Induce trial; fill pipelines; sales agents or commissioned salesmen; publicity	Plan a logistics system
Growth	Production	Start successor product	Centralize production Phase out subcontractors Expedite vendors' output; long runs	Channel commitment Brand emphasis Salaried sales force Reduce price if necessary	Expedite deliveries Shift to owned facilities
Maturity	Marketing and logistics	Develop minor variants Reduce costs through value analysis Originate major adaptations to start new cycle	Many short runs Decentralize Import parts, low-priced models Routinization Cost reduction	Short-term promotions Salaried salesmen Cooperative advertising Forward integration Routine marketing research: panels, audits	Reduce costs and raise customer service level Control finished goods inventory
Decline	Finance	Withdraw all R&D from initial version	Revert to subcontracting; simplify production line Careful inventory control; buy foreign or competitive goods; stock spare parts	Revert to commission basis; withdraw most promotional support Raise price Selective distribution Careful phase-out, considering entire channel	Reduce inventory and services

Source: Reprinted by permission from *Atlanta Economic Review* (now *Business* Magazine). "Operational View of a Product Life Cycle," exhibit from "A Framework for Functional Coordination," by Harold W. Fox, November/December 1973, pp. 10–11. Copyright 1973 by the College of Business Administration, Georgia State University, Atlanta.

2. *Allocate substantial funds to the maintenance and enhancement of their distinctive competencies, especially those in the marketing area;*

3. *Develop a strong service capability in their distribution systems; and*

4. *Seek to expand the geographic scope of their operations, if possible.*

Source: Charles W. Hofer, "Toward a Contingency Theory of Business Strategy," *Academy of Management Journal* 18 (December 1975): 803–805. Reprinted by permission of the *Academy of Management Journal*.

Observing these propositions should make the difficulties in formulating contingency statements increasingly clear. One of the major barriers to the formulation of a usable contingency theory is the large number of variables to be considered. Hofer suggests that more than fifty major variables exist which could affect strategy on a contingency basis. He admits that this list is probably incomplete in

Table 4.3 continued

Personnel	Finance	Management Accounting	Other	Customers	Competition
Recruit for new activities Negotiate operational changes with unions	LC plan for cash flows, profits, investments, subsidiaries	Payout planning: full costs/revenues Determine optimum lengths of LC stages through present-value method	Final legal clearances (regulatory hurdles, patents) Appoint LC coordinator	Panels and other test respondents	Neglects opportunity or is working on similar idea
Staff and train middle management Stock options for executives	Accounting deficit; high net cash outflow Authorize large production facilities	Help develop production and distribution standards Prepare sales aids like sales management portfolio		Innovators and some early adopters	(Monopoly) Disparagement of innovation Legal and extralegal interference
Add suitable personnel for plant Many grievances Heavy overtime	Very high profits, net cash outflow still rising Sell equities	Short-term analyses based on return per scarce resource		Early adopters and early majority	(Oligopoly) A few imitate, improve, or cut prices
Transfers, advancements; incentives for efficiency, safety, and so on Suggestion system	Declining profit rate but increasing net cash inflow	Analyze differential costs/revenue Spearhead cost reduction, value analysis, and efficiency drives	Pressure for resale price maintenance Price cuts bring price wars; possible price collusion	Early adopters, early and late majority, some laggards; first discontinued by late majority	(Monopoly competition) First shakeout; yet many rivals
Find new slots Encourage early retirement	Administer system, retrenchment Sell unneeded equipment Export the machinery	Analyze escapable costs Pinpoint remaining outlays	Accurate sales forecast very important	Mainly laggards	(Oligopoly) After second shakeout, only few rivals

terms of other explanatory variables such as management techniques or social responsibility. Nevertheless, taking only his variables into account gives us some 18,000,000,000,000,000 combinations of circumstances to consider. This means that in order to have a truly inclusive contingency variable theory, an almost infinite number of contingency statements would have to be formulated. Approaching the task from a life cycle stage basis, as Hofer has done, allows the number of situations to be reduced substantially. Even with these limitations, however, the number of possible situations which could exist is very high. This suggests that the future of contingency theory probably lies in identifying the major factors which should be considered, as has been done in Table 4.1, and combining them with hypothesized strategies such as those of Metzner, Watt, and Glueck (Table 4.2) or Fox (Table 4.3). (These are behavioral type strategies which will be defined later.)

Figure 4.4
Directional Policy Matrix

		Prospects for Market Sector Profitability		
Company's Competitive Position		Unattractive	Average	Attractive
	Weak	Disinvest	Phased Withdrawal Proceed with Care	Double or Quit
	Average	Phased Withdrawal	Proceed with Care Growth	Try Harder
	Strong	Cash Generation	Growth Leader	Leader

Source: Adapted from D. E. Hussey, "Portfolio Analysis: Practical Experience with the Directional Policy Matrix," Long Range Planning, Vol. 11 (August 1978), p. 3. Reprinted by permission.

The Directional Policy Matrix

One contingency business strategy technique (developed by Shell and used primarily in Europe) employs a nine-cell matrix as a means for determining strategies within a particular industry. The matrix approach is quite common in evaluating resource allocations among multiple businesses within the same firm (as you will see in Chapter 5), but has not been used that frequently in determining strategies within a particular industry. As you examine Figure 4.4, you will see that one of this matrix's axes characterizes the Prospects for Sector Profitability, the other characterizes the Company's Competitive Capabilities. Each of these two critical dimensions is viewed as having three levels of desirability. The prospects for sector profitability are unattractive, average, and attractive. The company's competitive capabilities are seen as either weak, average, or strong. The combinations of these three levels of the two critical dimensions then lead to eight advisable strategies (phased withdrawal appears twice on the matrix). In using this matrix, a firm would examine the prospects for sector profitability compared with its competitive capabilities, and then choose the indicated strategy at the intersection of the determined levels for each dimension. The resultant eight strategies are portrayed as follows:

1. *Disinvest.* These products are losing money in their long-term average performance, and should be eliminated from the product line.
2. *Phased Withdrawals.* Slowly, but surely, the business should eliminate these products from the product line. They may be earning money, but only a marginal amount. Any profits derived from these products is not justifiable in terms of relative investment.

3. *Cash Generator.* This product or service has no long-term future. Normally such products are in the late maturity stage of the product life cycle. No further investment should be allowed.
4. *Proceed with Care.* Two average levels on the two critical dimensions suggest caution in terms of future investment.
5. *Growth.* Where the company is strong and the industry averagely attractive, the firm should continue to support growth in this product or service. The business's position should allow the product or service to be self-financing.
6. *Double or Quit.* If the firm is weak in an attractive industry situation, it should either invest heavily in the product or service, or withdraw from the marketplace.
7. *Try Harder.* Where the firm finds itself in an attractive industry, but is only average in that industry, it should increase investment or withdraw from the marketplace.
8. *Leader.* At this intersection of the levels of the two dimensions, the business should attempt to maintain its leadership position in the market by investing, even though necessary investment funds may not be self-generating, because earnings will be above the average.[3]

This matrix seems to offer some very prudent, logical advice. But, as with any concept of strategic management, there are a number of factors to consider further. First, are there only two major sets of variables to consider? What are the specific product life cycles of the various products, and what are their impacts? Are there more than three levels of desirability characterizing the two dimensions noted? Are the recommended strategies the most satisfactory? Are there assumptions to this model which are not met in every situation? It is always best to be the leader, or can one make substantial profits as a follower? The point is that this model is only one approach to the determination of a business level strategy, and should not be taken as a recommended approach. Rather, it should be considered as a starting place.

An additional consideration should be used in determining an appropriate strategy. The behavioral theory of strategy formulation, which has often been labeled as part of the contingency theory, identifies certain behaviors which have been employed by the more successful firms in most, if not all, circumstances. The following paragraphs discuss some of the postulates of this strategy formulation theory.

The Behavioral Theory of Strategy Formulation

In the past few years, several studies utilizing regression analysis and other analytical techniques have demonstrated that successful firms engage in definite patterns of behavior in order to increase return on investment. While this research

---

[3] D. E. Hussey, "Portfolio Analysis: Practical Experience with the Directional Policy Matrix," *Long Range Planning* (August 1978): 1–9.

uncovered some surprises and some contradictions, most of its findings involved factors which theory would have identified as appropriate. The following paragraphs review some of these studies to determine which factors are of primary interest.

Profit Impact on Market Strategies, or PIMS, was a project organized in 1972 by the Market Science Institute, a nonprofit research organization affiliated with the Harvard School of Business. This project was a strategic information-sharing experience among 57 major North American corporations. The project had two phases. In Phase One, only 36 corporations supplied information on some 350 businesses. In Phase Two, 57 companies provided information on 620 businesses.

The original intent of the program was to determine the profit impact of market strategy. In addition, the project sought a basis upon which to estimate ROI for organizations in varying situations. Such a basis could help the organization to select businesses in which to diversify, projects in which to invest, and projects of which to divest and in general to balance the corporation's investment portfolio. Information relating to 37 major variables from these corporations was regressed against the ROI of the organizations. The intent was to determine which of these variables was the most explanatory. Some of the more significant contributory variables found included the following:

1. *Market Share*—the ratio of dollar sales by a business in a given time period to total sales by all competitors in the same market.
2. *Product (Service) Quality*—quality of each participating company's offerings appraised on several bases.
3. *Marketing Expenditures*—total cost for sales force, advertising, sales promotion, market research, and marketing administration.
4. *R&D Expenditures*—total cost of prior development of process improvement.
5. *Investment Intensity*—ratio of total investment to sales (has a high negative impact on sales).
6. *Corporate Diversity*—ratios which affect the number of different industrial categories in which most corporations engage.
7. *Other Company Factors*—characteristics of a company that owns a business; the primary concern here is organizational size.[4]

B. A. Kirchhoff believed that the interorganizational analysis used in the PIMS project was subject to methodological problems caused primarily by the difficulty of equating measurements contained in the different accounting systems employed by the PIMS project firms.[5] Therefore, he chose to analyze one organization through intraorganizational analysis. He analyzed two of four major divisions of a capital-intensive manufacturing firm within a mature industry. The firm manufactured separate but technologically similar products. In total, some 50 geographically separate

---

[4] S. Schoeffler, "Profit Impact on Marketing Strategy" (Internal memorandum, Marketing Research Institute, November 1972); S. Schoeffler, R. D. Buzzell, and D. F. Heany, "The Impact of Strategic Planning on Profit Performance," *Harvard Business Review* (March/April 1974): 137–145.

[5] B. A. Kirchhoff, "Empirical Analysis of Strategic Factors Contributing to Return on Investment," *Proceedings: Academy of Management*, 1975, pp. 46–48.

"So much for Plan A. Now . . ."

profit centers existed: 31 in division A, 13 in division B, 3 each in divisions C and D. Analysis applied only to divisions A and B, since divisions C and D were too small to allow regression to take appropriate effect.

Kirchhoff chose 17 factors, several of which were not used in the PIMS project—for example, personnel factors, which he believed would be important. These factors are displayed in Table 4.4 for Division A. Gross profit per unit and total profit per unit best explained ROI in Division A. These factors were surrogates for market price; therefore, market price was isolated as a major determinant of ROI. Several labor attitude and productivity variables were also shown to be significant. Absenteeism and accident frequency decreased ROI, and labor and machine productivity was shown to increase it. These are extremely important findings; personnel factors have been given little treatment in strategic literature, but Kirchhoff's results clearly suggest that these factors have a great impact on ROI. Production also emerged as a significant variable. In general, the most important factors can be summarized as cost control and price factors.

Noticeably absent was the market share variable reported as most important by the PIMS project. Kirchhoff suggests that this was a result of a very high demand in the market for products of most organizations at the time of the study, including all businesses of the organization he examined. Market share had limited impact. Less favorable economic conditions would probably cause market share to be more important.

Table 4.4
Independent Variables Included in Kirchhoff's Analysis

No.	Description	Division A	All Combined[a]
1	Labor/machine productivity index	Included	NCM
2	Gross profit per unit	Included	NCM
3	Units produced per labor hour	Included	NCM
4	Factory cost per unit	Redundant with 5	NCM
5	Total cost per unit	Included	NCM
6	Units sold per salesman	Redundant with 7	NCM
7	Sales revenue per salesman	Included	Included
8	Marketing expense as percent of sales revenue	Included	Included
9	Marketing expense per unit	Redundant with 8	NCM
10	Output to capacity ratio	Included	Included
11	Collection period	Included	Included
12	Inventory to sales ratio (dollars)	Redundant with 13	Redundant with 13
13	Inventory to sales ratio (units)	Included	Included
14	Market share	Included	NCM
15	Labor absenteeism	Included	Included
16	Accident frequency	Included	Included
17	Labor turnover	Included	Included

[a] NCM indicates that no common measurement was found for the variable.
Source: Bruce A. Kirchhoff, "Empirical Analysis of Strategic Factors Contributing to Return on Investment," *Proceedings: Academy of Management*, 1975, p. 47. Reprinted by permission of the Academy of Management.

With respect to the total corporation, the number of variables was reduced to eight because of inability to find common measurements for these variables across all four divisions. The inventory to sales ratio exerted the greatest influence on ROI; the less inventory a profit center had, the higher its ROI. Collection period had the second greatest influence; the longer the collection time, the lower the ROI. Sales revenue per salesman, a measure of salespeople's productivity, was the third major variable. Absenteeism had a similar effect on the total organization as it did on Division A. One interesting finding—accident frequency correlated negatively with ROI. That is, as accidents increased so did ROI. Obviously, this should not occur; some unforeseen moderator variable must be influencing these data. The three variables which did not have a significant impact were capacity utilization, marketing expenses as a percent of sales revenue, and labor turnover.

The major contribution of Kirchhoff's study is in showing the importance of internal variables as opposed to the external variables emphasized by the PIMS project. The study's finding that the market share variable is not universally important is also significant.

K. J. Hatten, employing multiple regression and other statistical techniques as well as case study investigation, closely examined strategic variables in 13 major breweries for the 20-year period 1952–1971.[6] Rather than emphasizing specific be-

---
[6] K. J. Hatten, "Strategic Models in the Brewing Industry" (Ph.D. dissertation, Purdue University, 1974); "Strategy, Profits, and Beer" (Paper presented at the Academy of Management Meetings, New Orleans, August 1975).

havior patterns for most firms, his results suggest that within a given industry certain strategies are successful for one group of firms, another set of strategies is successful for another group of firms, and so forth. For instance, he found that strategic success for large national brewers and strategic success for regional brewers were caused by different factors. His findings support the classical belief that size is an important factor in determining competitive strategy. More importantly, his findings point to the need to investigate claims that certain behaviors always ultimately lead to success, since his study indicates that appropriate behaviors vary among situations.

Some earlier studies provide limited evidence as to appropriate behaviors. For example, the Boston Consulting Group's (BCG) findings in 24 technology-oriented industries support the PIMS finding that market share is an important contributor to ROI.[7] BCG also notes the importance of price and price/cost relationships in various product life cycle stages.

Other early efforts support a more contingent point of view. W. E. Fruhan, Jr., found that the BCG results were not universal.[8] The strategies recommended by the BCG were not found to be applicable to the industries he examined. Government was observed to be a major determinant of which competitive strategy would be acceptable.

More recently, in a conceptual analysis of the underlying assumptions and related problems, Carl R. Anderson and Frank T. Paine concluded that PIMS was still the most viable strategic analysis methodology. They believed that it had several weaknesses, which if improved, would make it much more useful to researchers and practitioners alike. Several of these weaknesses are highlighted in the summary below.[9] Finally, Michael Lubatkin and Michael Pitts employed the PIMS analysis (limited information model) on beer industry data for the period 1952–1974. They found general support for the PIMS results, with PIMS explaining at least 60% of the variance in the data.[10] Note, however, the time period of the data analyzed coincides with much of the original PIMS research.

In summary, substantiation for the view that certain behaviors are applicable to all firms is limited empirically. As with any preliminary research, these findings are limited in their applicability until additional supporting research is reported. Furthermore, correlation/regression techniques such as those used in the PIMS project are not truly explanatory but rather indicate the strengths of relationships. And the variables mentioned above have several exceptions. Some are more applicable in certain situations than in others.

For example, these "universal truths," as the PIMS result are sometimes referred to, do not apply to all industries, nor to all firms in all industries, given factors such as market variables, the economy, and market position. Indeed, earlier and later in this chapter, various strategies for those in different positions within the

---

[7] The Boston Consulting Group, *Perspectives on Experience* (Boston: The Boston Consulting Group, 1968); the Boston Consulting Group, *Perspectives on Experience* (Boston: The Boston Consulting Group, 1970).

[8] W. E. Fruhan, Jr., *The Fight for Competitive Advantage: A Study of U.S. Domestic Trunk Air Carriers* (Boston: Division of Research, Harvard Business School, 1972); W. E. Fruhan, Jr., "Pyrrhic Victories in Fights for Market Share," *Harvard Business Review* (September/October 1972): 100–107.

[9] C. R. Anderson and F. T. Paine, "PIMS—A Reexamination," *Academy of Management Review* (July 1978): 602–612.

[10] M. Lubatkin and M. Pitts, "PIMS: Fact or Folklore?" *Journal of Business Strategy* (Winter 1983): 38–43.

market have been and will be noted. It is possible that the PIMS results would not be true in some other time period other than that examined. (Although the few later studies, support the PIMS results.) Furthermore, there is also a high probability of statistical methodological problems—multicollinearity to be specific. In addition, PIMS assumes only one performance objective.[11] Other explanatory variables exist that either were not included in the PIMS project or did not prove to be sufficiently explanatory in this particular study. However, this project has shown that for large, multifaceted business corporations, in varying industries and in differing situations, some common indicators of return on investment can be found. But the choice of a strategy is at least partially a function of industry. Additional research should isolate commonly successful behaviors for certain industries and for groups of firms within those industries.

The meek shall inherit the world, but they'll never increase market share.
　　　　　　　　—William C. McGowan, Chairman of MCI Communications

Porter's Competitive Strategies

Michael Porter, has suggested that three major business level strategies exist for outperforming other corporations engaged in similar activities: overall cost leadership, differentiation, and focus. These "generic" strategies are to be utilized in coping with the five competitive forces related to his competitor analysis approach discussed in Chapter 2.[12]

1. *Cost Leadership*—employs a set of functional policies to achieve the basic objective. This strategy "requires aggressive construction of efficient-scale facilities, vigorous pursuit of cost reductions from experience, tight cost and overhead control, avoidance of marginal customer accounts, and cost minimization in areas like R&D, service, sales force, advertising, and so on. . . . Low cost relative to competitors becomes the theme running through the entire strategy; tough quality, service, and other areas cannot be ignored."[13] By having the lowest costs, satisfactory returns will still accrue to this firm even after meeting the costs of competition. Competitors will not be able to make satisfactory levels of return.

2. *Differentiation*—involves creating a product or service that is perceived as being unique throughout the industry. Differentiation allows the firm to have sizable profit margins because of brand loyalty by customers, and their subsequent lower sensitivity to price. Entry barriers are created by customer loyalty. Fewer substitutes are possible than for competitors' undifferentiated products.

---

[11] T. Naylor, "PIMS: Through a Different Looking Glass," *Planning Review*," March 1978; M. Porter, "Market Structure Strategy Formulation and Firm Profitability: The Theory of Strategic Groups and Mobility Barriers," in *Marketing and the Public Interest*, J. Cady, ed., Cambridge, Mass.: Market Science Institute, 1978; C. R. Anderson and F. T. Paine, "PIMS—A Reexamination," *Academy of Management Review* (July 1978): 602–612; M. Lubatkin and M. Pitts, "PIMS: Fact or Folklore?" *Journal of Business Strategy* (Winter 1983): 38–43.

[12] M. E. Porter, *Competitive Strategy* (New York: Free Press, 1980), pp. 34–46.

[13] Ibid., p. 35.

Table 4.5
Requirements for Generic Competitive Strategies

Generic Strategy	Commonly Required Skills and Resources	Common Organizational Requirements
Overall cost leadership	Sustained capital investment and access to capital Process engineering skills Intense supervision of labor Products designed for ease in manufacture Low-cost distribution system	Tight cost control Frequent, detailed control reports Structured organization and responsibilities Incentives based on meeting strict quantitative targets
Differentiation	Strong marketing abilities Product engineering Creative flair Strong capability in basic research Corporate reputation for quality or technological leadership Long tradition in the industry or unique combination of skills drawn from other businesses Strong cooperation from channels	Strong coordination among functions in R&D, product development, and marketing Subjective measurement and incentives instead of quantitative measures Amenities to attract highly skilled labor, scientists, or creative people
Focus	Combination of the above policies directed at the particular strategic target	Combination of the above policies directed at the regular strategic target

Source: M. E. Porter, *Competitive Strategy* (New York: Free Press, 1980), pp. 40–41. Copyright © 1980 by The Free Press, a division of Macmillan Publishing Co., Inc. Reprinted by permission.

3. *Focus*—the thrust of this strategy is to serve a particular target market very well, be it a specific buyer group, a segment of the product line, or a geographic market. The underlying assumption is that by focusing, the firm can provide better service or a better product, and can do so more efficiently. The consequences of this strategy will be either lower cost or differentiation, or both. The narrow target market is the vehicle to achieve these ends.

Successfully implementing these three strategies requires differing skills, resources, and other common organizational requirements. Porter's perspectives on these requirements are contained in Table 4.5.

Comments on Porter's Generic Strategies.

"Generic" strategies are of modest help, at best. Most businesses consist of complex collections of product-market units which share production and/or marketing functions. The most profitable strategy for the business will depend on the relationships between product market units, market segment economics, competitive position, and the behavior of rivals. —James M. McTaggart, Marakon Associates

Porter's strategies are first of all behaviorally based, which means that they are suggested as appropriate in all situations rather than on a contingency basis, although he does allow for assessment of the situation to see which is most relevant. But, many of the complexities of each particular situation are overlooked by generic approaches. Many of the general criticisms made about PIMS could be applied to Porter's generic strategies and all other behavioral strategies for that matter. On the other hand, Porter's strategies are conceptually and intuitively sound. In examining the research, we find one study which lends support to Porter's cost and differentiation strategies. Roderick E. White, examined 69 business units and found, not surprisingly, that firms with both cost and price advantages had the highest ROI. The highest sales growth was achieved by those businesses employing a pure differentiation strategy. White also examined the relationship of the environmental context to these strategies and firm performance, and found that, indeed, a positive relationship appears to exist.[14]

Additional research by Gregory G. Dess and Peter S. Davis also supports the view that having generic strategies leads to higher performance than not having generic strategies on an intra-industry basis. Employing questionnaires, they examined 22 firms in the same industry.[15] However, not all research is supportive. Carolyn Y. Woo and Karel O. Cool reported that the preliminary analysis of their data was not supportive of Porter's generic strategies. They question whether "generic" strategies are viable descriptions of the strategic process.[16] Obviously more research is necessary in this field before conclusions may be drawn.

Additional Behaviorally Derived Strategies

Several authors have recommended strategies for firms in specific situations. Among them are strategies for firms seeking intensive growth, for low-market-share firms, for firms competing in stagnant industries, for dominant firms, and for firms in declining industries.

Strategies for Firms Seeking Intensive Growth. P. Varadarajan has developed a three-stage growth strategy.[17] The first stage involves choosing a growth strategy—market penetration, market development, or product development. In the second stage, the strategist chooses the elements on which to focus—number of buyers, frequency of purchase, or average quantity purchased each time. In the third stage, the process is continually reviewed, feedback is obtained, and modifications are made. Varadarajan provides brief summaries of each of the main strategies available under the three major types of growth strategies and indicates which variables are most likely to increase sales.

---

[14] R. E. White, "Generic Business Strategies, Organizational Context and Performance: An Empirical Investigation" (Paper presented to the Academy of Management, Dallas, 1983).

[15] G. G. Dess and P. S. Davis, "Porter's (1980) Generic Strategies as Determinants of Strategic Group Membership and Organizational Performance," *Academy of Management Journal* (September, 1984):

[16] C. Y. Woo and K. O. Cool, "Generic Competitive Strategies: Performance and Functional Strategy Complements," (Paper presented to the Strategic Management Society, Paris, October 1983).

[17] R. Varadarajan, "Intensive Growth Strategies," *Atlanta Economic Review*, November/December 1978, pp. 4–11.

Strategies for Low-Market-Share Firms. R. G. Hamermesh, M. J. Anderson, Jr., and J. E. Harris propose that low-market-share companies do one of the following:[18]

Segment Markets. Sell only to a particular segment of the market in which the firm has expertise and in which larger firms are not likely to compete. For example, Southwire, a very successful regional metal products firm, concentrated on the segment of the market that wanted immediate delivery. Timex concentrated on the segment of the market that wanted an inexpensive but dependable watch.

Use R&D Wisely, to Lower Costs or Innovate. Larger firms have substantial R&D budgets. Therefore, the low-market-share company must use its R&D funds wisely. These authors, for example, suggest that the funds should be used either to lower costs or to bring new products to the market.

Think Small. A third strategy is to think small. Many firms seem content to remain in their niche and focus on profits, not growth.

Philip Kotler has suggested these strategies for low-market-share firms.[19]

Filling a Vacant Niche. Find an area in the market on which large firms are not concentrating. For example, specialty automobile manufacturers are successful largely because they fill a niche too small for the major manufacturers to bother with.

"Ours-Is-Better-Than-Theirs." Weak firms can improve on the products of dominant firms and then capitalize on this strategic advantage. Cross pens, Smirnoff vodka, and Sony televisions took advantage of this strategy.

Channel Innovation. Weak firms can distribute the product in new ways that will satisfy customer needs. King Kola has proposed direct distribution of its cola to food stores' warehouses from major regional bottlers in an effort to cut costs and hence capture market share through price competition.

Distinctive Image Strategy. Weak firms can develop a strategic advantage through the use of some distinctive image; for example, Dr. Pepper has emphasized its distinctive taste and, more currently, its challenge to "Be a Pepper." Another example is the Pro Staff golf ball campaign to show that more winners on the professional golf tours use Pro Staff than any other ball.

Information Capsule 4.2 gives an interesting insight into the need for an "onside kick" strategy.

Strategies for Firms Competing in Stagnant Industries. Richard G. Hamermesh and Steven B. Silk suggest that successful firms in stagnant industries do three things:[20]

---

[18] R. G. Hamermesh, M. J. Anderson, Jr., and J. E. Harris, "Strategies for Low Market Share Businesses," *Harvard Business Review* (May/June 1978): 95–102.

[19] P. Kotler, *Marketing Management, Analysis, Planning and Control* (Englewood Cliffs, N.J.: Prentice-Hall, 1980), pp. 281–284.

[20] R. G. Hammermesh and S. B. Silk, "How to Compete in Stagnant Industries," *Harvard Business Review* (September/October 1979): 161–168.

Information Capsule 4.2
The Onside Kick

The cheerleaders were turning triple flips.
The bands were breaking the sound barrier.
The 102,000 fans were roaring.
Football underdog was meeting football powerhouse.
Underdog lost the toss and had to kick.
Whistle.
Roar.
Boot.
It was an "onside kick!"
A strategy usually used near the end of a game, rarely at the beginning.
Fans gulped.
Piccolo player swallowed his piccolo.
TV commentator got hiccups.
Underdog got ball.
Six plays later, touchdown!
If you're an underdog
and don't want to stay that way,
try the unexpected for a quick score.
If you're an overdog,
watch out for clever underdogs.

Source: Reprinted with the permission of United Technologies, Inc.

1. *They identify, create, and exploit growth segments in their industry.* Despite a decline in the number of motion picture theaters over a twenty-year period, General Cinema recognized that one segment, the shopping center segment, was growing. It moved into this market in full force, successfully avoiding the pitfalls of a stagnant industry.

2. *They emphasize product quality and product improvement.* Despite stagnation in the coffee industry, General Foods' innovative freeze-dried coffee has proved to be a big money maker. Perhaps one of the best firms at this strategy is Gillette, which somehow manages to improve either the blade or the razor every three to five years.

3. *They systematically and consistently improve the efficiency of their production and distribution systems.* The Japanese auto, camera, and steel industries epitomize this approach.

Strategies for Dominant Firms. Philip Kotler suggests that the following are advisable strategies for dominant firms:[21]

[21] Kotler, *Marketing Management*, pp. 273–281.

1. *Keep the Offensive.* Keep pushing for increased market share. Don't give competitors a chance to strengthen themselves. Be efficient, be innovative, don't be content. IBM does this well.
2. *Use a Fortification Strategy.* Introduce additional brands to compete with the company's already successful brands, keeping the competition from entering the market. Phillip Morris has been adept at this strategy. Or protect your product's technology, or patents. Coca-Cola has done this well; only three people at any one time know Coke's formula.
3. *Use a Confrontation Strategy.* Be prepared to beat the competition in advertising and in price. Ward off all price challenges of smaller firms by meeting or beating their prices. General Motors has pursued these strategies for years.
4. *Use a Maintenance Strategy.* Set objectives for the firm's market position and then maintain investment accordingly, using excess cash flows to support growth businesses.

Strategies for Firms in Declining Industries. Kathryn Rudie Harrigan suggests that firms in declining industries most frequently have alternatives consisting of the following:

1. *Early Exit.* We might call this getting out while the getting is good.
2. *Milking the Investment.* Remove all possible cash flows.
3. *Shrinking Selectively.* Choose the available remaining markets and advance into them strongly.
4. *Employing Holding Patterns.* Hold your own.
5. *Increasing Investments.* Investment should be increased only where a long-term advantage exists in doing so.[22]

These additional behavioral strategies, and some two to three hundred more that have been suggested by various authors, are based on the successes of a limited number of firms. This is not to discount their validity but only to remind you that, because of the sample size upon which the recommendations are based, these strategies are worthy of consideration but are not steadfast rules for action.

Strategic Recommendations According to Strength and Product Life Cycle Stage

Finally, Peter Patel and Michael Younger have developed a model, shown in Table 4.6, which suggests certain strategies as a function of product life cycle stage and the relative strength of the company.[23]

---

[22] K. R. Harrigan, "Strategy Formulation in Declining Industries," *Academy of Management Review* (October 1980): 599–604.

[23] P. Patel and M. Younger, "A Frame of Reference for Strategy Development," *Long Range Planning*, April 1978, pp. 6–12.

Table 4.6
Strategic Guidelines as a Function of Industry Maturity and Competitive Position

	Embryonic	Growing	Mature	Aging
Dominant	All-out push for share	Hold position	Hold position	Hold position
	Hold position	Hold share	Grow with industry	
Strong	Attempt to improve position	Attempt to improve position	Hold position	Hold position or harvest
	All-out push for share	Push for share	Grow with industry	
Favorable	Selective or all-out push for share	Attempt to improve position	Custodial or maintenance	Harvest
	Selectively attempt to improve position	Selective push for share	Find niche and attempt to protect	Phased withdrawal
Tenable	Selectively push for position	Find niche and protect it	Find niche and hang on or phased withdrawal	Phased withdrawal or abandon
Weak	Up or out	Turnaround or abandon	Turnaround or phased withdrawal	Abandon

Source: From Peter Patel and Michael Younger, "A Frame of Reference for Strategy Development," *Long Range Planning*, April 1978, p. 8. Reprinted by permission of Pergamon Press Ltd., Oxford, England.

Behavioral Theories: A Commentary

You have been exposed to a number of behavioral theories. Considered in total, they may seem somewhat bewildering. Indeed, there are overlaps and even contradictions among them. The various strategies were presented to provide you first with a feel for the alternatives and second with some ideas for your own strategy formulation as you do case work.

Functional Supportive Strategies

Functional strategies are designed to support the competitive effort of the business strategies. There are three types of functional strategies:

1. *Economic Functional Strategies*—involving the functions which allow the firm to exist as an economic entity, such as marketing, and the functions that support marketing and the basic action strategies, such as finance, operations, human resources management, information systems, research and development, and the like. These are vital to many "generic" or "behavioral" strategies.
2. *Management Functional Strategies*—involving the management functions of planning, organizing, implementing, controlling, staffing, leading, motivating, communicating, decision making, representing, and integrating.

3. *Strategic Issues Strategies*—used to monitor the environment. There are two major types. One functions to help the organization contend with known contingencies; the other is designed to help the organization overcome surprises. The latter normally involves the creation of several contingency strategies, which have become increasingly popular as the operating environment has become more turbulent and should continue to increase in popularity.

It might be helpful to mention here again that, while marketing is an economic function, it is included as the main part of the business strategy because it is basic to the SBU's central focus—to compete. The other economic functions are grouped here with the functional strategies because their purpose is to support the competitive effort of the business strategy.

It is important to think of the management functions as integrative rather than as separate from the economic functions. As Figure 4.5 reveals, the management functions are performed across all functions of the organization. Thus, marketing, finance, operations, human resources, and the like must all be managed—there must,

---

Figure 4.5
The Managerial Matrix

Economic and Managerial Functions

Managerial Functions	Marketing	Finance	Operations	Human resources	Information	Research and development	Planning	Organizing	Implementing	Controlling	Staffing	Leading	Motivating	Communicating	Decision making	Representing	Integrating
Planning																	
Organizing																	
Implementing																	
Controlling																	
Staffing																	
Leading																	
Motivating																	
Communicating																	
Decision making																	
Representing																	
Integrating																	

for example, be marketing planning, financial organizing, operations implementing, and human resource control. Similarly, the management functions must be managed—planning, organizing, implementing, and controlling must be planned, organized, implemented, and controlled.

In examining the role of functional strategies, this text will not define and describe each of the functions. That has been done in other courses. Rather, a few examples of how these strategies contribute to business success will be presented to illustrate how important they are. Extensive information as to the principal components of each of these areas is provided in the situation audit, Appendix II.

How Delta Combines Sound Financing and Good People Management

The excellent companies live their commitment to people . . .
—Thomas J. Peters and Robert H. Waterman, Jr.

Delta Airlines is, by measure of continued profit, the most successful airline in the United States. There are many reasons for this success. In terms of marketing strategies, "Delta is ready when you are." Delta has a product—a flight—available at the times people need it most. Delta also stresses service. Its planes are on time, its employees are courteous, and it strives to make the customer feel important. Behind its ability to succeed in these areas are two critical factors—its debt structure and its people strategy.

Delta purchased the right airplane fleet for its schedules. That was an operational consideration and an important factor in Delta's success. But perhaps more importantly, Delta purchased this fleet of airplanes at the right price, at the right time, on the right terms. Eastern Airlines, which competes virtually head-on with Delta in every major market, has to earn millions more than Delta just to break even, because Delta's debt maintenance is so much lower. This gap in debt maintenance has existed for almost ten years, although it has not always been so large. The difference in net available cash can be used by Delta to pay dividends, improve employee benefits, and improve capital assets.

The second key factor in Delta's success has been its people strategy. Delta attempts to maintain a "family feeling" among members of its work force to encourage employee loyalty and productivity. Information Capsule 4.3 describes this strategy in more detail.

Donnelly Mirrors' Low Prices and High Quality Depend on Productivity, Innovation, and People Management

Donnelly Mirrors now dominates what was once a highly competitive, virtually entry-proof industry, the automotive mirror industry. They succeeded by achieving lower prices and higher quality than their competition through management techniques and systems that emphasized productivity, quality, and innovation while rewarding the individual and providing job security. Donnelly encourages its workers

Information Capsule 4.3
"Family Feeling" at Delta Creates Loyal Workers, Enmity of Unions

In February 1979, James Burnett's paycheck came up $38 short. Delta Airlines hadn't paid him enough overtime for the day he came in at 2 a.m. to repair an L-1011 engine.

When his supervisor wouldn't help, the 41-year-old mechanic wrote Delta's president, David C. Garrett, Jr. He complained that "the pay problem we have experienced is bad and it has caused a lot of good men to go sour on the company." Three days later, Mr. Burnett got his money and an apology from top management. Delta even changed its pay policy, increasing overtime pay for mechanics called in outside normal working hours.

Such reaction from top executives to the little problems of Delta's 36,500 employes isn't an isolated incident. It's part of a sophisticated personnel policy to maintain what Delta calls its best asset: an unusually productive and loyal work force. The strategy, which includes virtual open-door access for all employees to top management, has kept Delta largely nonunion and made it a consistent money maker in an industry plagued with labor-management strife.

At the heart of Delta's philosophy is a concept it calls "the Delta family feeling." More than a slogan, it's an attitude that was nurtured by the airline's founder, the late C. E. Woolman, and then carefully institutionalized by W. Thomas Beebe, Delta's current chairman. "It's just a feeling of caring within the company," says Mr. Beebe.

The approach has its drawbacks. Because few people quit, it's tough to move up in seniority. A Dallas baggage handler on the night shift complains: "We figured we'd be 103 years old before we got day shift." And some employees say that because there isn't a clear-cut promotion system, they have to buddy up to supervisors to get ahead.

Nevertheless, it's difficult to find workers with serious complaints. Delta promotes from within, pays better than most airlines and rarely lays off workers. When other airlines cut employment during the 1973 oil embargo, Mr. Beebe told senior management: "Now the time has come for the stockholders to pay a little penalty for keeping the team together."

Delta makes sure employees embrace the family concept by carefully screening job applicants. Stewardesses, for instance, are culled from thousands of applicants, interviewed twice, and then sent to Delta's psychologist, Dr. Sidney Janus. "I try to determine their sense of cooperativeness or sense of teamwork," he says. At Delta, "you don't just join a company, you join an objective."

Delta holds yearly employee meetings with top management and lets workers make what would normally be considered management decisions. A committee of flight attendants chooses uniforms for Delta's 6,000 stewards and stewardesses. "That's important. You have to live in them," says flight attendant Pam Webb. Mechanics even choose their immediate supervisors.

But Delta can be tough. Recently it fired a flight attendant trainee because she complained about having to train between 10 p.m. and 12 a.m. on a Saturday night before an 8 a.m. company exam. "She had a little attitude problem," says Mary Ruth Rouse, supervisor of flight attendant training. "We had visions of her refusing to go out on flights."

And Delta can be downright prudish. In May it fired flight attendant Linda Lehner for exposing her derriere in Playboy magazine. "We attempt to hire young ladies for these jobs, and we expect them to act like that," says Mr. Garrett, Delta's president. On duty, stewardesses can't even wear open-toed shoes.

For years, union organizers have tried without success to organize Delta workers. "They have a relationship with their employees that's most difficult to break into," says Frank O'Connell of the Transport Workers of America. The last union vote at Delta occurred in 1955. There hasn't been a strike since 1947. Only pilots and flight dispatchers—about 1% of the work force—are organized.

A Free Trip

"If we ever become unionized, it will be because we've made mistakes," says Mr. Beebe. But the company didn't make mistakes with Arnie Rich. The Northeast Airlines mechanic worried about losing his union protection when Delta merged with Northeast in 1972. Delta flew him and his wife to Atlanta so he could talk to Delta employees. "I walked out into the hangar at three in the morning and talked to people," he says. "I asked, has anyone been fired? What do you get fired for? Everybody was just happy."

Without union work rules, Delta is free to switch employees to different jobs as needed. During the 1973 fuel crunch, for instance, Delta reassigned 700 pilots and flight attendants to jobs loading bags and taking reservations. The company believes cross-training helps employees understand how their jobs fit in with overall company goals.

Help From Colleagues

Delta will go to great lengths to get an employee's side of the story. Three years ago, the marketing manager in Fort Worth, Texas, "was in serious trouble," says C. P. Knecht, former vice president, marketing programs. "He kept reporting expenses we couldn't find. Everybody said we should fire him."

The Fort Worth man said medicine he was taking for a blood disease caused his memory to lapse. Mr. Knecht thought he was lying. But he flew to Fort Worth to meet with the man's doctor, who verified the story. Delta transferred the man to a less demanding job.

Such understanding seems to give employees a family-like esprit de corps. Mr. Burnett, the mechanic, lost a week of work last January when his 16-year-old daughter died in a car accident. Forty other mechanics each worked an hour on his time card so he wouldn't lose any pay.

During peak periods, pilots and gate agents help load bags to speed up departures. Robert Oppenlander, senior vice president, finance, says this is one reason Delta continually leads the industry in service and profits. Since 1974, according to the Civil Aeronautics Board, Delta has had the fewest complaints per passenger boarded of any major airline. And Delta's 1979 net income of $103.4 million accounted for more than a fourth of the entire industry's profit last year.

"At Christmas, you see top management come and pitch in," says Scotty McCarthy, 31, who started as a baggage handler 10 years ago. "I've gone over to Eastern at peak times and seen mountains and mountains of bags, and I've seen one guy trying to handle all this. Does anyone come over to help him? No ma'am."

Mr. Beebe says Delta holds firm on its policy of promoting from within. "We've got hundreds of college-degree graduates working on the ramp knowing they will be promoted if their work merits it," he says, but "we don't have any stars," such as Eastern's top man, Frank Borman. "Usually, it turns out to be an ego trip which is bad for the company. We want people who will enjoy and want to be working for the team."

Source: Reprinted from "'Family Feeling' at Delta Creates Loyal Workers, Enmity of Unions," by Janet Guyon, *The Wall Street Journal*, July 7, 1980, pp. 13, 16. Reprinted by permission of *The Wall Street Journal*, © Dow Jones & Company, Inc. All rights reserved.

to find new ways of saving money, doing the job faster or cheaper, or eliminating the job altogether. Its encouragement includes bonuses tied to productivity and guaranteed employment. Allowing employees to participate in decisions that affect the individual or group also plays an important role in its success. Without these strategies, Donnelly could not have been so competitive.[24]

Bank of America Emphasizes Open Communication to Improve Service

The Bank of America has created what it calls "people advocacy programs." In order to improve service and make the bank a better place to work, the bank has opened up communication between managers and their subordinates. The results indicate that the programs have been phenomenally successful. Like Delta's people policies, these programs show that employees are more committed to organizational goals when corporate concern for employees is perceived to be high. Included in the six people advocacy programs are the following three:

Employee Assistance Department. If work-related problems cannot be solved through routine company channels, an entire department is available to devote its time and energy to solving these problems.

Let's Talk It Over. A six-step formal problem-solving process through the bank's officers is another alternative.

[24] Participative Management at Work: An Interview with John F. Donnelly," *Harvard Business Review* (January/February 1978): 117–127.

Figure 4.6
Major Strategic Choices—a Decision Tree

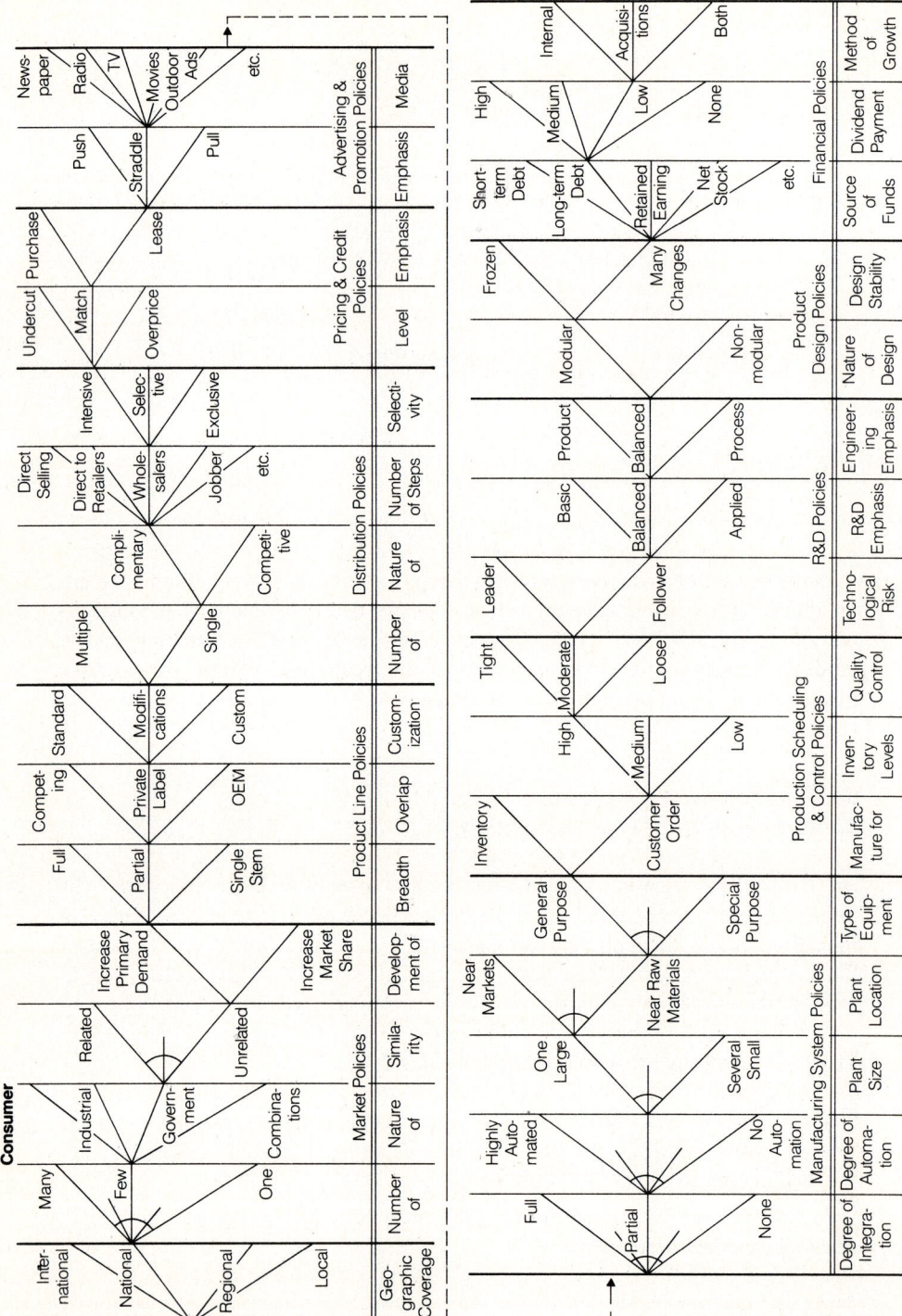

Source: C. W. Hofer, "Conceptual Constructs for Formulating Corporate and Business Strategy," Dover, MA: Case Teacher's Association, #BP-0041, p. 14. Copyright © 1971 by C. W. Hofer.

Open Line.   A telephone system is available to receive employees' questions. The person who asks the question receives a written answer in a short time.[25]

Using Production Technology to Cut Costs

One company which makes plastic bags and polyeurethane refrigerator storage containers found itself with high labor costs because of unionization of its employees. Because of the intense competition in these two industries and the domination in both by large firms, price was felt to be the key means of attracting business in both markets. The firm found that it could reduce costs most quickly by replacing the large labor force with capital production equipment. This classical economic labor substitution strategy provided the firm with a significant reduction in costs and the ability to stay in these markets.[26]

The Support Strategies

In each of the cases above, the supportive strategies were essential to the success of the marketing effort. Support strategies and basic action strategies are often integral components of the business strategy.

Charles Hofer has provided a vital perspective regarding functional strategies and their relevance to the business strategy. This perspective is revealed in Figure 4.6. This figure may be utilized as a resource in determining the types of functional strategies which a business organization should develop. Note also his guidance on marketing and certain basic action strategies.

International Master Strategies at the SBU Level

The fundamentals of the master strategy at the SBU level are applied internationally as they would be domestically, but the specifics of application and the bases upon which these applications occur are again significantly modified by multinational operations.

Each of the five major factors involved in the marketing mix is affected in some way by the international situation. For example, the size of the target market, its purchasing capabilities, and its identification are often much more difficult to determine because of varying demographic and socioeconomic factors. S. Majaro indicates that numerous potential problems exist with respect to the other factors, product, promotion, price, and distribution.[27] He emphasizes the impacts of environment, competition, institutions, and the legal system on the components of the marketing mix.

---

[25] A. W. Clausen, D. W. Ewing, and P. M. Banks, "Listening and Responding to Employees' Concerns," *Harvard Business Review* (January/February 1980): 101.

[26] As reported to the author by the firm's vice president for production.

[27] S. Majaro, *International Marketing* (London: Allen & Unwin, 1977), pp. 88, 111, 178.

Some of the major impacts of these four factors on the product, including its aesthetic design, branding, and packaging, are as follows: special needs for sizes, dimensions, and standards; attitudinal constraints; available supportive resources; attitude of local consumers to colors, shapes, and appearances; local tastes and traditions; acceptability of proposed product name and its pronounceability, recallability, and message conveyance; availability of desired packaging materials; compliance with various bodies which set standards for product and packaging; compliance with laws affecting the use of the product; safety rules; pollution rules; registration of design; constraints on shapes; registration of trademark; legal constraints on name; and requirements for labeling of packages.

Among the major factors relating to promotion are the following: language; literacy levels; readership details; attitudes towards advertising, sales personnel, and sales promotions; influencer patterns; demography; symbolism; media availability and other situational aspects of media; legislative bans on certain advertising; sales promotion or personal selling practices; and laws limiting expenditures on marketing.

Majaro goes on to suggest that many local market factors must be considered in pricing. Among them are: whether social and cultural taboos affect the amount of money that can be spent on a product; whether it is customary to overprice in anticipation of reducing the price; whether institutions exist that must be consulted before the price is set; whether there are legal constraints on price changes; whether legal limitations on margins exist; and finally, whether there is a legal requirement to print price details on the product or package.

Among the major factors relevant to distribution are: availability of roads and other transportation channels; customer buying habits; use of local agents versus a company sales force; whether channels are government controlled; what red tape must be managed before and during distribution; and whether special packaging, safety, size, material, or other rules exist.

These are lengthy lists, but critical ones. A few examples will show that firms have not always taken these factors into account and have suffered as a result. One U.S. auto manufacturer exported its sporty model to a Spanish-speaking country. In choosing a name for the car to replace its English name, the company wanted something that sounded sporty. The name they chose sounded sporty to them, but it meant slow or sluggish in Spanish. Another U.S. firm attempted to sell its razor blades in one foreign country in drugstores and supermarkets just as they had in the United States. Sales failed to materialize; people in that country at that time bought their razor blades in hardware stores. One fried-chicken firm scored an instant success in Japan. Apparently thinking that the Far East market was homogeneous, the firm attempted to sell its "finger lickin' good" chicken in Hong Kong. But several problems arose. The Chinese apparently expected to be served a towel with their meal, and they tended not to eat with their fingers. Finally, one U.S. cereal manufacturer attempted to sell its cereal in Brazil, where people do not eat breakfast. Not to be outdone, another division of the same company attempted to sell its gelatin dessert to a population of which only 3 percent owned refrigerators. Similar examples are numerous, although multinationals are improving in this regard.

With respect to the other functional strategies, many differences exist. Financial strategies must of course include some concern for currency translations. Production strategies must cope with numerous logistical problems resulting from differing and often inadequate transportation systems, the absence of suppliers, and the frequent absence of necessary skills in the work force. Personnel strategies must cope with differing laws and local customs regarding work and authority. For example, in much of Europe, it is virtually impossible to terminate employees; it is even illegal in many countries. Other external factors may influence personnel matters. For example, when John DeLorean built his car factory in Ireland, he was not fully prepared for the necessity of segregating the work force along religious lines, nor was he prepared for the firebombings his plant suffered as a result of religion-related labor disputes.

Finally, management functions differ in other countries. Managers often find themselves confronted with differing expectations about motivation and leadership styles. In much of Europe and Japan, participation in decision making by first-line employees is much greater than in the United States and Canada. Yet, in the Middle East, Central and South America, and most of the rest of the world, the manager's word is law and is seldom disputed. Long-range planning is important in Japan, where it is viewed as critical to the success of the organization; but it is not much practiced in China. Motivation techniques vary primarily with need levels, and the need levels of people outside major industrialized countries tend to be much lower on Maslow's scale than the needs of people in industrialized nations, who often seek high-level need satisfiers in their jobs. Control strategies are of special importance in the multinational enterprise because of the multitude of factors already noted, especially geographic separation and, in many cases, the absence of a manager familiar with the multinational's operation. (That is, the manager may be a host country national rather than a parent country employee.) Communication habits, decision-making skills and habits, and a host of other functional strategy factors vary as well. The multinational organization must be extremely adaptive if it is to survive and prosper.

Nonprofit Strategies at the SBU Level

Since competition and competitive strategies are the primary concerns of the grand strategy—the focal point of the master strategy at the single business level of strategy, it is appropriate to identify the nature of competition in the nonprofit organization. Ellen Greenberg identifies several key areas in which nonprofits compete: for funding; for personnel and other resources; for users-customers, clients, and audience; for influence and prestige. She suggests that nonprofits have recently entered a more turbulent environment. There is a related increased taxpayer, contributor, or other fund provider interest in decreasing taxes, contributions, or dues. Thus there will be an increased competition for funds,[28] and hence an increased need for marketing strategies. Indeed, with federal, state, and local government cutbacks, the number of solicitations of business for support for education, for the arts, and for charities has increased substantially. The competition for users would also seem to

[28] Ellen Greenberg, "Competing for Scarce Resources," *Journal of Business Strategy* (Winter 1982): 81–87.

be quite significant, for in many cases, as governments slash programs, the individual agency will seek to continue to justify funding based on the existence of a significant user base.

In short, the nonprofit sector represents a new and virtually untapped area for research and writing in strategic planning.

—Robert C. Shirley

The absence of related research prohibits this text from identifying specific nonprofit strategies, except for anecdotal evidence or prescriptive strategies. The key factor involved in all of these is much the same as it would be in a for-profit organization-identification of the proper target market. With respect to federal, state, and local government, it is apparent that a large number of publics must be satisfied, that society at large, political interest groups, legislators, and members of various government agencies all have major concerns regarding taxes and uses of funds. These groups must be marketed to. These marketing efforts can be substantive. Television, radio, and various forms of printed media may be utilized in order to secure approval and programs and their respective budgets. Millions of various mail pieces may be involved in one single campaign, at the federal level, with numerous issues being attacked in campaigns at various times throughout the year. The President, various congresspersons, lobby groups, and various societal constituents may attempt to influence each other and the general public on a host of issues. Similar efforts may take place at the state and local level.

In other nonprofits, marketing is also critical. In hospitals, for example, the marketing manager's position is vital. There are tremendous needs to raise funds, primarily from sources other than clients, largely to pay for the services provided to many clients at no cost to them. Similarly, most sizable colleges or universities have a professional fund raiser and/or staff, serving in the marketing capacity to a host of various target markets. This is especially true of the private institution, but increasingly true of public institutions as well, due to the ever-tightening budget. With respect to that budget, most major public institutions must maintain lobbyists in order to preserve funding needs as they proceed through the legislature. In most states, education is the single biggest expenditure in the budget, and is coming under closer scrutiny. Religious institutions, museums, clubs, and unions have all carefully selected target markets at which they aim their marketing strategies. Many of these strategies play upon historical ties, such as having graduated from a particular educational institution; many focus upon the individual's ethical or moral beliefs; and many focus on the individual's particular needs—for example, the need to help others. Some, such as those employed by clubs and unions, focus on needs for certain activities or factors such as security. These latter organizations, which depend on dues for funds, must of course market heavily the services they provide to the users and to potential users, in order to create funds. Unions especially find themselves losing power in the 1980s, and their marketing efforts are primarily aimed at new target markets, such as geographically in the South, or in different jobs, such as those held by white-collar employees. Obviously, a tremendous amount of personal selling is involved in virtually all of the marketing strategies of these nonprofits.

Philip Kotler has suggested that marketing for nonprofits has four distinctive characteristics:[29]

1. Multiple publics—clients and funders, both of whom must be marketed to.
2. Multiple objectives—difficult to find strategies that will satisfy all simultaneously.
3. Services rather than physical goods—these tend to be intangible, inseparable, variable, and perishable.
4. Public scrutiny—observed and pressured externally.

Yet, despite these and several other differences in major strategies, most not-for-profit organizations carry out Figures 4.1 and 4.2 much as do for-profit organizations. Figure 4.7 portrays the various stages of planning for one very representative non-profit . . . a college or university. As you can see, there is a value derived purpose, a matching of strengths and weaknesses (implied) against opportunities and threats, a classic mission statement, and an apparent grand strategy seeking some competitive advantage. There are functional strategies, organizational strategies, and implementation strategies. These are all adapted to the specific environment as they should be. Compare this process then to Figures 4.1 and 4.2 and you will see a significant number of similarities.

Summary

The principal focus of the master strategy at the SBU level is the marketing strategy. Each major component of the marketing mix offers opportunities for strategic (competitive) advantages.

The contingency theory of strategy formulation is conceptually appropriate but difficult to utilize because of the numerous variables involved. Several behavioral theories offer sound alternatives to the contingency theory. The behavioral strategies are based partly on research and partly on experience and suggest that, in most situations or in selected situations, certain strategies are best. The key to both contingency and behavioral theories is the life cycle stage of the particular product or service.

Supportive functional strategies are extremely critical to the success of the organization. For a few firms, these strategies do not just support the competitive effort but may become critical components of that effort. There are two major types of supportive strategies, the economic functional strategies and the management functional strategies. A third type is strategic issues functional strategies. All strategies, including the management strategies, must be managed.

---

[29] Philip Kotler, *Marketing for Non-Profit Organizations*, 2d ed. (Englewood Cliffs, N.J.: Prentice Hall), 1982, p. 9.

Figure 4.7
Levels of Strategy in a College or University

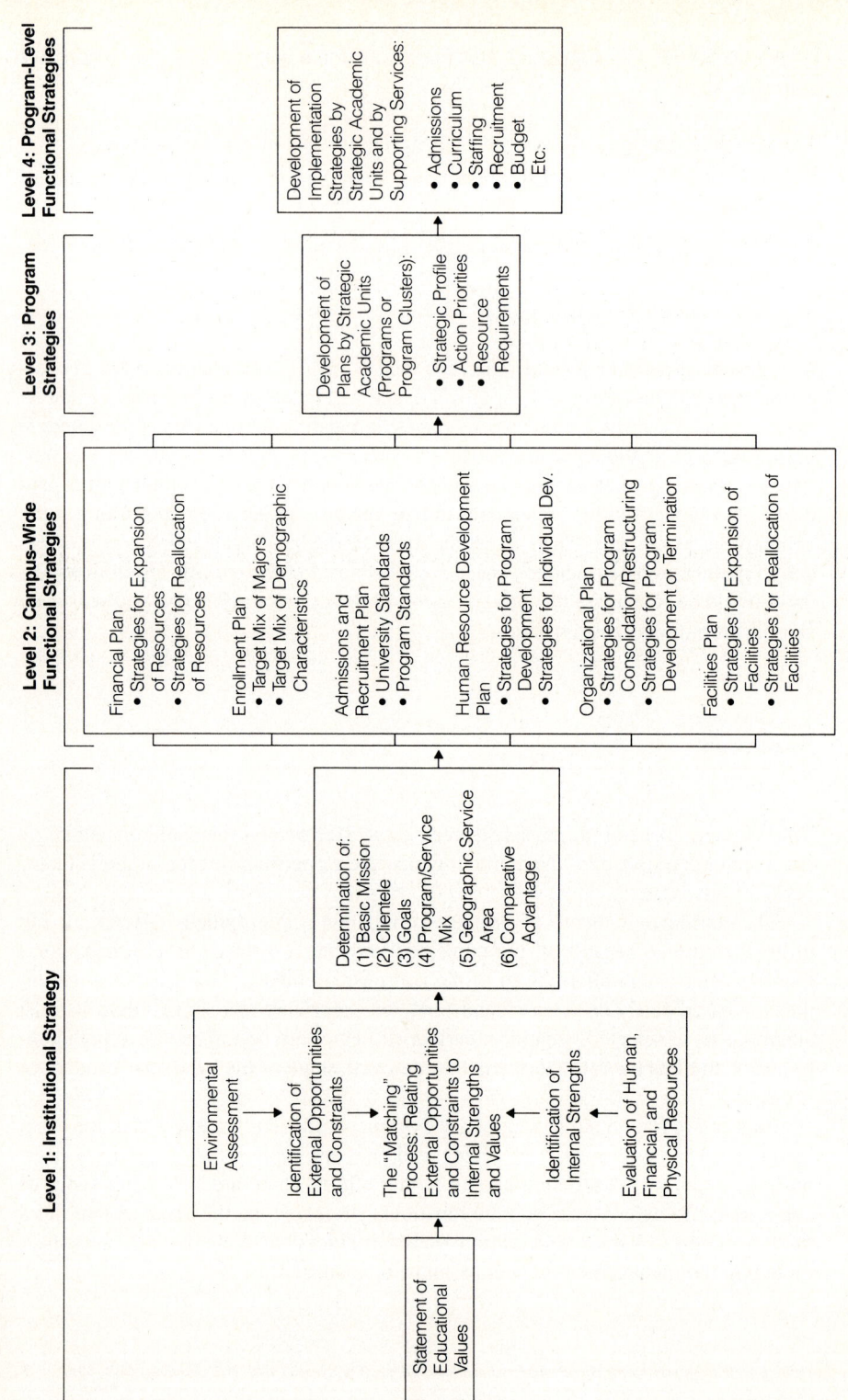

Source: Robert C. Shirley, "Identifying the Levels of Strategy for a College or University," *Long Range Planning*, June 1983, p. 94.

Key Terms and Concepts

By the time you have completed this chapter, you should be familiar with the following key terms and concepts: the business strategy, the marketing strategy, target market strategic advantages, product strategic advantages, promotion strategic advantages, price strategic advantages, distribution strategic advantages, the contingency approach to business-level strategy formulation, major contingency variables, the behavioral theory of strategy formulation, major behaviorally derived strategies, functional supportive strategies, economic functional strategies, management functional strategies, impacts of multinational and nonprofit situations on the major concepts in this chapter.

Discussion Questions

1. Discuss some target market and marketing mix strategies that aim to achieve competitive advantage for a product or service.
2. Discuss why the contingency theory is difficult to apply.
3. Discuss examples of the various behavioral theories with which you are familiar.
4. Provide examples of the importance of functional supportive strategies for both economic and management functions.
5. Provide examples of how international and nonprofit situations affect the master strategy at the SBU level.

Chapter 5
The Master Strategy in Multiple-SBU Firms

Destiny is not a matter of chance, it is a matter of choice; it is not a thing to be waited for, it is a thing to be achieved.
William Jennings Bryan

In the last chapter, the master strategy of the individual business unit was examined. This chapter identifies the ways in which multiple-SBU organizations can combine the strategic efforts of various component businesses to achieve organizational objectives. The master strategy in multiple-SBU organizations consists primarily of portfolio management techniques in combination with a limited number of master policy guidelines and a philosophy of substantial decentralization. In the conglomerate, each SBU usually operates as an independent company with only limited guidance from above.

The principal tasks that multiple-SBU firms' strategists must accomplish are

1. Establishing strategic objectives.
2. Determining whether current businesses are helping achieve those objectives and, subsequently, determining what actions to take regarding those businesses.
3. Determining what objectives remain to be accomplished.
4. Determining what actions to take to achieve the remaining objectives of the total organization.
5. Establishing support functions and master policies for SBUs.

Establishing strategic objectives was discussed in Chapter 3. This chapter reviews the processes involved in answering questions 2, 3, 4, and 5 above, focusing pri-

Figure 5.1
The Organization—a Strategic Management Process Model

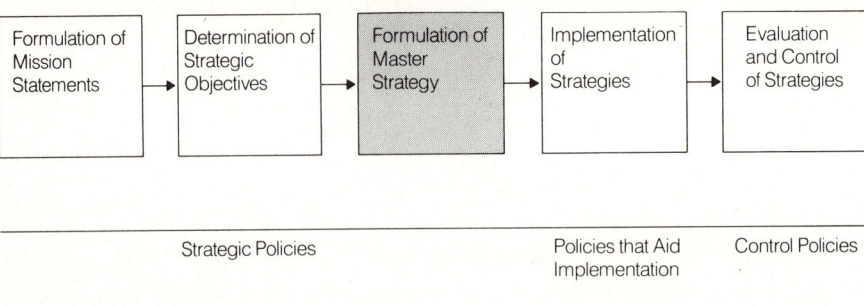

marily on the portfolio management matrix technique. In addition, it discusses policies, functional support, and decentralization as key elements in the successful strategic management of multiple-SBU firms. Finally, it presents a brief commentary on the differences in perspectives between organizational and divisional strategists.

Figures 5.1 and 5.2 indicate which portions of the major strategic processes are examined in this chapter. Figure 5.3 illustrates the relationships between the various types of strategies in a multiple-SBU firm.

Corporate Strategy at the Level of the Total Organization

The corporate strategy at the total organization level for the multiple-SBU organization is comprised of the components in Table 3.5 in a somewhat different fashion than is the strategy for the single-SBU organization which parallels Table 3.5 almost precisely. The multiple-SBU corporation acts primarily as a coordinating unit, providing direction and service to individual SBUs. It establishes policy guidelines for the enterprise strategy. Corporate headquarters also provides certain functional services and related policies for common areas of need—typically finance, personnel, and planning services. And it provides policy in virtually all business strategy and functional and economic strategy areas. But the primary concern of the multiple-SBU firm headquarters is the corporate strategy.

The essence of the corporate strategy and hence master strategy at the level of the total organization, for multiple-SBU firms, is portfolio management. Just as an investment counselor seeks synergy and balance in an individual's personal investment portfolio, the strategists for a conglomerate attempt to achieve these ends in terms of businesses in the total organization portfolio. But the same basic issues prevalent in any strategic situation must be addressed:

1. Where are we now?
2. Where do we want to be?
3. How do we get there?

Figure 5.2
Objective Determination and Master Strategy Formulation

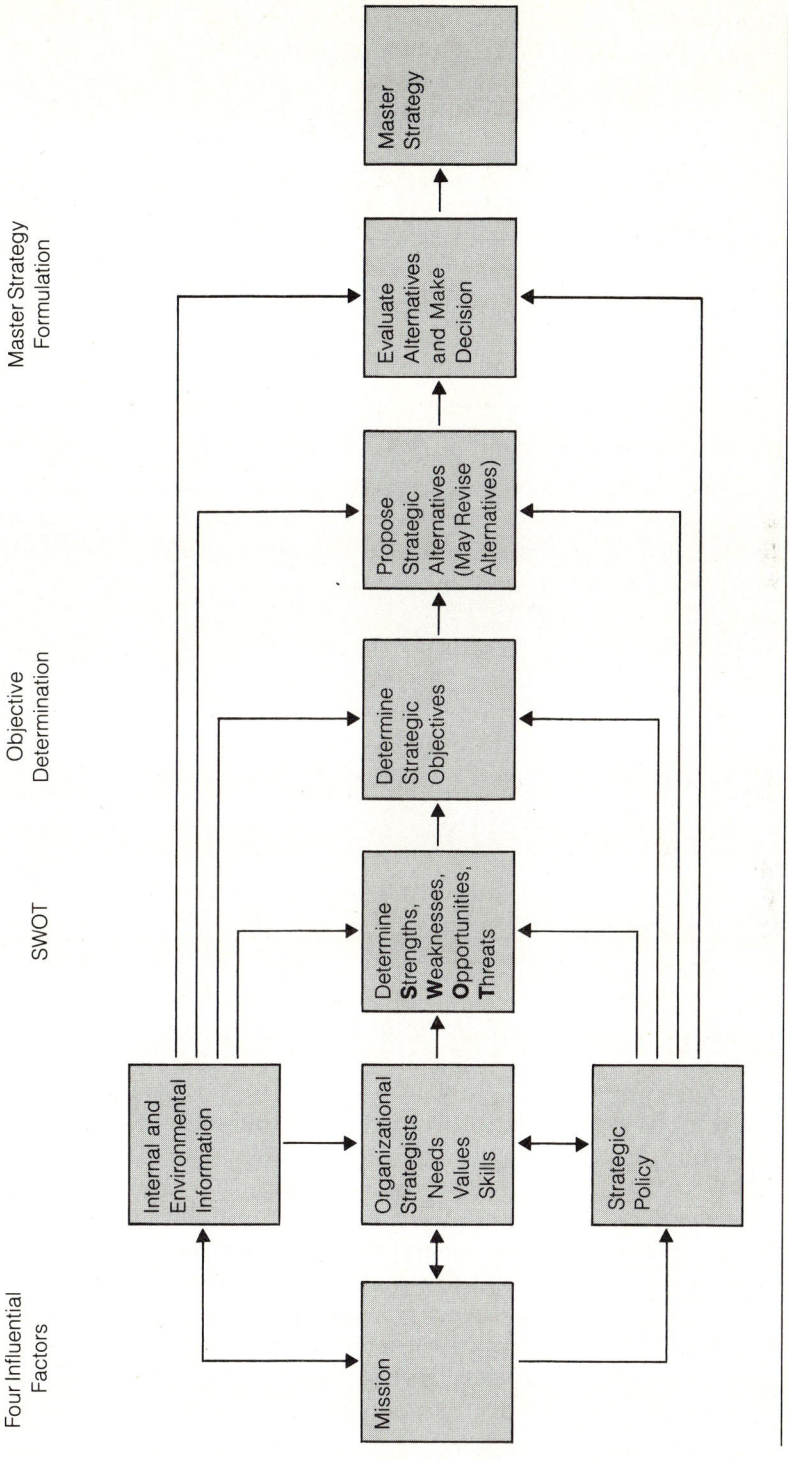

**Figure 5.3
Relationships among Strategies in Multiple-SBU Firms**

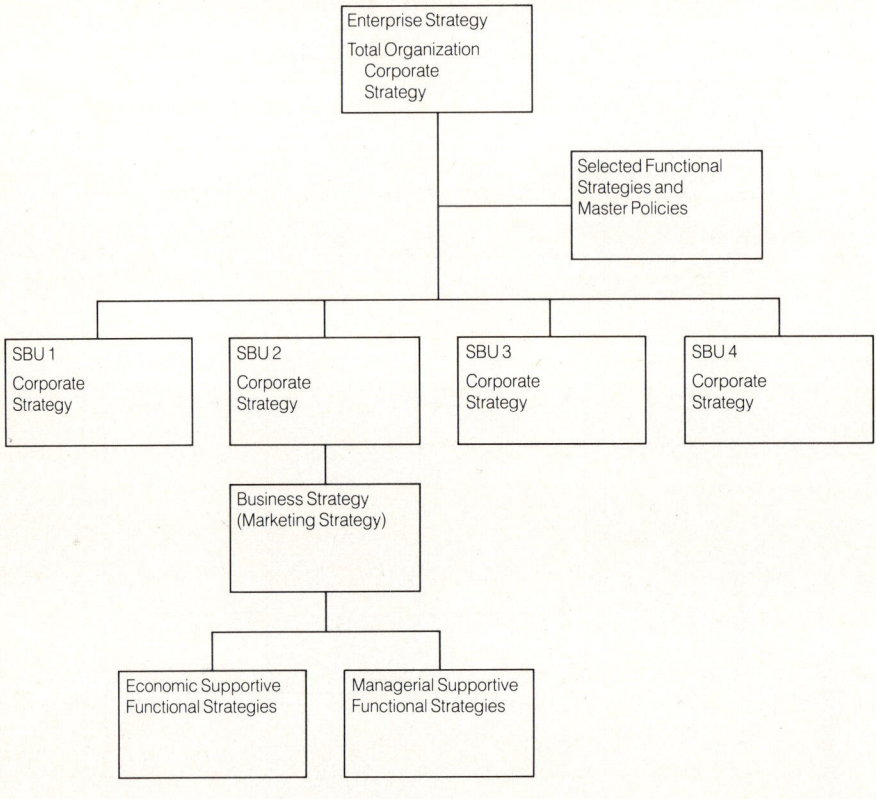

Portfolio Management Techniques

The portfolio matrix is the current principal portfolio technique used by multiple-SBU firms. There are several major types of portfolio matrices, but the most important of these include: the Boston Consulting Group (BCG) business portfolio matrix (Figure 5.4), the General Electric business screen (Figures 5.5 and 5.6), and the product/market/industry evolution portfolio matrix (Figure 5.7). Their applicability depends on the circumstances in which they are to be used.[1] Charles Hofer and Dan Schendel recommend that strategists use a two-stage process. The BCG matrix is used in the first stage because it is relatively simple to construct and its data requirements are low. Once this initial investigation has been completed, a GE-type matrix

---

[1] Y. Wind and V. Mahajan, "Designing Product and Business Portfolios," *Harvard Business Review*, January/February 1981, pp. 155–65; M. B. Coate, "Pitfalls in Portfolio Planning," *Long Range Planning*, June 1983, pp. 47–56.

Figure 5.4
The BCG Business Matrix

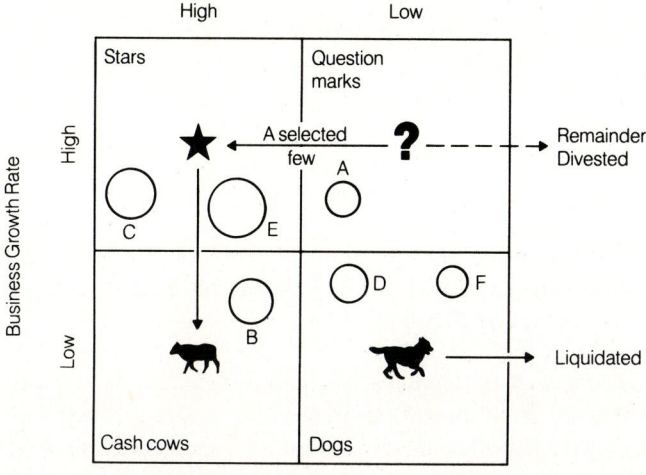

Source: Adapted from Barry Hedley, "Strategy and the 'Business Portfolio,'" *Long Range Planning*, February 1977, p. 10. Reprinted by permission of Pergamon Press Ltd., Oxford, England.

should be used where the products and market segments involved are diverse, and the product/market/industry evolution matrix should be used where the products and market segments involved are limited in type.[2]

Using any of the strategic matrices involves plotting two factors against one another on a grid in order to arrive at some appropriate strategy.

Merger fever is taking on epidemic proportions in board rooms of corporate giants. The trend is changing the face of American business, jolting stock markets and evoking howls in Congress. —U.S. News & World Report, *April 6, 1981*

The BCG Business Matrix

The BCG matrix is shown in Figure 5.4. To use it, the strategist plots the business's relative competitive position (horizontal axis) as expressed by relative market share against the business's growth rate (vertical axis), the industry growth rate for the business in question. The company is represented as a circle on the matrix, and the size of a circle represents that business's size (usually in terms of sales) relative to the sizes of other businesses in the portfolio. The matrix is subsequently divided into four cells according to the relative desirability of four combinations of competi-

[2]C. W. Hofer and D. Schendel, *Strategy Formulation: Analytical Concepts* (St. Paul, Minn.: West, 1978), Chapters 2–4.

tive position and growth, which are symbolized by stars, question marks, cash cows, and dogs. Once the firm is positioned in the matrix, the strategic actions that should be employed can be identified. The basic assumptions underlying this matrix are that market share in growth markets leads to profitability, but that in slow-growing markets, obtaining market share takes too much cash. Thus, firms in slow-growing markets should either be invested in or be milked of cash and divested.

Stars represent the best profit and growth potentials. These businesses show rapid growth and are self-sustaining with respect to cash flow. The company that owns such a business should continue full steam ahead. Acquiring such businesses—at the right price—is also vital.

Question marks usually have the poorest cash flows. They require large amounts of cash because they are growing; however, they are not self-sustaining because their market share is low. As their title indicates, their progress must be monitored closely. The organization that owns the business naturally hopes it will grow into a star; but if it does not, it should be divested. If a firm believes a business it does not already own may grow into a star, acquisition at the right price is desirable.

Cash cows have low growth and high market share. They also have large cash flows, because their market shares are high. They require little investment. Thus they can be "milked" of their cash to support other businesses, especially new enterprises—for example, question marks. If market share declines and cash flow consequently subsides, they may be divested. Or the firm may choose to invest in them once again. But the firm must be careful lest they become dogs. Seldom do cash cows become available for acquisition; however, if the opportunity for acquisition at a good price presents itself, it should be taken advantage of.

Dogs are not desirable investments. They require large cash flows but have poor competitive positions and are therefore either unprofitable or, at best, have low profitability. The owning firm should divest. Dogs are, obviously, not suitable targets for acquisition.[3]

The BCG matrix was an important development in multiple-SBU strategic planning because it determined three key factors in strategic success for such organizations—cash flow, market share, and industry growth. However, like most single management systems, the matrix oversimplifies many of the critical factors involved. For example, high and low positions on the two axes are simplistic. And, the dimensions of growth rate and market share are only one aspect of industry attractiveness and competitive position, respectively.[4] The GE business screen forces strategists to consider more of these variables.

The GE Business Screen

Most of the weaknesses inherent in the BCG matrix are eliminated in the General Electric business screen (Figures 5.5 and 5.6). The GE matrix employs composite measures of both business strength and industry attractiveness. These composites

---

[3] B. Hedley, "Strategy and the 'Business Portfolio,'" *Long Range Planning*, February 1977, pp. 9–15.
[4] C. W. Hofer and D. Schendel, *Strategy Formulation: Analytical Concepts* (St. Paul, Minn.: West, 1978), pp. 31–32.

Figure 5.5
General Electric's "Stoplight Strategy" for Planning

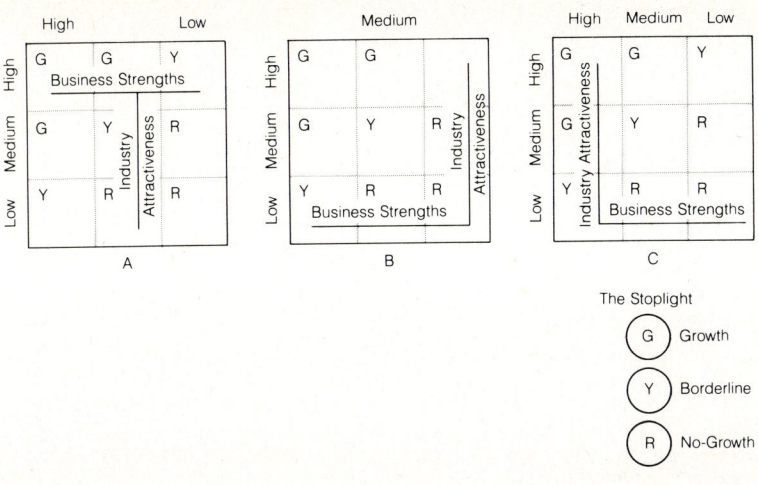

Figure 5.6
Alternative Related Strategies for GE Business Screen

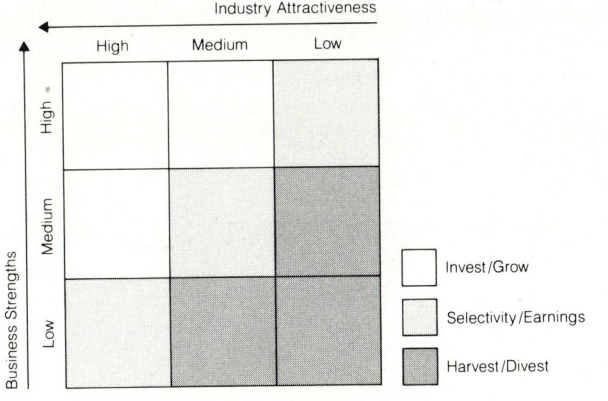

are essential additions. They allow nine possible positions or types of firms, with advisable strategies, to be identified, instead of four. Information Capsule 5.1 briefly summarizes the important points of the GE business screen.

Information Capsule 5.1
The GE Stoplight Portfolio Matrix

The General Electric Company has pioneered the development of an advanced portfolio matrix to determine which SBUs or major products it wishes to retain in its portfolio, which it wishes to delete, and how it wants to treat those that it retains. With minor adjustments in the criteria employed, this matrix can also be used to evaluate potential acquisitions, mergers, or new product developments. The GE Strategic Business Planning Grid, or "stoplight strategy" as it is known, employs the use of different colored cells in a nine-cell matrix to indicate which strategies it should follow for various businesses. SBUs or products are located on the grid based on an evaluation of the attractiveness of the industry in which these are found and upon GE's strengths in that business. Both industry attractiveness and GE business strength are rated as either high, medium, or low. The term "stoplight strategy" is applied to this matrix because of the green, yellow, and red color coding employed to identify various classifications of businesses or products according to their desirability. Those firms which turn up in the green (G), are to be invested in and will employ growth strategies. Those SBUs which turn up in the red (R) will no longer be invested in and may become cash cows and/or divested. Those which end up in the yellow (Y) are monitored for progress, for change in either industry attractiveness or business strengths. Large SBUs may have products that fall into each of these three categories.

In Figure 5.5, stoplight grid A indicates that the subject organization has medium business strengths but high industry attractiveness. Since the evaluations intersect in a green box, the business would receive an invest and grow strategy treatment. Stoplight matrix B portrays a business in which the business strength is low and the industry attractiveness is low. As a result, the business is in a red zone, and will be harvested and ultimately divested, with reduced or no investment occurring, and with cash extraction occurring where possible before divestment. Stoplight grid C characterizes a firm with low business strengths but high industry attractiveness. As a result, the firm lands in a yellow cell of the matrix and will thus be monitored for progress. Those firms that prove worthwhile from a potential earnings standpoint, will be selected for invest and grow strategies. Those that do not will be divested.

One intriguing point about the grid is that it allows the firm to compare apples and oranges using the same system. With some 50 SBUs, GE needs just such an ability. Perhaps more importantly, the grid allows GE to evaluate factors such as social responsibility and employee loyalty as well as such quantitative factors as return on investment, market share, and cash flow. Each SBU or major product is evaluated during the annual planning review. A consensus is almost always reached by those present. Final strategic decisions are made by the corporate policy committee which consists of several members of top management.

In using the business screen, GE's top management might assign values to these strategic factors:

For business strengths/competitive position:	For industry attractiveness:
Size	Size
Growth	Market growth, pricing
Share	Market diversity
Position	Competitive structure
Profitability	Industry profitability
Margins	Technical role
Technology position	Social factors
Image	Environmental factors
Pollution	Legal factors
People	Human factors

Note that the factors considered include not only competitive and supportive factors, such as sales, profit, and loss, but also factors more difficult to quantify, such as technology needs, social responsibility, and employee needs.

Like the BCG matrix, the screen is used primarily to manage the current or prospective businesses of the organization, especially in balancing the investment portfolio. GE uses the grid to determine the type of strategy it should employ based on the assessment of factors illustrated in Figure 5.5. Figure 5.6 shows the alternative related strategies. For current or potential businesses judged to be in the green sectors of the matrix, a growth strategy will be followed. For those positioned in the yellow sectors of the matrix, a selective strategy based on earnings will be pursued. For those in the red sectors, a harvest/divest strategy will be employed. The matrix can be used to reevaluate investments as the environment changes; the strategists simply change the criteria (the factors considered) and the relative weights given to the criteria.

The matrix technique is commonly used by large organizations for business project and product selection, although the color coding is perhaps unique to GE. For example, the PIMS (Profit Input of Market Strategy) Project organizations, some fifty of them, employ this type of matrix for market share analysis and project selection. McKinsey & Co. employs a similar nine-cell "business assessment array" matrix in its strategic consulting practice.

One of the major criticisms of the nine-cell matrices is that they do not provide sufficient information on market growth. The following matrix attempts to overcome this deficiency.

The Product/Market/Industry Evolution Matrix

As you can see in Figure 5.7, using a product/market/industry matrix involves plotting the firm's competitive position against the stage of product/market evolution in the product or industry life cycle. Various businesses are shown as pie slices (market share) of total industry (circles). The size of the circles indicates the relative size

Figure 5.7
A Product/Market/Industry Evolution Portfolio Matrix

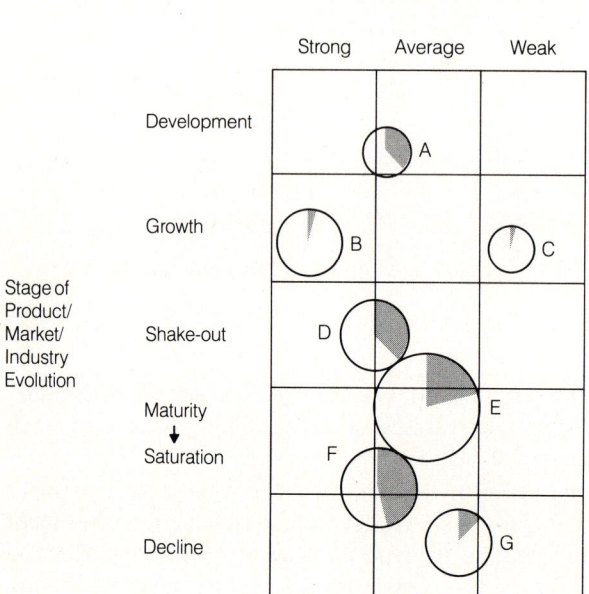

of the industries.[5] It is generally believed that conglomerate organizations should seek to have businesses in all stages of respective industry/product life cycles, with the largest and most profitable firms being in the maturity stage or the late growth stage. This is, of course, similar to the classic marketing strategy of having products in various stages of the product life cycle within the same industry. Arthur D. Little, Inc., has devised a modification of the product/market/industry evolution matrix which incorporates recommended strategies. This modification is shown in Figure 5.8. (Note that the axes have been rotated in their version.) Their strategies are essentially the same as those employed in the GE Business Screen or the McKinsey nine-cell business assessment array.

It is probably best to use all three of the matrices discussed above in the assessment process. Similar information can be used for all three; and the sophistication of the results is greatly enhanced when all three are used. However, while the underlying concepts of the matrices appear to allow for substantial precision, the actual mechanics of their use often involves a considerable amount of subjective estimation, as the following description of the assessment process reveals.

---

[5]C. W. Hofer, "Conceptual Constructs for Formulating Corporate and Business Strategies," #9–378–754 (Boston: Intercollegiate Case Clearing House), 1977.

Figure 5.8
The ADL Portfolio Planning Matrix

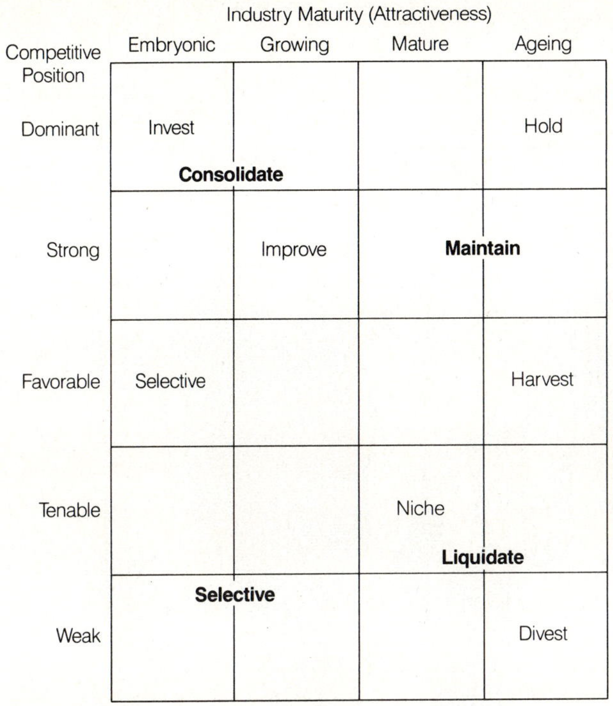

Competitive Position	Industry Maturity (Attractiveness)			
	Embryonic	Growing	Mature	Ageing
Dominant	Invest	**Consolidate**		Hold
Strong		Improve	**Maintain**	
Favorable	Selective			Harvest
Tenable			Niche	**Liquidate**
Weak	**Selective**			Divest

The Assessment Process

Like business strategy and corporate strategy for single-business organizations, the corporate strategy for multiple-SBU firms focuses on evaluating SWOT. Assessing competitive position (what GE refers to as business strengths) requires a thorough analysis of business strengths and weaknesses. Assessing industry attractiveness requires a thorough analysis of opportunities and threats. The matrices merely combine these factors in an organized fashion. Using the GE business screen as an example, we will now examine how a business's position on the matrices is determined. Note how both "where we are" and "where we want to be" are addressed in the information provided by the matrix.

The process begins with some statement of criteria for both business strengths (competitive position) and industry attractiveness. Developing these criteria is, of course, a complex and highly subjective process, although research, such as the PIMS project mentioned in Chapter 4, and experience can help. The information sources cited at the end of Chapter 2 should be used in this process.

"I don't know what's wrong with me, but I have this uncontrollable desire to acquire National Airlines!"

Source: Drawing by Joseph Farris: © 1979 *The New Yorker Magazine*, Inc.

As noted earlier, criteria often evaluated for business strengths include size, growth, share, position, profitability, margins, technology position, image, pollution, and people. The criteria believed to determine success vary from industry to industry; but as we saw in the PIMS results, some common criteria, such as market share, seem to be determinants of success in almost all businesses. Industry attractiveness criteria might include size, market growth and pricing, market diversity, competitive structure, industry profitability, technical role, social factors, environmental factors, legal factors, and human factors. The company using these criteria has determined that any business it chooses to enter must score well on them. These criteria also vary from company to company, depending on numerous variables—risk propensity, top management values, and so forth.

The actual mathematical calculations involved in the assessment process vary. Firms typically create checklists of the above factors and then note each of the factors according to some scale for measuring excellence. Firms often assign nonparametric values—checks, pluses, minuses, and zeroes—as a scale description. For example, a firm might assign strong plus, plus, neutral, minus, and strong minus to each line item in a strategic factors checklist: strengths and weaknesses, threats and opportunities. Or ordinal values such as +2, +1, 0, −1, −2 might be assigned. Various techniques are employed to interpret the meanings of these checklists. Simple scanning or mathematical summation of assigned values is normally employed. Some descriptive or mathematical cut-off point is usually established which will indicate the desirability of a strategic action, for example, investment. This is an extremely complex process and one which requires careful consideration. Frequently no value is assigned. Executives may simply vote based on their perceptions of each item's worth. Following is an example of how the mathematical computation process typically occurs.

Assessing Industry Attractiveness

According to Hofer and Schendel, there are four steps in assessing industry attractiveness once the attractiveness criteria have been chosen:[6]

1. The firm attaches priorities to the criteria factors in the form of weights.
2. Each industry in which the firm currently competes or might compete is rated according to these factors, typically on some scale—say, a scale of 1 to 5.
3. A weighted score is calculated for each industry.
4. The weighted scores are evaluated against some experience-based standard, against other industries, or both.

Table 5.1 illustrates this process.

The weights assigned to industry attractiveness criteria directly reflect how important top management perceives each to be in accomplishing objectives. The sum of all weights must add to 1. Because of the possible differences among executives in how they perceive the importance of these criteria, several iterations of assigning weights may be necessary before the 1 is reached. Often, using GO or NO GO, instead of using a weight, may suffice. For example, where negative social factors exist, the firm may decide on a NO GO position regardless of other factors.

Rating individual industries simply involves evaluating how well that industry is doing. Other industries should be kept in mind as this process occurs, as should the overall state of the economy. Once a weighted score is obtained, then the firm may be plotted on the matrix. The choice of a scale is important to where a firm ends up on the matrix; this issue will be discussed shortly.

[6] Hofer and Schendel, *Strategy Formulation*, pp. 72–75.

Table 5.1
An Industry Attractiveness Assessment Matrix

Attractiveness Criteria	Weight[a]	Rating[b]	Weighted Score
Size	.15	4	.60
Growth	.12	3	.36
Pricing	.05	3	.15
Market diversity	.05	2	.10
Competitive structure	.05	3	.15
Industry profitability	.20	3	.60
Technical role	.05	4	.20
Inflation vulnerability	.05	2	.10
Cyclicality	.05	2	.10
Customer financials	.10	5	.50
Energy impact	.08	4	.32
Social	GO	4	—
Environmental	GO	4	—
Legal	GO	4	—
Human	.05	4	.20
	1.00		3.38

[a] Some criteria may be of a GO/NO GO type. For example, many *Fortune 500* firms probably would decide not to invest in industries that are viewed negatively by our society, such as gambling, even if it were both legal and very profitable to do so.

[b] 1: very unattractive.
5: high attractive.

Reproduced by permission from *Strategy Formulation: Analytical Concepts* by Charles W. Hofer and Dan Schendel. Copyright © 1978 by West Publishing Company. All rights reserved.

Assessing Competitive Position

Like assessing industry attractiveness, assessing competitive position, according to Hofer and Schendel, involves identifying success criteria and then following a four-step process:[7]

1. For each industry, the firm must weight the relative importance of the various success factors to the specific industry in question.
2. For each of its businesses, the firm must rate the competitive position of that business in that industry for each factor.
3. A weighted average must be computed.
4. Comparisons with standards and other businesses must be made.

Table 5.2 illustrates the steps in this process.

Key success factors have two main characteristics: management can influence them; and changes in them could, at least theoretically, have a significant impact on

[7] Ibid., pp. 75–79.

Table 5.2
A Competitive Position Assessment Matrix

Key Success Factors	Weight	Rating[b]	Weighted Score
Market share	.10	5	.50
SBU growth rate	X[a]	3	—
Breadth of product line	.05	4	.20
Sales distribution effectiveness	.20	4	.80
Proprietary and key account advantages	X	3	—
Price competitiveness	X	4	—
Advertising and promotion effectiveness	.05	4	.20
Facilities location and newness	.05	5	.25
Capacity and productivity	X	3	—
Experience curve effects	.15	4	.60
Raw materials cost	.05	4	.20
Value added	X	4	—
Relative product quality	.15	4	.60
R and D advantages/position	.05	4	.20
Cash throw-off	.10	5	.50
Caliber of personnel	X	4	—
General image	.05	5	.25
	1.00		4.30

[a] For any particular industry, there will be some factors that, while important in general, will have little or no effect on the relative competitive position of firms within that industry. It is usually better to drop such factors from the analysis than to assign them very low weights.
[b] 1: very weak competitive position
5: very strong competitive position
Reproduced by permission from *Strategy Formulation: Analytical Concepts* by Charles W. Hofer and Dan Schendel. Copyright © 1978 by West Publishing Company. All rights reserved.

the firm's competitive position. The weighting process may once again involve several iterations before the desired sum of 1 is reached. In highly segmented markets, weights may vary significantly among market segments.

Placing the SBU on the Matrix

Once a total weighted score for both competitive position (business strengths) and industry attractiveness have been calculated, the location of these numbers on the matrix must be plotted. A key question involves what the scales of the two axes should be. Firms set these scales based on experience. The author has found that few firms ever score below 1.5 or above 4.5 on either axis; so setting a low point of 1.5 and a high point of 4.5 for each axis seems reasonable. Exceptions can be placed on the axis itself. This scaling yields a 1-by-1 interval per square on the matrix. Utilizing this method, Figure 5.9 portrays the firm (A) characterized in Tables 5.1 and 5.2 and several other firms.

Figure 5.9
Placing the SBU on the Matrix (Using the GE Business Screen)

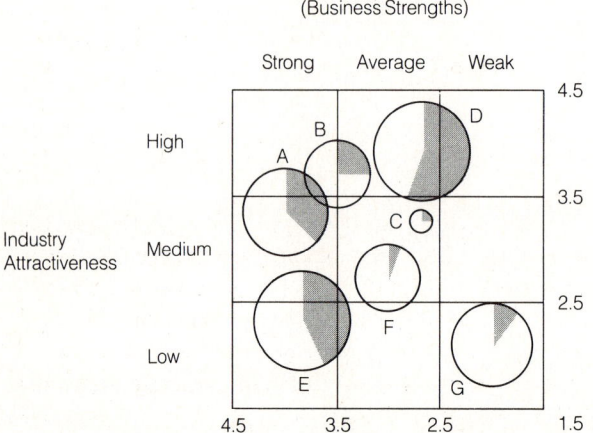

Gap Analysis

Often, a gap exists between SBU performance and corporate objectives. Gap analysis involves determining the contribution which current businesses are making or can make to present and future organizational strategic objectives. The various business matrices are good indicators of what is occurring and what may be expected to occur in the way of contribution. Contingency strategies recommended for each business are also portrayed by the matrices.

The most desirable portfolio of businesses obviously contains no money-losers. Certainly, having no more than one or two SBUs awaiting divestment is advisable. The organization's largest and most profitable businesses should be growing in sales or profit areas. All this portrays an ideal but infrequently obtainable profile. It is also possible that a firm may prefer a different type of portfolio—for example, one that focuses on long-term growth at the expense of current profit.

If current businesses are not contributing sufficiently to organizational objectives or are expected not to contribute in the future, then six possibilities for fundamental action exist, as identified by Hofer and Schendel:[8]

1. Change the investment strategies of some or all of the SBUs.
   Change the level of resources allocated to an SBU.
2. Change the business strategies of one or more SBUs.
3. Add some new SBUs to the corporate portfolio.
4. Delete some existing SBUs from the corporate portfolio.

[8] Ibid., Chapter 7.

5. Change the way the organization relates to external environmental stakeholders —for example, suppliers, consumers, government, and so on. This involves political strategies.
6. Change strategic objectives.

Most businesses overpay significantly for their acquisitions, and then they have the nerve to wonder why ROI declines. —James M. Higgins

Closing the Gap

The choice of which of these six actions to take is not based strictly on the portfolio matrix results. The portfolio is part of a broader group of considerations, including the mix of businesses in the current portfolio; recent portfolio actions; the ability to integrate new firms into the portfolio; cash position; major potential environmental threats and opportunities; current resource allocation policies; the value orientations of top management, especially their risk propensities; corporate objectives; and the existing strategies of the SBUs themselves.

In selecting the businesses in which the organization will engage, strategists look for synergy and balance among existing and future businesses. Synergy, you may recall, is the degree to which SBUs reinforce each other in pursuit of objectives. The strategist may consider whether the organizations' managerial skills are transferable; whether the firms are technologically similar; whether the businesses have some common theme, such as markets; whether compatability in distribution exists; and so forth. Information Capsule 5.2 reveals some of the intricacies involved in achieving synergy.

Balance refers to the degree to which business cash flows support one another. For example, firms in growth markets usually require more cash investment than do firms in older, more mature industries. The profits from the latter can be used to support the former. Similarly, a firm with strong summer revenues, such as a soft-drink firm, can be balanced against a firm with stronger winter revenues, such as a restaurant chain, to provide the total corporation with strong year-round cash flows.

Where necessary, prospective businesses can be plotted on matrices to help identify suitable investments. Of special concern are forecasted major environmental changes, both competitive and noncompetitive. Projected political events; expected changes in laws, forecasted major economic factors (GNP, interest rates, wages, controls, and so forth); and societal response to particular investments (for example, in chemicals or energy) must all be monitored for their potential impacts on the desirability of certain businesses as members of the portfolio. Table 5.3 lists some of the major external factors which should be considered.

Pitfalls in Portfolio Utilization

In the mid 1970s through 1981, portfolio analysis was a major new concept in strategic planning. It became very popular quite rapidly as major U.S. industries pursued avid programs of merger and acquisition, to which the portfolio techniques

Information Capsule 5.2
The Elusive Synergy

On a sunny Thursday morning last September, L. J. Sevin, the chairman of a thriving Texas-based semiconductor company called Mostek, climbed into the cabin of a Sabreliner jet parked on the tarmac at an airport near Dallas. He was there for a clandestine meeting with a stranger named Peter Scott, an executive vice president of United Technologies. For the next hour, Scott described the wonderful things that would happen if United acquired Mostek. Sevin, who was trying to fend off a takeover bid by Gould Inc., listened attentively, but told Scott he wasn't ready to sell to anybody yet. With that, Sevin climbed out and Scott jetted 1,500 miles back to United's Hartford, Connecticut, headquarters.

Apart from the fact that Scott flew all the way to Texas, United's "we're here if you want help" offer seemed almost half-hearted. And the possible purchase of Mostek certainly looked like small change in the affairs of United; Mostek's 1979 sales of $200 million or so would add only 2% to United's $10.4 billion in revenues. But Scott's mission was extremely important to Harry Gray, United's notoriously acquisitive chief executive. In many ways Gray coveted Mostek more than the much larger acquisitions he had made in the eight-year process of reshaping United Aircraft, a stagnating $2-billion jet-engine company, into United Technologies, an aggressive, rapidly expanding conglomerate.

The Knight and the Linchpin

Gray had wanted a semiconductor company since he arrived at United in 1971. But success in semiconductors depends largely on the brilliance of the manager-scientists who run most of the companies, and a hostile acquirer risks driving them away. Gray refused to go after a semiconductor company unless he could do so in the role of white knight. Gould's takeover attempt gave Gray his opening. Three weeks later, after four more meetings between Scott and Sevin, Mostek was his.

Mostek is the linchpin in the strategy behind the seemingly unrelated takeovers that preceded it. Gray has repeatedly said that he isn't building a garden-variety conglomerate—that the companies he has bought have a common ability to benefit from the enormous amount of research United must perform for its aerospace business. But few outsiders saw the link between United Aircraft's jet engines and, say, Otis elevators.

With Mostek, it suddenly became clear that the disparate acquisitions did share an important common element. Gray acquired companies that all stand to profit from the state-of-the-art expertise in electronics and controls that United's Hamilton Standard division has developed in its aerospace control-systems business. In addition to Otis, Gray's acquisitions include Carrier (air conditioning), Essex International (wire and cable, controls and switches for cars and appliances), and Ambac Industries (diesel fuel injectors, small electric motors, and scientific and medical instruments).

Source: Excerpted from A. F. Ehrbar, "United Technologies' Master Plan," *Fortune*, September 22, 1980, p. 97.
© 1980 Time Inc. All rights reserved.

Table 5.3
Some Strategically Significant Broad Environmental Variables

Economic Conditions	Demographic Trends	Technological Changes	Social and Cultural Trends	Political and Legal Factors
GNP trends	Growth rate of population	Total federal spending for R&D	Lifestyle changes	Antitrust regulations
Interest rates	Age distribution of population	Total industry spending for R&D	Career expectations	Environmental protection laws
Money supply	Regional shifts in population	Focus of technological effort	Consumer activism	Tax laws
Inflation rates	Life expectancies	Patent protection	Rate of family formation	Special incentives
Unemployment levels	Birth rates			Foreign trade regulations
Wage/price controls				Attitudes toward foreign companies
Devaluation/revaluation				
Energy availability				

Reproduced by permission from *Strategy Formulation: Analytical Concepts* by Charles W. Hofer and Dan Schendel. Copyright © 1978 by West Publishing Company. All rights reserved.

were highly suited. However, as experience with these techniques progressed, certain doubts about them began to arise. Malcolm B. Coate has proposed that several major pitfalls exist in the portfolio approach. He suggests the following concerns:

1. They are based on certain assumptions that must be examined in each particular situation:
   a. Each firm is divisible into independent business units. He questions the ease of defining these in the real world.
   b. The dominant firm earns the highest profits in each market. He suggests this is not necessarily true. (Other research cited elsewhere in this book suggests that his objection is correct.)
   c. Industries are more or less attractive based on their life cycle. This tends to ignore differences in capital intensities between industries.
   d. Investment funds are limited, and these must be allocated among all businesses in the organization. This tends to ignore the long-term perspective, where funds will not be limited as they are in the short run.
2. In addition to pitfalls with assumptions, Coate observes that portfolio models tend to overlook additional considerations that should be incorporated in an "optimal investment planning model":
   a. The funds invested in various SBUs should be allocated in such a way as to equate marginal rates of return.
   b. It is possible that where tacit collusion exists, firms would need to alter strategies recommended by these techniques and reduce investment in order to take advantage of market power.
   c. The liquidation value of the SBU is a better measure of its value than the

more commonly used cost basis. In that light, liquidation becomes a much more acceptable strategy.

d. Risk is given very little quantitative attention in portfolio models.

Coate then proceeds to identify the pitfalls which exist in the application of a portfolio model:

1. The actual process of business unit definition is quite complex, and something more akin to an art than a science.
2. Actually using the matrix involves considerably more time and attention than the conceptual perspective would allow. A large number of value judgments must be made about some very tenuous numbers. Measurements are often vague. Detailed information on each unit is vital to the success of the portfolio approach.
3. There is a question related to the validity of the strategies which are recommended by the model. Since some assumptions of the model noted earlier may not be true, there can be serious problems of pursuing these strategies. The availability of resources—financial, human, and others—always affects the ability of any business to implement strategy.[9]

Others have also pointed to the problems associated with using portfolio techniques. Philippe Haspeslagh surveyed the *Fortune* 1000. Among the 345 respondents, he found a wide variance in the degree to which these approaches were utilized, the rate of successful utilization, and the degree to which the individual SBUs involved adhered to recommended strategies. He indicates that these approaches were perceived by respondents to be useful in these primary ways: by generating better strategies through a more selective resource allocation process, and by adding a more differentiated approach to managing specific SBUs. He points out, however, that there are "complex realities" that face the user of these strategies when it comes time to implement them. For example, problems were reported involving the defining of a business. A large conglomerate might technically have 100 to 500 "businesses," but no one could comprehend the issues involved with that many simultaneously, so SBUs are typically grouped in similar categories for analysis purposes. This then causes all sorts of difficulties in terms of implementing strategies due to the differences among businesses within each group. Another problem with resource allocation is the power associated with these resources. He implies that power distribution or redistribution is going to be accompanied by behavioral adjustment. (I suspect resistance is what is most frequent.) He also found that while in theory, portfolio techniques should be used to allocate all resources, most firms focused singly on capital investment.[10]

While Haspeslagh did not discuss in depth additional implementation problems related to such factors as motivation, budgets, leadership, communication, and so forth, Walter Kiechel III, in an article in *Fortune*, has indicated just how critical

---

[9] M. B. Coate, "Pitfalls in Portfolio Planning," *Long Range Planning*, June 1983, pp. 47–56.

[10] P. Haspeslagh, "A Survey of U.S. Companies Shows How Effective Portfolio Planning Could Be But Often Isn't," *Harvard Business Review*, January/February 1982, pp. 58–73.

these aspects of implementation can be. This author, as have others, pointed to the fact that strategic planning can carry the organization only so far. The strategies deriving from the strategic management process have to be implemented.[11] This means that proper structures must exist, that programs and budgets must be derived in support, that motivation, leadership, and communication be properly conducted, that operational planning systems be effective, and that the culture must be receptive. There are, in short, many ifs in the process. These difficulties with implementation will have more meaning as you read Chapter 7. Similarly, Chapter 6 indicates the numerous types of behavioral problems associated with all stages of strategy: formulation, implementation, and control. You have already learned in this chapter that much of what transpires involves imprecision.

Multiple Point Competition

For a very few, large, select conglomerates, the central strategic question is how to compete with the other few, large, select conglomerates. This issue is raised in this text primarily to alert you to its existence. There are *very few* strategists involved in such concerns, but pragmatically, their endeavors do control a relatively signficant number of corporate resources. Hofer and Schendel, and Karnani and Wernerfelt, among others, have provided their guidance to those involved in such competition.[12] Both sets of these authors offer suggested strategies for responding to competitors or for initiating competition.

Difference in Perspective: Divisional versus Corporate Strategists

In the large business organization with numerous businesses (SBUs) or products, divisions are usually established based on these businesses or products. Normally, these divisions develop their own objectives and plans, choosing among new products, new marketing strategies, and new research and development projects as points of investment. All are subject, however, to the approval of top corporate management. To the division, these plans constitute strategy, but to the corporation, they are forms of intermediate planning. Strategic perspective at the division level differs significantly from that at the corporate level. The most obvious difference is that the division must respond to corporate objectives and policies, while the corporate top management establishes those objectives and policies. Furthermore, corporate level strategy emphasizes portfolio techniques while division level strategies emphasize the business strategy of marketing.

Because of this problem, the role of the division manager usually involves great responsibility with less than commensurate authority. The divisional general mana-

---

[11] W. Kiechel III, "Corporate Strategists Under Fire," *Fortune*, Dec. 27, 1982, pp. 35–39.

[12] C. W. Hofer and D. Schendel, *Strategy Formulation: Analytical Concepts* (St. Paul, Minn.: West, 1978), Chapter 7; A. Karnani and B. Wernerfelt, "Multiple Point Competition," *Proceedings: Academy of Management*, August 1983, pp. 27–31.

ger must translate objectives into action and action into measurement. He or she must satisfy superiors; compete and cooperate with peers; and lead subordinates—usually organization function managers, product managers, or geographic area managers. The division manager operates in a highly political environment. He or she is, in fact, a person in the middle. The division manager's position is most often filled by a former functional specialist. The transition to generalist is often too great, the viewpoint too different, for many who have been appointed to this position. The corporate general manager, in contrast to the division manager, acts primarily as a superior and as an objective and policy setter, a resource allocator.

Peter Lorange suggests that, as a result of the lack of appreciation of the differences in these perspectives, the resulting divisional strategies are perhaps too conservative given the total corporate investment portfolio. He believes that for a very large organization, a risky venture could be "averaged out." Often, divisional managers believe they cannot accept a product with high risk, because their performance is measured on return and their compensation is based on performance. The

Figure 5.10
Matrix for Determination and Evaluation of Business Line Product Strategy

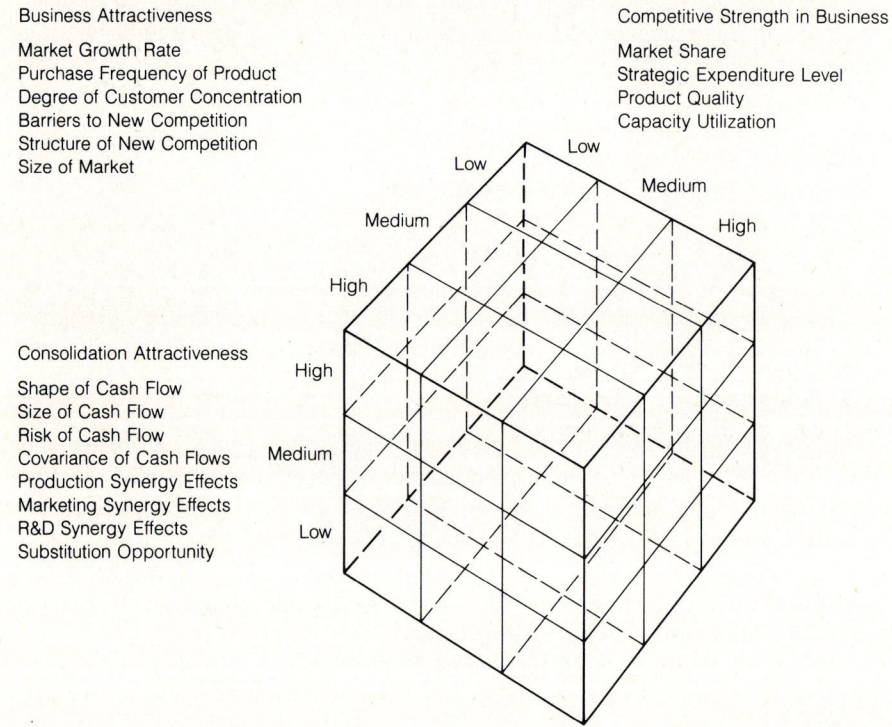

Business Attractiveness

Market Growth Rate
Purchase Frequency of Product
Degree of Customer Concentration
Barriers to New Competition
Structure of New Competition
Size of Market

Competitive Strength in Business

Market Share
Strategic Expenditure Level
Product Quality
Capacity Utilization

Consolidation Attractiveness

Shape of Cash Flow
Size of Cash Flow
Risk of Cash Flow
Covariance of Cash Flows
Production Synergy Effects
Marketing Synergy Effects
R&D Synergy Effects
Substitution Opportunity

Source: Reprinted from "Divisional Planning: Setting Effective Direction," by Peter Lorange, *Sloan Management Review*, Vol. 17, No. 1, Fall 1975, p. 87. Reprinted by permission of the publisher. Copyright © 1975 by the *Sloan Management Review* Association. All rights reserved.

Table 5.4
GE Criteria for Choice of Business Managers

Investment Category	Manager's Key Strengths
Invest/grow	Entrepreneur/leader
Selectivity/earnings	Sophisticated/critical
Harvest/divest	Solid/experienced

Source: Michael G. Allen, Vice-President, General Electric Co., "Strategic Problems Facing Today's Corporate Planner" (Paper presented to the Academy of Management, Kansas City, August 1976). Reprinted by permission of General Electric Company.

Figure 5.11
Bonus Matched to Business

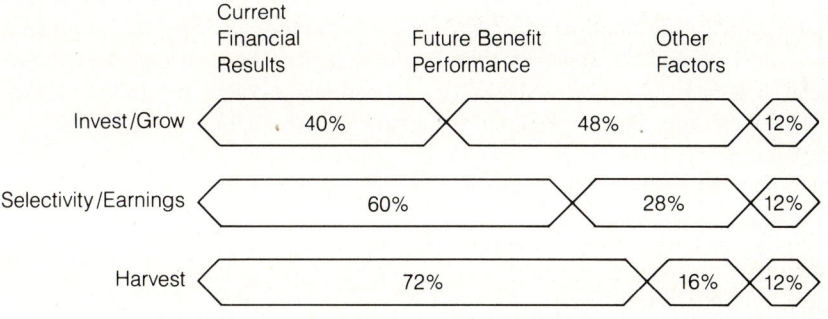

Source: Michael G. Allen, Vice-President, General Electric Co., "Strategic Problems Facing Today's Corporate Planner" (Paper presented to the Academy of Management, Kansas City, August 1976). Reprinted by permission of General Electric Company.

result is often the forfeit of considerable gain. Lorange has proposed that the business strategy (industry attractiveness/competitive strength) matrix be made three-dimensional to allow firms to account for the attractiveness of investment opportunities on a consolidated corporate basis. Figure 5.10 portrays this three-dimensional approach.[13]

The motivational scheme for divisional managers must be designed to incorporate the difficulty of the task and the need for attention to corporate as well as divisional interests. One such motivational scheme is that of General Electric. Both its choice of managers for various businesses (Table 5.4) and the motivational scheme for these managers (Figure 5.11) incorporate key factors related to the type of investment category (strategy). Such approaches are vital if the division level manager is to be of the utmost utility to the corporation. If the division or product manager is not motivated to support corporate efforts, then mission is not likely to be accomplished.

[13] P. Lorange, "Divisional Planning: Setting Effective Direction," *Sloan Management Review*, Fall 1975, pp. 77–91.

Note how GE's approach accounts for the differing environments confronting managers. Too few firms appreciate these differences. Many critics point to the compensation system as a major reason why strategic managers in most companies have a short-term outlook. General Electric has largely overcome that problem with this compensation system.[14]

The Master Strategy for Multinational Multiple-SBU Firms

The master strategy for multinational multiple-SBU firms is conceptually similar to the master strategy for other organizations. It is the specific content of the master strategy, the specific content of the four influential factors, and the specifics of the process that vary. In previous chapters, we noted the differences in mission, objectives, strategists, and, to some degree, information. We continue that discussion in this chapter.

With respect to the utilization of the techniques of matrix and portfolio management, the process for multinational use appears essentially the same as the process outlined in this chapter. However, the specific factors to be considered vary. For example, Derek F. Channon and Michael Jalland suggest that the following are often of critical importance when multinational enterprise is being considered:

Market characteristics.

Macroeconomic factors.

Political factors.

Infrastructure characteristics.

Labor factors.

Financial considerations.

Fiscal considerations.

Table 5.5 presents each of these important factors in more detail for the direct investment alternative.

Channon and Jalland also suggest that, in addition to direct investment, both licensing and joint ventures are sound methods for entering new geographic areas. Licensing, for example, usually requires very little capital investment and fewer parent country managers; is a relatively cheap method of marketing to a given market; involves fewer problems of exchange risk; is the only way to enter certain countries, for example, in eastern Europe; and finally, may be an important component of an overall strategy. Licensing does have its drawbacks: for example, every licensee is a potential competitor; control is more difficult to maintain than over a direct investment operation; the licensee usually comes out better than the licensor with regard to factors such as inflation; and finally, fiscal problems such as taxes or even refusal of the licensee to pay royalties are not uncommon.

[14]M. G. Allen, "Strategic Problems Facing Today's Corporate Planner" (Paper presented to the Academy of Management, Kansas City, August 1976).

Table 5.5
Checklist for Assessing a Nation's Investment Climate

Market Characteristics

Size of market and growth rate.
Key market characteristics.
Industry structure and competitive position.
Product adaptation needs.
Any price controls?
Level and type of price competition.
Channels used, controls and availability.
Media used, costs and availability.
Advertising controls, spending patterns.
Tariff position. Is protection available?

Macroeconomic Factors

Size of GNP and growth rate.
Inflation rate.
Attitude to private enterprise?
Fairness and honesty of administration of accepted standards of morality; corruption present or not?
Fairness and honesty of legal system.
Efficiency and operating speed of bureaucracy.
Details of corporate law affecting the MNC; monopoly control? Restrictions on ownership? Legal obligations? Consumer law? Product liability? Pollution control?

Infrastructure Characteristics

Geographic distribution of industry and population.
Availability, cost, and efficiency of transport systems.
Availability, cost, and efficiency of port facilities.
Availability, cost, and reliability of raw materials.
Availability, cost, and reliability of energy and utilities.
Site location prospects and proximities to raw materials? Markets?
Site costs? Building costs?
Climatic conditions?
Housing, educational, social/cultural facilities?
Ease of foreign trade imports? Exports?

Labor Factors

Availability of managerial, technical, linguistic, and skilled and unskilled production labor.
Labor productivity, historic? Expected?
Educational and skill levels.
Level of unemployment, historic and expected trends.
Degree of union membership.
Balance of payments position, historic? Future?
Stage of economic development.
Income per capita, historic? Future?
Size and demographics of population.
Number of households; percentage home ownership.

Political Factors

Type and stability of government.
Any dangerous internal strife?
Any particular ethnic, social class problems?
Economic ideologies of major political parties.
Historic attitude toward MNCs. Any nationalization? Unfair discrimination?

Table 5.5 continued

Trade union structure and attitudes.
Record of industrial relations.
Labor laws affecting the MNC; trade union participation? Employment protection? Social security payments? Hire and fire regulations? Redundancy costs? Other fringe benefits expected costs?
Wage rates, historic? Trend?
Attitudes to profit sharing?

Financial Considerations

Stage of development of local capital market.
Sources and type of funds available; costs?
Stability of local currency, historic? Future?
Exchange control regulations.
Treatments of leads and lags.
Investment incentive schemes available.
Stability of investment incentives.
Depreciation treatments.
Accounting and financial reporting requirements.
Availability and cost of risk insurance locally? In home country?

Fiscal Considerations

Tax rates (corporate and personal, income capital gains, withholding, excise duties, payroll tax, value added tax rates, other direct and indirect taxes).
Tax treatments on dividends, interest payments, technology, management fees, transfer policies, and other means of extractions.
Tax incentives for investment.
Customs and tax-free zones.
Joint tax treaties.
Treatment of losses.
Import-export tax drawbacks.
Attitudes to avoidance? Evasion?

Source: D. F. Channon with M. Jalland, *Multinational Strategic Planning* (New York: AMACOM, 1978), pp. 193, 194.

Joint ventures, too, offer both positive and negative features. On the positive side, the smaller firm gains a distinct advantage in terms of obtaining resources. The joint venture helps reduce host country prejudice against the parent country national. Joint ventures offer a chance to work with the host country government, which is absolutely essential to any type of entry in many countries. Large projects especially may require the pooling of resources, since many problems cannot be handled by a single firm. Finally, exchange controls may favor a joint venture where external capital influx or outgo is prohibited. On the negative side, joint ventures are difficult to integrate into a total master strategy because of the many problems that arise. Furthermore, a partner in the venture may attempt to maximize its own return at the expense of the other partner's. Objectives may become incompatible; and, management philosophies, staffing, and structures may come into conflict. Finally, tax interests often vary; and as a result, partners often seek different objectives and strategies.[15]

---

[15] D. F. Channon with M. Jalland, *Multinational Strategic Planning* (New York: AMACOM, 1978), Chapter 7.

The Master Strategy for Multiple Primary Mission Nonprofits

In reviewing the contents of the master strategy portrayed in Table 3.5, in light of the context of this chapter, we are concerned with the primary mission strategy. The focus of our concern is with nonprofit organizations that have various divisions, each possessing differing missions—defined as we would define them for businesses, in terms of product or service, target market, characteristics of product or service, and geographic location. As a consequence of these differences in missions, the manner in which these divisions' basic actions are conducted also varies. It is clear that primary mission strategies will vary with each agency. It is also clear that, as the next chapter reveals, in government, much of the resource allocation process is political. A rationally derived portfolio process does not exist per se, but rather, based on factors such as the power of coalitions, the strength of various leaders, the demands of society, and the requirements of the law, resources will be allocated among the various divisions of a government, in a typically slow, bureaucratic fashion. Thus, in addition to the local, state, and federal agencies which you might normally think of, such as those assisting in community or individual health and welfare, the military, police and fire departments, the commerce department, the transportation or highway department, and so forth, most schools including most major colleges and universities, hospitals, museums, and other public institutions, will allocate resources, or will have their resources allocated to them, on the basis of the aforementioned, often politically inspired bases. The following chapter reviews this process in much more detail.

Summary

In the multiple-SBU firm, the principal tasks of the strategist include establishing strategic objectives, determining the extent to which current and future businesses are helping or can help accomplish those objectives, examining what remains to be accomplished, determining strategies to accomplish those objectives, and establishing support functions and policies to accomplish those objectives. These activities center around portfolio management techniques.

The Boston Consulting Group matrix is a mechanism for relating two key factors—business or industry attractiveness and the firm's competitiveness within that industry—to help select businesses to enter or businesses in which to remain. The General Electric business screen has proved to be even more useful than the BCG matrix, because it isolates more specific considerations. The product/market/industry evolution matrix allows strategists to consider the additional critical variables related to product life cycle. A number of criteria exist to help the strategist assess both industry attractiveness and competitive position. Often, gaps exist between SBU performance and corporate objectives. As a result, corporate strategists may be required to adjust investment strategies or business strategies, add or delete SBUs from the portfolio, change enterprise strategies, or change strategic objectives. One should always keep in mind that a number of limitations exist with respect to both the concept of and implementation of portfolio approaches.

A difference in perspective often exists between the corporate and the divisional executive. Divisional managers often tend to be either function- or product-oriented. The corporate executive must be a generalist. It is often difficult for the specialist to make the transition to generalist.

With respect to international multiple-SBU firms, the concepts of master strategy formulation are essentially the same, although the specifics may cause problems. Similarly, for nonprofits, the concepts are the same, but the specifics are largely undocumented.

Key Terms and Concepts

By the time you have completed this chapter, you should be familiar with the following key terms and concepts: contents of the master strategy at the corporate level, BCG business matrix, GE stoplight strategy, business screen, business strength and business attractiveness, assessment process, placing the SBU on the matrix, product gap analysis, product/market/industry evolution portfolio matrix, difference in strategists' perspective, and the impacts of multinational and nonprofit situations on master strategy formulation.

Discussion Questions

1. Select a conglomerate and describe its major SBUs in terms of the BCG matrix, the GE business screen, and the product/market/industry evolution matrix. Utilize the major concepts discussed in this chapter.
2. Describe how the objective setting and master strategy formulation processes differ at the SBU and corporate levels.
3. Describe how multinational situations may affect the master strategy formulation process in multiple-SBU firms.
4. Discuss how master strategy formulation might differ for both mission determination and primary mission for nonprofits with multiple primary missions.

Chapter 6
The Strategic Decision Process—
A Behavioral View

All decision is compromise.
Herbert Simon

Decision making is the most important of all of the activities in which managers engage. It is through decision making that the other functions of management are accomplished. A decision is a choice among alternatives, but decision making also involves problem or opportunity recognition, identification, implementation, and control. In earlier chapters, the strategic decision process was viewed as it is normally conceptualized, and some of the techniques which may be employed in that process were noted. This chapter focuses on the behavioral aspects of strategic decision making. This includes discussions of specific components of the strategic decision process, especially the solution component. This chapter is concerned with those portions of the planning models indicated in Figures 6.1 and 6.2.

The Complexity of Organizational Decision Making

As shown in Figure 6.3, decision making is normally portrayed as a five-step process: recognition, identification, solution, implementation, and control. In the recognition phase, decision makers become aware of a problem or an opportunity. A problem exists when what is falls short of what should be. Problems result from many factors, but primarily from internal weaknesses or external threats. An oppor-

Figure 6.1
The Organization—a Strategic Management Process Model

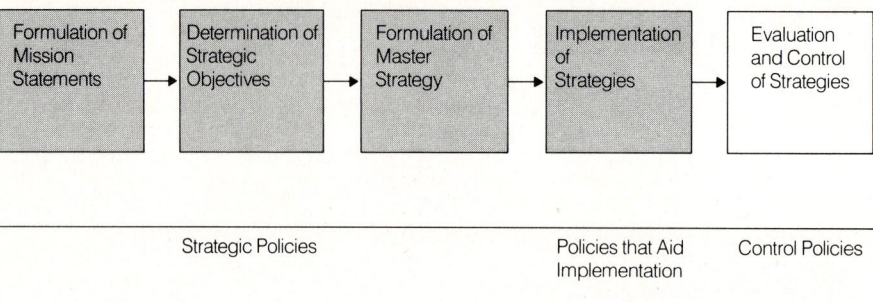

tunity exists when what is falls short of what could be. Opportunities result primarily from favorable environmental circumstances and are almost always expressed in terms of market/profit potentials.

In the recognition phase, problems and opportunities are not well understood. The decision maker simply becomes aware that a problem or an opportunity exists. In the identification phase, these problems or opportunities are better defined. In the solution phase, alternative objectives or plans of action are generated to solve problems or take advantage of opportunities. The decision maker evaluates these alternatives by using information; the constraints of policy; and for strategy, the constraints of the objectives. Finally a decision is made. Implementation of the decision occurs next. This decision will then be subject to control efforts that are intended to assure its effectiveness.

The five-part decision process model, while appealing because of its simplicity, understates the complexity of the organizational decision process. Decision making occurs within constraints, which include psychological, environmental, and decision-related factors. Psychologically, the decision maker is constrained by his or her own personality—primarily needs, but also knowledge, risk propensity, aspirations, values, skills, experience, perceptions, and limited cognitive ability. Environmental constraints include organizational factors such as objectives and policy, organizational environment and structure, reference groups and group dynamics, and roles. Decision-related factors include the importance of the decision, the time in which the decision must be made, the information available, and the involvement of multiple decision makers. As a result of these and numerous other factors, the decision process is much more complex than classically conceptualized. The following statements provide a more realistic view of decision making in an organization:

1. Objectives are often vague, conflicting, and not agreed upon.
2. Too frequently, managers are unaware that problems or opportunities exist.
3. When problems are recognized, managers often react to symptoms and not

Figure 6.2
Objective Determination and Master Strategy Formulation

Four Influential Factors

SWOT

Objective Determination

Master Strategy Formulation

- Internal and Environmental Information
- Organizational Strategists Needs Values Skills
- Strategic Policy
- Mission
- Determine **S**trengths, **W**eaknesses, **O**pportunities, **T**hreats
- Determine Strategic Objectives
- Propose Strategic Alternatives (May Revise Alternatives)
- Evaluate Alternatives and Make Decision
- Master Strategy

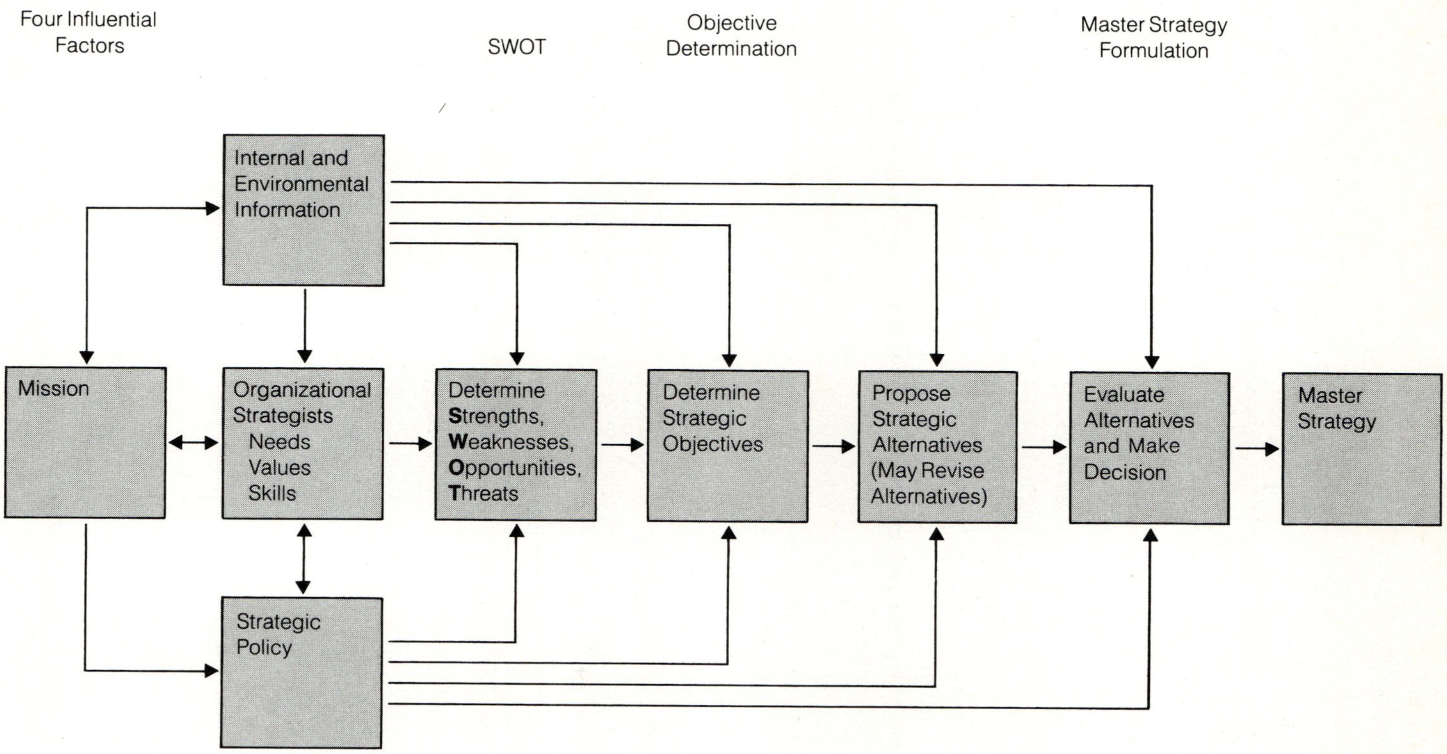

**Figure 6.3
Basic Decision Process Model**

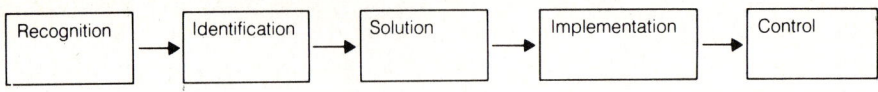

causes. J. Mitroff has labeled this phenomenon an "error of the third kind"—solving the wrong problem.[1]

4. Since decisions are based on models, rationality, if applied, can be applied only to the aspects of the situation perceived to be most important. Omission of vital data, variables, and relationships is not infrequent.
5. Since it is normally mentally and physically impossible to observe all or even most alternatives in complete detail, actual search behavior is much less extensive than that conceptualized. The decision maker's knowledge of the situation is limited.
6. Few managers have a maximizing criterion in mind. Most will settle for an alternative which satisfies minimal, and minimally considered, objectives. These are known as "satisficing" criteria.
7. Managers make decisions based on rules of thumb and frequently do not evaluate alternatives even by the satisficing criteria. Managers apparently believe that whatever worked last time will work this time.
8. Social relationships greatly affect the decision maker's rationality.

The Strategic Decision Process

The role of top management in strategy formulation is to review both policy and information related to internal factors and the external environment and then, through rational decision making, to translate mission into more specific objectives and establish major plans of action to reach those objectives. Often, the information indicates a need to reformulate strategy and thus triggers the strategic decision process. More often than not, the information indicates the need to change only certain objectives or certain elements of strategy.

The strategic decision process is characterized by the five phases common to other decisions. Research related to the first four phases, especially the solution phase, will be explored here in more detail. The control phase parallels that in Figure 6.1 and is not discussed in detail here. Control will be discussed in Chapter 8. Emphasis is placed on describing the actual strategic decision process as opposed to the classical conceptualization.

---

[1] J. Mitroff, "On Helping a Large Governmental Organization to Do Research on Planning on Itself: A Case Study" (Unpublished working paper, University of Pittsburgh).

Most discussions of decision making focus on problem solving. Note that in the strategic situation, decision making occurs not only as the result of problems but also as the result of opportunities. The discussion in this chapter treats both opportunities and problems as initiators of the strategic decision process. While it is questionable whether smaller businesses engage in opportunity searches, larger businesses clearly treat strategy as an exercise in opportunity exploration, routinely employing various portfolio management techniques.

A Strategic Decision Process Model

Examining the strategic decision process is important to actual organizational experiences because it leads to a better understanding of organizational objectives, plans, structure, and resulting everyday operations. This examination of the actual decision process will help you gain a better understanding of the objectives, plans, structure, and operations of organizations you may be required to analyze, for example, in case studies, or as top managers.

The behavioral aspects of strategic decision making are somewhat complex, but they can be modeled. Figure 6.4 presents a model for the first four components of the strategic process. The model incorporates the available research evidence and normative/descriptive literature.

The Component Phases of Strategic Decision Making: A Closer Examination

Let us now examine each of the four component phases of the strategic decision process model presented in Figure 6.4. (Again, the control phase will be discussed in Chapter 8.)

Recognition

Diagnosis is probably the single most important routine, since it determines in large part, however implicitly, the subsequent course of action. Yet researchers have paid almost no attention to diagnosis, preferring instead to focus on the selection routines. . . . —H. Mintzberg, D. Raisinghani, and A. Theoret

In order to know if a problem exists, the decision maker must know what *problem* means. A problem, as suggested earlier, occurs when objective accomplishment differs negatively from established objectives. (This implies that objectives have been established.) In theory, it is the function of information systems to alert the manager to such situations. Information systems should be designed to discover problems before they become serious. While we might assume that problems are precisely defined at this stage, it more often involves a vague feeling that something is not right. In the identification phase, more precise modeling of the problem occurs.

Figure 6.4
Strategic Decision Process Model

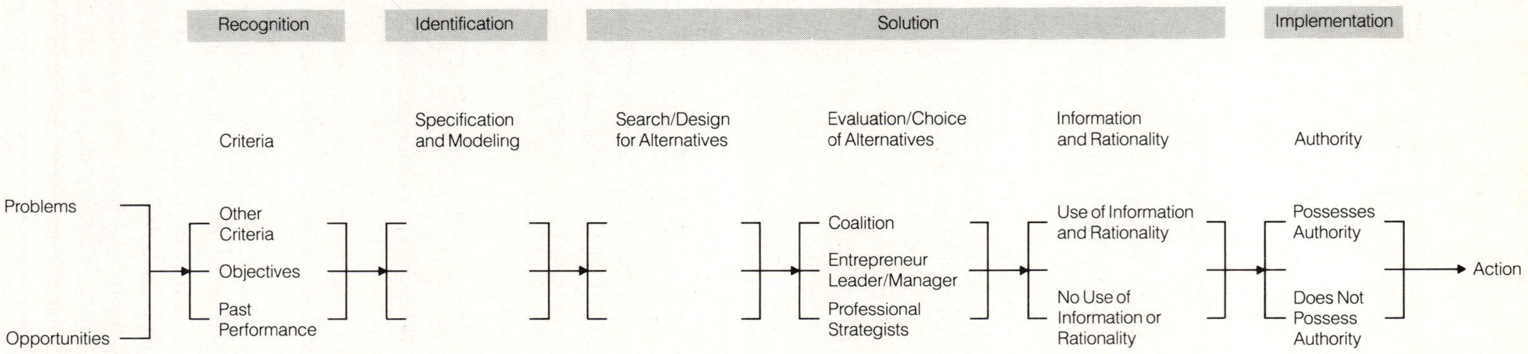

| Recognition | Identification | Solution | Implementation |

Criteria — Specification and Modeling — Search/Design for Alternatives — Evaluation/Choice of Alternatives — Information and Rationality — Authority

Problems
- Other Criteria
- Objectives
- Past Performance

Opportunities

Coalition
Entrepreneur Leader/Manager
Professional Strategists

Use of Information and Rationality
No Use of Information or Rationality

Possesses Authority
Does Not Possess Authority

→ Action

One of the weaknesses of the decision-making/problem-solving process as it actually occurs is the fact that too few organizations and too few decision makers have seriously approached the question "How do we know when we have a problem?" A study by W. E. Pounds, one of the few studies which has analyzed the problem recognition process, reveals that business managers do not utilize objectives to establish the existence of problems.[2] Theoretically, managers should know they have a problem when performance does not equal objectives. Objectives should be the benchmark against which progress is measured. But Pound's study revealed that managers most frequently use previous performances as a reference instead of using current objectives. This approach often results in problems not being recognized. Some managers may also compare performance to the performance of other organizations doing similar tasks or to some other external model. Of these four possible performance comparisons—objectives, previous performance, similar organizations, and external models—the first is the most appropriate for determining whether organizational goals have been accomplished. Yet, it is apparently seldom used.

In another study of 33 case histories of strategic problem and opportunity recognition and identification (they used the term problem formulation to identify these two stages), Marjorie Lyles and Ian I. Mitroff found that 80% of the managers involved believed themselves to be aware of the problem before formal indicators, such as financial figures, indicated the existence of a problem, or before a superior or a subordinate brought the problem to their attention. Their study supports the view that much decision making occurs as the result of, first, the use of informal information sources, and second, the use of intuition for recognition. They reported significant human behavioral factors being involved in the recognition and in the identification phases of decision making, including commitment, political maneuvering, denial, etc. They suggest that such factors may reduce the utilization of rational approaches to problem recognition and identification.[3]

An opportunity, as stated earlier, exists when a firm determines that what is falls short of what could be. First, of course, a firm must establish what could be. Little research has examined how firms determine opportunities. Organizations must scan their environments as suggested in Chapter 2 in order to be able to recognize opportunities. The comments by H. H. Stevenson referred to in that chapter are especially relevant; not all managers use the same criteria for identifying the various parts of SWOT.[4] Entrepreneurial ability plays an important role; although many might assess the same information, only one might see the opportunities revealed.

Identification

Once it is known that a problem or opportunity exists, then the causal factors must be identified or the opportunity more clearly defined. With the problem-solving system most managers employ, the real problem or opportunity is often overlooked. Managers often jump right in, assuming they know what the problem or opportunity

---

[2] W. F. Pounds, "The Process of Problem Finding," *Industrial Management Review*, (Fall 1969), pp. 1–19.
[3] M. A. Lyles and I. I. Mitroff, "Organizational Problem Formulation: An Empirical Study," *Administrative Science Quarterly*, (March 1980), pp. 102–119.
[4] H. H. Stevenson, "Defining Corporate Strengths and Weaknesses," *Sloan Management Review*, (Spring 1976), pp. 51–66.

is. Like recognition, identification has been little researched or considered. Information again plays an important role in this process.

C. Kepner and B. Tregoe, in one of the few discussions of problem identification, suggest that the process of specification is helpful.[5] In specification, decision makers must determine exactly what the specific problem is, where and when it occurred, whom or what it affected, and the extent of its effect. The decision maker must distinguish differences between the problem's consequences and other events in similar situations. This occurs as a result of examining the situational data.

Specification aims at factually separating what the problem is from what it is not. The uncovering the real problem then becomes a matter of deduction from what should be to what is. This process is not simple; it is at least partly intuitive and it also relies partly on experience. The decision maker must learn to ask a series of questions which aid in this process; for example: What is the urgency and severity of each problem? How are these problems related? Which problems result from other problems? What could uniquely produce these consequences? The end result of this phase will be a model of the problem. The model routinely summarizes and conceptualizes the situation under examination. Importantly, processes such as competition analysis (Chapter 4) and portfolio management (Chapter 5) help in the identification process.

Continued analysis by Lyles of the 33 case histories, discussed in the previous section on recognition,[6] revealed that many organizations are initially incorrectly identifying the problem, or are avoiding it all together. This suggests then a slowness to "trigger" identification processes even though there is clear recognition of the problem. Interestingly, she found that in 75% of the situations reviewed, a problem was explicitly identified, but then the identification process was reinitiated and a new definition was begun.

Based on additional findings in her research, Lyles suggests several propositions:

1. The more ill definied the nature of the problem, the more political will be the problem formulation process.

2. The more political the problem formulation process, the more debate should be used as a method of confrontation.

3. The more debate that is used, the more accurate will be the problem definition.[7]

Her propositions are especially relevant to strategic problems and opportunities, since many, if not most, strategic situations are typically ill defined and "open to divergent interpretations."

Solution

As suggested in Chapters 3, 4, and 5, in the solution component of the decision-making process, the decision maker first searches for alternative solutions, proce-

---

[5]C. Kepner and B. Tregoe, *The Rational Manager* (New York: McGraw-Hill, 1965).

[6]M. A. Lyles, "Formulating Strategic Problems: Empirical Analylsis and Model Development," *Strategic Management Journal*, (January–March 1981), pp. 61–75.

[7]Ibid., p. 74.

dures, or courses of action to solve the problem or exploit the opportunity and then arrays these alternatives in some fashion which will facilitate making a choice among them. The search for alternatives can be extremely time consuming and complicated. This section will examine in detail the social processes involved in the solution process. The emphasis will be on the nonrational aspects of decision making displayed by each of the three types of decision makers identified in Chapter 1.

Entrepreneurial Leader/Manager. Managers cannot separate their personalities from their decisions. Their needs, their values, their emotions, their ethics, their feelings, their risk propensities, their approaches to problem solving, their attitudes toward people, their attitudes toward life, and numerous other personality factors influence the decisions they make. The most frequently discussed behavioral determinant of organizational success or failure with respect to behavioral variables has been values.

Values conceptualize what their holders view as desirable. They reflect an individual's, a group's, an organization's, or a society's history of experiences. The perception processes trigger decision-making actions. Values enter into perceptions. Thus values play a critical role in decision making. Many times, managers are not consciously aware of utilizing values in making decisions; values nonetheless may at the subconscious level greatly affect decisions.

William D. Guth and Renato Taguiri have identified six primary types of value orientations:[8]

1. *Theoretical*: interested in the discovery of truth, in rationality, in reason.
2. *Economic*: practical; interested in what is practical; interested in the accumulation of wealth.
3. *Aesthetic*: values the artistic aspects of life; enjoys each event for its own sake, for its beauty.
4. *Social*: loves people; is sympathetic, unselfish, kind.
5. *Political*: oriented towards power; sees competition as vital.
6. *Religious*: has a "mental structure permanently directed to the creation of the highest and absolutely satisfying value experience"; seeks relationship with the universe.

Guth and Taguiri found that the business managers they sampled had values strongest on economic, theoretical, and political scales and weakest in aesthetic and social areas and that their religious value scores were moderately strong relative to the other values.

How are each of these values reflected in decisions? We can't be sure; but it seems likely that values enter into virtually every decision and that more than one value is usually involved. For example, when L. M. Clymer resigned as president of Holiday Inns in protest of the directors' decision to establish a gambling casino, he may have been motivated by "religious" values.[9] When John DeLorean left as

---
[8] W. D. Guth and R. Taguiri, "Personal Values and Corporate Strategies," *Harvard Business Review*, (September/October 1965), pp. 125–126.

[9] n.a., "Holiday Inns Sets its First Hotel—Casino, Prompting Clymer to Resign as President," *The Wall Street Journal*, October 2, 1978, p. 16.

president of the Chevrolet Division of General Motors in protest of top management's refusal to move as quickly to the small car as he wanted, it is likely that theoretical values were involved; DeLorean believed that, rationally, making more small cars was necessary. Later, his economic values apparently grew stronger than his religious values as he reportedly sought to keep his car company afloat through dealing in drugs. Political values—power struggles—may also have been an issue.[10] When resort owners hire Peter Dye to design a golf course, they do so, it would seem, primarily for his ability to create a course that is aesthetically pleasing as well as economically successful.[11] When Philip Friedman and Mickaell Keiser founded Recycled Paper Products, Inc., in 1971, they did so to help keep trees from being cut down to make greeting cards. They were satisfying a social or perhaps aesthetic value.[12] Many more examples could be cited; the point is that since values underlie managerial decisions, they have important impacts on these decisions.

Other managerial personality traits play an important role in strategic decisions as well. A study by Danny Miller suggests that top management traits such as conservatism or extremely arbitrary risk taking are significant in determining whether a firm is successful or unsuccessful.[13] Unsuccessful firms did not employ techniques such as environmental scanning, environmental analysis, or analysis of any kind in terms of strategic formulation as often as did successful firms. This study suggests that the human variable may be an important predictor of strategic success and that therefore strategy may be contingent upon this variable. For example, one firm's scenario was characterized by a bold and reckless entrepreneur who was proactive and a high risk taker.

Top Management Coalition. While the entrepreneurial leader/manager guides most organizations, not all such leaders are sufficiently strong to cope with all the forces they encounter. Where weaker chief executives head an organization or where especially strong power centers exist, the coalition is the dominant factor in strategy determination. This is especially true of larger organizations.

R. Cyert and J. March first noted the existence of the coalition.[14] Organizational objectives and strategies are determined in the coalition process through a bargaining mechanism—essentially a trading process involving exchanges of what have been termed "policy side payments" for alliance on some particular strategic objective or plan. These payments may take the form of money, a promise of agreement on some future policy matter or objective, personal favors, authority, and so forth.

Objectives set by this process tend to be vague and to vary over time and reflect the aspirations of various coalition members. Conflict within the organization is never fully resolved (because of the bargaining, compromising, and vagueness involved). This latter characteristic Cyert and March referred to as the "quasi-

---

[10] R. Lovins, Jr., "Automobile Industry has Lost its Masculinity," *Fortune*, September 1983, pp. 186–191, +.

[11] Pete Dye is known for his dramatic use of water and sand in combination with wood retainers. Among his courses are the Campo de Campo in the Dominican Republic; Amelia Island in Jacksonville, Florida; Oak Tree in Edmond, Oklahoma; and Harbor Town on Hilton Head Island, South Carolina.

[12] S. Graham, "I Think That I Shall Never See a Greeting Card Lovely as a Tree," *Wall Street Journal*, September 3, 1980, p. 29.

[13] D. Miller, "Towards a Contingency Theory of Strategy Formulation," *Proceedings: Academy of Management*, (1975), pp. 64–66.

[14] R. Cyert and J. March, *The Behavioral Theory of the Firm* (Englewood Cliffs, N.J.: Prentice-Hall, 1963).

resolution of conflict." As an example of this phenomenon, there often exists a constant struggle among marketing, accounting, and production subunits regarding the amount of inventory that should be maintained. The marketing director seeks high inventories of all items in order to be able to satisfy customers. The comptroller seeks low inventories to reduce carrying costs. The production executive may be aligned with either, depending on how his or her performance is judged and the rewards to be received for alliance. This problem is usually quasi-resolved; that is, no party achieves a clear victory. As a result, the issue remains as a roadblock to organizational mission achievement. However, if, say, the marketing manager finally wins and the company agrees to maintain in inventory a great number of products across a diversified number of product lines, then a policy side payment will be forthcoming. What emerges is a view of strategy formulation as an exchange process based on power.

While much of the following discussion on coalitions focuses on internal coalitions, organizations, their subunits, and individual members may also form coalitions with major stakeholder constituents, especially when they are dependent on these constituents. Coalitions with unions, government, competition (restraints of trade), and various pressure groups may exist. For example, many business organizations have attempted to work "with" environmentalists and minority interest groups rather than fight them. In so doing, they are forming coalitions, exchanging increased social responsibility commitments for decreased protest.

Surprisingly, there has been little research attempting to verify the coalition concept. Perhaps this is because most practitioners and researchers have experienced this phenomenon or because the concept seems so intuitively valid. Following are brief descriptions of the major studies which have dealt with this process.

J. D. Thompson was the first to elaborate on the coalition in his discussion of organizations. He observed that the relationship of the organization to its environment was important in determining coalition functioning. He also expressed the view that the future of the organization's objectives depended on the perceptions of the dominant coalition.[15]

E. E. Carter empirically tested Cyert and March's behavioral theory of decision making. He examined six different but related major decisions for a small computer firm. Carter's results essentially verified the Cyert and March hypotheses. However, he suggested certain changes in their theory. One such change was that, instead of a single, large, dominant coalition which resolved conflicts within itself, there existed a series of small groups engaged in bargaining at each level of the organization. As a decision passed through each level of the organization on its way to final executive approval, a new coalition might exert its influence on the eventual decision.[16]

C. B. Saunders reported that in an eight-year study of the planning process in a single firm, observed behaviors did not differ significantly from those described by Cyert and March. In reviewing the coalition process, he concluded that in complex organizations strategy formulation was a highly diffuse and highly political process. He viewed environmental factors as important determinants of an organization

[15] J. D. Thompson, *Organizations in Action* (New York: McGraw-Hill, 1967), pp. 127–128.
[16] E. E. Carter, "The Behavioral Theory of the Firm and Top-Level Corporate Decision," *Administrative Science Quarterly*, (December 1971), pp. 413–429; "A Behavioral Theory Approach to Firm Investment and Acquisition Decisions" (Ph.D. dissertation, Graduate School of Industrial Administration, Carnegie Mellon University, 1970).

member's efforts to influence the firm's activities. His research also supported the concept of a dominant coalition.[17]

H. Mintzberg, D. Raisinghani and A. Theoret closely scrutinized twenty-five strategic decisions—nine in service firms, five in quasi-governmental agencies, five in government agencies, and six in manufacturing firms. The results of their study also supported the coalition concept. Coalition bargaining behavior was reported in over half the decisions they observed.[18]

Finally, a study of strategic energy policy decision making in six large multidivisional firms by Liam Fahey supports the previous views of researchers related to the significant impacts of behavioral and political processes on strategic decision making. Several tentative propositions include the following: strategic decision making is predominantly political; it is iterative and interactive; it is more "problematical" than rational; the search process for alternatives is multilevel and highly political; a structured process of decision making does not necessarily lead to a "rational" decision.[19]

With the exception of these studies, much of what is known about the coalition results from studies of power relationships within the organization. The coalition is, after all, a power concept. In recent years, interest in power in the organization has increased as its significance has been recognized.

Power and the Political Aspects of Strategic Decision Making. The use of power (politics) to further one's own interests is not new to the organization. Its use in planning is certainly not new, nor is the recognition of its importance. Anthony Jay addressed this aspect of corporate life in his book *Management and Machiavelli*. He observed that while controlling this problem is not too difficult at the lower levels of organization, it is quite difficult at the higher management levels—the strategic decision levels.[20] According to a study by R. Stagner, business executives reported that key (strategic) decisions in their organizations were often settled by power rather than by rational maximization criteria.[21] J. V. Baldridge reported that the coalition model described decision making at New York University.[22] What has become increasingly clear is that while rationality may be a formally proclaimed method of making strategic decisions, power and personality play important roles in this process.

Much of the coalition phenomenon results from competition among organizational subsystems. Relative power among these subsystems is determined by such factors as how well each subsystem can help the organization to cope with uncertainty and the importance of each subsystem to the organization. Apparently the composition of the dominant coalition and its power distribution result to a great

---

[17] C. B. Saunders, "What Should We Know about Strategy Formulation," *Proceedings: Academy of Management*, (1973), p. 32.

[18] H. Mintzberg, D. Raisinghani, and A. Theoret, "The Structure of Unstructured Decision Processes," *Administrative Science Quarterly*, (June 1976), p. 258.

[19] L. Fahey, "On Strategic Management Decision Processes," *Strategic Management Journal*, (January–March, 1981), pp. 43–60.

[20] A. Jay, *Management and Machiavelli* (New York: Holt, Rinehart and Winston, 1967).

[21] R. Stagner, "Corporate Decision Making: An Empirical Study," *Journal of Applied Psychology*, (February 1969), pp. 1–13.

[22] J. V. Baldridge, *Power and Conflict in the University* (New York: Wiley, 1971).

"OK, Accounting agrees to bigger inventories, but we get to keep our offices in the upwind wing . . . !"

extent from the effects of environmental change. The point is that the organization is composed of interdependent subsystems: a problem for one is a problem for another. The coalition or coalition member who is able to provide the means for coping with change, has lower substitutability, or is more central to the work flow gains power. The implication is obvious: the subunit manager is in a position to gain power. Coping with uncertainty is one obvious basis for the increasing power of planning units in larger organizations. This power can lead to dominance by the planner.

While research regarding the coalition is not abundant, as indicated earlier, that which exists supports Cyert and March's postulations. More research is needed, especially to sample behavior across many firms of varying sizes in several industries and in nonprofit organizations. However, we must not overlook the abundant informal group research which is available. While this research mainly examines groups at lower levels of the organization, it should not be dismissed. In general, it also concludes that power is relative and is bargained for. It also suggests that an informal group at lower levels can counteract the power of the formal managerial leader. These findings support the coalition concept.

The role of power (and politics) cannot be overemphasized. Remember that a subunit of General Electric or a similar-sized organization may be larger than several entire companies against which it competes. Considerable resource allocations are involved in the coalition process. Much additional evidence of the importance of power can be found. The president of a large strategic planning consulting firm indicates that organizational politics often plays an important role in preventing the adoption of his firm's recommended planning models. And the recognition of the correlation between political behavior and success in the organization has been increasingly discussed in the strategic management literature. For example, F. F. Gilmore has outlined a four-stage strategy for assisting the executive in efforts to have plans adopted by the organization.[23] A. P. Brief and A. C. Filley have outlined a similar series of propositions for selling proposals for change before committees.[24] Several books are also available which offer advice to the aspiring manager in the political organization.

Coalition activity, power, and politics in strategic decision making are interdependent. As coalition power centers develop, admission to them becomes partially a function of politics. As objectivity in decision making is reduced, power and politics become increasingly important to those who aspire to and have a high need for achievement. Success becomes a function of power.

It's not so much what you know, but who you know that counts. —Anonymous

Corporate Planning Units. The third major strategist is the corporate planning unit. The comments related to values and other personality traits of the individual top manager are relevant here; and the coalition may also have an impact on these decision makers. This discussion focuses on some of the subtleties of organization structure and, hence, position power as they might affect these planners as strategists.

Organizational Structure and Corporate Planning Units. Every planning system is unique because it results from particular circumstances. Similarly, the position of the planning unit in the organization's structure varies in duties and responsibilities as well as in authority to carry out these duties and responsibilities. Interest in these differences stems from the need to predict which arrangement would be most appropriate for a particular situation. Numerous variations exist, and the research on this subject is too limited to permit a refined prediction as to which will be most appropriate. The limited research does help identify the alternatives available and some of the causes and implications of the various structures.

The following are common organizational structure arrangements for planning units:

1. **The Executive Group.** In this arrangement, there is no professional planner but rather the top executive group performs the planning function.
2. **The Functional Structure.** The office of the corporate planner is subordinated to a functional subsystem executive, for example, the executive in charge of finance.
3. **The Corporate Planning Group.** The corporate planner reports directly to the president.

---

[23] F. F. Gilmore, "Overcoming the Perils of Advocacy in Corporate Planning," *California Management Review*, (Spring 1973), pp. 127–137.

[24] A. P. Brief and A. C. Filley, "Selling Proposals for Change," *Business Horizons*, April 1976, pp. 22–25.

4. **The Corporate Planning Committee.** A committee is formed to perform the planning function.
5. **The Corporate Planning Group and Committee.** Both a planning committee and a professional planning unit are established.
6. **The Corporate Planning Group and Divisional Committees.** A divisional planning committee is added to the structure in Item 5.
7. **Corporate and Divisional Planning Groups.** A divisional planning group is added to the structure in Item 6.

With regard to the impacts that structural arrangements have on strategy formulation, the following observations can be made. An executive group or committee would not be expected to be able to devote the time to planning or possess the planning expertise which a professional planning group would possess. Access to the president or CEO is an obvious consideration in the political influence aspect of corporate strategy formulation. Potential for conflict exists where corporate and divisional planning groups or committees exist.

J. W. Dobbie has shown that the types of goals resulting from the strategic process vary according to structure.[25] Where the functional structure is employed, goals are routinely expressed in pro forma financial statement terms, reflecting the bias of the functional subsystem, which is usually the financial function. Dobbie also correlated CEO involvement in the planning process with the type of structure. He concluded that where the "corporate planner" reports to the president or where no planner exists, then strategic planning is more likely to occur at the president's level than where a committee or a functional area has the responsibility for planning. P. Lorange found that planners perceived their influence on strategy as high when direct reporting to the president occurred and low when reports were made to a functional subunit executive.[26]

It would seem appropriate to involve the chief executive in planning or at least to obtain top management support for strategic planning. It also seems appropriate to have the planning group report directly to the president. These recommendations have been supported by several empirical but largely descriptive examinations of corporate planning processes. Political bargaining often occurs in a planning committee of top executives. Such committees may interfere with the planning group. But since top management is involved, these committees can function partially to gain top management support for the resultant strategy.

In summary, evaluation and choice normally involve either a single entrepreneurial leader/manager, a coalition of top managers, or some sort of planning unit. Returning to Figure 6.4, you can see that each of these decision makers may or may not utilize information and follow a rational choice process. Normally, professional strategists would be expected to use information and rational decision processes more than other types of decision makers.

---

[25] J. W. Dobbie, "Guides to Foundations for Strategic Planning in Large Firms" (Paper presented to the Academy of Management, Seattle, August 1974).
[26] P. Lorange, "Divisional Planning: Setting Effective Direction," *Sloan Management Review*, (Fall 1975), pp. 82–83.

Implementation

When decision makers do not possess the authority to approve the decision, they must seek it if the decision is to be implemented. Decision-making processes may be repeated as an issue progresses upward through the decision levels of the organizational hierarchy. Often, however, the higher level decision process is abbreviated as decisions are based on lower level recommendations. Here we find what is known as incremental decision making. Once authority is possessed, implementation action ensues. Various interruptions and delays to this process may occur and may result in variances in the exact decision process in any particular situation.

Incremental Decision Making. Examination of the strategic decision process reveals that, in many organizations, decisions are made in a series of small steps—hence the term *incremental*. As portrayed by C. E. Lindblom and by Lindblom and D. Braybrooke, incrementalism is based on the belief that a rational approach does not account for people's limited problem solving capacity, their lack of information, the impact of their values on decisions, the openness of systems, the high cost of total rationality, the need for sequencing of decisions, and the variations in policy problem situations. Lindblom's and Braybrooke's idea of incrementalism is based on the concept that most governmental policy decisions involve small changes not guided by a high level of understanding.[27] Political decisions indeed proceed by small steps—a preliminary solution is attempted, performance is measured, and perceived shortcomings are corrected. Such an approach is best, because it allows for the recognition of the problems associated with the rational approach to decision making. Related research supports the existence of the incremental process in business but not necessarily all Lindblom's and Braybrooke's assumptions about it.

Y. Aharoni observed the foreign investment decision processes of 38 U.S. firms. His research suggests that incremental decision making is at least partially a function of organizational structure. His research is important because it substantiates the observations of Lindblom and Braybrooke as well as the coalition propositions of Cyert and March. He concluded that decision making in large, complex organizations was a continuous social bargaining process composed of many small parts. He observed that different people were involved at different points in the organization and at different times. Personal interests were found to play a key role in decisions.[28]

Two additional studies supporting both bargaining and incremental decision making are those of J. L. Bower and R. W. Ackerman. Both studies were concerned with investment decisions. Bower examined one firm's decisions extensively.[29] Subsequently, Ackerman, testing Bower's decision model, observed four firms extensively.[30] A third effort, by S. C. Gilmour, examined simultaneously the

---

[27] C. E. Lindblom, *The Policy-Making Process* (Englewood Cliffs, N.J.: Prentice-Hall, 1968); *The Intelligence of Democracy* (New York: Free Press, 1965); "The Science of 'Muddling Through,'" *Public Administration Review*, (Spring 1959), pp. 79–88; C. E. Lindblom and D. Braybrooke, *A Strategy of Decision* (New York: Free Press, 1963).

[28] Y. Aharoni, *The Foreign Investment Decision Process* (Boston: Division of Research, Harvard Business School, 1966).

[29] J. L. Bower, *Managing the Resource Allocation Process: A Study of Corporate Planning and Investment* (Boston: Division of Research, Harvard Business School, 1970).

[30] R. W. Ackerman, "Influence of Integration and Diversity on the Investment Process," *Administrative Science Quar-*

work of Cyert and March and Bower and traditional capital budgeting theory.[31] As the result of his study of divestiture in three large U.S. businesses in different industries, he postulated a revised theory which focused on the concept of individual commitment. He proposed that, an individual would become committed to a self-generated solution. This person would implement the decision if he or she had the power. If not, he or she would attempt to persuade others to follow the recommended course of action. E. W. Trevelyan, in researching strategic decision processes in two large organizations, substantiated the concept of incremental decision making.[32] Each successive commitment to a course of action was found to reinforce others of a similar nature.

Finally, James Brian Quinn, in a study of 10 major multinational firms, found extensive support, not only for the existence of, but also for the need for, incrementalism. He argues convincingly that it is necessary, that politics are a part of organizational life and should not be ignored. He also suggests that more attention be paid to the behavioral aspects of strategy formulation and implementation.[33]

The incremental decision process in business organizations appears to result from reviews of strategic decisions, taking place at every organizational level. Figure 6.4 reflects this process under the Implementation Component. When the individual does not possess authority, he or she refers the decision upward in the organization. Additional repetitions of the strategic decision process are then necessary. Incremental decision making for governmental decisions, while resulting partially from structure, appears to result primarily from the desire of the politician "not to rock the voter boat." Several repetitions of the model occur, but not necessarily because the decision maker did not possess the proper authority. In business, the initial impetus for strategic incrementalism (which, importantly, is not characteristic of all decisions) is the initiation of strategic commitments at lower levels, which, once approved by successively higher levels of management, leave little room for rejection at the highest level. But in government, incrementalism allows the politician who does not make waves to be reelected.

Three Common Strategic Planning Modes

With respect to the solution and implementation components of the planning process, Henry Mintzberg suggests that three common modes of planning exist. These modes summarize most of the research presented in this chapter and reveal the most common paths through the model in Figure 6.4.

The first mode he labels the entrepreneurial mode. The traditional concept of strategy formulation holds that it is the entrepreneurial leader who guides the organization to its destiny through strategic decision making. This view of the en-

---

terly, September 1970, pp. 341–352; "Organization and the Investment Process: A Comparative Study" (Ph.D. dissertation, Harvard Business School, 1968).
[31] S. C. Gilmour, "The Divestment Decision Processes" (Ph.D. dissertation, Harvard Business School, 1973).
[32] E. W. Trevelyan, "The Strategic Process in Large, Complex Organizations: A Pilot Study of New Business Development" (Ph.D. dissertation, Harvard Business School, 1974).
[33] J. B. Quinn, "Formulating Strategy One Step at A Time," *Journal of Business Strategy* (Winter 1981), pp. 42–63.

trepreneurial leader resulted primarily from the classical economic literature, which saw the entrepreneur as the risk taker, the decision maker. When corporations became the dominant form of enterprise, the characteristics were transposed to the CEO, who normally does not start the enterprise but rather manages it. Certainly many organizations, especially smaller business organizations, are headed by chief executives who fit this model and who do indeed guide almost single-handedly their organizations' fortunes. Among the characteristics of this mode Mintzberg lists the following:[34]

1. *Strategy-making is dominated by the active search for new opportunities.*
2. *Power is centralized in the hands of the chief executive.*
3. *Strategy-making . . . is characterized by dramatic leaps forward in the face of uncertainty.*
4. *Growth is the dominant goal.*

This model is congruent with how most conceptualize strategic management; but, as the material presented earlier in this chapter has shown, other modes exist. Another mode Mintzberg identifies is referred to as the adaptive mode, which is characterized by the coalition and by incremental decision making. Mintzberg characterizes this mode as follows:

1. *Clear goals do not exist . . . strategy-making reflects a division of power among members of a complex coalition.*
2. *The strategy-making process is characterized by the "reactive" solution to existing problems rather than the "proactive" search for new opportunities.*
3. *The adaptive organization makes its decision in incremental, serial steps.*
4. *Disjointed decisions are characteristic of the adaptive mode.*

Mintzberg also suggests a third mode—the planning mode. At the center of this mode are rationality and the corporate planner, especially the analyst. Mintzberg characterizes this mode as follows:

1. *The analyst plays a major role in strategy-making.*
2. *[It] focuses on systematic analysis, particularly in the assessment of the costs and benefits of competing proposals.*
3. *[It] is characterized above all by the integration of decisions and strategies.*

Mintzberg summarizes the key characteristics and conditions of these modes in Table 6.1. What appear to distinguish these three modes are: the source of power, especially single versus multiple decision makers; the decision process utilized, especially the use or absence of systematic planning and planning information; and the number and types of decisions made. These three modes, as mentioned earlier, represent the three most common paths through the model presented in Figure 6.4. Other variations exist, of course.

---

[34]H. Mintzberg, "Strategy Making in Three Modes," *California Management Review*, (Winter 1973), pp. 45–51.

Table 6.1
Characteristics and Conditions of the Three Modes

Characteristic	Entrepreneurial Mode	Adaptive Mode	Planning Mode
Motive for decisions	Proactive	Reactive	Proactive & reactive
Goals of organization	Growth	Indeterminate	Efficiency & growth
Evaluation of proposals	Judgmental	Judgmental	Analytical
Choices made by	Entrepreneur	Bargaining	Management
Decision horizon	Long term	Short term	Long term
Preferred environment	Uncertainty	Certainty	Risk
Decision linkages	Loosely coupled	Disjointed	Integrated
Flexibility of mode	Flexible	Adaptive	Constrained
Size of moves	Bold decisions	Incremental steps	Global strategies
Vision of direction	General	None	Specific
Conditions for use			
Source of power	Entrepreneur	Divided	Management
Objectives of organization	Operational	Nonoperational	Operational
Organizational environment	Yielding	Complex, dynamic	Predictable, stable
Status of organization	Young, small, or strong leadership	Established	Large

© 1973 by the Regents of the University of California. Reprinted from *California Management Review*, volume XVI, number 2, p. 49, by permission of the Regents.

Managerial Comprehension of the Behavioral Process

Top management must be attuned to the behavioral aspects of the organization's strategic process—formulation, implementation, and control. Strategy simply cannot be successfully implemented without organizational support. And, as this chapter demonstrates, the actual content of strategy will be affected by this process. Decisions reflect their decision makers. Strategies reflect their formulators, their implementers, and those who control them. The top manager who wishes to have strategies succeed must work within the behavioral/political environment as well as within the rational one. Information Capsule 6.1 provides an additional insight into one manager's understanding of this process.

Behavioral Aspects of Strategic Decision Making for Multinational Firms

For multinationals, behavioral aspects of decision making are basically the same as for other firms; but the degree of incrementalism and the degree of power sharing and usages of power may differ significantly. Recall from the discussion in Chapter 1 that in many countries, the government takes a much stronger role in business decision making than in the United States or Canada. Thus, for firms operating in such countries, the strategic decision process is often slowed by bureaucracy; and a fourth strategist—government—is added to the process.

Information Capsule 6.1
Commitment to Excellence in Aerospace

When the president of one of the United States' premier aerospace firms appraised the company's strategic situation, he identified two primary issues. First, the future of the aerospace industry was almost certain to hinge on a "fixed price" contract as opposed to the prevailing "cost plus" contract. Second, he foresaw significant competitive advantages accruing to foreign competitors, principally the Japanese, in nonproprietary domestic and in virtually all international contract situations because of their abilities to produce high quality products.

High quality had become an absolute necessity in this industry where a single product unit, for example a missile, might cost $50 million. Encouraged by his operations vice president, who directed the efforts of two thirds of the firm's 10,000 employees, and who was confronted with the tremendous task of managing the firm's manufacturing efforts for the five current major contracts, the president determined that a commitment to excellence (CTE) program was necessary. This program would require "zero defects" in all products, a gigantic undertaking when one considered the thousands of parts involved in individual product units. With the approval of the firm's top eight managers, the president sent the company's 200 foremost managers to the leading quality management educational institution. This represented an initial investment, in out-of-pocket expenditures, of more than $200,000. Each of these 200 managers attended a three-day seminar on the basics of quality management.

However, these seminars were only the beginning of a major educational process intended to ensure that all levels of management "signed up" for the CTE program. The major problem that the president foresaw with this quality management strategy was that many of the top managers in the firm remembered earlier, largely unsuccessful, attempts at similar programs. And, he was rightfully concerned that many managers within the organization would not support the program for any number of reasons. For example, the firm had been recently restructured into a matrix structure at the macro-level. Project managers had responded less than enthusiastically to this new structure since in the former project-based structure they had been more powerful. Consequently, programs initiated from the president's office were often viewed as suspect by some, regardless of their actual, long-term value to the firm. In addition, a number of powerful coalitions existed within the company. The president had only recently become president. Furthermore, since he had come from another division of the firm and had replaced most top managers within the firm, there existed a coalition of old-line top managers who felt that "outsiders" ran the firm. And while he was an engineer, there were those that felt the new operations emphasis of the firm was less than desirable; after all, for the past ten years, this had been a research and development firm based on engineering. And there were always those who thought they "had been passed over." Combined with the inevitable resistance to any change that occurs within organizations, much less a change of such major proportions, challenges to the CTE program were plentiful.

The president recognized that he faced considerable opposition in moving forward with his desire to change the organization. He knew that virtually all of this opposition was based on power and other behavioral factors. To him, the changes certainly made rational, empirical sense.

Because of this behavior resistance, the president encouraged key managers at all levels of the organization to take part personally in the educational process. He was especially careful to include those top managers whom he felt might not be totally supportive. He believed that by giving them active roles in the process, he would further their personal stake in its success. He was also careful to solicit their advice in developing the specifics of this process and the actual operational mechanisms to be employed. And, when necessary, he twisted a few arms to gain support for the CTE program. These actions occurred within the first six months of what he anticipated to be a three- to five-year program before total implementation would occur and zero defects would become a reality.

Source: This incident was related to the author by the firm's top managers.

The Soviet government, for example, is extremely slow to decide about foreign business or even domestic business investment. In Europe and South America, the process takes less time, but can still be quite involved. For example, the desire of persons in many countries in South America to socialize for long periods of time before making a business decision often causes problems for multinationals attempting to conduct business there. In much of the Middle East, a similar socializing requirement exists; and many locals will not do business except with well-established friends.[35] In Europe, unions often play a strategic role in the organization. Hence, there is frequent use of politics and power. For example, in England, unions have nullified the efforts of both businesses and government to arrive at strategic business decisions. The Triumph motorcycle essentially disappeared from the marketplace largely because of a union strike that negated a strategic decision jointly determined by business and government.[36] Finally, in Japan, everyone who has any stake in the decision must be consulted before the decision is made. This requirement adds a tremendous amount of time to the decision process. However, it does aid in implementation, since it ensures commitment. Thus the total time of decision and implementation is probably no greater in Japan than elsewhere.[37]

In summary, the multinational's decision processes are essentially the same as those of other organizations; but the number of strategists is often greater, the incrementalism is more pronounced, the usages of power are more frequent, coalitions abound, and the time taken for making decisions is often much greater than in the United States and Canada. Multinational managers must be alert to these differences and not expect to be able to make decisions as independently of social and political stakeholders as they otherwise might.

[35] J. Higgins, *Human Relations Concepts and Skills* (New York: Random House, 1982), Chapter 14.
[36] W. R. Sandberg, "Norton Villiers Triumph and the Meriden Cooperative," in W. F. Glueck, *Business Policy and Strategic Management* (New York: McGraw-Hill, 1980), pp. 436–442.
[37] W. J. Ouchi, *Theory Z* (Reading, Mass.: Addison-Wesley, 1980).

The Behavioral View of Strategic Decision Making in Nonprofits

This chapter differs from the others in that the conceptual and research material is heavily nonprofit oriented. Much of what we know about the impacts of behavioral factors on the strategic decision process has in fact been learned from examining nonprofit organizations. Indeed, the concept of incrementalism, later identified as existing in businesses, was first conceptualized and researched in government. Therefore, this section of the chapter is limited only to the observation that nonprofits tend to have multiple, major constituents, imprecise missions and objectives, and inherent bureaucracies. All of these factors typically lead to political rather than rational decisions. These characteristics frequently encourage the development of coalitions, of incrementalism, of decisions based on personality, rather than on information. To the extent that these same factors characterize businesses, we would expect them to have less rational and more political decision making.

Everything having to do with the government and everything the government does is political, for politics is the art and science of government. —Paul H. Appleby

Summary

The strategic decision process follows the classic decision model consisting of recognizing the problem, identifying the problem, solving the problem, implementing solutions to that problem, and controlling for results to make certain that the actions taken did solve the problem. But the behavioral factors involved make the strategic decision process much more complex, much less easy than it might first appear. Figure 6.4 and its accompanying narrative revealed just how complex the process can be. We discovered that both recognition and identification may be complicated by the availability of information and by the use of decision rules of thumb and decision criteria (last year's performance, for example) which may not be appropriate. The solution phase was characterized as dominated by three types of decision makers—the entrepreneur, the coalition, and the professional planner. Coalitions tend to make decisions in a series of small steps, known as increments, rather than making larger, grander scale decisions. Each may or may not use information and rational thinking. The values of the decision makers were found to have a significant impact on their decisions. Power and politics were also found to have significant impacts on strategic decisions, especially those in which a coalition dominates the organization's strategic decision-making process. Mintzberg has shown that three common strategic planning modes exist. These modes are: the entrepreneurial modes, the adaptive mode, and the planning mode. These three modes are dominated by the entrepreneur, the coalition, and the professional planner, respectively, and are comprised of varying degrees of objective setting, incrementalism, political maneuvering, use of information, and rationality. Internationally, the strategic decision process is again conceptually the same as the domestic model, but specific decision maker values, the composition of the decision-making unit, and other factors vary significantly.

Discussion Questions

1. How might social relationships among organizational strategists play a role in determining strategy content?
2. Describe the coalition, incremental decision making, and the adaptive mode.
3. Think of an organization with which you are familiar. Imagine a strategic decision of this organization. Now follow the route you think this decision might take through the model in Figure 6.4.
4. Which of the three modes of strategic planning do you suppose is most common? Why?
5. Discuss possible variances in the strategic decision process for U.S. and Canadian for-profits and nonprofits, and for those for-profits operating in foreign countries.

Key Terms and Concepts

Before you complete this chapter, you should become familiar with the following key terms and concepts: the classic five-part decision model; the definitions of and problems associated with recognition, identification, solution, implementation, control; the differences between problems and opportunities; the role of criteria in decision making; the uses of information and rationality in decision making; the three major types of decision makers; Mintzberg's three types of decision modes; the impacts of values on decision making; the coalition and how it functions; the nature of incrementalism.

References

Alexis, M., and Wilson, C. Z., eds. *Organizational Decision Making*. Englewood Cliffs, N.J.: Prentice-Hall, 1967.

Bauer, R. A., and Gergan, K. J. *The Study of Policy Formation*. New York: Free Press, 1971.

Hickson, D. I., et al. "A Strategic Contingencies Theory of Intraorganizational Power." *Administrative Science Quarterly*, June 1971, pp. 216–229.

Hill, W. "The Goal Formation Process in Complex Organizations." *Journal of Management Studies*, May 1969, pp. 198–208.

Hinings, C. R., et al. "Structural Conditions of Intraorganizational Power." *Administrative Science Quarterly*, March 1974, pp. 22–44.

Karda, M. *Power: How to Get It, How to Use It*. New York: Random House, 1973.

McMurry, R. N. "Power and the Ambitious Executive." *Harvard Business Review*, November/December 1973, p. 140.

"Machiavellian Tactics for B School Students." *Business Week*, October 13, 1975, p. 86.

March, J. G., and Simon, H. A. *Organizations*. New York: Wiley, 1958.

Mason, R. O. "A Dialectical Approach to Strategic Planning." *Management Science*, April 1969, pp. B403–B414.

Mintzberg, H. "Planning on the Left Side and Managing on the Right." *Harvard Business Review*, July/August 1976, pp. 49–58.

Narayanan, V. K., and Fahey, L. "The Micro-Politics of Strategy Formulation." *Academy of Management Review*, January 1982, No. 1, pp. 25–34.

Rondinelli, D. A. "Public Planning and Political Strategy." *Long Range Planning*, April 1976, p. 76.

Simon, H. A. "Theories of Decision Making in Economics and Behavioral Science." *American Economic Review*, June 1959, pp. 253–283.

———. *Administrative Behavior*. New York: Free Press, 1957.

Soelberg, P. "Unprogrammed Decision Making." In *Research toward Development in Management Thought: Proceedings of the 1966 Annual Meeting of the Academy of Management*, edited by H. P. Hottenstein and R. W. Williams, 1976, pp. 3–16.

Wu, F. H. "Incrementalism in Financial Strategic Planning." *Academy of Management Review*, January 1981, No. 1, pp. 133–143.

Zalesnik, A. "Power and Politics in Organizational Life." *Harvard Business Review*, May/June 1970, p. 47.

Chapter 7
Implementation

The proof is in the execution.
Robert H. Waterman, Jr.

The most elegantly conceived, most precisely articulated strategy is virtually worthless unless it is implemented successfully. Far too many firms and far too many managers forget this vital component of the strategic management process. Braniff chose a grand strategy of growth through market development, to be carried out by opening numerous new routes upon deregulation of the airline industry. It forgot that it did not have sufficient staff (pilots, cabin attendants, service and maintenance personnel) to execute that strategy successfully. Coleco wanted to become a major force in the personal computer market with its Adam. It chose a grand strategy based on a price lower than the competition's. To employ this strategy required consumer-acceptable hardware and software design features and efficient, technologically oriented manufacturing capabilities. Selling the product was not difficult at the projected price. But meeting the requirements of design, price, and quality at that price was. The firm had failed, as of January 1984, to achieve its strategic objectives, because it did not recognize its limitations in the design and manufacturing of this type of product. Fortunately, Coleco did know how to make toys, and the "Cabbage Patch" proved to be a bountiful garden in 1983, saving the company's beleaguered financial statements. These two firms and thousands of others, large and small, discover each year that setting objectives and formulating strategies is one thing, and making those strategies work to achieve their objectives is another.

This chapter examines implementation—the means by which strategy is translated into successful accomplishment. There are any number of approaches to achieving implementation. Most authorities, however, point to the matching of organization structure to strategy, to the development of appropriate systems for implementation, and to the proper management of the organization's human resources and the related organizational culture, as the key ingredients in successful implementation. These topics comprise then the three major parts of this chapter.

Organization and Implementation

A great many administrators and managers carry in their heads a pattern of the "ideal" organization. That pattern is the classic hierarchy, the family tree; one man at the top, with three below him, each of whom has three below him, and so on with fearful symmetry unto the seventh generation, by which stage there is a row of 729 junior managers and an urgent need for a very large triangular piece of paper.

—*Anthony Jay*

In the organizational structuring process, the tasks and jobs required to achieve objectives are determined; and authority is delegated to perform these tasks. This structuring process has a significant impact upon mission accomplishment:

1. Because structure defines the specific actions to be taken in implementation.
2. Because structure establishes the degree of autonomy each individual has in performing implementation activities.

Organization and implementation are highly interdependent processes. For example, the amount of authority a manager has places limits on his or her ability to lead and to motivate—two critical managerial implementation processes. Organizations are normally ongoing. Therefore, most organizations are not concerned with organizing for the first time, but rather with achieving an appropriate combination of strategy and structure in order to ensure the proper implementation. The components of the organizational process model discussed in this chapter are indicated in Figure 7.1.

Organizational Structure

An organization's structure is the combination of its formal and informal structures. Most perceive the organizational structure as those boxes and connecting lines depicted on the formal organization chart. But, if the actual concept and relationships portrayed there are to be realistically envisioned, then the informal organization must be considered. The primary dimensions of formal structure include

Figure 7.1
The Organization—a Strategic Management Process Model

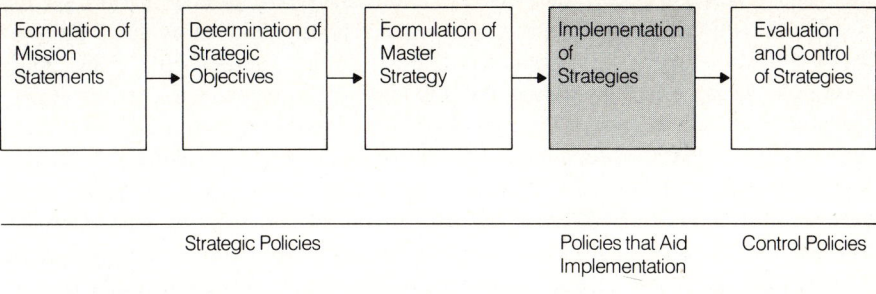

1. Roles as required by plans and successive divisions of labor (defining the task).
2. Delegation of authority to various individual roles and groupings of roles to enable people who fill the roles to accomplish them (delegating the authority to accomplish the task).

Other major structural dimensions include

1. The manager's span of control.
2. The grouping of roles and spans of control into departments on a functional, product, customer, project, geographic, or SBU division basis.
3. The formalization of processes as revealed in records and reports.
4. The existence of written policies, procedures, and rules governing behavior.
5. Written communications.
6. The number of levels of authority in the organization.

A formal, rationally organized social structure involves clearly defined patterns of activity in which, ideally, every series of actions is functionally related to the purposes of the organization.   —Robert K. Merton

The informal organization consists of all that is not formal, primarily

1. The personalities of the individuals who fill the roles prescribed by the formal structure.
2. The informal groups which develop within the formal structure.

While much of what follows in this chapter is primarily related to formal structure, the individual and the group as determinants of structure will be discussed where relevant, though not in great detail. The following paragraphs examine factors which are considered to be the primary determinants of structure. Proper combinations of strategy and structure will also be discussed.

Formal Structures

Three basic organizational structures exist: the classical pyramid, the matrix, and the team. (See Figure 7.2.) Each displays a different distribution of authority.

The pyramidal form is found in most organizations and is the product of classical organization theory. It is common in both single- and multiple-SBU firms. Staff positions may be added throughout the pyramid but do not change its basic shape. Both the team and the matrix are normally found as part of the pyramidal structure, rather than as separate structures unto themselves. Figure 7.3 indicates the major types of basic pyramidal forms. The simple structure is normally found in the small organization, in the early stages of its existence, or later stages if it does not grow. The economic functional structure is usually the next structure to be employed as an organization grows when it still has one major product, or only a few products. The third structure presented is the product structure. As firms reach certain sizes and various products become significant in terms of contribution to the firm, then it becomes desirable to structure on the basis of products. Once enough product lines in a specific industry or major target market area become sufficiently large, the organization will normally proceed to some type of SBU structure, such as indicated in Figure 7.4. Within any of these four major types of pyramids, departmentation of jobs may occur on the basis of geography, client, and by task specialization. The very large complex organization, pictured in Figure 7.4, often has all of these types of departmentations and basic structures as components. Additional comments on these structures occur later as we discuss in more detail the relationships between and among strategy, structure, and size.

The exact shape of a particular organization's pyramid is primarily a function of the spans of control which exist in the organization. A flat pyramid indicates large spans of control and a high degree of delegation of authority. A tall, slim pyramid indicates small spans of control and little delegation of authority. But shapes can be deceiving. Actual delegation may far exceed what the shape indicates. Decentralization is a matter of interpersonal relationships, not simply a matter of line drawings on an organization chart.

The matrix form of organization structure, further illustrated in Figure 7.5, in-

Figure 7.2
The Shapes of Organization Structures

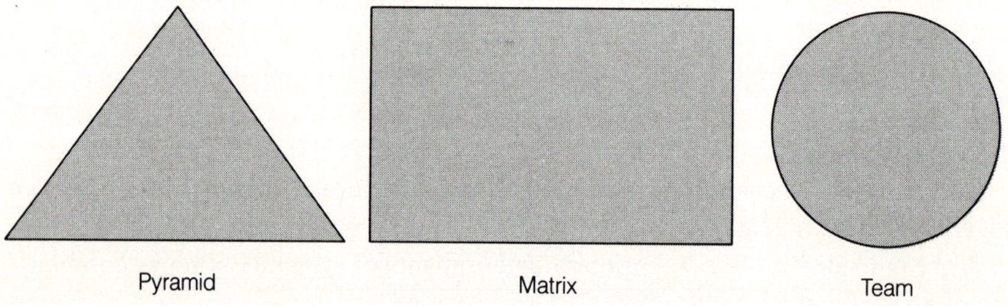

Pyramid   Matrix   Team

Figure 7.3
Types of Pyramids

I. Simple Structure

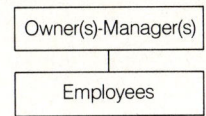

II. Economic Functional Structure

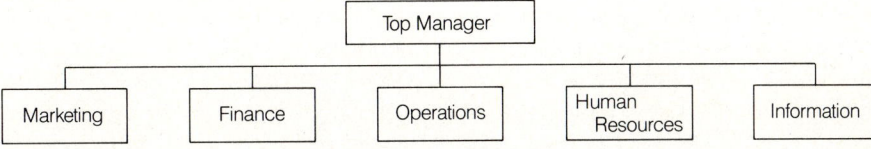

III. Product Structure

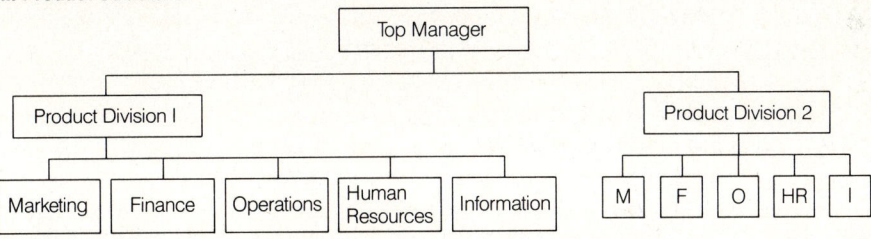

IV. Project Structure

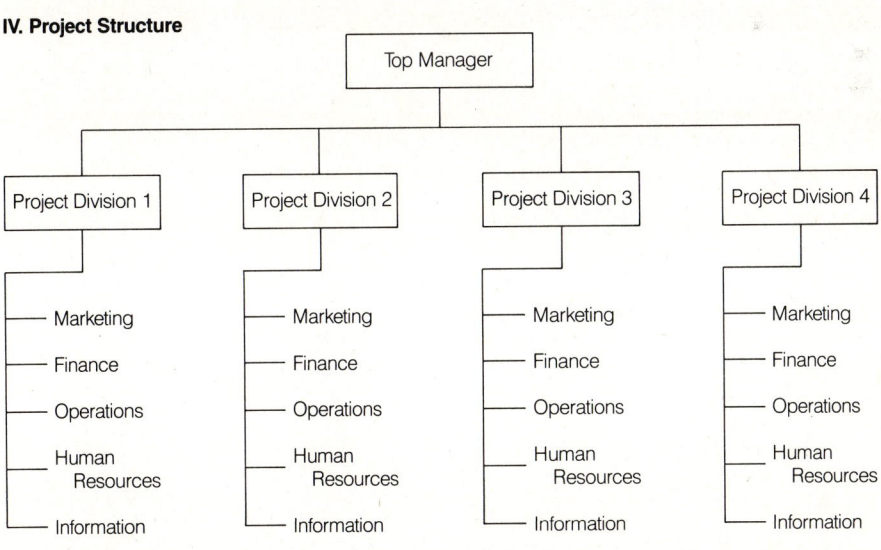

Figure 7.4
Typical Multidepartmental Organization

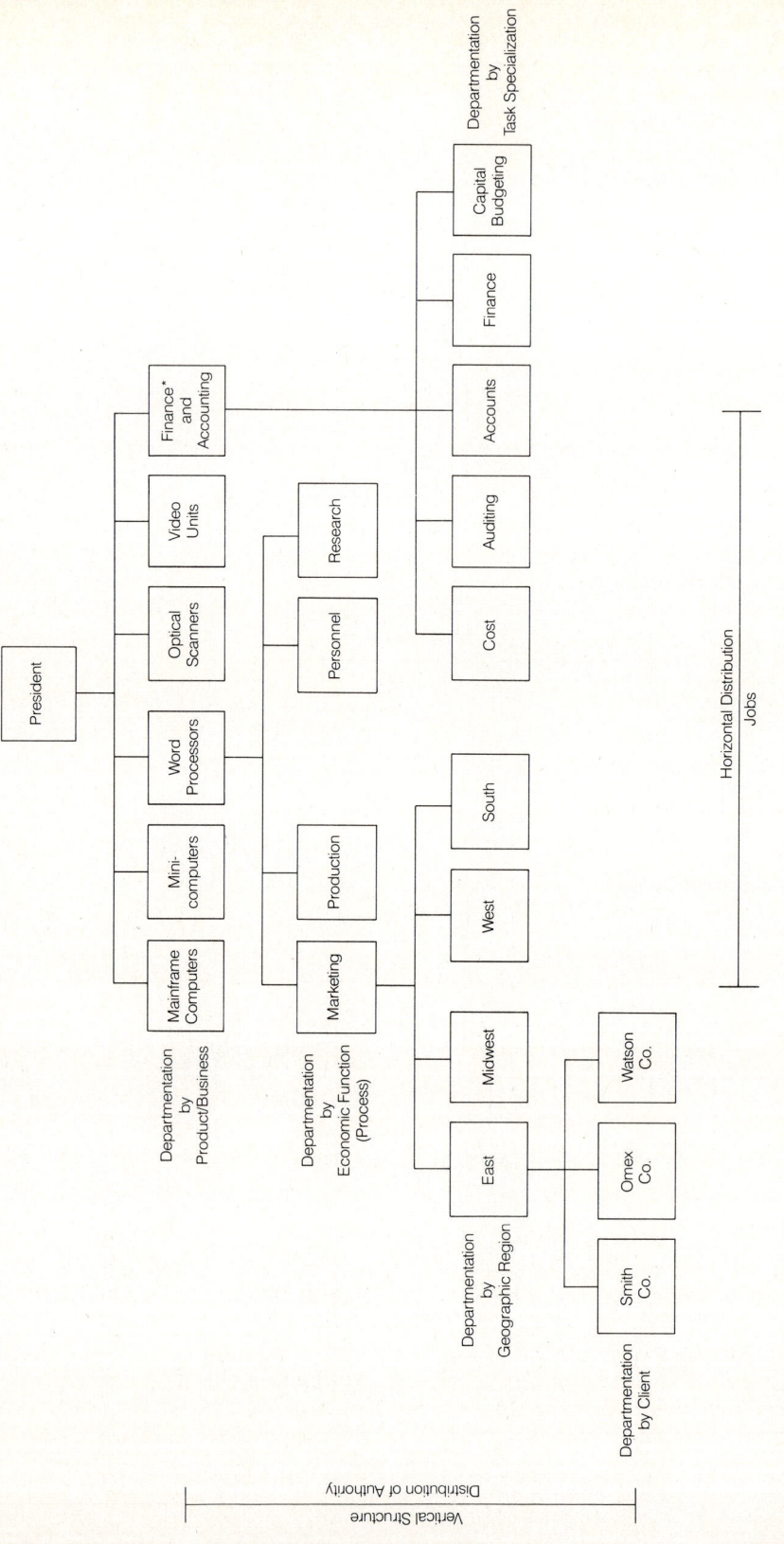

*This particular staff job is normally centralized, that is, operating divisions do not usually have their own finance department.
Source: J. M. Higgins, *Human Relations Concepts and Skills*. Copyright 1982, Random House, Inc., p. 237.

Figure 7.5
The Matrix Organization

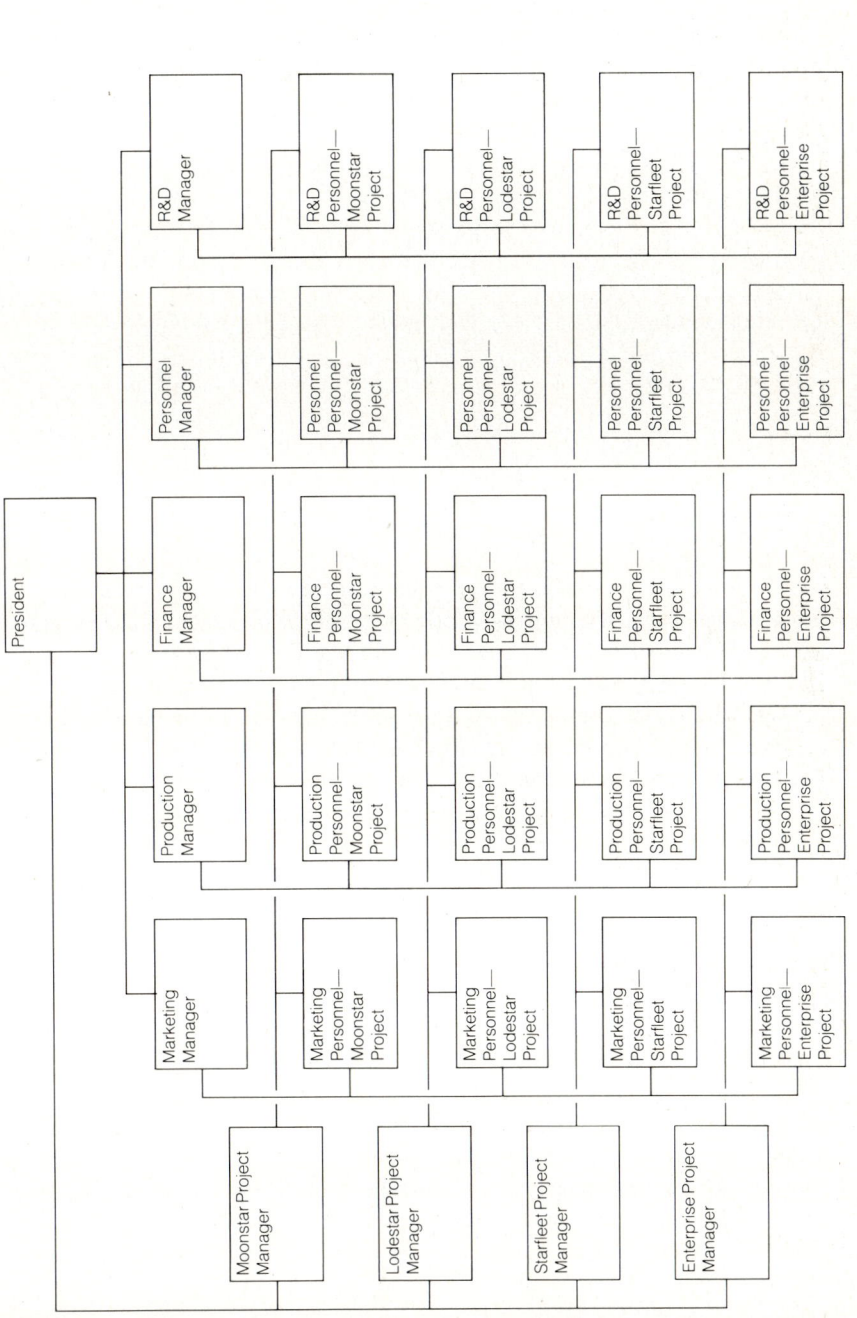

Information Capsule 7.1
The Sun Comes Up Matrix

In 1980, Sun Banks, the then third largest bank group in the state of Florida, found itself with numerous operational problems. Many of its branches had been acquired through purchase. As a result, numerous differing policies and practices existed in the Sun system. Reporting relationships were especially troublesome in acquired banks, as loan officers and other operating personnel reported to their former presidents, who were now branch managers. Lending limits varied substantially, and often were not acceptable to higher headquarters. But changes were slow to come through branch managers, many of whom naturally wanted to protect their individual banks since they had a personal interest in them. In reviewing what systems other major banks employed to overcome these problems, it became obvious that the matrix system was the solution. Loan officers and operations officers were placed in a dual reporting relationship. They were controlled in terms of loan and operational policies through the headquarters loan and operations officers, but they reported to the branch manager for routine day to day operations. This arrangement proved to be extremely beneficial in improving control over branch activities.

volves simultaneous authority over a line or staff employee by both a project or product manager and a functional manager. Matrix organizations are common in aerospace firms such as Lockheed or Martin Marietta, where it is necessary to use functional specialists for a period of time on a project, SBU, or product. Matrix management is also appropriate to firms where assignments by functional specialty are made within continuing organizational subunits and where both subunit and functional control are desired; for example, a loan officer at a Bank of America branch. Its use in banking is discussed in Information Capsule 7.1.

The matrix organization is used in many organizations to overcome the complex problems of business diversity of either projects or products. A strict project form of management structure differs from the matrix form in that the project structure is principally a temporary pyramidal form of management with line and staff personnel assigned to the project for a limited time period. (See Figure 7.3.) In matrix, the project is ongoing and the individual employee has two quasi-permanent bosses.

The team management concept, as illustrated in Information Capsule 7.2, emphasizes the sharing of authority among team members—hence the circle in Figure 7.2 to indicate an equal distribution of authority. The term *team* implies an attitude as much as a structure. The actual distribution of authority depends upon numerous factors; but the essence of team management is participation—the sharing of authority between leader/manager and followers/subordinates in an effort to increase both productivity and employee satisfaction. Teams are usually found as part of a pyramid or matrix. Each work group can be viewed as a team as long as the atti-

Information Capsule 7.2
The Quality Control Circle

The quality control circle is a team management approach being utilized increasingly in the United States and Canada today. The quality control circle is a voluntary group of employees, meeting periodically on company time to analyze and solve work related problems. Major features of the group include their heavy usage of statistical quality control methodologies and their use of participation in decision making. The supervisor of the work group participates in these meetings, but is more of a facilitator and resource person than a traditional "boss."

The quality control circle was started in Japan, but has been imported to the United States and Canada in an effort to improve sagging quality and productivity. It remains to be seen whether or not this approach can work well in these countries, but reported results in companies such as Lockheed, Quasar, Martin Marietta and others have been impressive.

tudes utilized in the work force favor participation. More and more organizations are adopting one type of team approach or another in an effort to achieve those objectives. In any organization, some chain of command must exist; but how the subordinates participate within that chain is the vital issue.

In addition to the three structures described above, another form exists—the venture. Ventures are basically partnerships between two distinct organizations which allow firms to combine their strengths and mitigate their weaknesses to accomplish jointly a task neither could achieve singly. Many times, capital or cash flow is a major consideration. Technology and management skills are also important factors. Quite often, a smaller, technologically innovative firm will combine with a larger, cash-rich, marketing-oriented firm to market a particular product, often for a set period of time. Edward B. Roberts suggests that two major problems occur in joint ventures.[1] First, both partners may misread the match; each may think the other is better suited to the joint purpose than it is. Second, there is often what Roberts calls an impedance mismatch; the firms simply do not manage the same way. The smaller firm, for example, may find itself ready to make decisions, while the larger firm's representatives must carry back information from meetings to superiors, who will ultimately decide on strategic matters. Nonetheless, the rewards from ventures can be great, and ventures are an increasingly popular form of organization structure.

[1] E. B. Roberts, "New Ventures for Corporate Growth," *Harvard Business Review*, (July/August 1980), pp. 134–142.

Choosing a Structure

Most decisions regarding structure are concerned with

1. What division of labor is appropriate for a given situation (defining the task).
2. Whether, how, and to what degree the organization should be centralized or decentralized (delegating authority to accomplish the task).

The determinants of structure have been examined extensively in both the normative and the empirical literature. It is evident that no single factor determines structure. Rather, multiple factors are responsible for the structures used by organizations. The primary determinants appear to vary from situation to situation. However, consideration of available information indicates that the following seven factors are the most important determinants of structure in most situations. Since these factors and related research should be familiar, they will not be reviewed here in depth.

1. *Size (Growth)*. Organizational size is a significantly explanatory variable. As organizations grow to certain sizes, they encounter various structural problems. The product or SBU division is a natural consequence of growth.
2. *Technology*. The types and complexity of the technology employed to accomplish an organization's tasks have been shown to be significantly related to structure. This complexity is not only an issue at lower organization levels, where much of the research has been performed, but also at upper levels, where the complexity of tasks facing top management often requires structural solutions.
3. *Environment*. Several environmental factors seem to help determine structure, but the amount of change in the environment appears to be the most important. Decentralized firms respond faster to the environment than do centralized firms, and are thus preferable in changing environments. Centralized structures fare well in stable environments. Information systems may soon allow centralized structures to be more appropriate to changeful environments.
4. *Top Management Prerogative/Philosophy*. Top management may intentionally choose to structure the organization in a certain manner for reasons related to technology, size, or environment. For example, in order to develop its managers' decision abilities, some firms may require large spans of control. In order to cut overhead, middle management may be virtually eliminated.
5. *Geographic Considerations*. As organizations expand geographically, either within a single country or into different countries, certain divisions of labor must obviously occur. Geographic decentralization does not necessarily require decision decentralization, although the latter often follows. However, geographic decentralization does require new divisions of labor. Martin Marietta, for example, has three SBU group divisions, one of them an international division.
6. *The Informal Organization*. The people who fill positions in the organization may, in fact, demand a particular type of formal structure. For example, profes-

sionals—engineers, accountants, and scientists—may not tolerate a mechanistic, formalized work situation.

7. *Strategy.* A. D. Chandler, in his classic book *Strategy and Structure*, was the first to expound the relationship between these two concepts.[2] His examination of the histories of General Motors, Dupont, Standard Oil of New Jersey, and Sears Roebuck & Company showed that their decentralized, multidivisional structures resulted largely from trial-and-error attempts to meet environmental conditions. He believed that outside market opportunity was the primary variable affecting structure, since structure followed strategy. Also, while supporting the view that size contributed to variations in structure, he observed that task complexity at top management levels also accounted for a significant amount of variation in organizational structure. It is logical that what an organization wishes to become and how it will become what it wishes to be while managing its interactions with the environment would to a great extent decide most of the other structural determinants as well—technology, size, environment, and geographic dispersion. Strategy, by definition and as noted in the organizational process model, leads to structure.

Little further research has been performed strictly on the strategy and structure relationship. However, both Parsons and Selznik have argued that a very definite relationship exists between organizational charter (mission) and structure.[3]

Structure follows strategy. —Alfred Chandler

Strategy follows structure. —David J. Hall and Maurice A. Saias

These seven factors are not mutually exclusive. Their interdependence has made scientific analysis difficult but not impossible. Clearly, strategy and top management prerogative are primary determinants. However, once these commitments are made, the other factors have varying impacts on the eventual structural pattern. Only in recent years, as multivariate techniques have been utilized, has the relative importance of these factors been better understood; and what has become apparent through extensive research is that their relative importance is situational. The following summary observations can be made:

1. All of these factors (plus some not mentioned) contribute to structure, but structure begins with strategy. As Chandler has noted, "Unless structure follows strategy, inefficiency results."[4]

2. Within departments (whether based on product, function, customer, project, or geography), operational technology usually plays a significant role in determining structure specifically impinged on by the work flow. Supportive (knowl-

---

[2] A. D. Chandler, *Strategy and Structure* (Cambridge, Mass.: MIT Press, 1962).
[3] T. Parsons, "Suggestion for a Sociological Approach to the Theory of Organization: I and II," *Administrative Science Quarterly*, (June 1956, pp. 63–85 and September 1956, pp. 225–239); P. Selznik, *TVA and the Grass Roots* (Berkeley: University of California Press, 1949).
[4] Chandler, *Strategy and Structure.*

edge) technology may also play an important role in determining structure. Technology has more of an impact on smaller organizations than on larger ones, on manufacturing organizations than on service organizations. Operational technology has little impact on administrative structures or decentralization.

3. Organizations vary substantially in their structures. Subsystems' structures also vary substantially, both within and among organizations. These differences result from the processes of differentiation and integration—coping with the environment while accomplishing mission.

4. Both size and task complexity affect structure. The more tasks, and the more specialized the tasks, the greater the need for structured arrangements of coordination and control—that is, formalization. Size and complexity of tasks are relevant to top management levels and result in the need for decentralization.

5. The routineness, predictability, or certainty of environment, tasks, or problem-solving orientation have all been depicted as the underlying factor which explains much of the variation in structure. These terms appear to describe the same phenomenon.

6. The Weberian structure model, while common and useful, is limited in its utility as a description of certain types of situations.

7. An organization is not independent of its environment. The degree of interaction and dependency varies, but no organization completely escapes bargaining or accountability. Structure changes as a result.

8. Structure is not and cannot be static in a changing environment.

9. The structure of staff as well as line components is governed by these factors, but in different degrees.

Designing organizations to meet the demands of the situation is not an easy task. There are few authoritative guidelines. The research is only now beginning to suggest what separates effective from ineffective organizations. It has often been assumed that for a given environment or technology a certain structure was appropriate. Empirical evidence to date does not support this view. Rather, many factors result in the selection of structure and in the proper combination of strategy and structure. The next few paragraphs review some of the more common problems associated with organization structure.

Strategy and Structure: Size, Growth, and Environment—a Discussion

Given the results of research and the nature of the strategy formulation process, the organization's primary concern with structure becomes one of matching strategy to structure and structure to size and environment. Size is invariably a direct result of growth. The importance of growth as a factor in structure determination is obvious, since most organizations, especially businesses, grow and have growth strategies. Growth has, of course, been discussed at length, and several theories of resultant structural relationships have emerged. Examining these theories and other data reveals several commonly occurring problem areas related to the relationship of growth, size, and structure.[5]

In its most rudimentary form, a firm begins as an individual entrepreneur with an idea. After a person starts a business, he or she soon realizes that one person cannot perform all of the tasks related to the product or service. The first structural problem arises. To solve it, the entrepreneur must institute a division of labor and hire additional employees on a functional basis. Soon, however, a second structural problem arises. The entrepreneurial leader has not delegated any authority. The functional area personnel are not allowed to manage. They have no autonomy. Eventually the leader must delegate. The amount of authority delegated varies but usually increases as the firm continues to expand. As the organization grows, it arrives at a point at which geographical expansion is desirable. The third structural problem arises. If the expansion occurs entirely within one country, geographic decentralization (division of labor) follows. Increased decision decentralization may or may not ensue. If the expansion involves entering other countries, then a somewhat different pattern of actions is employed. The fourth problem (or third, if it occurs before geographic expansion) is related to diversification. The organization may decide to offer additional product lines or services. The size and task complexity become too much for one leader to manage closely. A decision-decentralized product, project, or SBU division structure normally emerges. A fifth problem—control—is associated with all acts of decentralization. When authority is delegated, results must be assured. Formalization is pursued, but the organization may become mechanistic and unadaptive. Eventually, the organization must develop a means of control by specific objectives, with the division or functional area managers delegated authority to proceed within policy to accomplish those objectives. Other approaches, such as team management or the matrix, may be added, depending on various factors, such as complexity.

While this model is a simplification, it does point to the major problems normally encountered as organizations grow. Next, each of these problem situations will be discussed in more detail.

Entrepreneurial Start-Up—The Need for Functionalization. In practice, most firms begin with some type of functional structure. The problem at this stage of organizational growth is to determine the exact division of labor among the employees. Smaller organizations have difficulty in fully utilizing the efficiencies associated with the division of labor because these firms are just not large enough to take full advantage of all of the possible task simplifications. The cost-benefit tradeoff of hiring additional personnel to perform more efficiently is often not sufficiently positive to justify this action. The recruitment of a work force with multiple task skills is therefore required and unfortunately not easily accomplished.

---

[5]R. R. Blake, W. E. Avis, and J. S. Mouton, *Corporate Darwinism* (Houston: Gulf, 1966); L. E. Greiner, "Evolution and Revolution as Organizations Grow," *Harvard Business Review*, July/August 1972, pp. 37–46; J. R. Montanari, "Operationalizing Strategic Choice" (Paper presented at the Academy of Management Meeting, Kissimmee, Fla., August 1977); R. P. Rumelt, *Strategy, Structure and Economic Performance of the Fortune "500"* (Cambridge, Mass.: Division of Research, Harvard School of Business, 1974); M. Salter, "Stages of Corporate Development," *Journal of Business Policy*, (Autumn 1970); B. R. Scott, "The Industrial State: Old Myths and New Realities," *Harvard Business Review*, (March/April 1973), pp. 133–149; B. R. Scott, *Stages in Corporate Development: Part II* (Cambridge, Mass.: Harvard School of Business, 1971); D. H. Thain, "Stages of Corporate Development," (*Business Quarterly*), Winter 1969, pp. 32–45.

A Crisis of Autonomy—A Solution of Delegation. Some entrepreneurs never can relinquish authority. One clothing manufacturer who had 250 employees and annual sales of $6 million could be found working at 10 p.m. on weekends on the accounts payable ledger, even though he had an accounting staff. Six months after he was advised to use his time better, he was still performing this activity. In another case, an Air Force missile wing commander personally inspected Montana State Highway bridges for tonnage requirements because a bridge had collapsed under a truck carrying a missile. He also personally sanded the base gymnasium floor to make certain a good job was done. And he personally approved every purchase order over $50.

The syndrome is a common one. The question is: who will inform the leader of his or her faults? Just as importantly, how can his or her behavior be changed? A change agent (a consultant) may be requested, but often only after a catalyst, usually a serious downturn in organizational fortunes, has taken place. It is normally the catalyst which calls attention to the need for delegation. This pattern occurs in the largest multidivisional organizations as well as in smaller organizations. Managers have a natural propensity for holding onto power. Indeed, one of the major value orientations of managers is the political orientation, the desire for power, as discussed in Chapter 6.

The Problem of Geographic Expansion—A Solution of Decentralization. When expansion occurs within a single country, the structural patterns routinely include some decision decentralization as well as geographic decentralization. The greater the physical distance, the more the amount of decision decentralization which would seem naturally to follow. When expansion occurs into new countries, a somewhat different pattern of events normally transpires. M. Brooke and H. L. Remmers indicate that this sequence usually begins with the establishment of a base of operations.[6] This step is characterized by initial expansion and accumulation of resources. Second, a single executive is appointed to head foreign operations. Third, new organizational arrangements are developed to administer expansion and new products. A fourth stage of development is emerging, a type of structure in which functional departments service all divisions in all countries.

While decentralization is apparently effective in developed countries, research has suggested that it may be dysfunctional in certain developing countries. The structures of multinationals reveal cultural influences. The structures and succession of structures of multinational businesses may vary according to the country of origin.

Diversification—Decentralization with the Product/SBU Divisionalized Structure. When the business firm diversifies into additional products and services, the characteristic structure utilized is one known as the product/SBU division structure. In this structure, the product/SBU division is the first level of the corporate hierarchy below the CEO. These divisions usually have functional internal structures. The transition from an organization operating on a functional basis to an organization

---

[6]M. Brooke and H. L. Remmers, eds., *The Multinational Company in Europe: Some Key Problems* (Ann Arbor: University of Michigan Press, 1972).

operating primarily on a product/SBU basis is apparently required by the complexity of the top management process in highly complex situations.

A. H. Walker and J. W. Lorsch identified three criteria for choosing between product (SBU) and functional structures:[7]

1. Which approach permits the maximum use of special technical knowledge?
2. Which provides the most efficient utilization of machinery and equipment?
3. Which provides the best hope of obtaining the required control and coordination?

Recognizing, however, the extent of the problem, the behavioral aspects, and the significance of information obtained through research since the first set of criteria was formulated, they offer the following as more relevant criteria:

1. How will the choice affect differentiation among specialists? Will it allow the necessary differences in viewpoint to develop so that specialized tasks can be performed effectively?
2. How does the decision affect the prospects of accomplishing integration? Will it lead, for instance, to greater differentiation, which will increase the problems of achieving integration?
3. How will the decision affect the ability of organization members to communicate with each other, resolve conflicts, and reach the necessary joint decisions?

L. Wrigley found that among larger, diversified firms, the product/SBU divisionalized structure is quite common; it is the dominant form (approximately 90 percent) among *Fortune* 500 companies.[8] A whole series of studies performed at the Harvard School of Business reveals that the divisional form has in the past 15 to 25 years become the dominant form in the largest firms in the United States, Europe, and Japan.[9] L. G. Franko, in a separate survey, found similar results among European firms. However, he suggested that the divisional structure in Europe resulted primarily from competition and not from product diversification strategies, which seems to be the common cause in the United States.[10]

It may very well be that there is a point of diminishing returns with regard to size. As suggested previously, the product/SBU division structure may become tangled by mechanistic control systems which attempt to ensure that all activity is congruent with overall objectives. Commonly, people refer to these controls as red tape. Red tape is found in business, in government, and in nonprofit private sector

---

[7] A. H. Walker and J. W. Lorsch, "Organizational Choice: Product versus Function," *Harvard Business Review*, (November/December 1968), pp. 131–132.

[8] L. Wrigley, "Divisional Autonomy and Diversification" (Ph.D. dissertation, Harvard School of Business, 1970).

[9] D. F. Channon, "Strategy and Structure of British Enterprise" (Ph.D. dissertation, Harvard School of Business, 1971); R. J. Pavan, "Strategy and Structure: The Italian Experience," *Journal of Economics and Business*, (Spring/Summer 1976), pp. 254–260; R. J. Pavan, "Strategy and Structure of Italian Enterprise" (Ph.D. dissertation, Harvard School of Business, 1972); G. Pooley, "Strategy and Structure of French Enterprise" (Ph.D. dissertation, Harvard School of Business, 1972); H. Thanheiser, "Strategy and Structure of German Enterprise" (Ph.D. dissertation, Harvard School of Business, 1972).

[10] L. G. Franko, "The Move toward a Multidivisional Structure in European Organizations," *Administrative Science Quarterly*, (December 1974), pp. 493–506.

organizations. Various means of removing it have been suggested. The best at this time appears to be autonomy for the decision-decentralized divisions. Broad policy guidelines and specific objectives exist for the company, but plans of action are formulated by the divisions themselves. In this process, information and control systems play significant roles.

Team management has been offered as another solution to the problem. If team management should prove to be the appropriate device for controlling large, multidivisional organizations, then presumably another structure problem would result. Only time will tell what problems will result from team management.

In summary, organizational structure seems not to depend on any one factor. Rather, several factors act as determinants. The relevance of each is situational, although strategy begins with structure and management prerogative—two considerations often neglected in current research. Organizations pass through various stages of growth, each of which results in certain structural problems. Finally, it should be observed that we cannot yet determine what problems may be associated with growth beyond the team-managed stage of organization.

Little has been written and probably less is understood about successful implementation, once structure is determined, than about any other phase of strategic management. There is only limited research on this subject as such, and therefore much of what follows is conceptual. Importantly, however, much has been written and research has been undertaken with regard to the topics embodied in the process of implementation. Almost all the management functions—planning, controlling, organizing, motivating, leading, directing, integrating, communicating, and innovation—are in some degree applied in the implementation process. This text is not the appropriate medium for a long discourse on the nature of successful implementation. The focus of the following discussion, then, is on those aspects of implementation which are viewed as the most essential and which may not have been covered extensively in other courses. Where the reader is expected to be familiar with the topic, the discussion is brief and the emphasis is on relating how these familiar topics relate to successful implementation.

I used to keep a sign opposite my desk where I couldn't miss it if I was on the telephone (about to make an appointment) or in a meeting in my office: "Is what I'm doing or about to do getting us closer to our objective?" That sign saved me from a lot of useless trips, lunch dates, conferences, junkets and meetings. —Robert Townsend, Former President, Avis

Implementation Systems

Implementation is the process of translating strategic plans and policies into results. It is the summation of activities in which human resources use other resources to accomplish the objectives of the strategy. In conjunction with the choice of structures, two other key elements are necessary in order for strategy to be successfully implemented. First, as portrayed in Figure 7.6, management systems must be ade-

**Figure 7.6
Implementation**

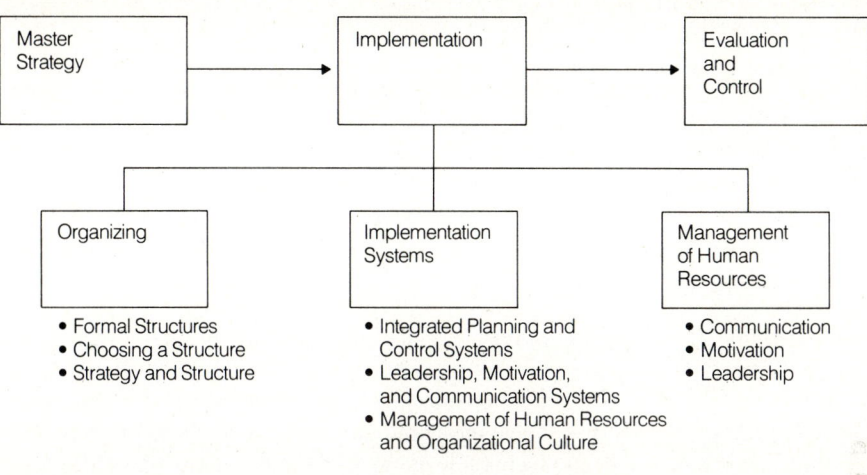

quate to the task. Integrated planning and control systems; appropriate leadership, motivation, and communication systems; and relevant human resource and culture management systems must be utilized. These systems function to ensure that implementation activities—for example, decision making or physical labor—are in accordance with strategy. Vital to this end are objectives, plans, and policies. In most organizations, the strategy is first further spelled out in terms of intermediate plans/ programs, and later in terms of operational plans. Individual and work group actions then follow. Operational planning is especially critical to successful implementation, since, in this planning effort, the exact actions to be taken by first-line employees are delineated. One of the major operational plans, a financial plan, is the budget, which guides the year-to-year expenditure of funds in pursuit of mission accomplishment. Second, once resources—human, financial, and capital—are committed to the tasks established in organizing, they must be properly managed. Appropriate human resource management by individual managers is the essence of this phase of implementation.

Integrated Planning and Control Systems.

Integrated planning and control starts with master strategy formulation and is of concern in the formulation of all plans derived from the master strategy. Successful implementation requires that precise objectives be stipulated for strategies and for the intermediate and operational plans derived therefrom. This is accomplished through the use of an MBORR-type system, as was discussed in Chapter 3. Precise objectives, by clarifying role prescription for executives, managers, and first-line employees, achieve the following:

1. They assure that these individuals will know what is expected of them.
2. They provide built-in standards against which performance can be compared for control purposes.
3. They assume that each action taken is in pursuit of mission.

Integration of the efforts of the organization's subsystems is assisted by these systems and by network planning models such as the now-familiar Program Evaluation Review Technique (PERT), Critical Path Method (CPM), and Gantt Charts. Since control is the subject of the next chapter, this chapter focuses on the planning aspects of these systems. The following sections discuss the following planning and control systems: intermediate planning programs, operational planning, and budgets.

Intermediate Planning Programs. In the intermediate planning phase, the broader plans of strategy are more specifically delineated in what are often referred to as programs. Large, diversified organizations make these more refined plans on an SBU/product division basis. The business/product divisions themselves, as well as firms that make a single product or few products, formulate these plans on a functional (marketing, production, finance, personnel) basis. Some firms attempt to skip the intermediate phase entirely, going directly from strategy to operation. This usually results in ineffective operations, since strategies are so broad and operations so specific that additional intermediate planning is necessary for a smooth transition. Intermediate plans vary greatly in scope, time, horizon, comprehensiveness, and degree of detail. Normally, several successive intermediate plans are required to translate strategy into operations. For example, in a large multinational firm, the master strategy might consist of a corporate strategy and several SBU/product division strategies. These in turn might consist of competitive, supportive, and strategic issues strategies. Each of these components has several substrategies, all requiring intermediate plans/programs. (Some prefer to use the term *program* as a designation for an SBU division grand strategy only.)

As an example, let us examine the production substrategy. An intermediate plan is required to translate the production strategy into requirements for the various countries involved. Another intermediate plan is required to allocate objectives and actions to plants within those countries. Then, another intermediate plan is required to allocate objectives and actions to departments within each plant. Finally, operational planning occurs to allocate objectives and tasks to individuals. At each of these levels, coordinated policies are generated to aid managers in decision making.

Planning—setting objectives and determining plans to reach those objectives—is what connects mission with individual performance. Intermediate plans play an important role in this process. By establishing successive levels of objectives, plans to reach those objectives, and coordinated policies to ensure proper implementation of those plans, organizations greatly improve their chances of success. The individuals who must perform operational tasks can do so correctly only if they know precisely what they are supposed to do. The intermediate planning process aids in forming proper individual role prescriptions by parceling strategic objectives, plans, and policies into more manageable dimensions at each successive level of

Chief, Production Has a Question for the Site Selection Committee. . . .

the firm. Note that what is strategic to divisions or SBU will be an intermediate plan/program to the total organization.

Operational Planning. Operational planning is a key component of implementation. Operational plans normally cover a period of one year, although the period varies among organizations. General Electric and many other organizations label these one-year operating plans Profit Plans. The plans are used to translate intermediate plans into definite, result-producing actions. The descriptions of these actions and their objectives are normally referred to as procedures, roles, or job descriptions. It is operational plans that give substance to strategy. They have the most detailed objectives and the most specific activity requirements of any plans. They specify the exact resources needed and the precise manner in which they are to be obtained and utilized. Operational planning involves the middle and lower levels of management.

As observed by T. A. Anderson, operating plans emphasize automatic decision rules, procedures, and integrative activity.[11] These plans are concerned with the adjustment of production, marketing, and financial capacity to the levels of operation. They aim to increase the efficiency of operating activities. They provide specific

---

[11] T. A. Anderson, "Coordinating Strategic and Operational Planning," *Business Horizons*, Summer 1965, p. 51.

details of short-term operations. Operational planning focuses on the ways and means of accomplishing strategic objectives.

Budgets. The most common of the specific operational planning and control systems is the budget. The budget is usually referred to as a financial operating plan. It translates plans of action, usually operating plans, into dollar commitments. Through the budget, the organization determines whether an operating plan is acceptable on the bottom line (anticipated profit).

There are normally two major types of budgets: the operating budget and the financial budget. The operating budget consists of various functional budgets. This budget begins with a revenue forecast. For business, this is the sales forecast; for government, it is the tax receipt estimate and the monetary manipulations forecast; and for nonprofit private sector organizations, it may be a forecast of contributions. In budgeting, estimated expenditures are matched against anticipated revenues and role expectations emerge. Usually, some provisions are made for unforeseen variations in budgeted performance expectations. The operational budget's impacts upon the financial health of the firm are portrayed in the financial budget, composed of various cash and capital budgets. These, in turn, are used to develop pro-forma financial statements. Figure 7.7 details the relationships of the major types of budgets.

Leadership, Motivation, and Communication Systems

Strategists must lead and motivate their subordinates in order to have successful implementation. Top management's leadership style has a tremendous impact on the success and failure rates of corporations. There are now only beginning to emerge a number of theories related to top management styles and their impacts on successful implementation. These are as yet too preliminary for discussion here, but comments on leadership made later in this chapter are generally relevant.[12] Equally as important as leadership are the motivation/compensation approaches employed to motivate managers to implement strategy. Part of Chapter 5 addressed this issue in terms of motivating SBU managers in multiple-SBU firms. On a broader scale, the strategists and the organization must provide some reason, normally monetary in nature, for the top managers (and all others) to want to implement strategy. Participative types of management also apparently motivate managers to want to implement strategy. Careful thought and attention must be given to the development of these systems. More detailed commentary, relevant here as well, follows on motivation as it applies in general. Finally, an entire range of communication systems—policies, rules, procedures, memorandums, marketing plans, program plans, bulletin boards, periodic meetings, company newspapers, retreats, action lines, and so forth—must be carefully employed in order to assure successful implementation. (Note that plans not only serve the function we normally envision, but also serve as communication devices as well.)

---

[12] For example, see J. G. Wissema, H. W. Van Der Pol, and H. M. Messer, "Strategic Management Archetypes," *Strategic Management Journal*, (1980), Vol. 1, pp. 37–47.

**Figure 7.7
The Budget**

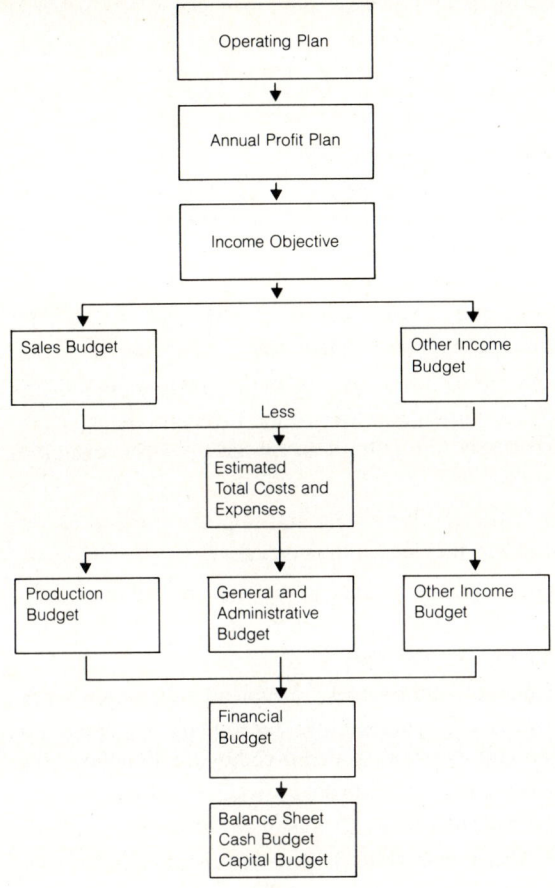

Management of Human Resources and Organizational Culture

From the systems perspective, much of these areas are managed through the personnel, or human resource management function, which is, in most organizations, assuming a much more significant role than it did years ago.

Human resources officers now play a key role and command top dollar.
—Business Week

A Note on the Personnel Function. The personnel department—or, as it is often called today, the human resources management department—is charged with two primary series of functions. The first focuses on placing the employee and includes

Personnel Planning. Determining the jobs necessary to carry out the mission; determining the number of people needed and where and when they will be needed and, with what capabilities, to fill those jobs.

Recruiting and Attracting. Obtaining a pool of applicants for those jobs.

Selecting. Choosing from among the applicants those best suited to perform those jobs.

Training and Developing. Preparing employees to perform those jobs.

Orienting. Integrating the individual into the work unit.

The second series of functions occurs once the employee has been placed in the job; it includes

Training and Developing. Training and development occur both before and after placement as employees continue to grow and seek new jobs.

Providing Compensation, Benefits, Motivation. One of the major functions of the personnel department is to motivate employees, most often through compensation and benefits systems but increasingly through other programs—for example, through improving managerial styles.

Ensuring Employees' Health and Safety. Monitoring and improving the work environment and providing insurance are included in this category.

Helping Group Relations. Group relations relates to unions and other specific groups, such as employees protected by equal employment opportunity laws, professional employees, youthful employees, and so forth.

Evaluating and Controlling. Evaluation and control are typically accomplished at the individual level through performance appraisal and disciplinary systems. Promotion, termination, and transfers, for example, are resolved by this function. The ultimate objective is to assure that organizational behavior leads to mission accomplishment. Human resource managers design the systems to do this.

Managing Change. Increasingly, the human resources management department is assuming the function of managing change through organizational development and related approaches for treating people within the organization.

Improving Productivity. In the United States and Canada, increasing concern exists for improving productivity. Through various systems, such as work redesign, changes in managerial styles and organizational structures, and improvements in technology, the personnel department is leading this effort in many organizations.

Improving Organizational Communication. Numerous programs to improve communication have been attempted. Among them are employee assistance programs, listening posts, company newspapers and magazines, bulletin boards, television broadcasts, discussion groups, meetings, and so forth.

The purpose of all of these functions is to assure that organizational behavior accomplishes strategic objectives. Personnel's role is an increasingly critical one, one which goes far beyond its traditional staffing functions. The organization's systems for managing organizational behavior are to a great extent designed and controlled by this department.

As a result, human resources departments, in conjunction with and as influenced by, the strategist(s)'s managerial style(s), determine to a great extent the nature of the organization's culture. In reexamining their functions, you will see that factors such as motivation, the management of groups and change, and the management of productivity, would have a tremendous influence on organizational culture.

Business performance therefore requires that each job be directed toward the objectives of the whole business. —Peter Drucker

Human Resource Management, Organizational Behavior, and the Individual Manager

After operational planning has been accomplished, what remains is to ensure that resources are appropriately utilized. The following paragraphs focus on how individual managers manage human resources, because if these resources are effective and efficient in fulfilling their roles, then the remaining resources will be effectively and efficiently managed as well.

An exhaustive treatment of organizational behavior is beyond the scope of this text. Organizational behavior is the subject of other texts and other courses. However, a brief review to relate its importance to strategy will be helpful.

Once the organization is committed to a course of action, communication, motivation, and leadership are needed to assure successful implementation. Therefore, a brief review of the major facets of these three important concepts is relevant. Moreover, the other functions of management should not be ignored. Lower-level managers, those primarily responsible for this phase of implementation, must plan—to an appropriate degree, organize, control, communicate, and make decisions. Also critical to this process are the actions of the personnel division as it obtains human resources for the organization and provides organizational systems to aid the individual manager in motivation and leadership efforts. If you will review Information Capsule 2.1, you will observe just how important human resource management can be.

Communication

Thirty to 70 percent of an individual manager's time in the organization may be spent communicating. Communication occurs verbally and nonverbally; nonverbal communication may account for as much as 70 percent of the message. Not only sending, but listening is critical to the success of the communication process. It is evident that more and more organizations will train their employees in this vital but often misunderstood practice.

Motivation

Motivation, in an organizational context, is the managerial influencing of subordinates to accomplish the objectives of the organization. This is accomplished by providing an environment in which the employee can satisfy needs and in so doing accomplish organizational objectives. Motivation begins with an individual's perception of needs. The organization may provide need satisfiers; so may the manager. Because of organizational motivation systems, managers often have limited latitude in providing need satisfiers. The manager's motivation dilemma may evolve into attempts to build satisfaction into a particular job and to provide rewards where no organizational opportunities exist. For example, to reward superior performance when no merit compensation is given by the organization, the manager may have to develop some enterprising recognition techniques.

The number of needs and hence need satisfiers is substantial. Typical needs include physiological, safety, social, esteem, self-actualization, power, achievement, objective accomplishment, and role fulfillment. And while needs appear to be ordered in a hierarchy, it is proving to be a different hierarchy than that conveyed by Maslow. Needs may be classified as intrinsic or extrinsic with respect to a particular position, but are not readily stereotyped into motivators or hygienic factors as originally proposed by Herzberg. Motivation is further complicated by the fact that individual needs are multiple, change over time, and vary from situation to situation. As need satisfiers are offered, certain moderator variables may impinge and prevent the need satisfiers from having the desired impact. Managers must be alert to these processes. For example, employees ask themselves questions before and after rewards are offered such as: Can I do the job? If I do the job, will I get the reward? What's the reward worth to me? Was the reward tied to performance? Were the rewards equitably distributed? Furthermore, there seems to be a major impact on continued motivation made by the process itself in terms of how the individual's self-image was affected.

The individual manager's role in motivation is to diagnose the situation correctly, determine the appropriate need satisfier or need satisfiers, offer them or effective substitutes, and ensure that consequences of the motivation process are congruent with expected results, all within organizational and nonorganizational constraints. This is obviously not an easy undertaking, but it is essential if employees are to fulfill their tasks. If individuals work to only a small part of their capabilities, then the organization will fall short of mission accomplishment. It is motivation which causes employees to work nearer their full potentials.

Leadership

Management is situational; leadership, a major function in the total management process, could hardly be otherwise. The situational approach to leadership proposes that managers identify the major factors in each situation and adjust their leadership techniques to match those factors. The difficulty lies in identifying the most critical factors. Some critical factors for the manager to consider in choosing a leadership style are the subordinates' needs and personalities, the nature of the subordinates' work groups, the types of tasks the subordinates perform, and the organization's structure and climate.

Having acknowledged the situational aspects of the leadership function, it is important to note that leaders then have a choice from among many types of leadership behaviors. The more or less continual pattern of these choices and resultant actions is known as leadership style. The major areas within which they must make leadership choices are[13]

Task. How much should I emphasize goals, objectives, the job, and how much should I control this person's, or this group's performance?
Relationship. How much do I want to attempt to build strong social friendships with subordinates; how much do I do to satisfy their social needs?
Rewards. How much should I and can I reward behavior?
Attitude. What type of attitudinal approach do I want to use with this person, this group?
Participation. How much do I let this person or group participate in decision making?

Obviously, not all behaviors are appropriate in all situations or for all managers. Again, leadership style is to a great extent explained by organizational climate. The individual manager's propensity for authoritarian versus democratic management style is tempered by how the organization prefers to be led. Organizational leadership style preferences are defined in policy and become a part of structure.

Not only is it difficult to effect changes in the styles of managers overnight, but the question that we raise is whether it is even appropriate. —Paul Hersey and Kenneth H. Blanchard

A Note on Implementation Policies.

Just as the organization establishes strategic policies to aid in formulating strategy, it must also establish implementation policies to aid in the implementing of strategy. The nature of implementation policies varies with the level of the organization at which they occur. Those at the top management level deal largely with management philosophies of staffing, leading, and motivating. By the time these policies reach the operational level of the organization, they may be quite detailed in terms of how employees will be developed, how managers will treat employees, what reward systems will be employed, how employees may progress in a career within the organization, how employees are recruited and selected, how groups should work together, what control measures can be expected to be utilized, and so forth. In addition, specific task instructions and procedures, detailed budget methodologies and performance evaluation systems would sometimes be included among these policies.

An Additional Perspective on Strategy/Structure/Implementation Relationships—The 7-S's Framework

McKinsey and Company have developed a model known as, "the seven elements of strategic fit," or the "7-S's." The 7-S framework is indicated in Figure 7.8. The

[13] J. M. Higgins, "The Management TRRAP," unpublished working paper.

Figure 7.8
McKinsey 7-S Framework

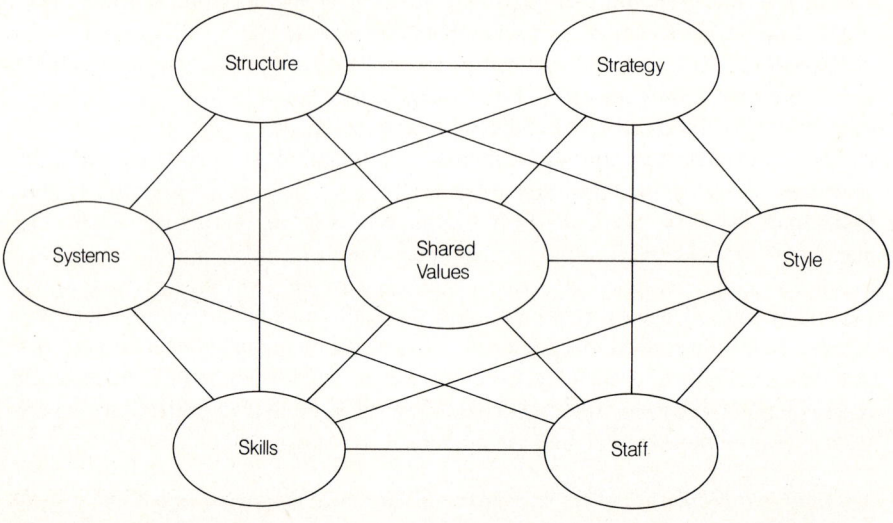

Source: R. H. Waterman Jr., "The Seven Elements of Strategic Fit," p. 70. Reprinted by permission from the *Journal of Business Strategy*, Winter 1982. Copyright © 1982, Warren, Gorhan & Lamont Inc., 210 South Street, Boston, Mass. All Rights Reserved.

EXHIBIT 7.1
A Summary of the 7-S's

1. *Strategy*. A coherent set of actions aimed at gaining a sustainable advantage over competition, improving position vis-à-vis customers, or allocating resources.
2. *Structure*. The organization chart and accompanying baggage that show who reports to whom and how tasks are both divided up and integrated.
3. *Systems*. The processes and flows that show how an organization gets things done from day to day (information systems, capital budgeting systems, manufacturing processes, quality control systems, and performance measurement systems all would be good examples).
4. *Style*. Tangible evidence of what management considers important by the way it collectively spends time and attention and uses symbolic behavior. It is not what management says is important; it is the way management behaves.
5. *Staff*. The people in the organization. Here it is very useful to think not about individual personalities but about corporate demographics.
6. *Shared values* (*or superordinate goals*). The values that go beyond, but might well include, simple goal statements in determining corporate destiny. To fit the concept, these values must be shared by most people in an organization.
7. *Skills*. A derivative of the rest. Skills are those capabilities that are possessed by an organization as a whole as opposed to the people in it. (The concept of corporate skill as something different from the summation of the people in it seems difficult for many to grasp; however, some organizations that hire only the best and the brightest cannot get seemingly simple things done while others perform extraordinary feats with ordinary people.)

Source: R. H. Waterman, Jr., "The Seven Elements of Strategic Fit," p. 71. Reprinted by permission from the *Journal of Business Strategy*, Winter 1982. Copyright © 1982, Warren, Gorham & Lamont Inc., 210 South Street, Boston, Mass. All Rights Reserved.

7-S's include: strategy, structure, systems, style, staff, skills, and shared values. These seven S's are defined briefly in Exhibit 7.1. The underlying concept of the model is that all 7 of these variables must "fit" with one another in order for strategy to be successfully implemented. The idea of "fit" is that successful strategy implementation depends on a proper "culture," and that only if all 7-S's are working in coordinated fashion, will this culture exist. A number of McKinsey clients have adopted this framework as a model for attempting to implement strategy.[14] And, from the conceptual viewpoint, the framework is appealing. It has yet to be shown, however, on the basis of research, as to whether or not successful implementation or failure in implementation can be predicted using this model. This model agrees generally with the major elements presented in this chapter, and their components—structure, systems, and the management of human resources by individual managers. Thus the 7-S's are in general agreement with much of the strategic management literatures as to the key factors for successful implementation.

Multinational Aspects of Organization and Implementation

The basics of structure are the same for multinationals as for other firms; but as noted earlier in this chapter, various macrostructures may be employed in different countries for different reasons.[15] Typically, multinationals add a "foreign subsidiaries" or "foreign business" division as one of their major SBUs. Then, depending upon growth, size, and the other structural determinants, other departmentations, such as geographic subdivisions or product subdivisions, may occur. It is almost always necessary to have special departments within the major staff functions of finance and personnel to cope with the problems encountered. With respect to delegation of authority, management styles, job design, and other microstructural phenomena, the multinationals find themselves subject to a set of rules quite different from those governing domestic firms.

When you go to a foreign country, much that you have learned about the meanings of people's behaviors will not apply. Not only the verbal languages but also the nonverbal languages are different. Furthermore, cultural patterns vary significantly among countries. Multinational managers are confronted with a bewildering array of changes. The following pages provide insights into a few of the problems which may be encountered.

Time. Probably nowhere is time so critical as in the United States and Canada. The Japanese use time especially well with Americans because they know our weak-

---

[14] R. H. Waterman, Jr., "The Seven Elements of Strategic Fit," *Journal of Business Strategy*, (Winter 1982), pp. 69–73; also see R. H. Waterman, Jr., T. J. Peters, and J. R. Phillips, "Structure is not Organization," *Business Horizons*, June 1980, pp. 14–26.

[15] A. Chandler, Jr., and H. Daems, "The Rise of Managerial Capitalism and Its Impact on Investment Strategy in the Western World and Japan" (Working paper, European Institute for Advanced Studies in Management, 1974); L. E. Fouraker and J. M. Stopford, "Organizational Structure and the Multinational Strategy," *Administrative Science Quarterly*, (March 1968), p. 62; A. R. Neghandi and B. C. Reimann, "A Contingency Theory of Organization Reexamined in the Context of a Developing Country," *Academy of Management Journal*, (June 1972), pp. 137–147; J. L. Simonetti and F. L. Simonetti, "The Impact of Management Policy and Organization Structure on the Management Effectiveness of Firms Operating in Italy," *Journal of Business and Economics*, (Spring/Summer 1976), pp. 249–252; H. Schollhammer, "Organization Structures of Multinational Corporations," *Academy of Management Journal*, (September 1971), pp. 345–365. Also see footnotes 6, 7, 8, 9, and 10 earlier in this chapter.

ness for it. "A Japanese once stated that Westerners have a most convenient weakness: If they are kept waiting long enough they will agree to almost anything. Consequently, negotiators visiting Japan will often be asked how long they have planned to stay. Once that is known, they will be pleasantly entertained, while negotiations are kept inconclusive until a couple of hours before they are scheduled to leave, when the real business starts."[16] In much of Eastern Europe, in China, in parts of South America, and in much of Africa, time is of little consequence. People may seem to take forever to make decisions and, indeed, may feel their esteem raised as the result of the time it takes them to decide.

Aspirations. In some countries, to strive for one's own objectives is discouraged. It is the community, the state, the religion that must be served first. Traditional western motivational systems may fail.

Authority. In much of South America, in much of Russia, and in much of the Middle East, the manager has absolute authority and no subordinate would ever dare practice participative management or even question the manager's orders. On the other hand, in Japan, there is much more participation than in the United States and Canada.

Rank and Social Status. Rank and status play a much more important role outside the United States and Canada than they do in these two countries. The ramifications are significant in terms of forms of address, amount of social space allowed between persons, right to speak one's opinions, and so forth.

Role of Women. Women play more important roles outside the home in the United States than in most of the rest of the world. Women cannot drive cars in Saudi Arabia. They cannot own property in many countries. Women have virtually no managerial roles in Japanese society. Indeed, women are seen and not heard in much of the world. They cannot therefore be multinational managers in many countries.

Discussion Topics. Europeans love to philosophize and analyze issues. Americans typically are not prepared for such discussions in social situations. Furthermore, Europeans are much more likely to accept communistic and socialistic economic philosophies than Americans. Again, problems may result.

Nonverbal Communications. In Greece, a nod of the head means no, not yes. In Italy, one must learn literally hundreds of hand gestures in order to assure that one understands the language. In Europe, it is common for men to embrace upon meeting; but traditionally that has not been acceptable in the United States.[17]

The examples are numerous, but by now, you have probably got the point. The task of implementation is compounded greatly in the multinational operation.

---

[16] H. K. Arning, "Business Customs from Malaya to Murmansk," *Management Review*, (October 1964), p. 11.
[17] These and numerous other cross-cultural human relations examples may be found in J. Higgins, *Human Relations Concepts and Skills* (New York: Random House, 1982) Chapter 14.

Implementation in the Nonprofit Sector

The basic organization structures are the same in nonprofits as in for-profit organizations. The choice as to the appropriate levels of centralization and decentralization is the same. In very large government organizations, there is more of a tendency to become bureaucratized and overrun with red tape than commonly occurs in businesses. There are also frequent differences in management systems and human resource management at the individual managerial level. Money can seldom be used as an extrinsic motivator.

Management systems in small nonprofits are often nonexistent, just as they are in small businesses, but more so. Funding seems to be a problem in many nonprofits, and thus management systems and management development often suffer. Similarly, there would appear to be an insufficient amount of funds to allow for a compensation reward for performance-type motivation systems. Since budgetary supervision is often used as a justification for administrative salary levels, empire building may result. In terms of managing the culture, there are many more constituents to satisfy, typically, than one would find in business. Thus, any major vested group may sabotage implementation efforts. And, there are probably differences in dominant needs between most nonprofit employees and most for-profit employees. This fact alone leads to very distinct changes in leadership, motivation and communication systems, and individual managerial styles. In summary, there are some very distinct differences, yet, there are numerous similarities.

Summary

Organization structure has several major determinants, whose importance varies with the situation. Organizations have a choice among three basic structures: the pyramid, the matrix, and the team. The decentralized pyramid is the most common structure in larger organizations. The product/SBU division structure is the most common structure in diversified firms. The choice of structures depends on seven key factors: size, technology, environment, top management prerogative/philosophy, geographic considerations, the informal organization, and strategy. Once structured, the organization must implement its plans. Successful implementation depends on proper integrative planning and control techniques and on appropriate managerial functioning—especially motivation and leadership. The relationships between organizational structure and implementation are of critical importance.

What can be said with certainty with regard to organization and implementation is that there is no one best way to organize or to implement. Various factors moderate the effects of actions taken. The primary factors affecting each individual situation should be determined and a course of action taken based on this analysis. Sound human resource management policies are critical to implementation, as are proper communication, motivation and leadership. Multinationals encounter many implementation problems related to differences in human relations factors among countries.

Key Terms and Concepts

By the time you have completed this chapter, you should be familiar with the following key terms and concepts: strategy follows structure, structure follows strategy, major structural dimensions, three major formal structures, ventures, seven factors upon which choice of structures depends, common major problems in structure, key elements in successful implementation, the roles of resource management and organizational behavior, the basic personnel functions, the basics of communication, motivation and leadership, and multinational and nonprofit aspects of organization and implementation.

Discussion Questions

1. Describe for each of the seven major determinants of organizational structure a situation in which that determinant plays the major role in determining structure.
2. What did Chandler mean when he said that structure follows strategy?
3. How are size (growth) and structure related?
4. What is the relationship of structure to implementation?
5. Why are systems so important to successful implementation?
6. Why is human resource management so critical to successful implementation?

References

Aldrich, H. B. "Technology and Organization Structure: A Reexamination of the Findings of the Aston Group." *Administrative Science Quarterly*, March 17, 1972, pp. 23–43.

Barrow, J. C. "The Variables of Leadership: A Review and Conceptual Framework." *Academy of Management Review*, April 1977, pp. 231–245.

Bourgeois, L. J., III, and D. R. Brodin, "Strategy Implementation: Five Approaches to an Elusive Phenomenon," *Strategic Management Journal*, July–September 1984 (in press).

Dewar, R. D., and Simet, D. P. "A Level Specific Prediction of Spans of Control Examining the Effects of Size, Technology, and Specialization." *Academy of Management Journal*, March 1981, pp. 5–24.

Ford, J. C., and Slocum, J. W., Jr. "Size, Technology, Environment and the Structure of Organizations." *Academy of Management Review*, October 1977, pp. 561–575.

Franklin, J. L. "Relations among Four Social-Psychological Aspects of Organization." *Administrative Science Quarterly*, September 1975, pp. 422–433.

Grinyer, P. H., and Ysai-Ardekani, M. "Strategy, Structure, Size, and Bureaucracy." *Academy of Management Journal*, September 1981, pp. 471–486.

———. "Dimensions of Organizational Structure: A Critical Replication." *Academy of Management Journal*, September 1980, pp. 405–421.

Jelinek, M., and P. Amar, "Implementing Corporate Strategy Theory and Reality" (Paper presented to the Strategic Management Society, Paris, October 1983).

Miner, J. B., and Dachler, H. P. "Personnel Attitudes and Motivation." *Annual Review of Psychology*, 1973, pp. 379–402.

Pugh, D. S. "The Context of Organizational Structures." Administrative Science Quarterly, December 1969, p. 91.

Chapter 8
The Evaluation and Control of Organizational Strategy

The best laid schemes o' mice an' men gang aft agley.
Robert Burns

There are three primary types of organizational control: strategic control, management control, and operational control. Strategic control, the process of evaluating strategy, is practiced both after strategy is formulated and after it is implemented. The organization's strategists evaluate strategy once it has been formulated to ascertain whether it is appropriate to mission accomplishment and again once it has been implemented to determine if the strategy is accomplishing its objectives.

Management control is the process of assuring that major subsystems' progress towards the accomplishment of strategic objectives is satisfactory. For example, is SBU/Product Division A's ROI performance acceptable? Or, is the Production Department meeting its quality control objectives? Operational control is the process of ascertaining whether individual and work group role behaviors (performance) are congruent with individual and work group role prescriptions. For example, is Tom reaching his sales quota?

Like the phases of planning, the types of control are not distinct entities. Rather, in various organizations, one type of control may be almost indistinguishable from another. Furthermore, the devices used in one type of control may also be employed in another. For example, management control devices such as ROI may be used to measure not only the performance of organizational components but the total organization as well. Finally, while most operational and many management control systems may possess automatic correction activities, the evaluation of strategy requires executive judgment.

**Figure 8.1
The Organization—a Strategic Management Process Model**

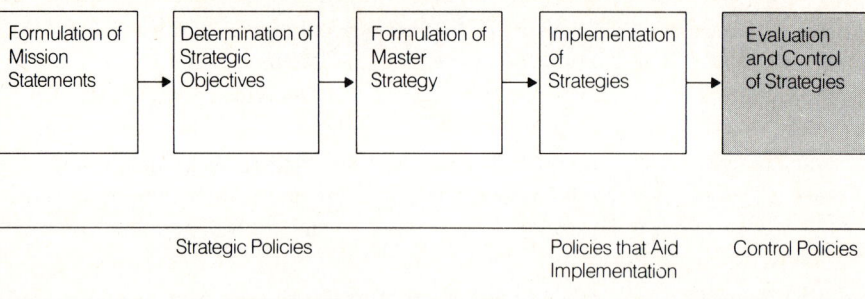

This chapter is concerned with those parts of the strategic management process indicated in Figure 8.1. The chapter begins with a discussion of control, followed by some observations on how to evaluate strategy. Next, some of the more common types of strategic/management control techniques are reviewed. Certain of the more relevant of these are discussed at length. Finally, the dysfunctional consequences of control are presented, followed by some concluding remarks on control and brief discussions of evaluation and control in multinational firms and in nonprofit organizations.

Control and Strategy

Strategic, management, and operational control systems perform an important integrative function. The measurement of performance as related to objective accomplishment coordinates activity. Experience and research have revealed that any number of variables may cause performance to be incongruent with strategy. For example, the assumptions under which strategy was formulated may change. Or, strategy, plans, and policies may not be adhered to. Deviations from either assumptions or guidance lead to unsatisfactory results. Therefore, the successful strategy must have control as one of its dimensions.

What is controlled varies from level to level in the organization. The organization's strategists are responsible for strategic control, as are the stockholders, theoretically. Management control is principally the function of top management, especially the CEO. Operational control is primarily the concern of lower-level managers. Strategic control and management control are concerned with perspectives broader than the details dealt with in operational control. Note, however, that "war" rooms and strategic information systems allow top management to view the details of operations if necessary. While much of what follows is related to formal control systems, informal control systems may suffice in the smaller organization, especially for operational control where personal observation is possible.

Control may be depicted as a six-step feedback model as follows:

1. *The Establishment of Standards of Performance.* Standards are specific points against which actual performance will be judged. As such they are more detailed expressions of strategic objectives and are the bases of role prescriptions. Establishing standards for organizational subcomponents is the first step in management control, and establishing them for individuals is the first step in operational control.

2. *The Statement of Acceptable Tolerances.* The standard is a single point on a continuum of possible behaviors, but it is not always necessary to perform exactly to that point. Normally, deviation from standards will be tolerated within certain control limits.

3. *Measurement of Actual Performance.* Measurement is the third step in management or operational control. It involves the identification of role behavior either for components or individuals. Measurement techniques vary from situation to situation and are often imprecise.

4. *Comparison of Standards and Performance.* While comparing standards and performance might appear to be a simple task, it is quite complex in the more qualitative performance areas because of the inability to quantify either standards or performance.

5. *Action.* Where performance is satisfactory—that is, congruent with standards—no action is necessary. But where it is not, corrective action must be taken.

6. *Preventive Action.* As Bill Greenwood has observed, it is insufficient simply to correct problems. Rather, action must be taken to assure that these problems do not occur again.[1]

This model focuses on results (outputs). In fact, most control systems—strategic, management, or operational—focus on results. Often, the consequence of utilizing these feedback control systems is that the unsatisfactory performance continues until the malfunctioning is discovered. One technique for reducing the problems associated with feedback control systems is "feedforward control." First suggested by Harold Koontz and Robert W. Bradspies, feedforward control focuses on the inputs to the system and attempts to anticipate potential problems with outputs.[2] (See Figure 8.2.)

With respect to strategy and planning, feedforward control has wide applicability. For example, the feedforward principle underlies the concept of simulation modeling. "What if" questions are, after all, examinations of hypothesized inputs to determine resultant effects on system outputs. Simulations of performance can be

---

[1] W. T. Greenwood, *Business Policy: A Management Audit Approach* (New York: Macmillan, 1967); W. T. Greenwood, *Decision Theory and Information Systems* (Cincinnati: South-Western Publishing, 1965); W. T. Greenwood, *Management and Organizational Behavioral Theories* (Cincinnati: South-Western Publishing, 1965).

[2] W. H. Koontz and R. W. Bradspies, "Managing through Feedforward Control," *Business Horizons*, June 1972, pp. 25–36.

Figure 8.2
The Organization as a Processing System

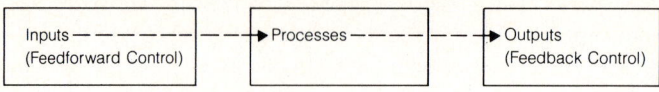

made in any number of strategic situations to test for changes in basic assumptions. In fact, any situation with identifiable inputs which can be modeled can and should utilize the feedforward approach.

Strategic Control: The Evaluation of Corporate Strategy

Once strategy has been formulated, it should be evaluated. Several criteria for evaluation have been suggested. The best known of these, the Tilles model, can be summarized as follows:[3]

1. Is the strategy internally consistent—for example, is it consistent with mission and consistent among its own plans? (other strategies in the master strategy?)
2. Is it consistent with the environment? (constituent demands, competition, economy, product/industry life cycle, suppliers, customers?)
3. Is it consistent with internal resources?
4. Does it have an appropriate amount of risk?
5. Does it have a proper time horizon?
6. Is it workable? Implementable? (The McKinsey 7-S approach discussed in Chapter 7 is applicable here.)

E. P. Learned and others, building on the Tilles model, suggest that the following are also proper evaluative questions:[4]

7. Is it identifiable? Has it been clearly and consistently identified and are people aware of it?
8. Is it appropriate to the personal values and aspirations of key managers?
9. Does it constitute a clear stimulus to organizational effort and commitment?
10. Is it socially responsible?
11. Are there early indications of the responsiveness of markets and market segments to the strategy?

---

[3] S. Tilles, "How to Evaluate Corporate Strategy," *Harvard Business Review*, (July/August 1963), pp. 111–121.
[4] E. P. Learned et al., *Business Policy: Text and Cases* (Homewood, Ill.: Irwin, 1969), pp. 22–25.

J. Argenti adds[5]

12. Does it rely on weaknesses or do anything to reduce them?
13. Does it exploit major opportunities?
14. Does it avoid, reduce, or mitigate the major threats? If not, are there adequate contingency plans?

Intuitively, these questions seem sound. More importantly, they relate directly to the strategic management process model constructed in Chapter 1. In fact, these questions, when considered in total, comprise a checklist to determine if the strategic management process model has been properly followed. All these questions can be applied as the strategy progresses through its various stages, including implementation. Progress and changes can thus be observed. Specific standards of performance are established by the strategic objectives of the master strategy and subsequent component objectives.

Once implementation occurs, measurements will be taken to determine if the objectives have been reached. The tolerances established in Step 2 of the model vary from firm to firm. Tolerances are primarily judgmental—they tell how much deviation from the standard management can live with. Corrective and preventive actions may require that strategy be changed.

Management Control

Management control becomes a distinct concern when decentralization occurs. Where management control is imposed, it functions within the framework established by the strategy. Management control focuses on the accomplishment of the objectives of the various substrategies comprising the master strategy and the accomplishment of the objectives of the intermediate plans. Normally these objectives (standards) are established for major subsystems within the organization, such as SBUs, projects, products, functions, and responsibility centers. Allowable tolerances vary from organization to organization. Typical management control measures include ROI, residual income, cost, product quality, efficiency measures, and so forth. These control measures are essentially summations of operational control measures. When corrective or preventive action is taken, it may involve very minor or very major changes in the strategy. Often, top management strategists may be removed from their positions as the consequence of poor performance as indicated by these control measures. One large firm has a policy for its European operating division managers: "Two consecutive quarters of declining ROI and you're fired!" Often, critical decisions for a company's future result from rather imperfect control information, as Information Capsule 8.1 reveals. Chrysler, in its recovery strategy, made important plant closing decisions based on admittedly imperfect information, some of which was based on assumptions of costs, schedules, and imports.

---

[5] J. Argenti, *Systematic Corporate Planning* (New York: Wiley, 1974), pp. 266–267.

Information Capsule 8.1
Chrysler, Considering Further Cutbacks, Is Using a New Tough Standard to Decide

Chrysler Corp. is considering further cutbacks in its manufacturing operations based on a new tough standard it is using to determine whether each of its plants is contributing to the bottom line.

During the past few months, Chrysler has been studying about 16 of its automotive plants to determine whether the parts they produce could be bought more cheaply from outside sources. The study has involved calculating the cost of each part and comparing it with bids submitted by outside suppliers. If the study finds that the plant's parts are more expensive, the plant will be sold or closed, Chrysler says.

There is already at least one casualty of the new evaluation procedure: a plant that makes power-train parts in New Castle, Ind., that Chrysler is trying to sell. Several other plants also are said to be about to get the ax.

All the plants involved in the evaluation have been considered borderline cases for some time. Chrysler has about 25 other plants, including its large assembly operations, that it believes are each critical to its survival.

Unusual Practice

Still, the practice of deciding whether to keep a plant based on its performance against outside suppliers is new for Chrysler and unusual in the industry. Though auto makers have long used such a standard for determining whether to build specific parts, they have only rarely applied it to whole manufacturing facilities. Chrysler, however, maintains that it has been forced to undertake such a study because it must continue to slash its fixed costs if it is to become profitable.

"We are continuing to look at our manufacturing operations to find ways to reduce overhead," says J. Paul Bergmoser, president. Adds another official: "In our position we certainly can't afford to be subsidizing inefficiency in our plants."

Viewed from another perspective, the Chrysler plant study raises questions about whether the No. 3 auto maker can afford to be a vertically integrated corporation, which its domestic counterparts are. "One has to wonder whether Chrysler will be able to come up with the financial resources to keep a full range of plants up to the new competitive standard," says a government analyst.

Swings in Consumer Demand

The analyst notes that Chrysler in recent years has been particularly hurt by swings in consumer demand that have forced the industry to spend huge sums of money retooling plants. Indeed, part of the purpose of the new Chrysler plant study is to determine which operations should get a share of Chrysler's limited funds, a company spokesman says.

The spokesman adds that most of the 16 plants that are being looked at build parts for rear-wheel-drive cars, which the company is gradually phasing out of production. "A lot of these plants are on the verge of becoming obsolete and we have to decide whether it is worth trying to convert them," he says.

Complicating the study, which is being conducted by John W. Day, Chrysler controller, are uncertain production schedules for the company's mid-size and full-size cars. Mr. Day wouldn't be interviewed for this story.

"One of the keys to the whole thing is what speeds Chrysler projects for the assembly lines that produce the big cars," a source says. He explains that the more big cars the company needs to produce, the more parts it needs to buy from the borderline plants. Selling more parts lowers a plant's costs and improves its chances of escaping the ax.

More Pressure on Dealers

Although Chrysler recently has been putting more pressure on its dealers to order the larger cars, there have been some signs that the effort is falling short of its goals. Chrysler, for instance, recently was forced to lower daily production of mid-sized Cordobas and Miradas at its Windsor, Ontario, assembly plant to 260 units from 380 units. There also has been persistent speculation that Chrysler may close its Lynch Road assembly plant in Detroit, which makes full-sized cars. Chrysler, however, says it plans to keep the plant open until at least the end of the model year.

A Chrysler official adds that the study also is taking into account the quality of parts made by outside producers and the number of alternative sources for each part. "We want to avoid a situation where there is only one supplier for a part who could eventually charge us monopoly prices," the official says.

Chrysler says it will try to sell the plants it doesn't want. A number of its suppliers have been asked by Chrysler if they'd be interested in buying plants. Sources say one possible candidate to buy the New Castle plant is TRW Inc., a maker of automotive, aerospace, industrial and electronic parts based in Cleveland. TRW wouldn't comment on that possibility.

Too Much Investment

An executive at one major supplier said it isn't interested in buying Chrysler plants because they would require too much investment to be competitive. He added, "Plus, Chrysler was talking about some kind of joint-venture. Who wants to do a joint-venture with Chrysler?"

An unwanted side effect of the Chrysler program has been widespread rumors of plant closings. Industry trade publications have been full of speculation about Chrysler plant closings, and a United Auto Workers official recently held a news conference to announce that he had learned that Chrysler planned to dispose of five plants. The union official then angrily flew to Washington to ask the Chrysler Loan

Guarantee Board to quit pressuring the company to get rid of more plants. Chrysler has since said that UAW's list of the five plants was incorrect.

A Chrysler spokesman said that the study doesn't have a timetable. "You won't be seeing a big D-day when we close a whole bunch of plants," he said. "This is a careful, ongoing evaluation."

Source: Reprinted from "Chrysler, Considering Further Cutbacks Is Using a Tough New Standard to Decide" by John Koten, *The Wall Street Journal*, October 27, 1980, p. 16. Reprinted by permission of *The Wall Street Journal*, © Dow Jones & Company, Inc. 1980. All rights reserved.

Operational Control

Operational control systems are designed to ensure that day-to-day actions are consistent with established plans and objectives. Operational control is concerned with individual and group role performance as compared with the individual and group role prescriptions required by organizational plans. Such control systems are normally concerned with the past (unless feedforward systems are being utilized). Operational control focuses on events in a recent period. Operational control systems are derived from the requirements of the management control system. Specific standards for performance are derived from the objectives of the operating plans, which are based on intermediate plans, which are based on strategy. Performance is compared against objectives at the individual and group levels. Corrective or preventive action is taken where performance does not meet standards. This action may involve training, motivation, leadership, discipline, or termination.

When all else is lost, the future still remains. —Christian Nestell Bovee

Strategic and Management Control Measures of Performance

Step 3 of the control process involves measurement of implemented strategy. For most firms, strategic and management control techniques that follow the implementation of strategy are identical. The most commonly used measures of strategic and management performance are financial statements and analyses of them. Included are considerations of profit, ROI, return on equity, ratio analyses, trends in the financial statement items, and several additional factors. Inspection of these factors may occur in routine reporting cycles, as the result of consulting efforts, or as the result of internal or external audits. Budgets, program planning budgeting systems, and zero based budgets and planning systems also serve as important financial indicators of strategic and management performance, but most often only for a specific operating period. The objective of all of these endeavors is financial control.

Financial control features include information on revenues, costs, profits, and funds flows within the control of responsibility centers and for the organization in total.

But financial control is only part of the total strategic or management control process. Why? Because much of the activity that affects financial performance is nonfinancial in nature. Recognizing this, firms have recently widely employed more comprehensive measures of strategic and managerial performance not normally found on traditional financial statements. They include considerations of labor efficiency and productivity (especially important to competing internationally); production quantity and quality; human resource factors such as absenteeism, turnover, and tardiness; on a very limited basis, human resources accounting and personnel satisfaction measures; more commonly, management by objectives systems; social performance measurements—social audits; cost benefit analysis; operational audits of any functional, divisional, or staff component; distribution cost and efficiency; network planning models; Gantt charts; market share analyses; inventory analyses; management audits; modeling; and so forth. The list is almost endless and there is not time to discuss each item here. In most instances, these measures stress short-run results. The obvious consequence is that managers place their emphasis on "looking good" in the short run, not the long run, as would be appropriate. One notable exception is at General Electric, which as part of its operational control standards for executives (and for the company and its components) emphasizes a balance between long-range and short-range objectives and emphasizes personnel development as well.

Most of the above-mentioned measures are familiar. However, in the following paragraphs a few of the more important or promising of these measures are reviewed in order to provide a common analytical base.

Ratio Analysis

Ratios of financial statement items (here, balance sheets and income statements) are widely used to measure strategic and management performance. With the exception of the current and quick ratios, few generally acceptable and appropriate ratio values exist. The exact number of ratios to use, the circumstances in which to use them, their components, and their exact meanings are often not agreed upon. Every financial analyst seems to have a preferred system.

Fortunately, there is common support for several ratios, which are presented in Table 8.1. These ratios are divided into four main subdivisions, each of which tells the analyst about a specific facet of corporate performance. Appendix III to this text explains each of these ratios in more detail. As Table 8.1 shows, a firm's ratios are normally compared with the ratios of other firms in the same industry. A firm's ratios may also be compared with its own historical ratios. Trends or deviations are the primary consideration. Comparative industry figures are often difficult to obtain, although certain organizational figures are available through services provided by Dun & Bradstreet and Robert Morris Associates. (While your library may have Dun & Bradstreet, you may find your local bank the only source of Robert Morris.) In addition, *Dun's Review* publishes annually (usually in November) "Ratios of Manufacturing"; annually in May and June, *Fortune* publishes selected ratios and

Table 8.1
Summary of Financial Ratio Analysis

Ratio	Formula for Calculation	Calculation	Industry Average	Evaluation
Liquidity				
Current	$\dfrac{\text{Current assets}}{\text{Current liabilities}}$	$\dfrac{\$700{,}000}{\$300{,}000} = 2.3$ times	2.5 times	Satisfactory
Quick, or acid test	$\dfrac{\text{Current assets} - \text{Inventory}}{\text{Current liabilities}}$	$\dfrac{\$400{,}000}{\$300{,}000} = 1.3$ times	1.0 times	Good
Leverage				
Debt to total assets	$\dfrac{\text{Total debt}}{\text{Total assets}}$	$\dfrac{\$1{,}000{,}000}{\$2{,}000{,}000} = 50$ percent	33 percent	Poor
Times interest earned	$\dfrac{\text{Profit before taxes plus interest charges}}{\text{Interest charges}}$	$\dfrac{\$245{,}000}{\$45{,}000} = 5.4$ times	8.0 times	Fair
Fixed charge coverage	$\dfrac{\text{Income available for meeting fixed charges}}{\text{Fixed charges}}$	$\dfrac{\$273{,}000}{\$73{,}000} = 3.7$ times	5.5 times	Poor
Activity				
Inventory turnover	$\dfrac{\text{Sales}}{\text{Inventory}}$	$\dfrac{\$3{,}000{,}000}{\$300{,}000} = 10$ times	9 times	Satisfactory
Average collection period	$\dfrac{\text{Receivables}}{\text{Sales per day}}$	$\dfrac{\$200{,}000}{\$8{,}333} = 24$ days	20 days	Satisfactory
Fixed assets turnover	$\dfrac{\text{Sales}}{\text{Fixed assets}}$	$\dfrac{\$3{,}000{,}000}{\$1{,}300{,}000} = 2.3$ times	5.0 times	Poor
Total assets turnover	$\dfrac{\text{Sales}}{\text{Total assets}}$	$\dfrac{\$3{,}000{,}000}{\$2{,}000{,}000} = 1.5$ times	2 times	Poor
Profitability				
Profit margin on sales	$\dfrac{\text{Net profit after taxes}}{\text{Sales}}$	$\dfrac{\$120{,}000}{\$3{,}000{,}000} = 4$ percent	5 percent	Poor
Return on total assets	$\dfrac{\text{Net profit after taxes}}{\text{Total assets}}$	$\dfrac{\$120{,}000}{\$2{,}000{,}000} = 6.0$ percent	10 percent	Poor
Return on net worth	$\dfrac{\text{Net profit after taxes}}{\text{Net worth}}$	$\dfrac{\$120{,}000}{\$1{,}000{,}000} = 12.0$ percent	15 percent	Poor

Source: From *Managerial Finance*, 5th edition, by J. Fred Weston and Eugene Brigham. Copyright © 1975 by The Dryden Press. Reprinted by permission of Holt, Rinehart and Winston, CBS College Publishing.

financial statement items and evaluations thereof for the *Fortune* 1000 and the *Fortune* 50s; annually in January, *Forbes*, in "The Annual Report on American Industry," provides evaluative commentary and analysis; *Business Week* reports selected large firms' financial information quarterly; the major investment banking firms provide studies on industries and individual firms; annual reports and 10Ks often provide useful information; Standard and Poor's *Industry Surveys* are helpful; and finally, Compustat and several other financial information firms will provide financial information on most large corporations.

The major problem with using these sources is finding the exact industry or group of firms against which to compare the subject firm. While data on large organizations is abundant, the multiplicity and diversity of products among firms make comparisons suspect. Data on small firms is available only from Robert Morris, and not all industries are covered. Data on intermediate-sized firms is virtually nonexistent. Even where comparative ratios are available, they must be used with caution. Financial statement information is subject to varying accounting practices which hamper comparisons. Footnotes to these statements often make significant differences as to the true value of certain items.

Return on Investment (ROI)

As a result of the positive aspects of decentralization, it has become a popular organizational design technique. As indicated in an earlier chapter, the need arises to control the resulting subsystems. Two primary types of control systems exist to exert financial control over these decentralized units: those that control projects and those that control responsibility centers. Anthony, Dearden, and Vancil describe five types of responsibility centers:[6]

1. Standard cost centers are those for which standard costs can be computed. By multiplying this cost times units, an output measure is devised.
2. Revenue centers are those for which revenues can be determined.
3. Discretionary expense centers are organizational units, normally staff units, whose output is not commonly measured in financial terms.
4. Profit centers are subsystems for which both costs and revenues can be measured and where responsibility for the difference—profit—has been assigned.
5. Investment centers are profit centers for which the assets employed in obtaining profit are identified. (These are SBUs or major project divisions.)

ROI (net income divided by total assets) is the performance measure most frequently used for the last of these responsibility centers—the investment center. As suggested in Chapter 7's discussion of top management motivation, ROI is a critical issue in large organizations. Inappropriate division control systems reduce execu-

---

[6]R. N. Anthony, J. Dearden, and R. F. Vancil, *Management Central Systems* (Homewood, Ill.: Irwin, 1972), pp. 200–203.

tive motivation. This can and usually does result in reduced profits. Indeed, while ROI analysis has several advantages, it also has several limitations.

Advantages of ROI analysis include the following:

1. ROI is a single comprehensive figure influenced by everything that happens.
2. It measures how well the division manager uses the property of the company to generate profits. It is also a good way to check on accuracy of capital investment proposals.
3. It is a common denominator which can be used to compare many entities.
4. It provides an incentive to use existing assets efficiently.
5. It provides an incentive to acquire new assets only when such acquisition would increase the return.

Limitations of ROI analysis include the following:

1. ROI is very sensitive to depreciation policy. Depreciation write-off variances among divisions affect ROI performance. Accelerated depreciation techniques reduce ROI, conflicting with capital budgeting discounted cash flow analysis.
2. ROI is sensitive to book value. Older plants with more depreciated assets and lower initial costs have relatively lower investment bases than newer plants (note also the effect of inflation on raising costs of newer plants and on the distortion of replacement costs), thus causing ROI to be increased. Asset investment may be held down or assets disposed of in order to increase ROI performance.
3. In many firms that use ROI, one division sells to another. As a result, transfer pricing must occur. Expenses incurred affect profit. Since in theory the transfer price should be based on total impact on firm profit, some investment center managers are bound to suffer. Equitable transfer prices are difficult to determine.
4. If one division operates in an industry with favorable conditions and another in an industry with unfavorable conditions, one will automatically "look" better than the other.
5. The time span of concern is short range. The performance of division managers should be measured in the long run. This is top management's time span capacity—how long it takes for their performance to realize results.
6. The business cycle strongly affects ROI performance, often despite managerial performance.

Despite these criticisms, ROI will likely continue as the leading index of management performance if for no other reason than its simplicity. Importantly, though, ROI must be supplemented with other decision information.

ROI is an important concept in terms of both total organizational control and subsystem control. As noted, it is the most widely used measure of a firm's operating efficiency. While ROI represents net income as a percentage of total assets, it is a function of many variables (see Figure 8.3). ROI results from two key factors,

Figure 8.3
Financial Analysis Using ROI

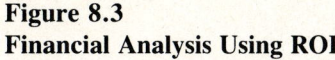

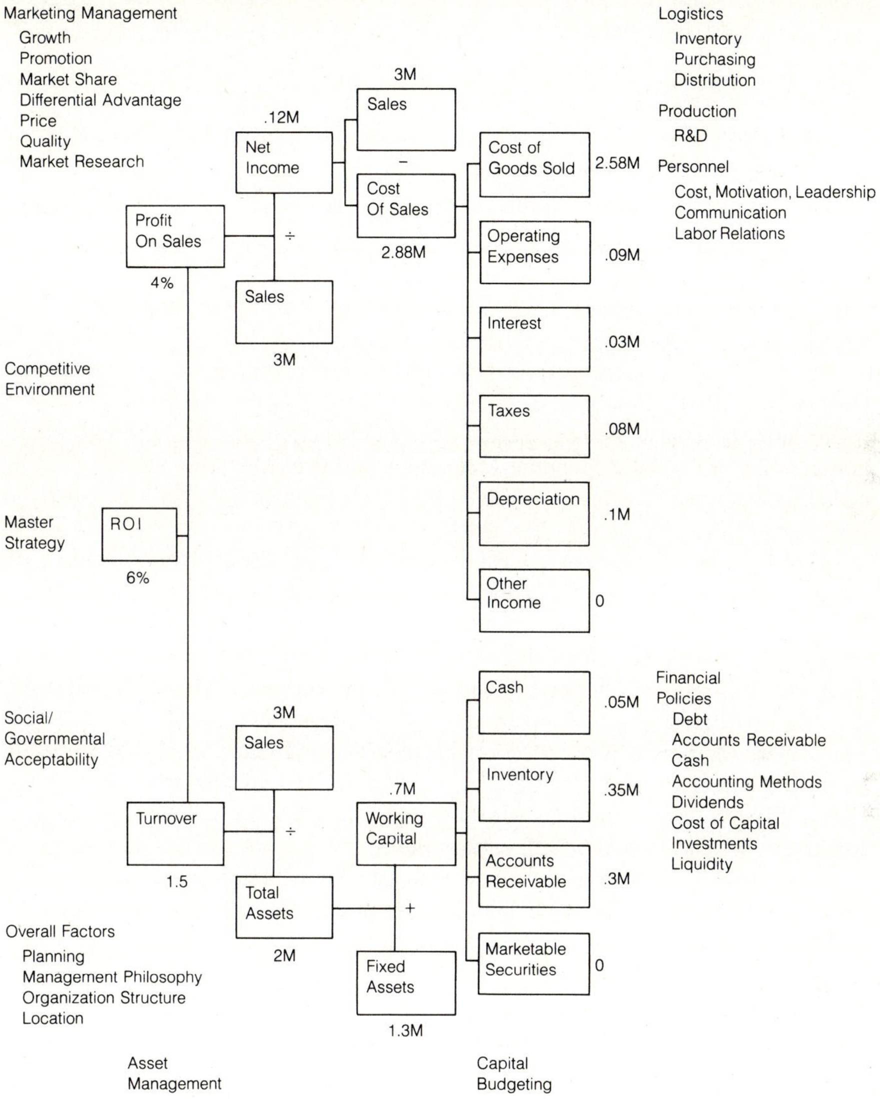

Source: Adapted from Ray Bressler, unpublished working paper, 1977.

profit margin on sales and assets turnover. Factors that contribute to these two ratios are outlined in the figure. These factors will not be discussed here at length, since most of you should already be familiar with the concept. You might want to work through the numbers given in the figure, relating the results to the contributive factors surrounding the model, as a review process.

Strategic and Management Audits

One of the major questions confronting organizations today is how to evaluate the performance of the top management team. In order for this end to be achieved, several factors must be considered:

1. Did top management accomplish the objectives it established?
2. How good were the objectives it established? How good were the strategies it employed to accomplish these objectives?
3. What factors beyond the control of top management affected its performance?
4. How well has it responded to and how well has it anticipated these factors?

These questions are operational control criteria for top management. Note, it is strategy that is at issue.

Several systems have attempted to measure top management's performance. One of the more promising is the management audit which examines all facets of organizational activity. A management audit familiar to many management practitioners is the one developed by the American Institute of Management (AIM). This audit examines ten categories perceived by AIM's founder, Jackson Martindell, to contribute to strategic success.[7]

The AIM audit consists of a questionnaire containing about 300 questions, each related to organizational performance in one of the ten categories. The questionnaires are completed by a team of AIM auditors. Questions are answered and additional information provided through interviews with organizational managers, analysis of reports, and third-party sources. At the end of the audit process, point values are assigned to the organization in each of the audit categories. An excellent rating is given if enough points are achieved. The audit has been widely used in many of the largest corporations and in smaller firms as well. Importantly, the audit can be adapted to organizations with missions other than profit, such as commonweal, service, and mutual benefit organizations.

Several additional approaches to the management audit have been suggested. Of interest is William Greenwood's management audit.[8] He suggests that a management audit should examine

1. Strategy and strategy determinants, especially environmental factors.
2. The major functional activities of a firm—marketing, operations (production), personnel, and accounting and finance.
3. Whether managers are performing the major functions of management—planning, organizing, staffing, directing, and controlling.

Finally, Greenwood recognizes the need for an annual organization policy audit. In this audit Greenwood has followed a management theory approach more traditional than Martindell's.

---

[7] J. Martindell, *The Appraisal of Management* (New York: Harper & Bros., 1962).
[8] W. T. Greenwood, *Business Policy: A Management Audit Approach.*

Management audits may also follow a format parallel to the content of the master strategy (see Table 3.5). Such an analysis is divided into four major parts: those for enterprise, corporate, business, and functional strategies. This approach includes recognition of product divisions but examines strategy on the basis of functional activities within divisions if they exist.

In observing any technique, it is important to note its weaknesses. While the strength of the management audit is that it often has been able to predict corporate performance successfully, it is not always accurate. Such audits have predicted success for some companies that failed miserably. Why? First, and probably most important at this time, the environment may change drastically. A management audit would probably have rated General Motors very high in 1973; yet in 1974, GM had a disastrous year. Strategic issues management must be monitored for surprises. Second, observing the manner in which ratings are assigned reveals that the process is rather arbitrary. There are no specific point values for responses to the questions, and such strict values would probably not be feasible. The auditors who audit a company and obtain responses to audit questions often disagree on the rating of the firm.

Regardless of its weaknesses, the audit serves an important function in its comprehensive examination of the organization. While examination of the "bottom line" indicates problems, the auditing of other areas is vital in explaining the causes of these problems. The audit is primarily effective because it looks beyond financial information and systematically appraises the performance of top management.

A brief example of a management audit that follows the master strategy format appears as part of an appendix to this book. This appendix should be a key part of your analyses of companies and their situations. Importantly, this management audit is part of a more comprehensive strategic audit. A strategic audit goes one step past the management audit and examines the external environment in which the organization finds itself. This allows for a full SWOT analysis. Furthermore, the questions employed in the management audit have been couched in such a way as to emphasize the firm's relationships with its environment. Many of the questions seek responses that require an examination of the firm's relationship to its external environment before they can be answered. This approach to performing a management audit was used in both the Martindell and Greenwood audits referenced earlier. The strategic audit is becoming an increasingly utilized technique in the formulation, and in the evaluation and control of strategy.

Human Resource Accounting (HRA)

The evaluation of human assets offers great promise, but to date this promise has been largely unfulfilled. The relevance of human resource accounting to strategic management is connected principally to evaluating the worth of the abilities, skills, knowledge, aspirations, and so forth of the strategic decision makers. But, in addition, the evaluation of corporate strengths and weaknesses requires an assessment of all employees and their potentials related to threats and opportunities.

To date, much of the implementation of HRA has involved calculations of the historical cost of human "assets" to the organization. A typical cost model observes the cost of recruiting and acquisition, formal training, orientation, development, familiarization, and related human resource expenses. Other HRA cost models exist. One might calculate opportunity cost—for example, and replacement cost—based on historical cost with operation costs added. In addition to cost models of HRA, one other major model—the economic value approach—exists in aggregate or on an individual basis. Ultimately, this latter is the information sought, but the difficulties, and even impossibilities of estimation, in this author's opinion, severely limit the applicability of the approach. The main problem with the economic value approach is one of validity. Such approaches require estimation of the worth of individuals to the organization. The question is, how can one be sure these estimations are meaningful?

In spite of the difficulties involved, the number of firms attempting HRA is growing and includes such firms as American Telephone and Telegraph, GTE in Michigan, and Texas Instruments. The increased emphasis on people and productivity which is anticipated in the 1980s should spur additional development of HRA systems.[9]

---

[9] P. H. Mirvis and B. A. Macy, "Human Resources Accounting: A Measurement Perspective," *Academy of Management Review*, April 1976, pp. 74–83; P. Ogan and S. Matulich, "Human Resource Accounting: Dead or Alive," *Atlanta Economic Review*, July/August 1976, pp. 13–16.

The Social Audit

In recent years, business's critics have demanded that social audits of corporations be conducted. The term *social audit* refers to any device which attempts to evaluate an organization's social performance. Areas which might be audited include environmental protection, equal employment opportunity, consumer satisfaction, governmental relationships, energy usage, and employee job satisfaction.

Ultimately the aim is to determine the social impact of the firm on its stakeholders. While some social areas are readily definable, a quantitative measure of both requirements and performance for many of these areas is extremely difficult, if not impossible, to obtain. Furthermore, it is difficult to obtain agreement as to exactly what business should accomplish. Each pressure group seems to have its own set of demands. Obviously, business cannot respond to all of them. Many corporations have audited their activities in several of the social responsibility areas, and the scoring systems which have been used are becoming more quantitatively oriented.[10]

Other Aspects of Control

Several additional factors should be considered with respect to control. The following paragraphs examine them.

Control Policies

Just as organizations establish strategic and implementation policies, they must also establish policies which guide control of the organization. Control policies naturally evolve from the objectives and standards established for performance. The organization must simply indicate to its managers and other employees, what the specific objectives are, how performance against these will be measured, what comparisons will ensue, and how differences between expectations and performance will be handled. Rewards must naturally be tied to results.

The organization needs policies establishing total performance measurements, intermediate organizational level performance measurements, and work group and individual performance measurements. Of principal concern is that the what and how of control is sufficiently definitive to motivate employees to perform.

A Note on the Role of Information in Control

A decision can be only as good as the information upon which it is based. In strategic control, management control, and operational control situations, for both feedforward and feedback control systems, comparison and adjustment occur as information is received. The absence of information, such as is the rule in manage-

Table 8.2
Information Requirements by Type of Control

Characteristics of Information	Operational Control	Management Control	Strategic Control
Source	Largely internal	Internal, partly environmental	Internal and environmental
Scope	Well defined, narrow	Moderately broad	Broad in scope
Level of aggregation	Detailed	Aggregated	Aggregated
Time horizon	Historical	Historical	Future and historical
Frequency of use	Very frequent, continuous	Periodic	Occasional, but with increasing frequency

Source: Reprinted from "A Framework for Management Information Systems," by G. Anthony Garry and Michael S. S. Morton. *Sloan Management Review*, Fall 1971, p. 59, by permission of the publisher. © 1971 by the Sloan Management Review Association. All rights reserved.

ment-by-exception control systems, is also important. There are differences in the characteristics of the information required in strategic control, management control, and operational control. These differences are portrayed in Table 8.2. The mass of information at operational levels must be meaningfully reduced before top management reports are prepared.

Integrated Planning and Control Systems

In a previous chapter, the importance of integrated planning and control was stressed from a planning perspective—objectives provide direction and motivation. Objectives are anticipated results. As such, for control purposes, they provide standards against which to compare performance. Program Evaluation Review Technique (PERT); Critical Path Management (CPM); Management by Objectives (MBO); Planning Programming Budgeting System (PPBS); budgets; and other planning and control systems can and should be applied to ensure successful mission accomplishment. It is essential that implementation be controlled if it is to be effective.

Dysfunctional Consequences of Control Systems

A certain amount of tension is desirable, but at many companies, the pressures to perform are so intense and the goals so unreasonable that some middle managers feel the only way out is to bend the rules, even if it means compromising personal ethics.
—Paul Lawrence

Control systems are sometimes formulated without consideration of the human beings who will be controlled by them. The behavioral results are often dysfunctional. For example, in the Vietnam War, an Air Force general falsified control reports submitted to the Pentagon regarding missions flown over North Vietnam. At least 28 unauthorized missions were flown before the military hierarchy became aware of these deviations from standard.[11]

More typically, in business, it is often observed that divisional managers may intentionally not invest in needed new plant and equipment in order to improve ROI results by reducing the size of total assets, the divisor in the ROI calculation. Or managers may not expend monies for the development of personnel, thereby increasing the dividend of the ROI calculation, net profit. Budgets have also been shown to result in undesirable consequences. For example, pressures associated with budgets may be resented by managers and their subordinates. Inefficiency may result. Pressure from the staff agencies requiring budget preparations may lead to staff-line conflicts. Examples of these dysfunctional consequences may be found in even the "best-managed" firms, such as Heinz, Ford and GM,[12] and Pepsico.[13]

In the nonprofit area, some universities highly restrict the number of days that business school faculty may spend each month in consulting activities. By insisting that faculty "get their forty hours in," rather than insisting on measurable results, university administrators fall victim to activity orientation. Professors do not necessarily contribute any more to the university by being there longer. It would seem to make more sense to require certain outputs than to legislate inputs.

Other examples could be cited. The point is this: if organizations have control systems, they must recognize that individuals can find ways to beat them, and will do so when the systems are unsound. Furthermore, control systems may often be so poorly designed that they are activity centered and not performance centered. Much of the behavioral literature addresses the identification and removal of such dysfunctional activities. Results, not activity, should be controlled.

What Should Be Measured?

Having just said that "it's results that count," it is appropriate to question if that is indeed all that should be considered in evaluating the success of a strategy. Or, are there other factors that are just as important as results? If so, what are they? We have already discovered that results-oriented systems are less applicable to service organizations and to nonprofits than they are to manufacturing and sales-type situations. Even there, results do not always tell the whole story. This, for example, is a major reason that management audits typically incorporate process questions, and strategic audits include environmental questions.

In the sense that an organization's effectiveness is in major part a measure of the effectiveness of its master strategy, the following conceptualization is highly

---

[10] For example see J. M. Higgins, "A Social Audit of Equal Employment Opportunity Programs," *Human Resource Management*, (Fall 1977), pp. 2–7.
[11] "Lavelle's Private War," *Time*, June 26, 1972, p. 14.
[12] G. Getshow, "Overdriven Execs: Some Middle Managers Cut Corners to Achieve High Corporate Goals," *Wall Street Journal*, November 8, 1979, pp. 1, 34.
[13] A. Hershmen, "Cooking the Books," *Dun's Business Month*, January 1983, pp. 40–47.

contributive to our understanding of the evaluation of strategies. J. Barton Cunningham, after reviewing the relevant literature, concluded that seven major ways of evaluating organizational effectiveness existed. These are defined as follows:[14]

1. The rational goal approach evaluates the organization's ability to achieve its goals.
2. The systems resource model analyzes the decision maker's capability to distribute resources efficiently among various subsystem's needs.
3. The managerial process model assesses the capability and productivity of various managerial processes—decision making, planning, and the like—for performing goal-related tasks.
4. The organizational development model appraises the organization's ability to work as a team and to fit the needs of its members.
5. The bargaining model measures the ability of decision makers to obtain and use resources for responding to problems important to them.
6. The structural functional approach tests the durability and flexibility of the organization's structure for responding to a diversity of situations and events.
7. The functional approach relates the usefulness of the organization's activities to its client groups.

It is evident that this text has stressed the first of these, but you may also observe that specific applications or examples of the others are noted throughout, and/or are queried in the strategic audit in Appendix II. Tables 8.3 and 8.4 provide additional information on Cunningham's analysis.

Descriptive Characteristics and *The Search for Excellence*

Another approach to analyzing the viability of a firm, more in the realm of why a firm is successful rather than measuring for success, is what one might call the descriptive characteristics approach. A number of authors have attempted to determine what characterizes the successful firm. In Chapter 4, we examined a number of behavioral strategies that predicted the success of a firm (noted for example in Tables 4.1, 4.2, and 4.3). In their book, *In Search of Excellence*, Thomas J. Peters and Robert H. Waterman, Jr., identify eight descriptive characteristics that, in their opinion, based on their research, are common denominators of the best-run companies. These denominators are business management practices that seem to enable the successful companies to be successful. Peters and Waterman examined, during a two-year period, through interviews and questionnaires, and through an examination of secondary information, the common characteristics of 36 successful, large, single-industry U.S. firms. These firms were part of an original sample of some 75

---

[14] J. B. Cunningham, "Approaches to the Evaluation of Organizational Effectiveness," *Academy of Management Review*, (July 1977), pp. 463–473.

firms, which was shortened on the basis of various performance criteria, or on representativeness in the case of 13 European firms. A number of standard performance criteria were employed. The resulting eight common characteristics are highlighted in Information Capsule 8.2.[15] The book itself, and Peters and Waterman, have become extremely successful. The book will probably sell over 2 million hardback copies, making it one of the all-time nonfiction best sellers; and Peters and Waterman are exceedingly active in speech making and in consulting. Many company presidents swear by the book, encouraging and often requiring their executives to read it. But it is not without its critics.[16]

Daniel T. Carroll provides us with a critical profile of the methodological and conceptual problems in Peters and Waterman's book. Their sample is not truly representative of American business, and is small. Perhaps most tellingly, the sample does not contain a group of unsuccessful companies for comparison. Thus, there is no guarantee that unsuccessful companies are not also characterized by these same eight common denominators. There is really no detailed description of how these characteristics were derived nor of how each firm was analyzed. The book depends heavily on secondary data. The study also focuses primarily on management practices, and fails to examine truly the impacts of other factors, both internal and environmental, which might affect the success or failure of a firm. For example, technology, market share, and competitor actions are not considered. Finally, Peters and Waterman attack the rational model with, unfortunately, somewhat biased and unsystematic arguments.[17]

In balance, *In Search of Excellence* must be considered a major contributor to management thought, perhaps intuitively sound, but limited in a number of critical ways in terms of research design. Its findings are suspect and its commentaries on the need for improvement in the rational model, though perhaps well founded, are not sufficiently supported by hard evidence. (The latter may, of course, be more difficult to come by than rationally and empirically oriented researchers would admit. I personally feel that they make a good point about the need to be more concerned with the human aspects of the organization opposed to what seems to be a penchant for number crunching, although they needed to have made a more research-based argument.) As a consequence of these arguments and similar ones made by other critics, those who would use these eight characteristics must do so with caution.

The Emergent Strategy

Henry Mintzberg has cautioned us to recognize that there is quite often going to be a difference between our intended strategy and our realized strategy. He suggests, in fact, that the strategy that is formulated is more properly entitled an "intended strat-

---

[15] Thomas J. Peters and Robert H. Waterman, Jr., *In Search of Excellence*, (New York: Harper and Row, 1982).
[16] S. Benner, "Peter's Principles: Secrets of Growth," *INC*. July 1983, pp. 34–38.
[17] D. T. Carroll, "A Disappointing Search for Excellence," *Harvard Business Review* (November/December 1983), pp. 78–88.

Table 8.3
Criteria Appropriate to Specific Applications of Evaluation Approaches

	Evaluating the Performance of the Organizational Structure	Evaluating the Performance of the Organization's Human Resources		Evaluating the Impact of Organizational Functions or Activities	
Rational Goal	Systems Resource	Managerial Process	Organizational Development	Bargaining	Structural Functional	Functional

Rational Goal	Systems Resource	Managerial Process	Organizational Development	Bargaining	Structural Functional	Functional
Accomplishments: Goals of the Esso Standard Oil Company for Preparing Employees for Retirement: 1. Increasing industrial efficiency, prestige, worker satisfaction; reducing costs; increasing public good will. 2. Aiding the nation and community to solve problems of the aged. 3. Helping the worker be well-adjusted in retirement.[a]	*Efficiency and Satisfaction Criteria for the Systems Need of Adapting to a Changing and Turbulent Environment:* 1. Adaptability—the ability to solve problems and to react with flexibility to changing internal and external circumstances. 2. Identity—knowledge and insight on the part of the organization of what it is and what it is to do. This involves (a) determining to what extent the organizational goals are understood and accepted by the personnel and (b) ascertaining to what extent the organization is perceived vertically by the personnel. 3. Capacity to test reality—the ability to search out, accurately perceive, and correctly interpret the real properties of the environment.[b]	*Productivity and Capability Criteria (Managerial Principles):* 1. Planning—shaping the future direction of the organization. 2. Organizing—recognition of the organization's personnel needs, and attempting to place people so that individual and organizational needs are in harmony. 3. Staffing—recognition of the organization's personnel needs, and attempting to place people so that individual and organizational needs are in harmony. 4. Leading—motivation of people to teach goals without deterioration of morale both of themselves and the organization.	*Interpersonal Competence and Job Satisfaction Criteria:* 1. Improvement in interpersonal competence. 2. Development of the norm that human factors and feelings are legitimate. 3. Increased understanding between and within working groups in order to reduce tensions. 4. Development of more effective team management. 5. Development of more rational and "open" methods of conflict resolution rather than suppression, compromise and unprincipled power. 6. Development of organic rather than mechanical systems.[d]	*Resource Utilization Criteria (Dimensions of Exchange):* 1. The parties to the exchange—their affiliation, function, prestige, size, personal characteristics, and numbers and types of clients served. 2. The kinds of quantities exchanged—the actual elements exchanged (consumer, labor services and resources other than labor services), and information on the availability of these organizational elements and on rights and obligations regarding them. 3. The agreement underlying the exchange—terms explicitly defined by one party or mutually defined by a number of parties. 4. The direction of the exchange—the direction of the flow of organizational elements (unilateral, reciprocal, or joint).[e]	*Structural Viability—Performance (Functional) Elements:* 1. Satisfying the interests of members and clientele groups. 2. Producing a quantity, quality, and mixture of outputs. 3. Investing in the system through hard goods, people, subsystems, and external relations. 4. Using inputs efficiently to achieve potential and profitability. 5. Acquiring resources such as money, people, goods. 6. Observing codes of laws and organizational rules. 7. Using relevant technical knowledge and administrative methods to behave rationally. *Structural Elements:* 1. Number and character of people. 2. Physical and monetary assets of nonhuman resources.	*Functional Criteria:* 1. Goal attainment—planning, programming, scheduling, rule making. 2. Adaptation—procurement, property management, office services, budgeting, personnel. 3. Integration—work flow procedures, internal rule-making process, informal or organizational status system, wage determination system. 4. Pattern maintenance—consideration given to agency's legal mandate, clientele needs, public interest, professional and mission oriented values of the organization, employee satisfaction and morale, social norms of informal groups within the organization.[g]

5. Controlling—activity that checks actual progress against planned progress and suggests ways of modifying activities falling below expected levels of performance.[c]

The principles are John G. Hutchinson's suggested redefinition of Henri Fayol's ideas using more modern terminology.

3. Type, location, form, and differentiation of subsystem.

4. Conflict, conflict resolution, superior/subordinate relations, bargaining procedures, formal and informal communications defining the organization's internal relations.

5. External organizations, agencies, roles, and environment characterizing the organization's external relations.

6. Values describing the organization's orientation; i.e., competitive, active.

7. The internal structure support base defining the guidance system.[f]

(These criteria, although defined in Bertram Gross' social systems model, are appropriate within Philip Selznick's definition of structural-functionalism.)

[a] Bass, Bernard M. "Ultimate Criteria of Organizational Worth," in Jaisingh Ghorpade, *Assessment of Organizational Effectiveness* (Pacific Palisades, Calif.: Goodyear, 1971).
[b] Bennis, Warren. "Toward a Truly Scientific Management: The Concept of Organizational Health," in *Changing Organizations* (New York: McGraw-Hill, 1966), 32–63.
[c] Gross, Bertram H. *The State of the Nation: Social Systems Accounting* (London: Tavistock, 1966).
[d] Bennis, Warren. *Organizational Development: Its Nature, Origins and Prospects* (Reading, Mass.: Addison-Wesley, 1969), p. 15.
[e] Jaques, Elliot. *Equitable Payment* (Heinemann Educational Books, 1961).
[f] Gowler, Dan, and Karen Legge. "Stress, Success, and Legitimacy," in Dan Gowler and Karen Legge, *Managerial Stress* (1975), pp. 34–51.
[g] Fremont, James Lyden. "Using Parsons' Functional Analysis in the Study of Public Organizations," *Administrative Science Quarterly*, Vol. 20 (1975), 59–70.
Source: J. B. Cunningham, "Approaches to the Evaluation of Organizational Effectiveness," *Academy of Management Review*, July 1977, p. 464. Reprinted by permission of the Academy of Management.

Table 8.4
Summary of Organizational Effectiveness Approaches

Organizational Effectiveness Model	Organizational Situation	Central Focus or Purpose	Assumption	Limitations
Rational Goal	Evaluation of performance of organizational structures.	Determine degree to which organizations are able to achieve their goals.	An organization is rational if its activities are organized to achieve its goals.	The model frequently shows that organizations do not reach their goals. There is also a difficulty in identifying and defining organizational goals.
Systems Resource	Evaluation of performance of organizational structures.	Determine decision maker's efficiency in allocating and utilizing resources for fulfilling various systems needs.	An organization, in order to survive, must satisfy some basic needs: 1. Acquiring resources, 2. Interpreting the real properties of the external environment, 3. Production of outputs, 4. Maintenance of day-to-day internal activities, 5. Coordinating relationships among the various subsystems, 6. Responding to feedback, 7. Evaluating the effect of its decisions, 8. Accomplishing goals.	Measures of all systems needs are difficult to develop.
Managerial Process	Evaluation of performance of organization's human resources.	Determine capability or productivity of managers or managerial processes.	An organization can be considered rational when its various managerial processes and patterns enhance the individual's productivity or capability to obtain objectives.	Measures of productivity and capabilities pinpoint personal problems and limitations.

Approach			
Organizational Development	Evaluation of performance of organization's human resources.	Determine organization's ability to work as a team and fit the needs of its individual members.	Work which is organized to meet people's needs as well as organizational requirements tends to produce the highest productivity.	Emphasis on the informal organization takes precedence over the formal. Individuals may be reluctant to accept interpersonal feedback supplied by the model.
Bargaining	Evaluation of impact of decisions.	Determine use or uses which various decision makers make of their resources in achieving organizational goals.	An organization is a cooperative, sometimes competitive, resource distributing system.	The model deals with a very specific part of the organization's activities.
Structural Functional	Evaluation of impact of organization's structure on performance	Determine organization's ability to develop structures to maintain and strengthen performance.	A system's survival is equated to satisfying five basic needs: 1. Security of organization in relation to environment, 2. Stability of lines of authority and communication, 3. Stability of informal relations in organization, 4. Continuity of policy making, 5. Homogeneity of outlook.	The model deals with a very specific part of the organization's activities.
Functional	Evaluation of impact of organizational activities.	Provide information on social consequences of organizational activities and on organization's ability to meet needs of key client groups in its environment.	Every system must define its purpose for being (goal attainment), determine resources to achieve its goals (adaptation), establish means for coordinating its efforts (integration), and reduce strains and tensions in its environment (pattern maintenance).	The model deals with a very specific part of the organization's activities.

Source: J. B. Cunningham, "Approaches to the Evaluation of Organizational Effectiveness." *Academy of Management Review* (July 1977) p. 464. Reprinted by permission of the Academy of Management.

Information Capsule 8.2
The *In Search of Excellence* Excellence Characteristics

1. *A Bias for Action*—for getting on with it. Even though these companies may be analytical in their approach to decision making, they are not paralyzed by that fact (as so many others seem to be). In many of these companies the standard operating procedure is "Do it, fix it, try it." Says a Digital Equipment Corporation senior executive, for example, "When we've got a big problem here, we grab ten senior guys and stick them in a room for a week. They come up with an answer *and* implement it." Moreover, the companies are experimenters supreme. Instead of allowing 250 engineers and marketers to work on a new product in isolation for 15 months, they form bands of 5 to 25 and test ideas out on a customer, often with inexpensive prototypes, within a matter of weeks. What is striking is the host of practical devices the excellent companies employ, to maintain corporate fleetness of foot and counter the stultification that almost inevitably comes with size.

2. *Close to the Customer.* These companies learn from the people they serve. They provide unparalleled quality, service, and reliability—things that work and last. They succeed in differentiating—*à la* Frito-Lay (potato chips), Maytag (washers), or Tupperware—the most commodity-like products. IBM's marketing vice president, Francis G. (Buck) Rodgers, says, "It's a shame that, in so many companies, whenever you get good service, it's an exception." Not so at the excellent companies. Everyone gets into the act. Many of the innovative companies got their best product ideas from customers. That comes from listening, intently and regularly.

3. *Autonomy and Entrepreneurship.* The innovative companies foster many leaders and many innovators throughout the organization. They are a hive of what we've come to call champions; 3M has been described as "so intent on innovation that its essential atmosphere seems not like that of a large corporation but rather a loose network of laboratories and cubbyholes populated by feverish inventors and dauntless entrepreneurs who let their imaginations fly in all directions." They don't try to hold everyone on so short a rein that he or she can't be creative. They encourage practical risk taking, and support good tries. They follow Fletcher Byrom's ninth commandment: "Make sure you generate a reasonable number of mistakes."

4. *Productivity Through People.* The excellent companies treat the rank and file as the root source of quality and productivity gain. They do not foster we/they labor attitudes or regard capital investment as the fundamental source of efficiency improvement. As Thomas J. Watson, Jr., said of his company, "IBM's philosophy is largely contained in three simple beliefs. I want to begin with what I think is most important: *our respect for the individual.* This is a simple concept, but in IBM it occupies a major portion of management time." Texas Instruments' chairman Mark Shepherd talks about it in terms of every worker being "seen as a source of ideas, not just acting as a pair of hands"; each of his more than *9,000* People Involvement

Program, or PIP, teams (TI's quality circles) does contribute to the company's sparkling productivity record.

5. *Hands-on, Value Driven*. Thomas Watson, Jr., said that "the basic philosophy of an organization has far more to do with its achievements than do technological or economic resources, organizational structure, innovation and timing." Watson and HP's William Hewlett are legendary for walking the plant floors. McDonald's Ray Kroc regularly visits stores and assesses them on the factors the company holds dear, Q.S.C. & V. (Quality, Service, Cleanliness, and Value).

6. *Stick to the Knitting*. Robert W. Johnson, former Johnson & Johnson chairman, put it this way: "Never acquire a business you don't know how to run." Or as Edward G. Harness, past chief executive at Procter & Gamble, said, "This company has never left its base. We seek to be anything but a conglomerate." While there were a few exceptions, the odds for excellent performance seem strongly to favor those companies that stay reasonably close to businesses they know.

7. *Simple Form, Lean Staff*. As big as most of the companies we have looked at are, none when we looked at it was formally run with a matrix organization structure, and some which had tried that form had abandoned it. The underlying structural forms and systems in the excellent companies are elegantly simple. Top-level staffs are lean; it is not uncommon to find a corporate staff of fewer than 100 people running multi-billion-dollar enterprises.

8. *Simultaneous Loose-Tight Properties*. The excellent companies are both centralized and decentralized. For the most part, as we have said, they have pushed autonomy down to the shop floor or product development team. On the other hand, they are fanatic centralists around the few core values they hold dear. 3M is marked by barely organized chaos surrounding its product champions. Yet one analyst argues, "The brainwashed members of an extremist political sect are no more conformist in their central beliefs." At Digital the chaos is so rampant that one executive noted, "Damn few people know who they work for." Yet Digital's fetish for reliability is more rigidly adhered to than any outsider could imagine.

Source: *In Search of Excellence: Lessons from America's Best-Run Companies* by Thomas J. Peters and Robert H. Waterman, Jr. Reprinted by permission of Harper & Row, Publishers, Inc.

egy," and the realized strategy is the actual strategy that results and is, in fact, "a pattern in a stream of decisions," sometimes deliberate, sometimes simply happening. His concept is pictured in Figure 8.4. The basic viewpoint expressed here is that many intended strategies become unrealized, and emergent strategies take their place. Intended strategies that were realized he terms as deliberate. When we are examining for the success of strategies, we are typically seeking to measure performance related to deliberate, realized strategies. But we must be alert to the fact that many times we are in effect measuring something not planned, but that just happened along the way . . . that pattern of decisions over time that emerged.[18] In most

---

[18] H. Mintzberg, "Patterns in Strategy Formation," *Management Science*, (1978), p. 945.

**Figure 8.4
Types of Strategies**

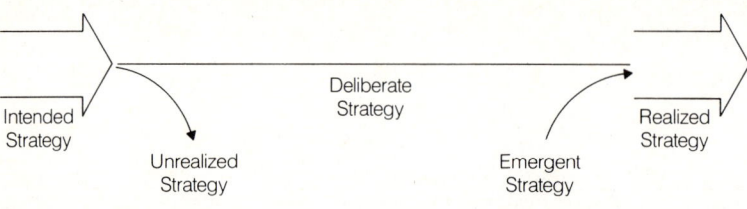

Source: H. Mintzberg, "Patterns in Strategy Formulation," *Management Science*, 1978, p. 945.

cases, this is not a critical point, but when it comes to measuring the performance of a specific unit or a specific manager, those involved should, in terms of their own corporate security, be quite concerned with this distinction.

Evaluation and Control in Multinational Enterprises

Control is absolutely critical in the multinational enterprise. The vagaries of this marketplace cannot be overestimated. In each of the preceding chapters, the problems associated with multinational enterprise have been noted. Control of the multinational enterprise depends, as does all control, upon information. When language, distance, politics, and a host of other exotic variables intervene, the difficulty of obtaining valid information is heightened.

James Hulbert and William Brandt suggest that the multinational is interested in achieving two objectives with its control systems—first to assure that its investment provides adequate returns, and in that same sense, is therefore protected. The second objective is to be able to coordinate all multinational marketing, production, financial, personnel, distribution, and related strategic processes. They suggest that the primary tool for achieving these ends is the budget, combined with standard total organizational performance measures such as ROI and cash flow. Control policies and requirements must be built around the organization's structure, with the amount of centralization and decentralization in foreign subsidiaries playing a major role in the development of control systems.[19] Michael Brooke and H. Lee Remmers, in examining the control systems of 30 American multinationals, found no fundamental differences between their systems for their multinational operations and those which were used domestically. These authors caution, however, that several major differences in operating environments cause the specifics of reporting systems to vary. The major factors they identify include

---

[19] James M. Hulbert and William K. Brandt, *Managing the Multinational Subsidiary* (New York: Holt, Rinehart and Winston, 1980), p. 112.

1. Wide variations in rates of inflation encountered from country to country.
2. Changes in the valuation of the currency of a country of investment.
3. The influence of intercompany transactions on the short-run performance of an operating unit.
4. Wide differences in cost structures among affiliates in different countries.[20]

Strategic and Management Control in Nonprofit Organizations

To this point, this chapter has addressed the issues involved with control in the profit-oriented organization. Normally, these techniques are also appropriate for nonprofit organizations. However, management control measures—especially financial control measures, specifically profit and ROI—are not very relevant to the nonprofit organization.

The problem of control is made more complex by the nature of the planning system employed by nonprofit organizations. Such organizations generally have vague objectives and ill-defined plans of action. Because of the inability to quantify objectives, and on many occasions the unwillingness to do so, these organizations employ the budget as the principal control device. Unlike the business firm, however, the nonprofit organization has far too little linkage between objectives and the budget. This approach, then, is often unsound. The primary concern should be objective accomplishment—not expenditure. When activity is equated with achievement, the results are often inefficiency and waste. Anyone who has experienced military service or been employed by the federal government is familiar with the rush to spend as much as possible at the end of each fiscal year (whether the items are needed or not) in order to assure that the budget amount is not reduced for the next fiscal year.

Planning Program Budgeting Systems (PPBS) are designed to eliminate some of these problems by requiring that programs be matched more closely to budgets and that the need for programs and budgeted amounts be verified each year. Several states have adopted the zero-based budgeting programs normally associated with PPBS. But the inescapable truth remains—it is virtually impossible to delineate what it is that many of these organizations are supposed to accomplish. Therefore, it is difficult to control performance towards this nonentity. Responsibility, one of the keys to control, is difficult to affix in such situations.

While it is encouraging that public management is now being accepted and even taught in the major universities (with some significant successes reported), the major problem—how to establish measurable objectives—remains. Until this problem can be solved, improvements will be limited. Furthermore, the problem is not one which many politicians in the public nonprofit sector seem eager to solve. Vague objectives and reactive decisions allow politicians to be reelected. Some govern-

---

[20]Michael Z. Brooke and H. Lee Remmers, *International Management and Business Policy* (Boston: Houghton Mifflin, 1978), p. 179.

ment agencies have never established objectives before. The coalitions which form and the political promises to various power groups which must be kept often prohibit meaningful plans of action and objective accomplishment as well as suitable administration. If performance measures were available and accountability became possible, performance would be more common. If tax revolts continue, demands for accountability, and use of managerial skills, should increase.

Summary

Control techniques are employed to ensure that mission is accomplished. Three principal types of control systems are created to that end: strategic control, management control, and operational control. Strategic control is concerned with the appropriateness of strategy to mission accomplishment. Such control is ongoing. Management and operational control systems control extensions of the strategy. That is, once the strategy has been more specifically defined and implemented, it must be ascertained whether the planned results, or objectives, have been achieved, both at the major component or total organizational level, via management control, and at the individual or group level, via operational control. Management and operational control systems, then, are designed to control the more articulated objectives and plans of action which emanate from strategy. These systems also provide indications of changes in the premises upon which the strategy was formulated, an important contribution.

Much of the organizational control system depends on financial information—information provided by the accounting system. The most sophisticated of the techniques are financial, ROI, and profit related, but other types of control measures such as management audits are being increasingly utilized and are proving essential, especially the objective-oriented techniques. The essence of the various control systems is accountability and responsibility. Control is critical in multinational environments, but control in these organizations occurs through the same systems as used in the domestic operation.

An organization can survive so long as it adjusts to its situation. . . .
—James D. Thompson and William J. McEwen

Key Terms and Concepts

By the time you have completed this chapter, you should be familiar with the following key terms and concepts: control, strategic control, management control, operational control, measures of performance, ratio analysis, ROI, advantages of ROI, limitations of ROI, management audits, human resource accounting, social audit, strategic audit, role of information in control, integrated planning and control systems, role of information in control, intended strategy, emergent strategy, control in multinational enterprises, control in nonprofits.

Discussion Questions

1. What is controlled by each of the three types of control? Why are three different types of control necessary?
2. Describe each of the strategic and management control measures mentioned in the chapter. Why is each necessary?
3. Try to define in specific terms the objectives of the U.S. Department of Health and Human Services. Now, how would you measure performance for each of these objectives?
4. How can the dysfunctional consequences of control be overcome?

References

Anthony, R. N. *Planning and Control Systems: A Framework for Analysis*. Boston: Harvard University Graduate School of Business Administration, 1965, pp. 24, 27, 29.

Anthony, R. N., Dearden, J., and Vancil, R. F. *Management Control Systems*. Homewood, Ill.: Irwin, 1972, pp. 200–203.

Argyris, C. "Human Problems with Budgets." *Harvard Business Review*, January/February 1953, pp. 97–110.

Bales, C. F. "Practice of Business Strategic Control: The President's Paradox." *Business Horizons*, June 1977, pp. 17–28.

Berkwitt, G. J. "Do Profit Centers Really Work?" *Management Review*, July/August 1969, pp. 15–20.

Cammann, C. and Nadler, B. A. "Fit Control Systems to Your Managerial Style." *Harvard Business Review*, January/February 1976, pp. 65–72.

Cunningham, J. B. "Approaches to the Evaluation of Organizational Effectiveness." *Academy of Management Review*, July 1977, pp. 463–474.

Dalton, G. W. "Motivation and Control in Organizations." In *Motivation and Control in Organizations*, edited by G. W. Dalton and P. R. Lawrence. Homewood, Ill.: Irwin, 1971.

Dearden, J. "Appraising Profit Center Managers." *Harvard Business Review*, May/June 1968, pp. 80–87.

———. "The Case against ROI Control." *Harvard Business Review*, May/June 1969, pp. 124–135.

deNoya, L. "How to Evaluate a Long Range Plan." *Long Range Planning*, June 1978, pp. 36–40.

Garry, G. A., and Morton, M. S. S. "A Framework for Management Information Systems." *Sloan Management Review*, Fall 1971, pp. 55–70.

Mintzberg, H., and Waters, J. A. "Tracking Strategy in an Entrepreneurial Firm," *Academy of Management Journal*, Vol. 25, No. 3, pp. 465–499.

Rumelt, R. "Evaluation of Strategy: Theory and Models." In *Strategic Management: A New View of Business Policy and Planning*, edited by D. Schendel and C. Hofer. Boston: Little/Brown, 1979.

Appendix I
Introduction to the Case Method

We learn best by doing.
Anonymous

The content of strategic management and organizational policy courses may vary substantially given the diversity of the objectives of such courses. (See the preface for a discussion of these objectives.) This book uses text to teach these subjects. Having reviewed strategic management and organizational policy through the use of text material, it is now time to apply this knowledge, to the real world and to cases. For use with cases, an introduction to the case method is in order. The following pages review the case method and explore some of its dimensions to acquaint you as a student with the case method in order that you will be better able to utilize any cases which you are assigned.

The case method has become a popular tool in teaching strategic management and organizational policy because it brings realism to the classroom. Reading theories and concepts is the beginning of knowledge, but in order to complete your education, it is believed necessary that you gain some practical experience. The case method involves the examination of an actual organizational event or series of events. These situations usually involve statements that reveal problems or opportunities. These problems (internal weaknesses or external threats) or opportunities must be recognized, identified, and solved. In short, strategic decisions must be made.

Cases are usually written by management consultants or by other individuals who were involved in the problem. They are almost always derived from real life occurrences, but occasionally cases may be hypothetical. Not infrequently, the identity of the firm involved is disguised in order to protect the firm from unwanted publicity.

While attaining access to internal corporate information is difficult for most students, it is relatively easy to observe an organization through the use of the case method. The case method as a presentation of a real situation does have one weakness, and that is that the student is not allowed to interact with the data—that is, the student does not change the data, nor does the data change. However, this is not a major problem; and some actions can be taken to reduce its effects—for example, certain assumptions of the case can be changed.

Cases are occasionally accompanied by notes, which are usually industry data and survey information to be used with more than one case.

Objectives

The case method's objectives are

1. To add realism to the classroom.
2. To cause the student to integrate knowledge of the functional areas and to employ principles of strategic management.
3. To improve the decision-making ability of the student, primarily through having the student practice making decisions.
4. To cause the student to see interrelationships of facts and what they mean in a practical as well as a theoretical sense.
5. To encourage students to be self-assertive. This occurs when the student is required to respond in class by attracting the professor's attention through both physical and mental assertion. The student who does not "seize the floor" will probably never be heard from and will not do well in the course.
6. To improve students' communication skills.

Approaches

There are two general approaches to the case method. In the first, students follow a set format in analyzing a case. They read the case and attempt to identify the principal problems and the principal factors involved in these problems by utilizing a specific list of predetermined key factors which are believed relevant to proper management functioning. This is referred to as the structured approach. In the second approach, students are not provided with a particular format but are left to derive their own methodology. This is commonly referred to as an unstructured approach. Individual instructors will indicate which is to be utilized. Case analyses for class may be either written or oral, or a combination.

Types of Organizations Encountered

Three primary types of organizations, according to size, are encountered in cases: large national or multinational firms, medium-sized organizations and entrepreneurships, or small businesses. They tend to have differing types of problems and opportunities, requiring somewhat different types of resultant analyses. And two primary types of organizations, according to mission, are also encountered: profit-oriented organizations, and nonprofit organizations. Again, these types often have differing problems and opportunities.

Planning Level of Problems, Opportunities Encountered

Most of the problems and opportunities which confront the case analyst occur at the strategy formulation level. However, in most texts, a limited number of cases are presented that involve other stages of the planning cycle, so that their interrelationships may be interpreted. In fact, many cases involve multiple stages, since stages are so highly interdependent. For example, control information points to the need to reformulate strategy, strategy leads to structure, and so forth. Cases on international business and nonprofits are often included.

Classroom Pedagogy

Group versus Individual Analyses

Students can engage in preclass and class analysis of a case in two ways. The first is in a group. This method is appropriate when students are able to come together for lengthy periods of time to analyze the case. As with all group activities, there may be those who work on the group's project and those who do not. Appropriate peer group evaluations should be carried out. Working in a group does not require conformity. Here too, strength of personality can be developed. Prior to the group analysis, the individual should go through the recommended steps of analysis which conclude this introduction.

To use the second method, students study the case by themselves and must cover all its facets individually.

Student Classroom Participation

In some classes, students must seize the floor in order to be heard. Here it becomes imperative that the individual become self-assertive. The student must also realize that he or she may make a mistake and must be either willing to learn to accept criticism or able to avoid making mistakes in judgment (a tough task for anyone). The student should anticipate that the instructor will attempt to find people who disagree with the student's position and analyses. The risks of nonassertion (failing grades) are, of course, motivating.

Specific questions may also be asked of a student on a nonvoluntary basis. Finally, analyses prepared by the student may be read and debated in class. Some combination of these three approaches is common.

Instructor's Role

Normally the instructor leads the discussion; he or she may also participate in it. Instructors usually are viewed as resource persons.

Preclassroom Analysis

As in real life situations, there is never enough data in any case to enable a perfect decision to be made. One of the most important factors to remember is that decision making is a function of time and data availability. No one ever has enough time or enough data. Therefore, the common criticism by students that the case may leave out data is not an acceptable one.

Students are allowed to undertake extra research; but for most cases the decision can and should be made based on the data presented. Furthermore, while students are encouraged to find information, especially industry information, relevant to the time the case was occurring, they should not seek to find out what happened subsequent to the time of the case, for example when using the second Appendix to this text.

Answers

There are no right answers in a case situation. There are, however, better answers. The only true test of the decision is in its implementation; and unfortunately, the case method does not allow for implementation of decisions. The right answer, then, is an unknown. Only the better answer can be determined. Students who make decisions based on insufficient analysis usually come up with worse answers and correspondingly worse grades. It is the facts upon which decisions are made that are important; several acceptable solutions may be derived from them.

Degree of Difficulty

Sometimes the point of the case will be obvious. At other times it will be necessary for the individual to read, reread, and reanalyze the case in order to determine what is the major problem or opportunity. Often, cases contain numerous technique problems which are not the major problems, only symptoms of a major problem.

Viewpoint

One factor to be considered is the viewpoint of the student. Should he or she envision himself or herself as a consultant or as a member of the organization? The ease with which solutions might be implemented is related to the choice of viewpoints.

Results

One important factor to consider is this: in many situations, no matter what the decision, the results may be ineffective. There are many factors, especially environmental factors, which are completely out of the control of the organization. In such situations, the best decisions may be those which allow an organization to minimize the loss it might incur.

Strength of Analyses

Most students will not uncover all the factors which will eventually be revealed in the classroom discussions. This constitutes one of the most important learning factors gained from use of the case method—the realization that there is always something the individual will overlook. This is very much like real life.

Perspective

For both the student and the instructor, the case method is a difficult process. In traditional classroom learning situations, students have been assigned the roles of listeners and nonparticipants. To be effective, the case method requires that students think, act, and participate. In order for students to receive a good grade, they must achieve these more active levels of learning as opposed to being merely receptive and passive members of a lecturer's audience. The role of a strategic manager, too, demands this kind of behavior.

Case Bias

One must be aware of the inherent bias in a case. The case is related as it is perceived by someone else, the case writer. The reader of a case does not have the benefit of knowing how the information was obtained or what factors the individual considered in writing the case. What is presented as fact may not be as clear-cut as it seems. How facts are presented, which facts are included, and which facts are left out are critical factors. Occasionally facts may be distorted, especially facts related to statements about the personalities of individuals. Often, individuals' personalities are the key problems in a case; yet the reader can never be sure that the statements about these personalities are exactly accurate.

A Suggested Course of Action

1. Read the case; become familiar with the situation. If possible, put the case aside for awhile.
2. Reread the case and
    a. Summarize pertinent information.
    b. Pay special attention to information in tables and figures—for example, financial statements, sales figures, and the like.
    c. Think of the questions your professor may have given you. Do they give clues as to what to do next? What are these clues?
3. Establish a decision framework:
    a. What is the major area of concern—strategy formulation, intermediate planning, organization, implementation, evaluation, or control?

b. What are the organization's missions, objectives, policies, and strategies?
c. What are the decision constraints?
4. If this is a strategy formulation problem, normally you should
a. Determine current master strategy.
b. Identify strengths, weaknesses, opportunities, and threats (SWOT).
c. Analyze substrategies if necessary.
5. Ask yourself if you really understand what's happening. If not, retrace your steps.
6. Search for and delineate alternatives. If the strategy must be reformulated, follow the strategic management process procedures discussed in the text. Be especially careful to match strengths and weaknesses against threats and opportunities. The alternative generation process involves examining the basic action strategies available and choosing the most appropriate. Next, the marketing strategy should be generated. In both these actions, the product life cycle should be observed for its impacts. Finally, supportive and strategic issues strategies should be formulated. Table 4.1 lists factors which should be considered in formulating strategy, while Table 4.2 lists classical marketing strategies. Both tables provide information for each stage of the product life cycle. Table 4.3 suggests possible supportive strategies by product life cycle stage. Numerous additional possible strategies exist, but these tables are a good place to begin. If the tables fail to yield what you consider to be appropriate strategies, then use your creativity to formulate additional ones.
7. Choose the appropriate alternatives. The evaluation process involves examining proposed alternatives to determine how well they match SWOT, mission, objectives, policies, the dominant planning mode, and other relevant criteria. The GE Strategy Matrix, or Stoplight, is one approach which may be used in this endeavor when multiple alternatives are available. The evaluation process is partly rational, partly intuitive, and partly dependent on skill. In many situations, it is also partly social. Once choices are made, the total master strategy should be viewed for compliance with the strategic control items noted in Chapter 8. Think through its consequences.
8. Set priorities for your solutions.
9. Be prepared to implement these decisions—that is, consider if they would and could be implemented. Eliminate "pie in the sky" solutions and marshal sufficient evidence to defend your solutions. Do your solutions solve the problems or exploit the opportunities? Budget for your decisions.
10. If written or class presentation is required, be professional. Use charts, handouts, slides, and the like.

The list above is a suggested series of general actions. Questions at the end of each case may direct that other actions be taken. The instructor may also choose other courses of action. Use what you have learned; for example,

1. Use the strategic audit in Appendix II.
2. Use the information in Table 8.1, Appendixes III and IV.

3. Determine the stage of the product life cycle.
4. Determine the contingency factors for this stage.
5. Decide what actions are appropriate in this situation.
6. Use a strategy matrix (like the GE Stoplight) where applicable.
7. Make certain you determine what it is your decision is supposed to accomplish.
8. Review the strategic control checklists in Chapter 8.
9. Review the 7-S's and other implementation materials in Chapter 7.
10. Accomplish spread-sheet pro formas where necessary.

Appendix II
The Strategic Audit– a SWOT Approach

The strategic audit is concerned with identifying the firm's current position relative to its industry, the economy, and other major variables such as its stakeholders. It involves a management audit of the firm in conjunction with an environmental analysis. In this appendix, the general format of the analysis follows this pattern: Determine the firm's current position in terms of its mission, objectives, master policies, and master strategy. Next, determine the firm's strengths, weaknesses, opportunities, and threats (SWOT). By employing this audit, we are fulfilling the role of organizational strategists examining mission, policy, and information in order to determine SWOT.

Immediately following then, is our version of the strategic audit. It begins with a brief version of a management audit checklist, which generally follows the master strategy format presented in Table 3.5 of the text. Many more questions could be asked; but since this tool is primarily for use in case analysis, its length has been kept to a usable minimum. Most cases will not contain enough information for all the questions to be answered; but in most cases, the major points will be determinable. Following the master strategy analysis part of the checklist is a brief environmental analysis. The environmental portion of the checklist is brief since much of the environment has been considered in management responses to it as found in the management audit. By using this checklist, you should be able to identify the firm's SWOT.

Management Audit

Mission

1. Has the firm identified its mission? If so, how appropriate is it?
2. What is its mission?

Objectives

1. Does the firm have strategic objectives? If so, how good are they?
2. What are they?

Enterprise Strategy (Societal Response)

Known Contingencies

1. What is the history of the firm's social responsibility efforts? Consider responses to EEO, EPA, consumerism, community and pressure groups, and so on.
2. Is the firm ethical?
3. What is the firm's relationship with government?

Unknown Contingencies

1. What possible surprises might occur for this firm—for example, with government, competition, the economy, pressure groups, and so forth? What weak signals exist?

Corporate Strategy (Mission Determination)

1. Is this firm competing or seeking a niche? Is this action appropriate?
2. Does this firm have a plan for growth? How good is it? What type of growth is it? How appropriate is it?
3. Have the following been considered or are they being used: diversification, vertical or horizontal integration, retrenchment, stability, investment reduction, turnaround, product expansion, product concentration, combinations, and the like? If any are being considered or used, are they appropriate?
4. Does the firm really know what business it is in?
5. Is the firm's location strategy sound?
6. Is the firm's product quality strategy sound?
7. Are the firm's basic action strategies appropriate to the industry, the economy, its resources? What else should be considered or undertaken?
8. Does the firm have a strategic advantage? What is it? How good is it?

Business Strategy (Primary Mission)[1]

Competitive Strategies

Economic Functional Strategies—Marketing

1. Product
   a. Has the firm identified the basic consumer need it wishes to satisfy? Is it appropriate? Is introduction of new products advisable?
   b. Are width, depth, differentiation, product life cycle, image, packaging, and the like satisfactory?
   c. Is technical support satisfactory?

---

[1] Business strategy can apply to a product, product line, SBU, or the total of these, whichever applies in a particular case.

d. Is the product competitive? If not, why?
   e. Are any changes to the product necessary?
2. Distribution
   a. Are purchasing, inventory control, and final distribution coordinated? Are they standard for the industry? If not, why? Are they too costly, too burdensome on the sales effort, or the like? Is a make-or-buy decision necessary?
   b. Does the firm really know who its customers are and how to distribute the product to them? Would vertical integration help, hinder?
   c. Does the firm use sound management techniques in this area (EOQ, ROP, ABC, modeling, simulation)?
   d. Are product distribution channels appropriate, effective, too long, too short, fully developed?
   e. Does the firm shop for better prices, discounts, and so on?
   f. Does it keep control of the flows and stocks at various points in the process? Are they sufficient?
   g. Does the firm evaluate systems, distributors, results?
3. Promotion
   a. Is promotion strategy relevant to product life cycle, target market, packaging, available funds?
   b. Is promotion push or pull, and which would be best? Both?
   c. Does selling emphasize personal selling, mass marketing, or sales promotion? Which would be best? All? How are salespersons and media selected and evaluated?
   d. How are salespersons rewarded? How effective are territories, sales goals, sales managers?
   e. Is the promotion strategy effective? If not, why?
4. Price
   a. What is the basis for the firm's pricing strategy? Is this strategy satisfactory given the industry, economy, and so on?
   b. Is the product price sensitive? Has the firm considered this?
5. Target Market
   a. Does the firm know the product market? Is it a correct target market?
   b. Has the firm established a marketing mix (product, distribution, promotion, and price) appropriate to this market?
   c. Has the firm correctly segmented the market? What is the future of its markets?
   d. How do the firm's customers make purchasing decisions? Does it know how its customers make such decisions?

Functional Strategy (Mission Supportive)

Economic Functional Strategies

Operations

1. Facilities and Equipment
   a. What factors have determined where facilities have been located? Are these factors appropriate?

b. In what condition are organizational facilities and equipment? How does their condition compare with conditions typical in the industry? What implications can be drawn?
c. Are buildings properly designed and equipment arranged according to major relevant variables?
d. What is the impact of OSHA and EPA on buildings and equipment?

2. Work Design
a. Is work design satisfactory? What options exist?
b. Do production standards exist for workers? If not, why? If so, how good are they?
c. Is satisfactory use made of operating leverage?

3. Operations Control
a. Is the firm properly scheduled, routed, in coordination with materials acquisition? If not, why?
b. What types of cost controls and production controls exist? How good are they?

4. Quality Assurance (QA)
a. Does the firm have QA programs for design, inputs, production, distribution, installation? How good are they?
b. Does the firm use appropriate QA methods? What are its rejection rates? How do they compare with industry averages?
c. What is the firm's customers' opinion of its products? Does the firm know customers' opinions for sure? What implications can be drawn?

5. Logistics
See comments under marketing distribution.

6. For service-related organizations, modify the above operations questions to fit the situation.

Finance

1. Performance Measurements
a. See the comments on ratio analysis and ROI in Chapter 8 of the text and in Appendix III.
b. Are any trends in balance sheet items, income statement items, cash flow statement items apparent? What implications can be drawn?
c. Are there any unusual items in financial statements? Why?
d. Are there any trends in company fortunes? Is this fact significant?
e. Is the firm aware of profit per product, per line, and so on? How good are these profits?
f. Does the firm target for ROI, gross margin, profit, or the like?

2. Policies
a. What is the firm's policies and how appropriate are they for the following: debt, dividends, cash usage, liquidity, taxes, growth, working capital, capital assets acquisition, budgets, depreciation, accounts receivable, accounts payable, credit, collections, funds acquisition, transfer pricing?

3. Overall Situation
a. What is the firm's working capital situation?

b. Does the firm have sufficient working capital for growth? If not, why?
c. Is the firm sales oriented or profit oriented?
d. Can it acquire funds? If not, why? Does it have a funds strategy? How good is this strategy?
e. Is stock ownership an important factor? How?
f. What external factors affected the firm's profits in recent years, and how well did the firm handle those factors?
g. Does the firm use appropriate analysis techniques in the financial area?

Personnel

1. Overall Personnel Practices
   a. Does the firm have a personnel department? If not, who handles personnel functions?
2. Employment Planning
   a. Does the organization have employment planning? How good is it?
   b. Do job descriptions and specifications exist? Are they up-to-date and realistic?
3. Recruitment and Selection
   a. Does the firm recruit appropriately?
   b. Does it select on some scientific basis or does it just seem to guess? Is its testing valid, reliable?
   c. Are interviews, performance ratings valid, reliable?
4. Employee Rewards and Benefits
   a. How are employees rewarded? Is this method appropriate?
   b. How do pay and benefits compare with those in the industry? In the firm's geographic area? What implications can be drawn?
5. Orientation and Development
   a. Does the firm have an orientation program? How good is it?
   b. Does the firm have employee and managerial development programs? How good are they?
6. Employment Security, Evaluation, and Control
   a. How does the company perform in these areas: absenteeism, turnover, safety, pensions, profit sharing, insurance, layoffs, terminations?
   b. How is employee performance rated, controlled for various jobs? Are these systems appropriate?
7. Labor Relations
   a. How good are the company's labor relations?
   b. Is the firm unionized? What are the impacts of unionization? What is the firm's relationship with the union?
   c. Could this firm be unionized? Why?
   d. What do employees think of this firm? What impacts does their opinion have?
8. Equal Employment Opportunity (EEO)
   a. Does the firm have an EEO program? If not, why? If so, how good is it?
9. How good is the firm's productivity management program?

Information Systems
1. Do managers get the information they need to make decisions? Is this information accurate and timely? Is the information related to objective accomplishment? Does the firm have a human resource information system?

Other
1. What else in the economic functional area should be considered? For example, what role does R&D play in the industry and how sound is the firm's R&D program? What is the status of its market research effort?

Management Functional Strategies

Planning
1. Does the organization have objectives and plans to reach those objectives for each of the major economic functional and management functional areas? For its major products? How good are those plans and objectives?
2. Does this organization have a plan for the planning function vs. a haphazard approach?
3. Do its plans meet the criteria suggested in the text?
4. Are planning studies, feasibility studies performed? How good are they?
5. How are planning and control coordinated? How well?

Organizing
1. Division of Labor, Establishment of Roles
   a. How are roles established? Is this procedure appropriate?
   b. What evidence, if any, is there that employees are dissatisfied with their jobs? What impact does this have?
2. Distribution of Authority
   a. Is the distribution of authority correct for this firm? If not, what distribution would be better?
3. Structure
   a. How do size, technology, environment, geographic factors, informal organization, management prerogatives and philosophy, and strategy affect the organization's structure? What impacts do these effects have?
   b. Does a better structure exist for this firm? What is it?

Implementing
1. Staffing
   See comments under personnel.
2. Leading
   a. What is the dominant leadership style of the organization? Of its top managers? Are these styles appropriate?
   b. Should there be some change in the distribution of authority?
   c. What is the climate of the organization? What impact does this climate have on productivity?
3. Motivating
   a. How does the firm motivate its employees? Is this method appropriate?

b. Does the firm rely on organization-wide systems such as compensation, or do managers also provide motivation?

c. Would recognition be a useful form of motivation in this firm?

Controlling

1. How does the firm control each of the economic and management functional areas? Are these controls appropriate?
2. Are strategic, management, and operational controls satisfactory?

Communicating

1. Does the firm have a communication strategy, policies, and so on? Are they satisfactory?

Decision Making

1. Does the firm use appropriate decision techniques? To what extent are decisions determined by social relations? What impacts does this have?

Integrating

1. How does the firm integrate and coordinate? Are its actions in this area effective and efficient?

Other Considerations

Management and Key People

1. Are managers providing the necessary leadership?
2. Are managers performing the management functions?
3. How would you rate the top managers? Based on what criteria?
4. What impact do coalitions have on this firm?
5. What changes in top management have occurred recently? How do they affect the firm's performance?
6. How do value orientations affect managers' decisions? What impact does this have?
7. Is top management keeping up with changes in the environment, management techniques, and the like?
8. How is integration accomplished at top levels?
9. Has top management been making the correct strategic decisions?
10. What impact does ownership/family have on this firm?
11. Is there a management development program in this firm? If so, how good is it?
12. Are managers adequately compensated and motivated? What impact does this have?

Overall Performance (Nonfinancial)

1. Does the firm use appropriate human resources, social, and environmental performance measures?
2. How good is their performance in these areas?

Environmental Analysis

Marketing Environment

1. Who are the firm's major competitors and what are their strategies, market shares, ROIs? Has a competitor analysis been performed? Results?
2. What distinguishes the good performers in this industry from the poor performers?
3. What is the industry's product life cycle stage? Is the firm's strategy appropriate to this stage? What are the implications of the life cycle stage?
4. What trends can be discerned in the economy and the industry? What are the firm's plans for coping with them? Are the plans appropriate? What is the relationship between the economy and product demand?
5. What are the major relevant factors with respect to demography, technology, style, culture, income, and government? What will the firm do about these factors? Are its actions sound?
6. How important are market segmentation, product differentiation, customer loyalty, new product introduction?
7. What other major factors characterize the industry?
8. What are relationships with suppliers, customers, clients, and creditors? Possibility of new entrants?

Marketing Management vis-a-vis the Environment

1. Does the firm have a marketing plan? How well is it implemented?
2. Does the firm use appropriate market research and forecasting methods?

Performance of Marketing Effort

1. What is company's market share? Its profit margin on sales?
2. What is company's image with consumers, customers? Is the company aware of this image? Is the image consistent with company intents?
3. What is the recent history of the company's products? How is this history related to the economy, to industry activity?

Other Environmental Factors

1. What other major environmental factors not previously mentioned affect or are likely to affect this organization? What are these impacts? Examine: pressure groups, government, international aspects, cultural phenomena, unions, technology, society, national resources.

Appendix III
Financial Ratio Analysis

Two types of financial statements, the income statement and balance sheet, are generally used for financial ratio analysis. From these statements come the figures used to calculate the four categories of financial ratios: liquidity, leverage, activity, and profitability.

Liquidity

Current Ratio. The current ratio measures the liquidity of the firm—that is, its ability to handle short-term debts and liabilities. It is found by dividing current assets by current liabilities. The result shows how many dollars of current assets exist per dollar of current liabilities. A rule of thumb for manufacturing firms is to maintain a current ratio of at least 2:1 (assets to liabilities), but each firm must compare its position with the industry average. Service firms require a lower ratio due to absence of inventories.

Quick, or Acid-Test, Ratio. The quick, or acid-test, ratio is the result of subtracting inventories from current assets and then dividing this figure by current liabilities (CA − Inventories/CL). This ratio is sometimes seen as a more accurate indicator of liquidity than the current ratio, since a firm with large but obsolete inventories included as part of its current assets could be misrepresenting its ability to meet short-term obligations. The quick ratio is also expressed as asset dollars per liability dollars. It is generally believed that a quick ratio of 1 is typical.

Leverage

Debt–to–Total Assets. The debt–to–total assets ratio equals total debt divided by total assets and is represented as a percentage. Thus, a ratio of .50 means that the firm's debt equals 50 percent of the value of the firm's assets. Generally, the lower this percentage is, the better, since a high ratio could mean that the firm has little ability to withstand losses. A low ratio indicates that the firm has a buffer of funds available to creditors should it become insolvent. For many a high ratio is good.

Times Interest Earned. To find the times interest earned ratio, profit before taxes plus interest charges is divided by interest charges. This figure gives an indication of how well the firm is able to cover its interest payments. Net income before taxes is used because the firm's ability to pay interest is not a function of taxes payable. This ratio varies from industry to industry. Thus a ratio of six times interest earned may be adequate in one industry and poor in another.

Fixed Charge Coverage. The fixed charge coverage ratio serves the same basic purpose as the times interest earned ratio. It shows how well the firm is able to meet its fixed costs. The ratio is the result of dividing income available for meeting fixed charges by the amount of the fixed charges. Again, there is no standard for this ratio; and each firm should compare its position with that of others in its industry.

Activity

Inventory Turnover. Dividing sales by inventory will indicate how many times per year the firm has been able to sell its inventory. A general average for U.S. companies is nine times, but this figure can vary. More expensive items such as autos, major appliances, and jewelry normally have lower turnover rates than less expensive items.

Average Collection Period. The average collection period is the number of days that, on the average, the firm takes to collect on its credit sales. It is found by dividing receivables by sales per day. A good indicator of whether the collection period is adequate is the firm's own credit policy. An average collection period of 41 days is unsatisfactory for a firm with a 30-day credit collection policy but adequate for a firm with a 60-day credit collection policy.

Fixed Assets Turnover. Like inventory turnover, fixed assets turnover measures how effectively the firm is using its resources and thus gives a measure of overall efficiency. This ratio is the result of dividing fixed assets into sales. The resulting turnover calculation is then compared with the industry average to find out if the firm is employing its fixed assets more or less efficiently than competitors.

Total Assets Turnover. Total assets turnover is found by dividing sales by total assets. It serves the same purpose and is evaluated in the same way as fixed assets turnover. This ratio will be smallest in capital-intensive industries.

Profitability

Profit Margin on Sales. The profit margin on sales, expressed as a percentage, is calculated by dividing sales into net profits after taxes. The percentage shows how much of each dollar of sales the firm realizes as profit. The U.S. average profit margin is 5 percent, but this percentage varies by industry.

Return on Total Assets. The return on total assets is a percentage determined by dividing net profit after taxes by total assets. This percentage is compared with the industry average and, when used in conjunction with the profit margin of the firm, is an indicator of earning power. It shows the rate of return the firm is getting per dollar invested in assets.

Return on Net Worth. The return on net worth is the result of dividing net profit after taxes by net worth and is also expressed as a percentage. Net worth is defined as total equity; thus, this ratio indicates the return the stockholders are receiving on their investments. This percentage, again, is compared with the industry average and evaluated by stockholders and other firms to determine the desirability of investing in the firm.

Appendix IV
Economic and News Information

Information to Be Used with Cases Whose Decision Year Is 1984

Forecast for 1984:
Interest rates may rise somewhat. Federal budget deficit will remain at almost constant level. Lower inflation rate. Personal consumption expected to slip. Domestic investment expected to rise. Increase in housing starts. Business investment expected to increase.

Important economic data predictions for 1984:   GNP: up 4–6%; civilian unemployment rate: over 8%; Rate of inflation: 4–5%; Growth of real disposable income: 3–4%; Wages up about 7–8%.

Top news stories of 1983:   241 U.S. servicemen killed in Beirut by suicide bomber in truck loaded with explosives; Beirut situation worsens; Soviet jet fighters shoot down Korean Airlines jetliner that strayed over Soviet air space; U.S. paratroopers and marines invade Island of Grenada; unemployment rate falls to two-year low; Anne Burford resigns as director of the Environmental Protection Agency; Interior Secretary James Watt resigns; Benigno Aquino is assassinated as he steps off a plane at Manilla Airport; global oil glut results in all out price war; housing market shows strong recovery; economic recovery strengthens.

Table 1.   Summary of Recent Data and Current Changes for Principal Indicators—1983

Series title	Timing classification	Unit of measure	Basic data							
			Average 1982	Average 1983	2d Q 1983	3d Q 1983	4th Q 1983	Oct. 1983	Nov. 1983	Dec. 1983
910. Twelve leading indicators	L,L,L	1967=100	136.8	156.0	154.8	159.1	162.3	162.2	161.9	162.9
920. Four roughly coincident indicators	C,C,C	do.	136.3	139.7	137.8	141.5	145.5	144.3	145.6	146.5
930. Six lagging indicators	Lg,Lg,Lg	do.	123.0	111.8	111.5	110.4	110.2	109.8	109.9	110.8
37. Total unemployed	L,Lg,U	Thousands	10,678	10,717	11,240	10,529	9,507	9,896	9,429	9,195
43. Unemployment rate, total	L,Lg,U	Percent	9.7	9.6	10.1	9.4	8.5	8.8	8.4	8.2
30. Chg. in business inventories, 1972 dol.	L,L,L	do.	−9.4	−2.4	−5.4	3.8	7.5	—	—	—
85. Change in money supply (M1)	L,L,L	do	0.69	0.72	0.94	0.35	0.26	0.15	0.08	0.54
119. Federal funds rate	L,Lg,Lg	Percent	12.26	9.09	8.80	9.46	9.43	9.48	9.34	9.47
114. Treasury bill rate	C,Lg,Lg	do.	10.72	8.62	8.42	9.19	8.79	8.71	8.71	8.96
67. Bank notes on short-term business loans	Lg,Lg,Lg	do.	14.69	10.64	10.31	11.09	10.97	—	—	—
109. Average prime rate charged by banks	Lg,Lg,Lg	do.	14.86	10.79	10.50	10.80	11.00	11.00	11.00	11.00
320. Consumer prices (CPI), all items		1967=100	289.1	298.4	296.9	300.5	303.1	302.6	303.1	303.5
330. Producer price index (PPI), all commodities		do.	299.3	303.1	301.5	304.4	306.0	306.3	305.6	306.0

Series title	Unit of measure	Basic data							
		1981	Average 1982	Average 1983	3d Q 1982	4th Q 1982	1st Q 1983	2d Q 1983	3d Q 1983	4th Q 1983
50. GNP in 1972 dollars	do	1513.8	1485.4	1534.8	1485.7	1480.7	1490.1	1525.1	1553.4	1570.5
200. GNP in current dollars	A.r., bil. dol.	2954.1	3073.0	3309.5	3090.7	3109.6	3171.5	3272.0	3362.2	3432.0
293. Personal saving rate	Percent	6.6	5.8	4.8	5.6	5.4	5.4	4.0	4.9	5.1

Sources: *Business Conditions Digest, Fortune, Forbes, Business Week, Time,* and *U.S. News and World Report.*

Information to Be Used with Cases Whose Decision Year Is 1983

Forecast for 1983:
Economy has bottomed, should be entering a strong recovery. Short term interest rates expected to stay down. Inflation rate relatively low, expect 20% gain in corporate profits. Decline in dollar expected, deficits to remain very high—perhaps $180 billion. Ten billion dollars required now to save Social Security; a long-term fix is needed. Food and housing prices to remain relatively stable.

Important economic data predictions for 1983: GNP: up 3.4%; Unemployment rate: over 10%; Inflation: 5–6%; Growth of real disposable income 2–3%; Wages up less than 8%.

Top news stories of 1982: U.S. auto production fell to a 35-year low in February; Sen. Harrison Williams, New Jersey Democrat, resigned due to involvement in the Abscam corruption probe; Argentina seized the Falkland Islands; Federal budget deficit for fiscal 1982 was a record $110.66 billion; the Dow Jones Industrial average posted its largest one-day gain; Soviet leader Leonid Brezhnev, 75, dies in Moscow, Yuri Andropov takes over; Lech Walesa, leader of the outlawed Solidarity Union, was released by the Polish government; the Senate passed a five-cent increase in the Federal tax on gasoline and diesel fuel. Continued problems in Beirut. Disney's Epcot opens. E. T. goes home.

Table 1. Summary of Recent Data and Current Changes for Principal Indicators—1982

Series title	Timing classification	Unit of measure	Basic data							
			Average 1981	Average 1982	2d Q 1982	3d Q 1982	4th Q 1982	Oct. 1982	Nov. 1982	Dec. 1982
910. Twelve leading indicators	L,L,L	1967=100	133.1	128.4	127.4	129.8	131.4	130.6	130.8	132.8
920. Four coincident indicators	C,C,C	do.	141.3	132.2	134.1	131.4	128.3	128.5	128.3	128.2
930. Six lagging indicators	Lg,Lg,Lg	do.	187.8	177.4	184.1	176.7	165.1	168.4	165.0	161.9
37. Total unemployed	L,Lg,U	Thousands	8,273	10,678	10,369	11,025	11,839	11,576	11,906	12,036
43. Unemployment rate, total	L,Lg,U	Percent	7.6	9.7	9.4	10.0	10.7	10.5	10.7	10.8
28. New private housing units started, total	L,L,L	A.r., thous.	1,087	1,061	952	1,118	1,253	1,126	1,404	1,229
30. Chg. in business inventories, 1972 dol.	L,L,L	do.	9.0	−8.5	−4.4	3.4	−17.7	—	—	—
85. Change in money supply (M1)	L,L,L	Percent	0.52	0.69	0.23	0.67	1.29	1.72	1.41	0.74
119. Federal funds rate	L,Lg,Lg	Percent	16.38	12.26	14.51	11.01	9.29	9.71	9.20	8.95
114. Treasury bill rate	C,Lg,Lg	do.	14.08	10.72	12.36	9.71	7.93	7.75	8.04	8.01
67. Bank notes on short-term business loans	Lg,Lg,Lg	do.	19.56	14.69	17.11	13.27	11.26	—	—	—
109. Average prime rate charged by banks	Lg,Lg,Lg	do.	18.87	14.86	16.50	14.72	11.96	12.52	11.85	11.50
320. Consumer prices (CPI), all items		1967=100	272.4	289.1	287.3	292.8	293.4	294.1	293.6	292.4
330. Producer price index (PPI), all commodities		do.	293.4	299.3	298.6	300.0	300.3	299.9	300.4	300.6

Series title	Unit of measure	Basic data								
		1980	Average 1981	Average 1982	3d Q 1981	4th Q 1981	1st Q 1982	2d Q 1982	3d Q 1982	4th Q 1982
50. GNP in 1972 dollars	A.r., bil. dol.	1474.0	1502.6	1475.5	1510.4	1490.1	1470.7	1478.4	1481.1	1471.7
200. GNP in current dollars	do	2633.1	2937.7	3057.5	2980.9	3003.2	2995.5	3045.2	3088.2	3101.3
293. Personal saving rate	Percent	5.8	6.4	6.5	6.5	7.5	6.6	6.7	6.9	5.8

Information to Be Used with Cases Whose Decision Year Is 1982

Forecast for 1982:
Upswing in business activity throughout the year. Energy prices steady and labor costs moderate due to increased productivity. Federal budget deficit $125 billion by end of fiscal year. Increase in government defense spending and in interest payments. Corporations and consumers cut down use of short-term credit; rates remain steady. Consumers savings rate increases to 6%. Business spending remains steady to counteract the decreases of 1981. Housing turnaround by midyear; makes a solid contribution to renewed economic growth. Interest rates decline by midsummer, but federal budget deficit may keep them high.

Important economic data predictions for 1982:   Economic growth: 3.3%; GNP: up 1.4%; Unemployment rate: over 9%; Inflation: 7%; Wages: between 8.5–9.5% increase.

Top news stories of 1981:   Iranian hostages come home; space shuttle; Reagan and Pope John Paul II shot; Sadat assassinated; Atlanta child murders; Sandra O'Connor appointed to Supreme Court; medflies; Kansas City hotel collapse; British royal wedding; Poland declares martial law.

Table 1.   Summary of Recent Data and Current Changes for Principal Indicators—1981

Series title	Timing classification	Unit of measure	Basic data							
			Average 1980	Average 1981	2d Q 1981	3d Q 1981	4th Q 1981	Oct. 1981	Nov. 1981	Dec. 1981
910. Twelve leading indicators	L,L,L	1967=100	131.2	133.3	135.6	132.9	128.9	128.8	128.6	129.4
920. Four coincident indicators	C,C,C	do.	140.3	141.3	142.3	142.4	138.3	139.9	138.5	136.6
930. Six lagging indicators	Lg,Lg,Lg	do.	176.8	187.7	186.5	193.6	185.4	189.7	184.9	181.5
37. Total unemployed	L,Lg,U	Thousands	7,448	8,080	7,900	7,708	8,995	8,520	9,004	9,462
43. Unemployment rate, total	L,Lg,U	Percent	7.1	7.9	7.4	7.2	8.4	8.0	8.4	8.9
28. New private housing units started, total	L,L,L	A.r., thous.	1,292	1,087	1,176	968	903	867	863	978
30. Chg. in business inventories, 1972 dol.	L,L,L	do.	−2.9	8.2	10.8	14.9	8.5	—	—	—
85. Change in money supply (M1-B)	L,L,L	Percent	0.52	0.52	0.25	0.23	0.77	0.28	1.13	0.91
119. Federal funds rate	L,Lg,Lg	Percent	13.36	16.38	17.78	17.58	13.59	15.08	13.31	12.37
114. Treasury bill rate	C,Lg,Lg	do.	11.61	14.08	14.83	15.09	12.02	13.87	11.27	10.93
67. Bank notes on short-term business loans	Lg,Lg,Lg	do.	15.17	19.56	19.99	21.11	17.23	—	—	—
109. Average prime rate charged by banks	Lg,Lg,Lg	do.	15.27	18.87	18.93	20.32	17.01	18.45	16.84	15.75
320. Consumer prices (CPI), all items		1967=100	246.8	272.4	269.0	276.7	280.7	279.9	280.7	281.5
330. Producer prices (PPI), all commodities		do.	268.8	293.4	294.1	296.0	295.8	296.0	295.5	295.9

Series title	Unit of measure	Basic data								
		1979	Average 1980	Average 1981	3d Q 1980	4th Q 1980	1st Q 1981	2d Q 1981	3d Q 1981	4th Q 1981
50. GNP in 1972 dollars	A.r., bil. dol.	1483.0	1480.7	1509.6	1471.9	1485.6	1516.4	1510.4	1515.8	1495.6
200. GNP in current dollars	do.	2413.9	2626.1	2922.2	2637.3	2730.6	2853.0	2885.8	2965.0	2984.9
293. Personal saving rate	Percent	5.2	5.6	5.3	6.1	5.1	4.6	5.4	5.2	6.0

Sources: *Business Conditions Digest, Fortune, Forbes, Business Week, Time,* and *U.S. News and World Report.*

Information to Be Used with Cases Whose Decision Year Is 1981

Forecast for 1981:
Economy surface turbulence covers more fundamental improvements occurring beneath. Unemployment rises as business and industry cut down labor costs to stabilize cash flows. Recession expected in March as capital expenditures, consumer goods spending, and buying plans for homes, autos, and major appliances decline. Economy causes capital goods decline due to short cash flows of most businesses. Federal funds decrease by summer. Situation reverses itself in the second half. 1981's economy at least as unstable as 1980's. Effect of new administration's outlook on inflation and unemployment unclear.

Important economic data predictions for 1981: Economic growth: about 4%; GNP: up 2–3%; Unemployment rate: at or above 10%; Inflation: near 10%, probably climbing higher; Wages: up 8–9%.

Top news stories of 1980: Reagan elected President; U.S. Summer Olympic boycott; Shah of Iran dies; U.S. Olympic hockey team beats Russians; John Lennon killed; pictures of Saturn from space; Mary Cunningham scandal; Mt. St. Helen's erupts; Polish workers unionize; MGM Grand Hotel fire; record inflation.

Table 1. Summary of Recent Data and Current Changes for Principal Indicators—1980

Series title	Timing classification	Unit of measure	Average 1979	Average 1980	2d Q 1980	3d Q 1980	4th Q 1980	Oct. 1980	Nov. 1980	Dec. 1980
910. Twelve leading indicators	L,L,L	1967=100	140.1	131.4	124.1	131.2	136.7	135.7	137.7	136.6
920. Four coincident indicators	C,C,C	do.	145.1	140.4	138.4	137.4	141.1	140.3	141.0	141.9
930. Six lagging indicators	Lg,Lg,Lg	do.	166.4	177.6	182.7	163.2	181.3	168.2	175.3	200.3
37. Total unemployed	L,Lg,U	Thousands	5,963	7,448	7,652	7,921	7,897	7,961	7,946	7,785
43. Unemployment rate, total	L,Lg,U	Percent	5.8	7.1	7.3	7.5	7.5	7.6	7.5	7.4
28. New private housing units started, total	L,L,L	A.r., thous.	1,744	1,291	1,053	1,412	1,556	1,557	1,563	1,548
30. Chg. in business inventories, 1972 dol.	L,L,L	do.	10.2	−1.2	1.3	−5.0	−0.2	—	—	—
85. Change in money supply (M1-B)	L,L,L	Percent	0.60	0.53	0.02	1.40	0.32	0.98	0.73	−0.75
119. Federal funds rate	L,Lg,Lg	Percent	11.20	13.36	12.69	9.84	15.85	12.81	15.85	18.90
114. Treasury bill rate	C,Lg,Lg	do.	10.04	11.61	10.05	9.24	13.71	11.58	13.89	15.66
67. Bank rates on short-term bus. loans	Lg,Lg,Lg	do.	13.18	15.17	17.75	11.56	15.71	—	—	—
109. Average prime rate charged by banks	Lg,Lg,Lg	do.	12.67	15.27	16.32	11.61	16.73	13.79	16.06	20.35
320. Consumer prices (CPI), all items		1967=100	217.4	246.8	245.0	249.6	256.2	253.9	256.2	258.4
330. Producer prices (PPI), all commodities		do.	235.6	268.6	264.2	272.8	278.6	277.0	278.4	280.3

Series title	Unit of measure	1978	Average 1979	1980	3d Q 1979	4th Q 1979	1st Q 1980	2d Q 1980	3d Q 1980	4th Q 1980
50. GNP in 1972 dollars	A.r., bil. dol.	1436.9	1483.0	1481.8	1488.2	1490.6	1501.9	1463.3	1471.9	1490.1
200. GNP in current dollars	do.	2156.1	2413.9	2628.8	2444.1	2496.3	2571.7	2564.8	2637.3	2741.4
293. Personal saving rate	Percent	5.2	5.2	5.7	5.4	4.7	4.9	6.2	6.1	5.6

Appendix IV: Economic and News Information 301

Information to Be Used with Cases Whose Decision Year Is 1980

Forecast for 1980:
Year shows shallow recession in first half. Slow recovery begins end of August. Consumer borrowing cut back. Business borrowing increases in long-term debt; decreases in short-term credit. Treasury and state/local borrowing increases. Expenditures by groups level off. Consumer spending cutbacks shift from cars, trucks and gasoline to clothing, home goods and durables. Consumer services experience sharp rise. Energy prices incline steeply, continuing yearly increases of 25%. Equipment orders fall back as capital good purchases by businesses decline. Auto and steel industries suffer the most. Short-term interest rates soften by midyear; long-term rates hit peak in autumn; start down by year end.

Important economic data predictions for 1980: Economic growth: 2.5%; GNP: up 0.3%; Unemployment rate: 6% by election day; 8% by year's end; Inflation: likely to reach 13%; Wages: up 9%.

Top news stories of 1979: Pope John Paul II appointed; Ayatollah Khomeini in power; hostages taken in Iran; Soviets invade Afghanistan; gas shortages, record high gas prices; United States and China establish diplomatic relations; Margaret Thatcher first woman prime minister in England; Vietnamese boat people; President Carter's cabinet resigns; Sadat and Begin continue talks over Mideast; gold reaches new high prices.

Table 1. Summary of Recent Data and Current Changes for Principal Indicators—1979

Series title	Timing classification	Unit of measure	Basic data							
			Average 1978	Average 1979	2d Q 1979	3d Q 1979	4th Q 1979	Oct. 1979	Nov. 1979	Dec. 1979
910. Twelve leading indicators	L,L,L	1967=100	141.8	139.9	139.9	139.7	137.4	138.5	136.8	136.8
920. Four coincident indicators	C,C,C	do.	140.1	145.0	144.9	144.9	144.8	144.7	144.6	145.2
930. Six lagging indicators	Lg,Lg,Lg	do.	143.1	166.6	162.7	167.3	178.2	176.1	179.6	178.9
37. Total unemployed	L,Lg,U	Thousands	6,047	5,963	5,890	6,008	6,084	6,121	6,044	6,087
43. Unemployment rate, total	L,Lg,U	Percent	6.0	5.8	5.8	5.8	5.9	5.9	5.8	5.9
28. New private housing units started, total	L,L,L	A.r., thous.	2,018	1,742	1,834	1,834	1,604	1,764	1,522	1,527
30. Chg. in business inventories, 1972 dol.	L,L,L	do.	14.1	10.2	18.1	7.1	3.2	—	—	—
85. Change in money supply (M1)	L,L,L	Percent	0.54	0.46	0.95	0.79	0.26	0.21	0.11	0.45
119. Federal funds rate	L,Lg,Lg	Percent	7.94	11.19	10.18	10.95	13.58	13.77	13.18	13.78
114. Treasury bill rate	C,Lg,Lg	do.	7.22	10.04	9.37	9.63	11.80	11.47	11.87	12.07
67. Bank rates on short-term bus. loans	Lg,Lg,Lg	do.	9.80	13.18	12.34	12.31	15.81	—	—	—
109. Average prime rate charged by banks	Lg,Lg,Lg	do.	9.06	12.67	11.72	12.12	15.08	14.39	15.55	15.30
320. Consumer prices (CPI), all items		1967=100	195.4	NA	214.1	221.1	227.6	225.4	227.5	229.9
330. Producer prices (PPI), all commodities		do.	209.3	235.5	231.8	239.0	247.2	245.2	246.9	249.4

Series title	Unit of measure	Basic data							
		1977	Average 1978	1979	3d Q 1978	4th Q 1978	1st Q 1979	2d Q 1979	3d Q 1979	4th Q 1979
50. GNP in 1972 dollars	A.r., bil. dol.	1340.5	1399.2	1431.1	1407.3	1426.6	1430.6	1422.3	1433.3	1438.4
200. GNP in current dollars	do.	1899.5	2127.6	2368.5	2159.6	2235.2	2292.1	2329.8	2396.5	2455.8
293. Personal saving rate	Percent	5.0	4.9	4.5	4.8	4.7	5.0	5.4	4.3	3.3

Information to Be Used with Cases Whose Decision Year Is 1979

Forecast for 1979:
Expected recession will not take place in 1979. No relief from inflation either. High interest rates restrain capital spending; long-term rates go up twice as much as last year. Short-term rates rise less drastically; possibly start down by year end. Debts repayments rise steeply; new borrowings level out. Final sales of goods slow. Economy hits double digit inflation. Consumers cut back due to purchasing power decline. Consumers cut back on mortgage and installment borrowing. Business buying rises sharply. Wage increases depend on compliance to Carter guidelines. Unions make important decisions regarding voluntary cutbacks.

Important economic data predictions for 1979: Economic growth: 2.5–3.9%; GNP: up 4.1%; Unemployment rate: 5.5%; Inflation: a little less than 9%, average; Wages: up 9%.

Top news stories of 1978: Pope John Paul I appointed; Pope John Paul I dies; Guyana suicides; 3-Mile Island nuclear accident; Mideast peace treaty signed; Nobel Peace Prize to Sadat and Begin; Cambodia and Vietnam at war; Rhodesia agrees to majority rule; Aldo Moro kidnapped and murdered in Italy by Red Brigades; OPEC raises oil prices.

Table 1. Summary of Recent Data and Current Changes for Principal Indicators—1978

Series title	Timing classification	Unit of measure	Basic data							
			Average 1977	1978	2d Q 1978	3d Q 1978	4th Q 1978	Oct. 1978	Nov. 1978	Dec. 1978
910. Twelve leading indicators	L,L,L	1967=100	130.9	136.7	136.9	137.0	138.0	138.7	138.0	137.3
920. Four coincident indicators	C,C,C	do.	130.2	138.6	138.2	139.6	142.6	141.6	142.7	143.6
930. Six lagging indicators	Lg,Lg,Lg	do.	126.9	145.4	141.9	146.9	155.2	150.5	155.7	159.4
37. Total unemployed	L,Lg,U	Thousands	6,855	6,047	5,962	6,054	5,931	5,870	5,912	6,012
43. Unemployment rate, total	L,Lg,U	Percent	7.0	6.0	5.9	6.0	5.8	5.8	5.8	5.9
28. New private housing units started, total	L,L,L	A.r., thous.	1,987	2,018	2,114	2,073	2,129	2,106	2,155	2,125
30. Chg. in business inventories, 1972 dol.	L,L,L	do.	8.9	10.4	12.7	9.0	7.7	—	—	—
85. Change in money supply (M1)	L,L,L	Percent	0.64	0.54	0.95	0.76	0.02	0.30	−0.39	0.14
119. Federal funds rate	L,Lg,Lg	Percent	5.54	7.93	7.28	8.10	9.58	8.96	9.76	10.03
114. Treasury bill rate	C,Lg,Lg	do.	5.26	7.22	6.48	7.32	8.68	8.13	8.79	9.12
67. Bank rates on short-term bus. loans	Lg,Lg,Lg	do.	7.97	9.85	9.13	9.95	11.43	10.65	11.43	12.22
109. Average prime rate charged by banks	Lg,Lg,Lg	do.	6.82	9.06	8.30	9.14	10.81	9.94	10.94	11.55
320. Consumer prices (CPI), all items		1967=100	181.5	195.3	193.3	197.8	201.8	200.7	201.8	202.9
330. Wholesale prices (WPI), all commodities		do.	194.2	209.3	208.0	211.2	216.0	215.0	215.7	217.4

Series title	Unit of measure	Basic data							
		1976	Average 1977	1978	3d Q 1977	4th Q 1977	1st Q 1978	2d Q 1978	3d Q 1978	4th Q 1978
50. GNP in 1972 dollars	A.r., bil. dol.	1271.0	1332.7	1385.1	1343.9	1354.5	1354.2	1382.6	1391.4	1412.2
200. GNP in current dollars	do.	1700.1	1887.2	2106.6	1916.8	1958.1	1992.0	2087.5	2136.1	2210.8
293. Personal saving rate	Percent	5.7	5.1	5.3	5.6	5.4	5.9	5.3	5.2	4.8

Information to Be Used with Cases Whose Decision Year Is 1978

Forecast for 1978:
Housing starts peak; then fall into a gradual decline. Purchases lag as short-term lending rate rises again. Volume of oil imports stops growing. U.S. trade deficit comes close to balancing out. Limited credit use by consumer and by business ends. Clothing and home goods do well. Federal spending increases at a slower rate. State and local public construction increases as smaller governments deplete surpluses from past 18 months. Rise in capital spending led by manufacturing concerns but not substantial.

Important economic data predictions for 1978: Economic growth: 4–5%; GNP: up 4.9%; Unemployment rate: down to 6%; Inflation: 6.5%; Wages: rise above 9% increase from last year.

Top news stories of 1977: Elizabeth II Silver Jubilee; 747 crash in Canary Islands; Elvis Presley dies; Sadat-Begin start peace talks; Son of Sam; Floods in Pennsylvania vs. California drought; "Roots"; Women's Rights marches begin; NYC blackout; "Star Wars" era.

Table 1. Summary of Recent Data and Current Changes for Principal Indicators—1977

Series title	Timing classification	Unit of measure	Average 1976	Average 1977	2d Q 1977	3d Q 1977	4th Q 1977	Oct. 1977	Nov. 1977	Dec. 1977
910. Twelve leading indicators	L,L,L	1967=100	124.7	131.1	130.2	131.8	134.6	134.2	134.3	135.3
920. Four coincident indicators	C,C,C	do.	122.3	130.1	129.6	130.8	133.0	132.4	132.9	133.8
930. Six lagging indicators	Lg,Lg,Lg	do.	120.7	126.7	124.6	127.9	132.1	131.1	132.6	132.5
37. Total unemployed	L,Lg,U	Thousands	7,288	6,855	6,816	6,814	6,676	6,872	6,818	6,337
43. Unemployment rate total	L,Lg,U	Percent	7.7	7.0	7.0	7.0	6.8	7.0	6.9	6.4
28. New private housing units started, total	L,L,L	A.r., thous.	1,538	1,986	1,905	2,059	2,206	2,203	2,121	2,295
30. Chg. in business inventories, 1972 dol.	L,L,L	do.	8.5	11.6	13.2	15.7	7.7	—	—	—
85. Change in money supply (M1)	L,L,L	Percent	0.48	0.60	0.68	0.87	0.50	1.00	−0.12	0.63
119. Federal funds rate	L,Lg,Lg	Percent	5.05	5.54	5.16	5.82	6.51	6.47	6.51	6.56
114. Treasury bill rate	C,Lg,Lg	do.	5.00	5.26	4.83	5.47	6.14	6.19	6.16	6.06
109. Average prime rate charged by banks	Lg,Lg,Lg	do.	6.84	6.82	6.47	6.90	7.67	7.52	7.75	7.75
320. Consumer prices (CPI), all items		1967=100	170.5	181.5	180.7	183.3	185.3	184.5	185.4	186.1
330. Wholesale prices (WPI), all commodities		do.	183.0	194.2	194.7	194.9	197.2	196.3	197.0	198.2

Series title	Unit of measure	1975	Average 1976	1977	3d Q 1976	4th Q 1976	1st Q 1977	2d Q 1977	3d Q 1977	4th Q 1977
50. GNP in 1972 dollars	A.r., bil. dol.	1202.1	1274.7	1337.6	1283.7	1287.4	1311.0	1330.7	1347.4	1361.4
200. GNP in current dollars	do.	1528.8	1706.5	1890.4	1727.3	1755.4	1810.8	1869.9	1915.9	1965.1
A7. Saving										
293. Personal saving rate	Percent	7.4	5.6	5.2	5.4	4.6	4.1	5.3	5.5	5.7

Information to Be Used with Cases Whose Decision Year Is 1977

Forecast for 1977:
No significant improvement expected in unemployment this year; not enough plant capacity available to accommodate further jobs. Inflation remains steady throughout year. Capital spending increases due largely to machinery acquisitions by businesses. Total credit use increases; short-term interest rates rise 1–2%. Federal spending increases as economy expands; state/local governments follow suit. Federal grants to state/local governments increase. Imports hold steady; net exports increase. Union activity increases; demands for higher benefits for working women and cost of living protection. Consumer goods buying rises, with foods and services following.

Important economic data predictions for 1977: Economic growth: 5.7%; GNP: up 5.2%; Unemployment rate: 7%; Inflation: 5+%; Wages: up 8%.

Top news stories of 1976: U.S. Bicentennial; Jimmy Carter elected President; Mao Tse-tung dies; Howard Hughes dies; Tutankhamen exhibit opens; Viking I lands on Mars; women cadets enter West Point; Legionnaire's disease; Elizabeth Ray scandal; 1976 Montreal Olympics/Nadia Comaneci.

Table 1. Summary of Recent Data and Current Changes for Principal Indicators—1976

Series title	Timing classification	Unit of measure	Basic data							
			Average 1975	Average 1976	2d Q 1976	3d Q 1976	4th Q 1976	Oct. 1976	Nov. 1976	Dec. 1976
910. Twelve leading indicators	L,L,L	1967=100	114.1	125.2	124.7	126.1	128.0	126.4	127.7	129.8
920. Four coincident indicators	C,C,C	do.	114.1	122.1	122.2	122.6	123.6	122.2	123.6	124.9
930. Six lagging indicators	Lg,Lg,Lg	do.	128.6	120.5	119.9	121.2	120.8	121.7	120.9	119.7
37. Total unemployed	L,Lg,U	Thousands	7,830	7,288	7,014	7,439	7,632	7,569	7,769	7,558
43. Unemployment rate, total	L,Lg,U	Percent	8.5	7.7	7.4	7.8	8.0	7.9	8.1	7.9
28. New private housing units started, total	L,L,L	A.r., thous.	1,160	1,540	1,433	1,586	1,823	1,814	1,716	1,940
30. Chg. in business inventories, 1972 dol.	L,L,L	do.	−12.0	9.1	11.1	10.2	4.7	—	—	—
85. Change in money supply (M1)	L,L,L	Percent	0.34	0.47	0.57	0.34	0.61	1.14	0.0	0.68
119. Federal funds rate	L,Lg,Lg	Percent	5.82	5.05	5.20	5.28	4.88	5.03	4.95	4.65
114. Treasury bill rate	C,Lg,Lg	do.	5.82	5.00	5.17	5.17	4.70	4.93	4.81	4.35
109. Average prime rate charged by banks	Lg,Lg,Lg	do.	8.65	7.52	7.44	7.80	7.28	—	—	—
320. Consumer prices (CPI), all items		1967=100	161.2	170.5	169.2	171.9	173.8	173.3	173.8	174.3
330. Wholesale prices (WPI), all commodities		do.	174.9	182.9	182.1	184.2	186.0	185.2	185.6	187.1

Series title	Unit of measure	Basic data								
		1974	Average 1975	1976	2d Q 1976	3d Q 1976	4th Q 1976	1st Q 1977	2d Q 1977	3d Q 1977
50. GNP in 1972 dollars	A.r., bil. dol.	1217.8	1202.1	1274.7	1271.5	1283.7	1287.4	1311.0	1330.7	1347.4
200. GNP in current dollars	do.	1412.9	1528.8	1706.5	1691.9	1727.3	1755.4	1810.8	1869.9	1915.9
293. Personal saving rate	Percent	7.3	7.4	5.6	6.0	5.4	4.6	4.1	5.3	5.5

Appendix IV: Economic and News Information   305

Information to Be Used with Cases Whose Decision Year Is 1976

Forecast for 1976:
Economic recovery continues. Demand for cars, housing and capital goods leads to more aggressive production schedules. Consumers spend more. Inflation decreases; consumers need to save less to maintain value of assets. Prime lending rate increases, as will short-term corporate and personal credit. New plant contracts and manufacturer's capital appropriations rise progressively. Treasury Bill yield goes up as federal government recovers; state/local government expenditures increase moderately, a few tenths of a percentage point behind GNP. Consumer goods and service buying patterns increase faster than those for goods. Moderate increases across the board.

Important economic data predictions for 1976:   Economic growth: 6%; GNP: up 5.8%; Unemployment rate: 8% by election day; Inflation: 5%; Wages: up 8%.

Top news stories of 1975:   America pulls out of Viet Nam; Fromme attempt on Ford's life; Jimmy Hoffa disappears; Chiang Kai-Shek dies; Baryshnikov defects; Karen Anne Quinlan case; Emperor Hirohito visits; Aristotle Onassis dies; POWs come home; "Jaws" breaks box office records.

Table 1.   Summary of Recent Data and Current Changes for Principal Indicators—1975

Series title	Unit of measure	Basic data				
		Average 1974	Average 1975	2d Q 1975	3d Q 1975	4th Q 1975
12 leading indicators	1967=100	154.7	144.9	142.0	151.7	153.4
4 coincident indicators	do.	169.8	152.7	148.3	154.0	158.5
6 lagging indicators	do.	190.7	180.5	180.9	174.7	172.8
Unemployment rate, total	Percent	5.6	8.5	8.9	8.4	8.4
Number of persons unemployed	Thousands	5,076	7,830	8,203	7,802	7,824
New private housing units started, total	A.r., thous.	1,336	1,162	1,068	1,258	1,372
Change in bus. inventories, all indus.	A.r., bil. dol.	9.7	−14.2	−29.6	−2.1	−0.2
Change in money supply (M1)	Ann. Rate	4.56	4.95	9.65	3.56	1.78
Treasury bill rate	Percent	7.87	5.82	5.40	6.33	5.68
Bank rates on short-term bus. loans	Percent	11.28	8.65	8.16	8.22	8.29
Consumer prices all items	1967=100	147.7	161.2	159.5	162.9	165.5
Wholesale prices, all commodities	1967=100	160.1	174.9	173.0	176.7	178.6

Series title	Unit of measure	Basic data							
		1973	Average 1974	1975	3d Q 1974	4th Q 1974	1st Q 1975	2d Q 1975	3d Q 1975	4th Q 1975
GNP in 1972 dollars	A.r., bil. dol.	1233.4	1210.7	1186.4	1210.2	1186.8	1158.6	1168.1	1201.5	1217.4
GNP in current dollars	do.	1306.3	1406.9	1499.0	1424.4	1441.3	1433.6	1460.6	1528.5	1573.2

Information to Be Used with Cases Whose Decision Year is 1975

Forecast for 1975:
Ongoing slide in business continues. Ford administration tax cut certain. Federal spending rises but less sharply than last year. Same is true of spending on state/local levels. Capital spending decreases, but picks up by year end due mostly to purchases made by electric utilities, communications, and commercial/service companies. Heavy bond flotations by corporations as businesses try to restructure debt. Personal loans decrease due to lack of confidence in future. Short-term interest rates finish out the year at about 6%. Purchases by consumers hit new highs in spring; decline due to autumn manufacturing cutbacks. Consumer goods big losers; food and services suffer little. Auto sales expand by ⅓; housing starts up by 50%. Consumers opt for installment buying and mortgage plans.

Important economic data predictions for 1975: Economic growth: 6%; GNP: down 2.9% after some mid-year ups and downs; Unemployment rate: 7–7.5%; Inflation: 7% in spring; 6% by year's end; Wages: up 7–8%.

Top news stories of 1974: Patty Hearst kidnapping; Watergate; Ford takes over as Nixon resigns; energy crunch/gas lines; Hank Aaron breaks home run record; Jupiter seen from Pioneer II; sugar prices hit all time high; Golda Meir no longer in power.

Table 1. Summary of Recent Data and Current Changes for Principal Indicators—1974

Series title	Unit of measure	Basic data				
		Average 1973	Average 1974	2d Q 1974	3d Q 1974	4th Q 1974
12 leading indicators, reverse trend adj	1967=100	163.4	171.9	175.2	177.2	164.9
5 coincident indicators	do.	155.5	165.9	165.8	169.2	166.0
6 lagging indicators	do.	164.4	204.2	199.4	212.9	217.9
Unemployment rate total	Percent	4.9	5.6	5.1	5.5	6.5
Number of persons unemployed	Thousands	4,306	5,076	4,667	5,014	6,008
New private housing units started, total	A.r., thous.	2,042	1,336	1,566	1,207	989
Change in bus. invent. all ind.	A.r., bil. dol.	15.4	13.4	13.5	8.7	14.4
Change in money supply	A.r. percent	5.98	4.45	6.51	1.57	4.26
Treasury bill rate	Percent	7.03	7.87	8.27	8.28	7.33
Bank rates on short-term bus. loans	do.	8.30	11.28	11.15	12.40	11.64
Consumer prices, all items	1967=100	133.1	147.7	145.4	149.9	154.2
Wholesale prices, all commodities	1967=100	134.7	160.1	154.5	165.4	171.2

Series title	Unit of measure	Basic data							
		Average 1972	Average 1973	Average 1974	3d Q 1973	4th Q 1973	1st Q 1974	2d Q 1974	3d Q 1974	4th Q 1974
GNP in 1958 dollars	A.r., bil. dol.	792.5	839.2	821.1	840.8	845.7	830.5	827.1	823.1	803.7
GNP in current dollars	do.	1158.0	1294.9	1396.7	1308.9	1344.0	1358.8	1383.8	1416.3	1428.0

Information to Be Used with Cases Whose Decision Year Is 1974

Forecast for 1974:
Oil embargo expected to continue; only modest impact on overall business during first quarter. By mid-year shortages' effects hit home as more workers laid off, and auto buying plans begin to fall off again. Capital expenditures by business hold their own, substituting energy research expenditures for car, truck and plane purchases. Home building decreases. By mid-year consumer credit tightens. Government expenditures rise on federal and state/local level; federal government increases energy research and state/local governments run down accumulated surpluses.

Important economic data predictions for 1974: Economic growth: nearly 7%; GNP: up 2.4%; Unemployment rate: 5.2%; Inflation: 8%, falling to 4% by December; Wages: up 7%.

Top news stories of 1973: Lyndon Johnson dies; Vietnam ceasefire signed; U.S. consumers boycott meat; Skylab launched; Watergate; Agnew criminal probe; Allende dies in Chile coup; Peron elected in Argentina; Middle East war; Ford becomes vice-president; oil problems.

Table 1. Summary of Recent Data and Current Changes for Principal Indicators—1973

Series title	Unit of measure	Basic data				
		Average 1972	Average 1973	2d Q 1973	3d Q 1973	4th Q 1973
12 leading indicators, reverse trend adj	1967=100	142.7	163.6	162.1	165.8	167.9
5 coincident indicators	do.	136.6	155.4	153.1	157.2	162.0
6 lagging indicators	do.	134.8	164.3	158.8	170.5	178.9
Unemployment rate, total	Percent	5.6	4.9	4.9	4.8	4.7
Number of persons unemployed	Thousands	4,840	4,304	4,357	4,230	4,256
New private housing units started, total	A.r., thous.	2,357	2,042	2,221	2,030	1,566
Change in bus. inventories all industries	A.r., bil. dol.	6.0	7.4	4.5	4.7	15.9
Change in money supply	A.r., percent	7.97	5.06	10.20	0.31	8.00
Treasury Bill rate	Percent	4.07	7.03	6.61	8.39	7.46
Bank rates in short-term business loans	Percent	5.82	8.30	7.35	9.24	10.08
Consumer prices all items	1967=100	125.3	133.1	131.5	134.4	137.6
Wholesale prices all commodities	1967=100	119.1	135.5	133.6	139.3	142.2

Series title	Unit of measure	Basic data							
		1971	Average 1972	1973	3d Q 1972	4th Q 1972	1st Q 1973	2d Q 1973	3d Q 1973	4th Q 1973
GNP in 1958 dollars	A.r., bil. dol.	745.4	790.7	837.3	796.7	812.3	829.3	834.3	841.3	844.1
GNP in current dollars	do.	1055.4	1155.2	1288.2	1166.5	1199.2	1242.5	1272.0	1304.5	1334.0

Index

Abernathy, M. J., 54
Ackerman, R. W., 206
Ackoff, Russell L., 34, 81
Adams, C. R., 47
ADL portfolio planning matrix, 172, 173
Aerospace industry, 210–211
Agethe, K. E., 28
Aguilar, F. J., 24, 48
Aharoni, Y., 206
AIM audit, 258
Aldrich, H. B., 244
Alexis, M., 213
Allegheny, Ludlam, 105
Allen, Michael G., 185, 186
Amar, P., 244
American Institute of Management (AIM), 258
AMF, 103
Analytical forecasting techniques, 71
Anderson, Carl R., 141, 142
Anderson, M. J., Jr., 145
Anderson, T. A., 233
Andrews, K. R., 21
Ansoff, H. I., 8, 34, 118
Anthony, R. N., 255, 275
Appleby, Paul H., 212
Aqua-Chem, Incorporated, 104
Arby's, 103
Argenti, J., 249
Argyris, C., 275
Armstrong, J. S., 8
Arning, H. K., 242
Art-publishing business, 128–129
AT&T, 13
Audits:
  AIM, 258
  management, 258–260, 285–292
  social, 261
  strategic, 258–260, 285–292
Austin, J. Paul, 22
Avis, W. E., 227

Baldridge, J. V., 202
Bales, C. F., 275
Banco, 13
Bank of America, 153, 155
Banks, P. M., 155
Barrow, J. C., 244
Baruch, Bernard, 119
Bass, Bernard M., 267
Bauer, R. A., 213
BCG business matrix, 167–168
Beatrice Foods, 109
Beebe, W. Thomas, 151–153
Behavioral theory, 137–148
Bender, P. S., 69
Bendix, 91
Benner, S., 265
Bennis, Warren, 267
Berg, N. A., 93

Bergmoser, J. Paul, 250
Berkwitt, G. J., 275
Blake, R. R., 227
Blanchard, Kenneth H., 239
Blau, Peter M., 11
Blinder, Martin, 128–129
Blomstrom, Robert L., 96
Blount Brothers Construction Company, 105–106
Blustein, P., 42
Board of directors, 17–21
Borman, Frank, 125, 153
Boulden, J. B., 69
Boulton, W., 21
Bourgeois, L. J., III, 244
Bouton, W., 68
Bovee, Christian Nestell, 252
Bower, J. L., 206
Box Jenkins, 71
Bracker, J., 35
Bradspies, Robert W., 247
Brandt, William K., 272
Braniff Airlines, 12–15
Braybrooke, D., 206
Bressler, Ray, 257
Brief, A. P., 204
Brigham, Eugene, 254
Brodin, D. R., 244
Brooke, Michael, 228, 272–273
Bryan, William Jennings, 163
Bryson, J. M., 35
Budgets, 234, 235
Buffa, E. S., 69
Bulkeley, W. M., 70
Bulova Watch Company, 42
Burnett, James, 151, 152
Burns, Robert, 245
Burt, D., 8
Business strategy, 94, 95, 108
  behavioral theory and, 137–148
  contingency approach to, 129–135
  directional policy matrix for, 136–137
  management audit and, 286–287
  Porter's competitive strategies, 142–144
  for single-business enterprise, 123–155
Business Week, 48, 255
Buzzell, R. D., 8, 138
Byrom, Fletcher, 270

Cady, J., 142
Cammann, C., 275
Campo-Flores, F., 26
Cannon, J. Thomas, 3
Carroll, A., 35
Carroll, Daniel T., 265
Carroll, Lewis, 81
Carter, E. E., 201
Case method, 277–283

CEO. *See* Chief executive officer
Chambers, J. C., 68
Chandler, Alfred, 225, 241
Chandler, M., 21
Chang, Y. N., 26
Channon, Derek F., 186–188, 229
Chief executive officer (CEO), 16, 21–22
Christensen, C. Roland, 93
Chrysler, 249–252
Churchill, N. C., 21
Clausen, A. W., 155
Cleary, M. J., 79
Clendenin, W. D., 21
Clymer, L. M., 199
Coalition, 22–24, 200–202
Coate, Malcolm B., 181–182
Coca-Cola Company, 41, 104, 105, 124
Coleco, 215
Columbia Pictures, 104
Commitment to excellence (CTE) program, 210–211
Communication systems, 234, 237–239
Competitive position assessment matrix, 177
Competitor analysis, 55–62
  information needed for, 61
  Porter on, 56–59
  sources of data for, 59, 62
Computers:
  forecasting and, 68–71
  Japanese market for, 55
Concentration, 101
Consumer laws, 51
Contingency theory, 129–135
Control, 246–275
  feedback model of, 247
  information and, 261–262
  integrated planning and control systems and, 262–263
  management, 249–252
  in multinational firms, 272–273
  in nonprofit firms, 273–274
  operational, 252
  strategic, 248–249
  strategy and, 246–248
Control policies, 261
Cool, Karel O., 144
Cooper, Arnold C., 42, 54
Cooper Industries, 42
Corporate planning units, 204–205
Corporate strategy, 94, 95, 97–107
  management audit and, 286
  for multiple-SBU firm, 164
  for single-business enterprise, 120–123
  See also Grand strategy
Critical Path Method, 71
Crouse-Hinds Company, 42

Crummer School of Business, 14
Cunningham, J. Barton, 264, 267, 269, 275
Cyert, R. M., 35, 200

Dachler, H. P., 244
Daems, H., 241
Dalton, G. W., 275
Dana Corporation, 18–20
Datsun, 102
Davis, Keith, 96
Davis, Peter S., 144
Day, John W., 251
Dearden, J., 47, 255, 275
DeButts, John, 22
deCarbonnel, Francois E., 79
Decentralization, 228
Decision making, 191–214
   behavioral aspects of, 209–212
   complexity of, 191–194
   component phases of, 195–207
   incremental, 206–207
   by management coalition, 200–202
   by managers, 199–200
   in multinational firms, 209–211
   in nonprofits, 212
   planning modes, 207–209
   power and political aspects of, 202–204
   strategic decision process, 194–212
   values and, 199
Decision tree, 154
Delegation, 228
De Lorean, John, 157, 199–200
Delta Airlines, 49, 150, 151–153
Demographic changes, 67
deNoya, L., 275
Descriptive characteristics, 264–265, 270–271
Dess, Gregory G., 144
Dewar, R. D., 244
Directional policy matrix, 136–137
Dirsmith, M. W., 32, 115
Disney Corporation, 42, 53, 102, 109
Diversification, 103–105, 228–230
Dobbie, J. W., 89–90, 205
Donance, Roy G., 79
Donnelly Mirrors, 150, 153
Doz, Y. L., 26, 27
Dresser Industries, 13
Drucker, Peter, 86, 88, 123, 237
Dun & Bradstreet, 253
Duncan Foods Company, 104
Dun's Review, 253
Dye, Peter, 200

Eastern Airlines, 125
Eastlack, J., Jr., 8
Eckerd, Jack, 22
Economic information, 64, 78, 297–307
Economics, laws affecting, 51
Ehrbar, A. F., 180
Energy laws, 51
Engledow, Jack L., 38
Enterprise strategy, 6, 94, 95, 96–97, 286
Environmental information:
   competitor analysis, 55–62
   on demographic changes, 67
   on the economy, 64
   on government, 50–53

   on international events, 66–67
   on labor, 65
   management audit and, 292
   for multinational corporations, 71–72
   on natural resources, 65–66
   on society, 63–64
   sources of, 48–49, 62, 77–79
   on technology, 53–55
   See also Information
Environmental laws, 51
Environmental Planning Systems, 71
Equal Employment Opportunity Commission (EEOC), 117
Equal Employment Opportunity laws, 51
Evaluation, 248–273
   audits, 258–261
   criteria for, 266–267
   descriptive characteristics and, 264–265, 270–271
   human resource accounting, 260
   in multinational firms, 272–273
   ratio analysis, 253–255
   return on investment, 255–257
Ewing, D. W., 155
Excalibur specialty car, 100–101

Fahey, Liam, 202, 213
Farris, Joseph, 174
Federal Express, 99
Federal laws, 51–52
Felton, S. M., Jr., 21
Filley, A. C., 204
Financial ratio analysis, 253–255, 293–295
Firstenberg, P. B., 21
First Northern Bank, 105
Forbes, 255
Ford, Henry, 22
Ford, J. C., 244
Forecasting, 67–71
   analytical, 71
   computers and, 68–71
   simulation modeling, 68–70
Fortune, 48, 253, 255
Fouraker, L. E., 241
Fox, Harold W., 134
Frankenhoff, W. P., 35
Franklin, J. L., 244
Franko, L. G., 229
Frederick, G. D., 35
Friedman, Philip, 200
Fruhan, W. E., Jr., 141
Fulmer, Robert M., 8, 33
Functionalization, 227
Functional strategy, 94, 95–96, 108
   management audit and, 287–291
   for single-SBU organization, 148–155

Galeese, L. R., 25
Gap analysis, 178–179
Garrett, David C., Jr., 151, 152
Garry, G. Anthony, 262, 275
General Electric (GE), 41, 99, 185
General Electric business screen, 168–171
General Electric stoplight portfolio matrix, 170
General Motors, 259
Gergan, K. J., 213

Getshow, G., 263
Gilmore, F. F., 204
Gilmore, S. C., 206–207
Glueck, William F., 132, 135
Goeldner, C. R., 79
Goldsmith, Jeff Charles, 74, 116
Gonzales and Company, 104
Government, information on, 50–53, 77
Gowler, Dan, 267
Graham, S., 200
Grand strategy, 5, 95, 101, 108–110
   See also Corporate strategy
Granger, C. H., 35
Grant, W. T., 12, 17, 49, 106
Gray, Harry, 180
Greenberg, E., 30, 32, 74, 157
Greenwood, William T., 247, 258
Greiner, L. E., 24, 227
Grinyer, P. H., 244
Groobey, J. A., 21
Gross, Bertram H., 267
Growth, 102–106
   diversified, 103–105
   integrative, 103
   intensive, 102
   speed of, 106
   types of, 102–105
Guth, William D., 199
Gutmann, P. M., 118
Guynes, C. S., 8

Hall, David J., 225
Hall, W. K., 68
Hamermesh, Richard G., 145
Haner, F. T., 72
Harness, Edward G., 271
Harper, Marion, Jr., 43
Harrigan, Kathryn Rudie, 147
Harris, J. E., 145
Harvard Business Review, 48
Haspeslagh, Philippe, 182
Hatten, K. J., 140
Hatten, M. L., 32, 35
Heany, D. F., 8, 138
Hedley, Barry, 168
Hegarty, H. W., 8, 35
Henderson, Bruce D., 60
Henke, J. W., Jr., 21
Heraclitus, 37
Herold, D. M., 8
Hersey, Paul, 239
Hershmen, A., 263
Heublein, 93, 105
Hewlett-Packard, 85
Hickson, D. I., 213
Higgins, James M., 86, 179, 211, 221, 238, 242, 263
Hill, W., 213
Hinings, C. R., 213
Hitt, Michael A., 109
Hofer, Charles W., 35, 68, 76, 82, 84, 94, 96, 109, 130, 131, 133–134, 155, 166, 167, 172, 175, 176, 177, 178, 181, 183
Hoffman, R. C., 35
Holt, D. D., 103
Hospitals, 73–74, 116–117
   See also Not-for-profit organizations
House, R. T., 8
Howell, R. A., 24
Hulbert, James M., 272

Human resource accounting (HRA), 260
Human resource management, 235–239
Hussey, D. E., 136, 137

IBM, 93–94, 124
Implementation, 215–244
 multinational aspects of, 241–242
 in nonprofit sector, 243
 organizational structure and, 216–230, 239–241
Implementation policies, 239
Implementation systems, 230–239
 communication, 234, 237–239
 human resource management, 235–239
 integrated planning and control, 231–234
 leadership, 234, 238–239
 motivation, 234, 237–238
Industry attractiveness assessment matrix, 176
Information, 43–79
 competitor analysis, 60–67
 control and, 261–262
 economic, 64, 78, 297–307
 external, 50–59, 77–79, 297–307
 forecasting and, 67–71
 internal, 49
 in the international arena, 71–72
 nonprofit usage of, 73–75
 sources of, 47–49, 77–79
 Strategic Information Systems, 43–47
Information capsules:
 behaviorally derived strategy, 146
 Chrysler's management control, 250–252
 Coca-Cola diversification, 104
 commitment to excellence in aerospace, 210–211
 Dana policy, 18–20
 Delta's employee policies, 151–153
 GE stoplight portfolio matrix, 170
 Hewlett-Packard's strategic objectives, 85
 information gathering, 45
 Japanese computer market, 55
 Japanese management, 23
 marketing strategy, 128–129
 mission statements, 13–14
 quality control circle, 223
 Sun Banks' organizational structure 222
 synergy, 180
Ingrassia, Laurence, 45
In Search of Excellence (Peters and Waterman), 264–265, 270–271
Integrated planning and control systems, 231–234, 262–263
Integrative growth, 103
Intensive growth, 102
Intermediate planning, 232–233
Internal information:
 for multinational corporations, 71–72
 sources of, 47–48
 types of information sought, 49
 See also Information
International corporations. *See* Multinational corporations
International events, information on, 66–67, 78
InterNorth, Inc., 42
Investment reduction, 106–107
Ireland, Duane, 109

Jablowsky, S. F., 32, 115
Jalland, Michael, 186–188
Janus, Sidney, 151
Japanese management, 23
Japanese market, 55
Jaques, Elliot, 267
Jay, Anthony, 202, 216
Jelinek, M., 244
Johnson, George E., 22, 124
Johnson, Robert W., 271
Johnson Products, 124

Karda, M., 213
Karnani, A., 183
Kay, Mary, 22
Keiser, Mickaell, 200
Kendrick, J. G., 12
Kennell, J. D., 47
Kentucky Fried Chicken, 72, 105
Kepner, C., 198
Kiechel, Walter, III, 182–183
King's restaurant chain, 105
Kirchhoff, B. A., 138–140
Kirks, Laura M., 79
K-Mart, 17
Knecht, C. P., 152
Koontz, W. Harold, 247
Koten, John, 252
Kotler, Phillip, 12, 29–30, 102, 145, 146–147, 159
Krasner, O. J., 68
Kroc, Ray, 22
Kudla, R. J., 8

Labor, information on, 65, 79
Labor laws, 52
LaForge, R. L., 8
Lanford, H. W., 79
Latham, G. P., 87
Launstein, M., 21
Lawrence, Paul, 262, 275
Laws, 51–52
Leadership, 234, 238–239
Learned, E. P., 248
Lebell, D., 68
Lee, James E., 26
Legge, Karen, 267
Lehner, Linda, 152
Lenz, R. C., Jr., 79
Lenz, R. T., 38
Leontiades, Milton, 16
Levi Strauss, 103
Lewis, V., 21
Lincoln, Abraham, 94
Lindblom, C. E., 206
Lindsay, W. M., 8
Linnemann, R. E., 47
Lockheed, 222, 223
Lone Star Industries, 103
Lorange, P., 47, 184–185, 205
Lorsch, J. W., 229
Lovins, R., Jr., 200
Lubatkin, Michael, 141, 142
Luzi, A. D., 32, 115
Lyles, Marjorie A., 197, 198

McCarthy, Scotty, 153
McCaskey, M. B., 87
McDonald, P., 8
McEwen, William J., 274
McGowan, William C., 142
McLean, E. R., 69
McMahon, Donald A., 41
MacMillan, Ian C., 110–112
McMurry, R. N., 213
McTaggart, James M., 143
Macy, B. A., 260
Mahajan, V., 166
Majaro, S., 155–156
Makridakis, S., 68
Malkiel, B. G., 21
Management and Machiavelli (Jay), 202
Management audits, 258–260, 285–292
Management control, 249–252
Managerial matrix, 149
Managers:
 decision making by 199–202
 values of, 199
March, J. G., 35, 200, 213
Market development, 102
Marketing strategy, 123–129
Market penetration, 102
Marlboro cigarettes, 125
Marriott, J. Willard, 22
Martindell, Jackson, 258
Martin Lawrence Limited Editions, 128–129
Martin Marietta, 17, 91, 222, 223, 224
Mason, R. Hal, 29, 113–114
Mason, R. O., 213
Master strategy, 119–190
 components of, 5
 defined, 4
 formulation of, 7, 8, 39
 in international arena, 113–114, 155–157, 186–188
 levels of, 94–96
 for multiple-SBU firms, 163–190
 not-for-profit organizations and, 114–117, 157–159, 189
 portfolio management, 166–183
 for single-SBU, 119–161
 See also Strategy
Matrix organization, 218, 221–222
MBORR (management by objectives, results, and rewards), 85–87
Mee, John, 87
Melvill Shore Corporation, 107
Merton, Robert K., 217
Messer, H. M., 234
Metzner, Henry E., 132, 135
Microsoft Corporation, 55
Miller, Danny, 200
Miller Brewing Company, 102
Miner, J. B., 244
Mintzberg, Henry, 17, 35, 76, 195, 202, 207–208, 213,, 271, 272, 275
Minute Maid Corporation, 104
Mirvis, P. H., 260
MIS (management information systems). *See* Strategic Information Systems
Mission, 11–15
 in multinational corporations, 27–28
 in not-for-profit organizations, 31–32

Mission statements, 13–14
Mitroff, Ian I., 197
Mitroff, J., 194
Mizruchi, M. S., 21
MNC. *See* Multinational corporations
Montanari, J. R., 227
Montgomery, J., 21
Morris, Robert, Associates, 253, 255
Morton, Michael S. S., 262, 275
Mostek, 180
Motivation, 234, 237–238
Mouton, J. S., 227
Mueller, R., 21
Mullick, S. K., 68
Multinational corporations (MNCs):
   control in, 272–273
   evaluation in, 272–273
   implementation in, 241–242
   information for, 71–72
   master strategy and, 113–114,
      186–188
   organizational structure of,
      241–242
   strategic decision making in, 209–211
   strategic management in, 26–29
   strategic objectives and, 113–114
Multiple-SBU organization, 5, 163–190
   corporate strategy for, 164
   divisional vs. corporate strategists,
      183–186
   multinational, 186–188
   nonprofit, 189
   portfolio management techniques,
      166–183
Murphy, John A., 22
Murray, E. A., Jr., 63

Nabisco Brands, 105
Nader, Ralph, 52, 96
Nadler, B. A., 275
Najjar, M. A., 8
Narayanan, V. K., 213
Natural resources, information on,
   65–66, 79
Naylor, T., 142
Neale, G. L., 69
Neghandi, A. R., 241
Newman, William H., 32, 35, 92
Niche strategies, 100–101
Northrup, W. D., 69
Northwest Bancorporation, 13
Not-for-profit organizations, 29–33
   control in, 273–274
   environment of, 33
   implementation in, 243
   information and, 73–75
   master strategy and, 114–117,
      157–159, 189
   mission in, 31–32
   strategic decision making in, 212
   strategic objectives and, 114–117
   strategic policy in, 32
   strategists in, 32–33
Nulty, P., 38
Nutt, A. B., 79

Objectives:
   established, 88–91
   levels of, 84–85
   MBORR and, 85–87
   in plans, 88
   prioritizing, 91

typical, 84
   See also Strategic objectives
O'Connell, Frank, 152
Odiorne, George, 86, 118
Operational control, 252
Operational planning, 233–234
Oppenlander, Robert, 152
Organizational policy, 15–17
   defined, 4
   at strategic level, 16–17 (*see also*
      Strategic policy)
Organizational strategists, 17–26
Organizational strategy. *See* Strategy
Organizational structure, 216–230,
   239–241
   formal, 218–223
   matrix, 218, 221–222
   pyramids, 218, 219
   selection of, 224–226
   shapes of, 218
   strategy and, 225, 226–230
   team management, 222–223
   venture, 223
Ouchi, W. J., 211

Paine, Frank T., 141, 142
Palia, K. A., 109
Parsons, T., 225
Patel, Peter, 147, 148
Patton, A. C., 107
Patton, George, 129
Pavan, R. J., 229
Pearce, John A., II, 8, 15, 108
PepsiCo, 105, 126
Performance measures, 252–261
   audits, 258–261
   human resource accounting, 260
   ratio analysis, 253–255
   return on investment, 255–257
Personnel. *See* Human resource
   management
Peters, Thomas J., 150, 241, 264–
   265, 271
Phillip Morris, 102, 124
Phillips, J. R., 241
Pillsbury, 45
PIMS. *See* Profit Impact on Market
   Strategies
Pitts, Michael, 141, 142
Planners, professional, 24–26
Planning:
   budgets, 234, 235
   intermediate, 232–233
   operational, 233–234
   pro-forma statements used in, 89
Planning modes, 207–209
Planning units, corporate, 204–205
Plans, characteristics of, 112–113
Policy, 15
   See also Organizational policy
Pooley, G., 229
Porter, Michael E., 56–59, 93, 109,
   142–144
Portfolio management techniques,
   102, 166–183
   assessment process, 173–177
   BCG business matrix, 167–168
   competitive position assessment
      matrix, 177
   gap analysis, 178–179
   General Electric business screen,
      168–171

industry attractiveness assessment
   matrix, 176
   pitfalls of, 179–183
   product/market/industry evolution
      matrix, 171–172
Pounds, W. F., 197
Preemptive strategies, 110–112
Product development, 102
Product life cycle, 130–133
Product/market/industry evolution matrix, 171–172
Profit Impact on Market Strategies
   (PIMS), 138–142
Profit Plans, 233
Program Evaluation Review Technique, 71
Pugh, D. S., 244
Pyramidal organizational structure,
   218, 219

Quality control circle, 223
Quasar, 223
Quinn, James Brian, 207

Radio Shack, 105
Raisinghani, D., 195, 202
Ramsay, C., 21
Ratio analysis, 253–255, 293–295
Reilly, D., 100
Reimann, B. C., 241
Remmers, H. Lee, 228, 272–273
Resources, information on, 65–66, 79
Responsibility centers, 255
Retrenchment, 106
Return on investment (ROI),
   138–141, 255–257
Revson, Charles, 124
Rhyne, L. C., 8
Rich, Arnie, 152
Richards, M., 113
Rickenbacker, Eddie, 22
Ringbaak, K. S., 47
Roberts, E. B., 223
Robinson, R. B., 8
Robock, S. H., 72
Rodgers, Francis G., 270
Rondinelli, D. A., 213
Ross, Larry, 128–129
Rothschild, W. E., 58, 60, 61, 62
Rouse, Mary Ruth, 152
Royal Crown Cola, 103
Rue, Leslie W., 8, 88, 89
Rumelt, R. P., 227, 275

Saias, Maurice A., 225
Salter, M., 227
Sandberg, W. R., 211
Saunders, C. B., 201–202
Savas, E. S., 30
SBU. *See* Strategic business units
Schendel, Dan E., 35, 42, 68, 82, 94,
   96, 107, 109, 166, 167, 175,
   176, 177, 178, 181, 183
Schlitz Brewing Company, 105
Schoeffler, S., 8, 138
Schollhammer, H., 241
SCOA Industries, Inc., 107
Scott, B. R., 227
Scott, Peter, 180
Scott, W. Richard, 11
Sears, Richard W., 21
Sears, 103, 125

Selznik, P., 225
7-S's framework, 239–241
Shaffer, Richard A., 55
Shapiro, J. R., 69
Shepherd, Mark, 270
Shetty, Y. K., 90
Shirley, Robert C., 158, 160
Shuman, J. C., 35
Silk, Steven B., 145
Simet, D. P., 244
Simmons, K., 72
Simon, H., 191, 213, 214
Simonetti, F. L., 241
Simonetti, J. L., 241
Simulation modeling, 68–70
Single-SBU organization, 5, 119–161
   business strategy for, 123–155
   corporate strategy for, 120–123
   functional strategies for, 148–155
   international master strategies for, 155–157
   nonprofit strategies for, 157–159
SIS. *See* Strategic Information Systems
Sloan, Alfred P., 22
Slocum, J. W., Jr., 244
Smirnoff vodka, 125, 127
Smith, D. D., 68
Smith, Frederick W., 99
Smith, G. A., Jr., 93
Social audits, 261
Society, information on, 63–64, 77–78
Soelberg, P., 214
Software, for simulations, 69–70, 71
Springer, C., 35
Stabilization, 106
Stagner, R., 8, 202
Standard and Poor's *Industry Surveys*, 255
Steiner, G. A., 35, 76
Sterling Vineyards, 104
Stevenson, Howard H., 40, 42, 197
Stopford, J. M., 241
Strategic audit, 258–260, 285–292
Strategic business units (SBUs), 5–6
   business strategy for, 123–155
   corporate strategy for, 120–123, 164
   functional strategies for, 148–155
   multinational, 186–188
   multiple, 5, 163–190
   portfolio management techniques, 166–183
   single, 5, 119–161
Strategic control, 248–249
Strategic decision process, 194–212
   component phases of, 195–207
   managers in, 199–202
   model of, 195, 196
   in multinational firms, 209–211
   in nonprofits, 212
   power and political aspects of, 202–204
   values in, 199
Strategic Information Systems (SIS), 43–47
Strategic management, 3–35
   defined, 3–4
   international, 26–29
   Japanese, 23
   in not-for-profit organizations, 29–33

   in the organization, 6–9
   process model for, 6
   in SBUs, 5–6
   See also Master strategy
Strategic objectives:
   components of, 82
   defined, 4
   determination of, 7, 8, 82–85
   Hewlett-Packard's, 85
   model of determination, 7
   multinational corporations and, 113–114
   not-for-profit organizations and, 114–117
   typical, 84
   See also Objectives
Strategic planning modes, 207–209
Strategic plans, 4
Strategic policy, 16–17
   in multinational corporations, 28
   in not-for-profit organizations, 32
Strategists, 17–26
   board of directors, 17–21
   chief executive officer, 21–22
   coalition, 22–24, 200–202
   corporate planning units, 204–205
   divisional vs. corporate, 183–186
   managers, 199–200
   in multinational corporations, 28–29
   in not-for-profit organizations, 32–33
   professional planners, 24–26
Strategy:
   behavioral theory and, 137–148
   business, 94, 95, 108, 123–155, 286–287
   contingency approach to, 129–135
   control and, 246–248 (*see also* Control)
   corporate, 94, 95, 97–107, 120–123, 164, 286
   defined, 92
   emergent, 265, 271–272
   enterprise, 6, 94, 95, 96–97, 286
   functional, 94, 95–96, 108, 287–291
   grand, 5, 95, 101, 108–110
   levels of, 94–96
   marketing, 123–127
   niche, 100–101
   organizational structure and, 225, 226–230
   overview of, 92–94
   Porter's competitive strategies, 142–144
   portfolio management, 166–183
   preemptive, 110–112
   for product life cycle, 130–133
   See also Master strategy
Summer, C. E., 76
Sun Banks, 222
Suzuki, Y., 114
SWOT (strengths, weaknesses, opportunities, threats), 40–43
   in multinational corporations, 72
   nonprofits and, 73–75
   strategic audit and, 285–292
Synergy, 179, 180

Taguiri, Renato, 199
Tandy, Charles, 22
Taylor, R. N., 47

Taylor Wine Company, 41, 104
Team management, 222–223
Technology, information on, 53–55, 77
Texas Instruments (TI), 40–41, 103, 127
Thain, D. H., 227
Thanheiser, H., 229
Theoret, A., 195, 202
Thomas, R. David, 22
Thompson, James D., 201, 274
Thoroman, D. G., 94
Thune, S. S., 8
Tilles, S., 248
Tipgos, M. A., 76
Tosi, H., 118
Townsend, Robert, 230
TransAmerica, 105
Trans World Airlines, 105
Tregoe, B., 198
Trevelyan, E. W., 207
Turnaround strategies, 107

Union Carbide, 92–93
United Technologies, 180
U.S. Department of Defense (DOD), 64
U.S. Steel, 14
Utterback, J. M., 54, 68

Values, 199
Vancil, R. F., 24, 255, 275
Van Der Pol, H. W., 234
Varadarajan, R., 144
Ventures, 223
von Clausewitz, K., 17

Walker, A. H., 229
Wallender, H. W., III, 32
Wall Street Journal, 48
Walters, Jim, 22
Waterman, Robert H., Jr., 150, 215, 240, 241, 264–265, 271
Waters, J. A., 275
Watson, Thomas J., Jr., 270, 271
Watt, Jerry L., 132, 135
Webb, Pam, 151
Wendy's, 99, 101, 125
Wernerfelt, B., 183
Weston, J. Fred, 254
Wheelwright, S. C., 8, 68
White, Roderick E., 144
Wilson, C. Z., 213
Wilson, Joseph, 21–22
Wind, Y., 166
Winegardner, Roy E., 12
Wissema, J. G., 234
Wommack, W. W., 21
Woo, Carolyn Y., 144
Wood, D. R., Jr., 8
Woodruff, John, 22
Woolman, C. E., 151
Wrigley, L., 229
Wu, F. H., 214

Xerox, 97

Yao, M., 38
Younger, Michael, 147, 148
Ysai-Ardekani, M., 244
Yukl, G. A., 87

Zalesnik, A., 214